Edited by Allan Pritchard

Vancouver Island Letters of Edmund Hope Verney, 1862-65

UBC PRESS / VANCOUVER

Printed in Canada on acid-free paper ∞

ISBN 0-7748-0554-4 (hardcover)
ISBN 0-7748-0573-0 (paperback)

Canadian Cataloguing in Publication Data

Verney, Edmund Hope, 1838-1910.
Vancouver Island letters of Edmund Hope Verney, 1862-65

(Pioneers of British Columbia, ISSN 0847-0537)
Includes bibliographical references and index.
ISBN 0-7748-0554-4 (bound)
ISBN 0-7748-0573-0 (pbk.)

1. Verney, Edmund Hope, 1838-1910. 2. Vancouver Island (B.C.) — History. 3. Vancouver Island (B.C.) — Social conditions. 4. British Columbia — History — 1849-1871.* 5. British Columbia — Social conditions — To 1871. 6. Great Britain. Royal Navy — Biography. I. Pritchard, Allan. II. Title. III. Series: The pioneers of British Columbia.

FC3822.1.V47A4 1996 971.1'202'092 C96-910020-5
F1088.V47 1996

This book has been published with the help of a grant from the Social Science Federation of Canada, using funds provided by the Social Sciences and Humanities Research Council of Canada.

UBC Press gratefully acknowledges the ongoing support to its publishing program from the Canada Council, the Province of British Columbia Cultural Services Branch, and the Department of Communications of the Government of Canada.

Typeset in Palatino by Arifin A. Graham, Alaris Design
Printed and bound in Canada by Friesens
Book design: Arifin A. Graham
Copy-editor: Susan Reaney

UBC Press
University of British Columbia
6344 Memorial Road
Vancouver, BC V6T 1Z2
(604) 822-3259
Fax: 1-800-668-0821
E-mail: orders@ubcpress.ubc.ca

Vancouver Island Letters of Edmund Hope Verney, 1862-65

In this previously unknown collection of letters, we see colonial British Columbia through the eyes of a young naval officer who spent three years on Vancouver Island commanding a Royal Navy gunboat during the Cariboo gold rush. A keen observer of life in the new world, Edmund Hope Verney corresponded on a regular basis with his father, a prominent British MP. The letters are highly engaging and provide an interesting record of many aspects of colonial life, including political and social history, civic and eccleciastical affairs, the impact of the gold rush, the establishment of European settlements, relations with Natives, and comments on the personalities and activities of leading figures in colonial British Columbia. The excellent introduction by Allan Pritchard provides the biographical and historical contexts and identifies the individuals mentioned in the letters.

Vancouver Island Letters of Edmund Hope Verney is a welcome new source for the history of colonial British Columbia as well as for British Imperial naval history, and it is a book that belongs in the library of anyone who enjoys reading about the province's early days.

ALLAN PRITCHARD is Professor Emeritus of English, University of Toronto. He was born and grew up in Comox and now divides his time between Victoria and Galiano Island.

Edmund Hope Verney, Victoria, 1863. BCARS 7434

Contents

Illustrations

Acknowledgments

I am grateful to Sir Ralph Verney and the Claydon House Trust for permission to publish Edmund Verney's letters and related material from the archive at Claydon House. I am indebted likewise for permission to reproduce previously unknown historical British Columbia photographs from Claydon House. Susan Ranson, archivist at Claydon House, has frequently provided essential assistance, and Mr. and Mrs. Michael Sandford, National Trust custodians at Claydon House during my periods of research there, have also been very helpful. I am indebted to the Public Record Office at Kew, especially for the use of Admiralty records, and to the British Library in London, for many printed sources. The resources of the British Columbia Archives and Records Service in Victoria have been invaluable, and the staff there have been generous in their help. I owe a special debt to Douglas Lister of Leigh-on-Sea, Essex, who transcribed in normal script two long letters and some shorter passages written by Edmund Verney in a now archaic system of shorthand, and made it possible to include them in this edition. Ruth Wallace has assisted my work greatly through her computer skills. My final debt is to expert readers and editorial staff of the University of British Columbia Press.

Abbreviations

BCARS	British Columbia Archives and Records Service
Colonist	*The Daily British Colonist*
DAB	*Dictionary of American Biography*
DCB	*Dictionary of Canadian Biography*
DNB	*Dictionary of National Biography*
PRO	Public Record Office

Vancouver Island Letters of Edmund Hope Verney, 1862-65

Introduction

In his *Reminiscences*, J.S. Helmcken, the pioneer Victoria doctor and Speaker of the colonial House of Assembly, describes the officers of ships of the Royal Navy at Esquimalt in the mid-nineteenth century as

> generally well off and connected with the landed gentry of England – they had been accustomed to firearms and so were good sportsmen and thus enjoyed themselves. They were quite at home here and had the run of the place – horses and what not – and having now the Langfords, Skinners, McKenzies and the HBCo's people to call on, times with them were pleasant.[1]

Helmcken could scarcely have known that one of the officers who fits his description wrote back to his family in England regular reports of his experiences and impressions of colonial life on Vancouver Island which on occasion included critical remarks about Helmcken himself.

This officer, Lieutenant Edmund Hope Verney, served as commander of the gunboat HMS *Grappler* on Vancouver Island between 1862 and 1865. During the whole of this period he wrote regularly to his father, Sir Harry Verney, at Claydon House in Buckinghamshire. Since the mail steamers left only at intervals of about two weeks, he often wrote his letters in dated instalments every few days like journals. His letters constitute a very full record of his three years in the colonies of Vancouver Island and British Columbia from his arrival in May 1862 to his departure for England in June 1865.

Verney had wide interests and wrote not only about naval matters but about many aspects of colonial life. He wrote much about the coastal scenery and climate as well as the diverse inhabitants of the colonies. He wrote about colonial society and politics, and about ecclesiastical and civic affairs in Victoria. In addition to public matters, he wrote about the more private aspects of his life, including his enjoyment of hunting (or 'shooting'), fishing, and picking berries, and the interest he took in gardening and raising fowls at a cottage he rented in Esquimalt. Mixed with this is his constant concern with news of events back in England and family affairs at Claydon that came to him in letters from home. The special quality of his letters is in the combination of the most diverse elements: navy, politics, scenery, weather, and more private and personal matters. Typically he moves on October 11, 1862 from expressing anxiety about the state of his sister Emily's health in one sentence to urging in the next that the San Juan Islands dispute should be settled.

Verney's three years in Vancouver Island and British Columbia were an important and interesting period of the colonies' history. He arrived in the spring of 1862 at the height of the Cariboo gold rush, and his letters give an account of the variety of people it brought, and the excitement, fermentation, and high prices it caused in Victoria. Victoria's population had suddenly doubled. With the aid of a panoramic photograph taken two years earlier, Verney provided a description of the recent changes and the current appearance of the town, and continued to record its progress in later letters. On the mainland, he described New Westminster in 1862 as no more than a few huts in a clearing of the forest, but noted in 1864 that a road was being built to Burrard Inlet, which would encourage ocean-going ships to come there rather than to Victoria or Esquimalt. In colonial administration and politics, he arrived toward the end of the long Douglas regime: he gave his critical impressions of it in some candid letters, and he subsequently recorded the transition to the administration of the two new governors, Kennedy and Seymour in 1864. He commented much on the jealousy that prevailed between the two colonies, but wrote in his later letters about the movement toward their union.

The letters give some sense also of the relation between the two colonies and their Russian and American neighbours. They are the record of a British Columbia where the hope was still sometimes expressed that the southern Alaska coastline, the "panhandle," might pass from Russian to British possession, and of a time when the San Juan Islands, where Verney occasionally visited the English Camp, was still a disputed territory between Britain and the United States. During nearly all his time in the colonies the American Civil War was raging, and he recorded various aspects of its impact, including the celebration of the Emancipation Proclamation by the black population of Victoria, the reception in Victoria of the news of Lincoln's assassination, and the occasional threats of war between the United States and Britain.

The letters convey the sense of a British Columbia that was still very remote and isolated from the outer world. During the "stirring European times" of the Schleswig-Holstein crisis, Verney felt he was in "an unheeded out-of-the-way part of the world," on "a little gunboat in the uttermost parts of the earth" (February 7, March 28, July 1, 1864). Until the arrival of the telegraph at Seattle and New Westminster near the end of his period in British Columbia, the only regular communication with the outside world was by American steamer two or three times a month to San Francisco. This city had an early telegraph link with the east, and letters went to the east and Europe either via Panama or overland by stage coach to the existing railheads.

As Verney's letters frequently complain, the mail steamers between Vancouver Island and San Francisco were really far from regular in their schedules; indeed, the vagaries of the mail service are a leading subject of his correspondence with his father. He wrote on February 6, 1865 that "of all the uncertain things of this world there is nothing beats the Vancouver mails." He pointed out to his father the advantages of addressing letters from England via New York, rather than the older route via St. Thomas in the West Indies. He experimented with the Wells Fargo Express route from San Francisco, but the letters normally took at least six weeks and often more than two months between Vancouver Island and England. Verney was able to economize by sending letters in Admiralty despatch bags, but these were subject to the same irregularities and delays as the remainder of the mail.

Partly no doubt because of the very wide range of his subjects, Verney's letters are inevitably uneven in interest and value. Sometimes he chose subjects that do not seem particularly interesting today. For example, on his arrival in Victoria, he wrote at length about a headless living chicken in San Francisco. In the later part of his time on Vancouver Island he wrote with obsessive and monotonous regularity about his desire for promotion in naval rank. He often apologizes for the inadequacy of his letters to his father. Sometimes he complains that he can find nothing to write about that he thinks will interest his father, or he has to work hard to fill out a letter. On the other hand, during periods of naval action, such as the search in the spring of 1863 for the Indians believed responsible for murders in the Gulf Islands, he has to explain that he has been kept too busy to write. But his apologies are prompted by the fact that his family had high standards for letter writing, and he often displays a talent for lively narration, description, and commentary that satisfies such standards.

That Sir Harry Verney appreciated the value of the letters is shown by the fact that he carefully preserved them and added them to the archive at Claydon House, where they still remain. Among English country houses, Claydon House has two special claims to fame: it contains eighteenth-century state rooms with magnificent rococo decoration, and it holds a great collection of Verney family papers, especially letters. The letters include some thirty thousand from the seventeenth century, probably the most extensive English domestic correspondence surviving from that period, and for many years included four thousand by Florence Nightingale, who was connected with the nineteenth-century Verneys and spent much of her time at Claydon. Partly no doubt because of the great size and importance of other parts of the Claydon House archive, Edmund Verney's Vancouver Island letters attracted little attention in later times and their existence has remained generally unknown.[2]

While Verney's letters to his father have been preserved, with one or two apparent gaps, few of those he wrote from Vancouver Island to other members of his family have survived, although he mentions many such letters in those to his father. Only a relatively small number of those written to him by his father and other relatives still exist. The Claydon archive, however, contains other material relating to Vancouver Island in the 1860s, including an interesting letter to Sir Harry Verney from Governor Arthur Kennedy, a series of letters to him from George Hills, first Anglican Bishop of Columbia, and two official *Grappler* letterbooks. Use has been made of these papers, together with the surviving letters of Sir Harry Verney to his son, in the introduction and notes to the present edition.

Among the letters preserved at Claydon House are those written by Edmund Verney to his father during his voyage from England to Vancouver Island in 1862 and during his return journey in 1865. They have not been given in full in this edition, but summaries and extracts are provided in the introduction. They record what is in a sense part of the Vancouver Island experience, and they illustrate two principal routes between England and the colony, the sea route by way of Panama, and the more adventurous overland route between San Francisco and the east coast.

All of Edmund Verney's letters to his father for the whole of his actual period in Vancouver Island and British Columbia are given complete in this edition, and a letter to his stepmother, Parthenope, Lady Verney, preserved with them (apparently the only surviving one) is also included. Manuscript enclosures found with the letters are given complete in some cases of special interest; in other cases their nature is indicated in notes. Verney's enclosures include many clippings from Victoria newspapers, and some from San Francisco newspapers, and these have also been indicated in notes.

Preparation of the text of the letters has not provided many problems, apart from those caused by the presence of a few passages of shorthand. The letters reveal that Verney's father sometimes criticized his handwriting but that Bishop Hills praised it (March 5 1863). It is in fact admirably clear, far superior both to his father's and the bishop's. The only common problems caused by his handwriting are in distinguishing between capitals and small forms of letters (W w, N n), and between marks of punctuation, such as colons and semicolons.

Verney's spelling is generally orthodox, but there are occasional irregularities. Sometimes these are mere slips resulting from haste: "beadstead," "liesure," "their" for "there," but sometimes he more consistently favours an unorthodox form: "agreable," "prarie," "managment." His use of capital letters is often eccentric, and he is quite inconsistent in capitalizing days of the week, for example. In the present text the irregularities of his spelling and punctuation have been retained, and "*sic*" has been inserted only sparingly. Some minor emendations which occur in the manuscripts of the letters have been silently incorporated,[3] and a few slight editorial emendations have been inserted within square brackets. Underlining has been indicated by italics. Beginning late in 1863, Sir Harry Verney marked on the letters the dates on which he

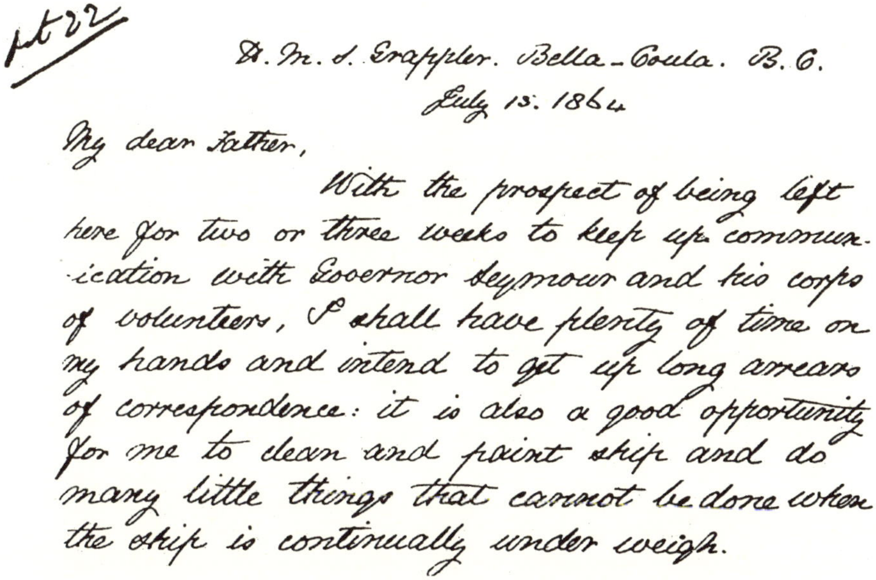

pt 22

H.M.S. Grappler. Bella-Coula. B.C.
July 15: 1864

My dear Father,

With the prospect of being left here for two or three weeks to keep up communication with Governor Seymour and his corps of volunteers, I shall have plenty of time on my hands and intend to get up long arrears of correspondence: it is also a good opportunity for me to clean and paint ship and do many little things that cannot be done when the ship is continually under weigh.

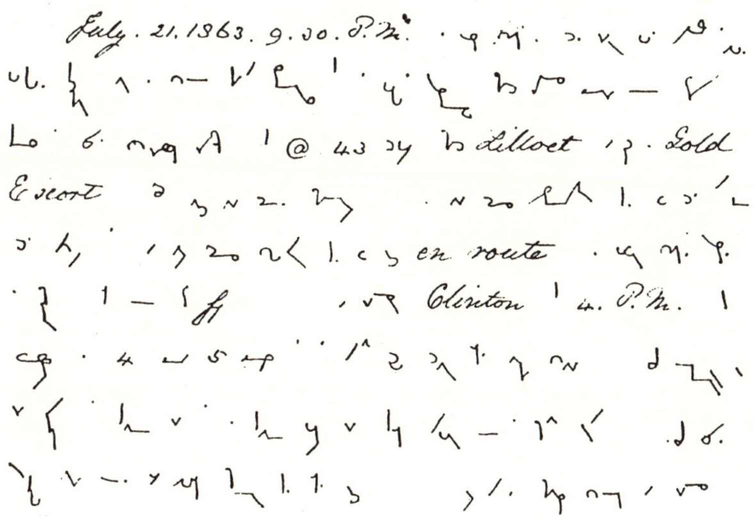

Samples of Verney's longhand and shorthand from his letters.
CLAYDON HOUSE TRUST

received them. Since the letters already contain much information about the speed and delay of the mails, these dates of receipt have not been recorded in this edition.[4]

Most of a very long letter about an excursion into the interior of British Columbia, which opens on July 14, 1863, and the whole (apart from dates, proper names and a few other words) of a letter of September 1, 1864 about the Chilcotin uprising, as well as two short passages in other letters, are written in an early nineteenth-century version of Gurney's shorthand, used by various members of the Verney family. In the Vancouver Island letters Edmund several times expressed the hope that his father would learn shorthand, but fortunately for us Sir Harry Verney did not do so. The text in the present edition follows transcripts of the shorthand provided by Douglas Lister.

Family and Early Life

Lieutenant Edmund Hope Verney was the eldest son and heir of Sir Harry Verney, second baronet, who had been born a Calvert but had taken the name Verney on inheriting the Claydon estate. He was conscious not only of distinguished military and naval traditions that existed on both sides of his family but also of bearing a name famous in English history: an earlier Sir Edmund Verney, Standard Bearer to Charles I, had died nobly defending the standard at the Battle of Edgehill in 1642. The nineteenth-century Edmund Verney was born on April 6, 1838, and after a short period at Harrow entered the Royal Navy in 1851 at the age of twelve years and ten months. Although only twenty-four when he arrived on Vancouver Island in 1862 to take command of the *Grappler*, he had already seen extensive service and had established a good reputation during the Crimean War and with a naval brigade in India at the time of the Mutiny.

In the Vancouver Island letters Verney mentions from time to time the ships on which he had served from the beginning of his naval career: HMS *Calliope* and HMS *Havannah* in South America and Australia (1851), and HMS *Arethusa* in the Mediterranean (1851-52). He joined HMS *Britannia*, the flagship of Admiral Dundas in the Mediterranean in October 1852, and was promoted midshipman a few months later. During the Crimean War in 1854-56 he served on the paddle-wheel steam-frigate HMS *Terrible* in bombardments of Sebastapol and Odessa, and was awarded the Crimean medal with clasp and the Turkish medal. In July 1856 he was appointed to HMS *Shannon*, a screw steam-frigate, commanded by Captain (later Sir) William Peel. He proceeded in this vessel to Hong Kong, where he was graded mate (i.e., sub-lieutenant), and then to India in August 1857 on the outbreak of the Mutiny, where he remained for a year. He served with Peel's naval brigade in inland actions including the final recapture of Lucknow. He was mentioned in despatches by Peel, and awarded the Indian medal with the Lucknow clasp. In March 1858 he was promoted lieutenant for good service in the field, recommended by Peel as "zealous and well conducted,"[5] and he was given temporary command of HMS *Pearl*, whose naval brigade was still up-country. In the autumn he returned to England and served on HMS *Emerald* in the Channel and West Indies before his posting to Vancouver Island.

During his period in India Verney had not only sustained well his family's military and naval traditions, but he had also maintained the Verney tradition that made Claydon House such a great repository of historically interesting correspondence. He had revealed himself as a frequent and fluent writer of letters, and just before his arrival in British Columbia he had published a book, *The Shannon's Brigade in India: Being Some Account of Sir William Peel's Naval Brigade in the Indian Campaign of 1857-1858* (1862), based on letters and journals he had written during the Indian Mutiny. His Indian letters in more recent times have provided the main basis for another book, by his great-nephew, Major-General G.L. Verney, *The Devil's Wind: The Story of the Naval Brigade at Lucknow from the Letters of Edmund Hope Verney and Other Papers concerning the Enterprise of the Ship's Company of HMS Shannon in the Campaign in India. 1857-58* (1956).

Verney's Vancouver Island letters to his father are shaped by the character of their recipient as well as that of their writer, and they embody many of the values and interests he shared with his father. Sir Harry Verney (1801-94) was the son of General Sir Harry Calvert, first baronet, who had been Adjutant-General of the Army during the Napoleonic wars. Harry Verney first followed a military career but then spent an adventurous year in South America, an experience which Edmund's family sometimes regarded as a kind of precedent for his period on Vancouver Island. After his return to England, Harry Verney gradually improved the Claydon estate, which was large and included several villages, but was in a financially overburdened condition when he was bequeathed it by a relative in 1827. He became a model landlord. In politics he was a Liberal and sat as Member of Parliament for Buckingham for fifty-two years, from 1832 to 1885, excepting two short intervals. In the last year he was made a Privy Councillor. He was high-minded and altruistic and a supporter of the good causes associated with his friend and former school-fellow, Lord Shaftesbury. During his long career he worked for many reforms, including the abolition of the slave trade, factory legislation, and the successive extensions of the franchise. He devoted himself especially to working for Florence Nightingale, whose sister Frances Parthenope he had married as his second wife after Edmund's mother died; he became known in the House of Commons as the member for Florence Nightingale. As well as having the strong local interests of a large landowner, he possessed a remarkable knowledge of geography and was one of the early members of the Royal Geographical Society.[6]

Sir Harry Verney was an evangelical Anglican, and the family circle at Claydon House was notable for its piety as well as for the support of liberal causes. He was an active member of the Bible Society, the Church

Missionary Society, and the Evangelical Alliance. His daughter-in-law, Margaret Verney, states: "In religious opinion he was of the old evangelical school, but his sympathies were broad."[7] Edmund Verney in his youth appears to have been subjected to a harsher and narrower religious influence from his mother Eliza, who died in 1857. She was a member of a distinguished naval family. Her father, Rear-Admiral Sir George Hope, had been one of Nelson's captains at Trafalgar, and her brother, Sir James Hope, rose to become Admiral of the Fleet.[8] She is described by her grandson, a later Sir Harry Verney, as "a mighty Protestant and Fundamentalist."[9] As a result of such influences, Edmund Verney emerges in his Vancouver Island letters not merely as one of the well-connected sporting naval gentlemen of the type described by Helmcken but also as one of those strongly pious Victorian naval officers, like Captain James Prevost, who a few years earlier had prompted William Duncan's coming to the coast as a missionary.

In addition to his father, other members of Edmund's immediate family figure prominently in his correspondence. During his period on Vancouver Island this family consisted of his stepmother, Frances Parthenope (Nightingale) (1819-90) – known by her second name and referred to by Edmund in the letters as "Mama" – and one sister and two brothers.[10] The sister Emily (b. 1843), to whom Edmund was closely attached and who regularly wrote him on Vancouver Island letters that have not survived, was an invalid or semi-invalid, afflicted with consumption, often absent from Claydon in Devonshire, Malta, or elsewhere for the sake of her health. She was greatly loved by Florence Nightingale as well as by the Verneys.[11] Edmund's brother George (b. 1842) was an ensign in the army in India. His youngest brother Frederick (b. 1846) was a schoolboy at Harrow when the Vancouver Island correspondence opens, and an undergraduate at Christ Church, Oxford, when it closes. The family centre was always Claydon House, but the Verneys also had a London house, 32 South Street, Park Lane, used particularly during sessions of Parliament, which is occasionally mentioned in the letters.

As well as the immediate family, Edmund's aunts and uncles on both his father's and his mother's side are mentioned from time to time in the letters. "Uncle Fred" was his father's brother, Frederic Calvert, a prosperous barrister; the Cunninghams were the family of his father's sister Mary and her husband, Rev. John W. Cunningham, Vicar of Harrow; "Uncle and Aunt Fremantle" were his father's sister Emily and her husband, Rev. William R. Fremantle, Rector of Middle Claydon, later Dean of Ripon; and "Aunt Abel" or "Aunt Fanny" was his father's sister Frances, the widow of Abel Smith, a banker. On Edmund's mother's side of the family were the important figure of her brother, "Uncle Hope," Rear-Admiral Sir James Hope, and the admiral's unmarried sister, "Aunt Helen" Hope.

In British Columbia there is a special reason in addition to the elucidation of Edmund Verney's letters for taking note of his family connections, for they have provided the place names that appear on maps and charts

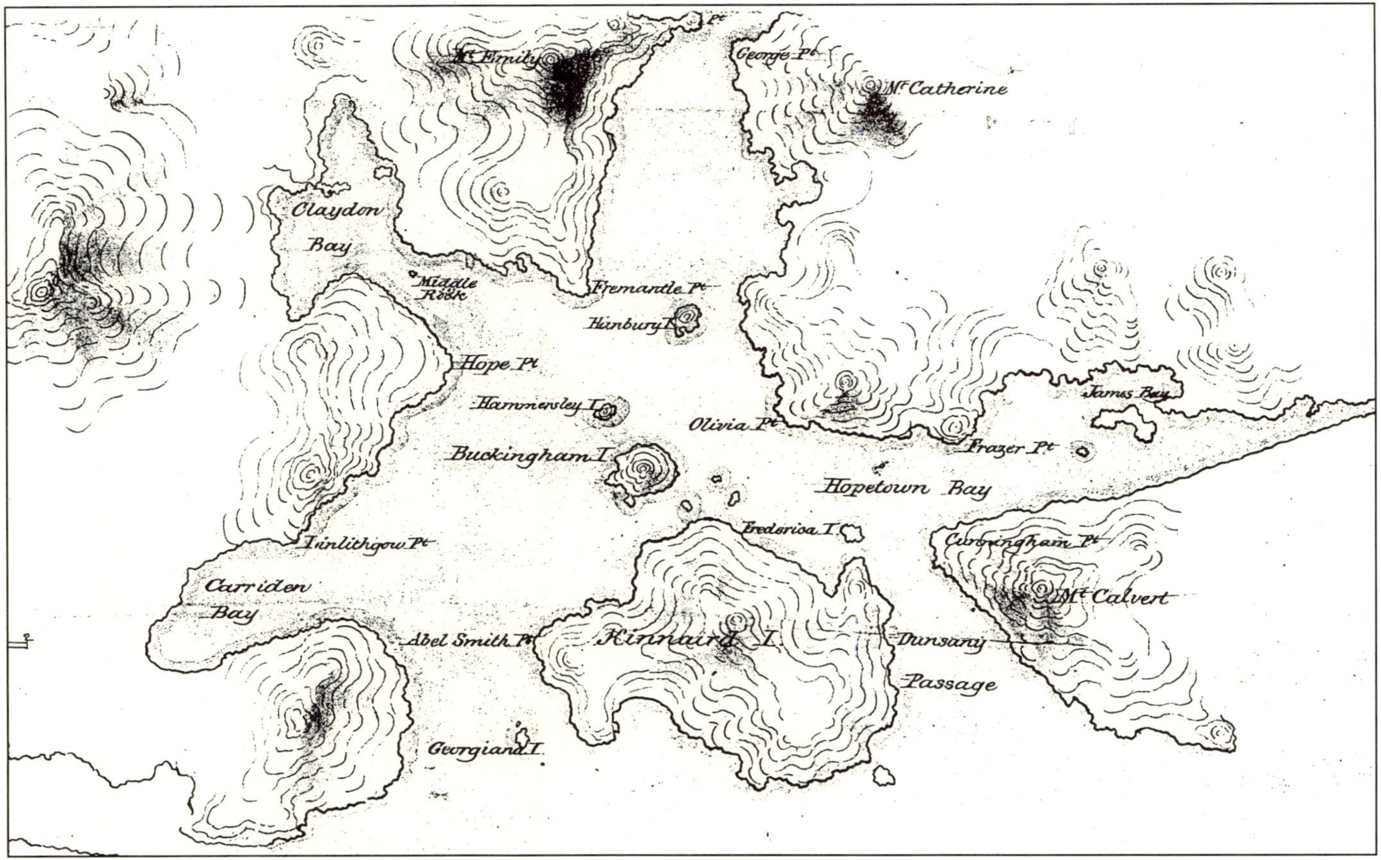

Part of Verney's copy of Pender's chart of Grappler Sound, Wells Passage, Queen Charlotte Strait, enclosed with a letter of January 17, 1864, showing some of the place names connected with Verney and his family. CLAYDON HOUSE TRUST of part of the coast.[12] This came about in October 1863 when Edmund in the *Grappler* made a rendezvous with his former shipmate, Daniel Pender, while the latter in the old Hudson's Bay Company ship, the *Beaver*, was engaged in coastal surveys in the Wells Passage area. Edmund subsequently enclosed with a letter to his father (January 17 1864) a copy of the new chart showing the numerous Verney family names placed on geographical features in this area.

Edmund Verney's family seat is commemorated in Claydon Bay, and his home county in Buckingham Island, his father in the Sir Harry Range, his father's original family name in Mount Calvert, and his father's mother's family in Hammersley Island. The aunts and uncles on the father's side are honoured with Fremantle Point, Cunningham Point, and Abel Smith Point, while Hanbury Island was given the married name of a daughter of the Abel Smiths. Verney's mother and her family are commemorated in Mount Eliza and Hope Point, as well as James Bay for her brother, Admiral Hope, Frederica Island for the admiral's late wife, and Helen Bay for his sister. Carriden Bay is named for Admiral Hope's family estate in Scotland, Hopetown Bay for the Scottish earl who was the head of the senior branch of the Hope family, and Linlithgow Point for the county where the Hope estates lay. Dunsany Passage and Kinnaird Island were both named for peers to whom Edmund was related through the Hope family, and Olivia Point was named for the late Lady Kinnaird. Edmund's stepmother's family was commemorated with Mount Nightingale, Mount Parthenope, and Mount Florence; the Nightingale's Hampshire estate gave its name to Embley Lagoon. For himself and his brothers and sisters Edmund named Edmund Point, Mount Emily, George Point, Frederic Island, and (for two sisters who died young) Georgiana Island and Mount Catherine. A peerage once held by the original Verney family provided Fermanaugh Passage. When the family names presumably had been exhausted, the steward and land agent of the Claydon estate, Alexander Frazer, was honoured with Frazer Point. Even Middle Rock in Claydon Bay may mark a Verney connection: it was probably so named not only because it was in the middle of the bay but as an allusion to the village of Middle Claydon on the Verney estate.[13]

The presence of these names on the map is one of the lasting results of Edmund Verney's period in British Columbia, but his family's connection with the region had actually preceded his arrival on Vancouver Island. Sir Harry Verney's interest in the area had begun more than two years earlier. It was specially prompted by his concern with religious matters and missionary activities, and probably originated with the foundation of the Anglican bishopric of Columbia in 1858-59. He was a friend of Angela Burdett-Coutts, whose endowment made the new bishopric possible, and he was a cousin of the first Bishop of Columbia, George Hills.[14] Edmund Verney's Vancouver Island letters do not at first make this relationship clear, but Bishop Hills addressed Sir Harry in his letters as "my dear Cousin": their mothers were both members of the Hammersley family. The Claydon House archive contains letters to Sir Harry from

Angela Burdett-Coutts in 1861-62 about the bishopric of Columbia, as well as letters from Bishop Hills in Vancouver Island and British Columbia beginning in 1860. The letters reveal that Sir Harry sometimes served as an intermediary between Angela Burdett-Coutts and Bishop Hills; he may well have influenced his relative's appointment to the new bishopric.

Bishop Hills' letters to Sir Harry Verney from the two western colonies are interesting both in themselves and in relation to Edmund's letters. They provide an indication of the information the Verneys had already received about the colonies before Edmund's arrival, and Edmund clearly had them in mind when he began to write to his father from Vancouver Island, for he excused deficiencies in his own letters on June 1, 1862 by stating he had seen little "but what I had been led to expect from the Bishop's letters, and from Vancouver's account." In the first of Hills' surviving letters to Sir Harry on April 17, 1860 the bishop described the laying of the cornerstone of the church of St. John in Victoria by Governor Douglas, while "Indians in some number sat and watched the proceedings," which took place "near the edge of the Forest": "thus following close upon the axe with the Gospel." On June 12, 1860 he wrote to Sir Harry from Yale a detailed description of a visit to the gold-mining areas of the Fraser, and to Lady Verney on such subjects as his desire to open a school for girls in Victoria. He enclosed newspapers to show the progress of the colonies. On July 14, 1860 he sent Sir Harry a copy of a long letter to Angela Burdett-Coutts describing two months travel on the mainland of British Columbia. In 1861 he wrote Sir Harry more than once about the problems of his diocese. He wrote Edmund, after the latter's arrival, from Williams Lake in July 1862 about a visit to the Cariboo, and he wrote Sir Harry from the *Grappler* at Deep Bay in October about a visit to the new Comox settlement and about his recent travels in the Cariboo. After Bishop Hills made a visit to England in 1863-65, when he married and spent his honeymoon at Claydon House, he resumed his correspondence with Sir Harry, which continued until the time of his resignation of his bishopric and his final return to England in 1892. His extensive accounts of his journeys in mainland British Columbia in the early 1860s, which display as well as a stern morality a good eye for details of frontier life and a strong interest in recording change, provided the Verneys with a specially valuable complement to Edmund's Vancouver Island letters, since Edmund had no opportunity of penetrating very far into the interior of the mainland.

Bishop Hills' letters also serve to elucidate various comments in Edmund Verney's. They show what Edmund meant, for example, when on his arrival on Vancouver Island he commented on the difficulties which faced the bishop there: "he has his troubles" (May 28 1862). Hills had written to Sir Harry Verney a year earlier (May 20 1861) about the "rancorous feeling & abuse" he encountered: "the English Bishop seems the constant object of attack." He stated that he had thought he was "pretty well seasoned" by his earlier experiences in Yarmouth and Leeds "but a Radical Corporation in Yarmouth is love & peace compared to the fierce hate of our strangely mixed society here."

In his letters to Sir Harry and Lady Verney about his travels on the mainland of British Columbia, however, Bishop Hills emphasized the good feeling that prevailed among the gold miners and their respect for law (June 12 1860), and their favourable reception of him when he preached in the open air, billiard saloons, restaurants, stores, log huts, and Indian lodges (August 1 1861). He wrote also of his admiration for the skill, courage, and high spirits of the Indians who took him by canoe up the Fraser from Hope to Yale in June 1860: he was impressed by the intelligence of the Indians and hoped to found schools for them.

Despite the difficulties Bishop Hills experienced, his letters corroborate Edmund Verney's warning to his father (February 5 1863) that the bishop was "a little bit of an enthusiast" in his view of the two colonies. Hills wrote to Sir Harry from Yale on June 12, 1860 that, in contrast to some adverse accounts, he was "fully satisfied of the vast resources" of British Columbia, and that the roads being built by the Royal Engineers would not only open up the mining district but also "a fine pastoral region" for stock farming. On July 15, 1862 he wrote Edmund from Williams Lake about "the magnificent country of Lakes La Hache & Williams" and the "magic change" brought about by the rapid progress of road-making. He had, he stated, "passed many farms newly taken up" and had "no doubt this year will see the commencement of considerable agricultural enterprises." When he wrote to Sir Harry Verney thirty years later on his resignation of his bishopric in 1892, he was able to show that his early enthusiasm was fully justified as he described the remarkable progress British Columbia had made during his long sojourn there. Through Bishop Hills the Verney family connection with British Columbia which had begun before Edmund's arrival was to continue long after his departure.

Letters of Sir Harry and Lady Verney

While Edmund Verney's letters to his father survive almost complete, only sixteen of those written to him on Vancouver Island and during his return journey by his father, Sir Harry, and only a dozen by his stepmother, Parthenope, Lady Verney, have been preserved.[15] But together with the frequent allusions in Edmund's own letters they are enough to reveal the nature of the other side of the correspondence. They show that Sir Harry normally wrote at fortnightly intervals to catch the mail steamers – he apologizes when he misses a mail – and that his and Lady Verney's letters were substantial ones, as Edmund commented on August 20, 1863: "you write to me long, long letters."

Edmund Verney wrote to his stepmother on October 11, 1862 that he liked above all things to know "little details of your life at Claydon," and the parental letters are naturally much concerned with family news and local matters, what Lady Verney terms "the Claydon chronicle"

(November 15 1864), and she states that this was the special subject also of the now lost letters to Edmund of his sister Emily when she was at Claydon. Sir Harry and Lady Verney wrote constantly about Emily's precarious health, which was the cause of much anxiety. They wrote from time to time of the academic failures and successes of Edmund's youngest brother Frederick, and in the earlier part of 1865 they wrote much about the other brother George, his return on leave from India, and what they considered to be an imprudent engagement to marry contracted there. They wrote of other relatives, retainers and servants, and of changes and improvements in the Claydon estate. Lady Verney kept Edmund informed not only about relatives and visitors but even about the family's horses. Sir Harry gave Edmund a very detailed account of the making of a great lawn and terrace at Claydon, paid for by his brother Frederic Calvert. He wrote also of his financial problems, such as the many requests from tenant farmers for improvements. He expected that the cost of the parliamentary election of 1865 would cause him to incur debt.

Sir Harry and Lady Verney did their best also to keep Edmund informed about public affairs and their views of political events and personalities in England and abroad. They wrote about the parliamentary sessions in London. On March 4, 1865 Lady Verney reported that Sir Harry was diligently attending the House of Commons, and frequently in the company of the Prime Minister: "He walks home very often with Lord Palmerston who is in high feather." The Nightingale estate of Embley Park was so close to Palmerston's country house, Broadlands, that Sir Harry could walk across to see the Prime Minister there, and Lady Verney mentions occasions also on which she and her husband were overnight guests at Broadlands. After a stay there she wrote in January 1863 that despite some signs of age Palmerston was energetically shooting and hunting, and she concluded that he and Lady Palmerston were "the most extraordinary couple in England for activity & enjoyment – & going on for 80."

In late 1864 Sir Harry and Lady Verney both expressed thanksgiving for the exceptionally fortunate condition of the nation. "This has been a most prosperous year for England," Lady Verney wrote on November 15: "Gladstone the rising & Palmerston the setting star are making progress through their dominions in great satisfaction." She mentioned a hopeful development on the other side of North America from Edmund: "This Confederation of Canada & the provinces sounds capitally. We have had Sir Edmund Head here [Claydon], who greatly desired it, tho' he said the difficulties were enormous of carrying it through."[16] In contrast, they wrote of the troubled conditions in other parts of the world: insurrection in Poland, the Schleswig-Holstein Crisis (as allusions in Edmund's letters reveal), and especially the Civil War in the United States. Sir Harry commented on April 1, 1865: "all the reports that we hear of the war are terrible, & the evils inflicted by Federals & Confederates on each other equal in atrocity any known in history."

Sir Harry and Lady Verney made a particular point of keeping Edmund on Vancouver Island informed about the health and activities of the family's famous relative, Florence Nightingale. On January 27, 1863 Sir Harry wrote that she had moved from the Verneys' London house, which she had been occupying: "She is extremely engaged with the Reports on Hospitals & Barracks in India." On March 15, 1865 he wrote from London:

> Miss Nightingale I see sometimes – from her sick bed she is working incessantly in many ways – setting the Indian Barracks into order – & now the Hospitals of Workhouses in England – I believe there never was a sick woman who has done what she is permitted to accomplish ... her administrative ability, & the influence she obtains over people, & her knowledge, are all wonderful.
>
> & there she lies on her sick bed. I have not seen her out of it for 5 years – She gets up & lies on a Sofa, when Ld Stanley comes to see her, or Sir J. Lawrence, or Mr Massey, on Indian financial affairs, or Mr Villiers on Poor Law Matters, or Garibaldi.[17]

Sir Harry also provided in this letter various additional details about Florence Nightingale's current work.[18]

The letters kept Edmund well informed about the great social network his family maintained not only in London and at Claydon but also at Lady Verney's parental home, the Nightingale estate of Embley. Lady Verney's social activities were limited because of her poor health, but she wrote of Sir Harry's dining at Lady Palmerston's and Miss Coutts', and about entertaining eminent Victorian religious figures, including Dean Milman and Archdeacon Ferrar. It is especially interesting to note the large number of persons connected with Vancouver Island and British Columbia who were or became socially linked with the Verneys during Edmund's period there. In several of their letters Sir Harry and Lady Verney wrote of the honeymoon that their relative Bishop Hills and his wife spent at Claydon. Other guests included from time to time both governors and admirals. As Edmund mentions in his letters, Governor Kennedy had visited Claydon and brought gifts from his family when he arrived on Vancouver Island. Sir Harry commented on the other new governor (November 30 1864): "I hope that Govr Seymour will do well. He visited formerly at Embley." Seymour too brought Edmund gifts from the Verney family. After Admiral Kingcome's return to England from Vancouver Island he was invited by the Nightingales to Embley where the Verneys were staying, because of his kindness in writing favourably of Edmund to the Admiralty, as Sir Harry informed his son (January 13 1865). Kingcome's successor, Admiral Denman, was already well known to the family. Lady Verney wrote to Edmund on November 15, 1864: "I hope you will see a good deal of the Denmans, they are old friends of ours, Derbyshire people, & both earnestly desiring to do right I truly believe."[19]

Persons of lower rank connected with Edmund Verney's sojourn on Vancouver Island also enjoyed the hospitality of Claydon House or were received by his father in London. Edmund's letters reveal that his predecessor as commander of the *Grappler*, A.H.P. Helby, visited Claydon in 1862, and Sir Harry refers in his letters to the later visit there of the *Grappler*'s gunner: "Marshall made many friends here" (November 30 1864). On February 13, 1863, Sir Harry reported to his son his conversations with Major Gossett about "Columbia" and Vancouver Island.[20] When Dr. John Ash of Victoria came to England, Sir Harry held conversations with him also, and he forwarded to his son Ash's advice about sightseeing en route home in the vicinity of San Francisco (February 16 1865). From Edmund's own letters we know that he recommended to his father the Victoria businessman and member of the colonial House of Assembly, Robert Burnaby. Edmund also expressed the hope that his father would see Sir James Douglas during the latter's visit to England after his retirement, but the existing letters of Sir Harry and Lady Verney make no allusion to this.

Sir Harry Verney's letters confirm his statement: "My thoughts are seldom away from the Cabin or Deck of your little Gunboat," which Marshall's visit had brought vividly before him (November 30 1864). His letters are filled with fatherly advice and admonition to his son on a great variety of subjects. As will be noted below, he strongly urged discretion on Edmund in connection with colonial affairs, politics and personalities, and wrote much also on the subject of Edmund's desire for naval promotion. At times he advised Edmund to concentrate his intention increasingly on his professional naval duties, but he frequently urged him also to make the most of his time on Vancouver Island by gaining as much knowledge and experience as possible, including the kinds of experience that would prepare him for his position in later life as a country gentleman. Toward the end of Edmund's stay he considered that, valuable though his time on Vancouver Island had been, three years was quite long enough. He wanted Edmund to return to a position where he would have more contact and association than was possible on Vancouver Island with superiors from whom he might learn much. He underlined the statement in his letter of November 16, 1864: "Every man is the better for the Discipline of good Society – the Society of those far his Superiors."

As an example of the kind of people he wished Edmund to cultivate, he gave his old friend Lord Chichester and his family. This was not, he stated, because they were lords and ladies but because of their refinement, their religious, moral, and intellectual qualities (January 13 1865). Among the distinctions he mentioned of Lord Chichester, whom he viewed as the ideal Christian gentleman, was his service as president of the missionary society that sent William Duncan to northwest America.[21] Some of Sir Harry's advice was no doubt prompted by the imprudent engagement of his younger son George; he was clearly anxious that when Edmund looked for a wife he should be fully aware of the social and financial as well as the other dimensions of his marriage.

Sir Harry Verney was candid in criticizing the faults or potential faults of his son, including vanity and indiscretion, but the tone of his letters is always warm and affectionate. The tone of Lady Verney's letters to her stepson is usually cordial too. Thus she wrote on February 16, 1865 that she considered his life on Vancouver Island comparable in interest to his father's youthful travels, she sympathized with him on having lost his best men when the *Grappler* was paid off, and hoped he would soon be back in England. But as occasional somewhat rueful comments in Edmund's letters indicate, she was sometimes quite sharp in her criticisms of him.[22]

When Edmund expressed regret that Mary Ann (or Marianne) Tyler, the sister of his personal servant Henry, was apparently no longer employed at Claydon House, Lady Verney responded (January 30 1865): "I wonder if you ever will be old & wise enough to conceive it possible that other people *may* do what is right & kind without your instructions, & that if they have not, the said instructions, 8 months after the event, will not be very serviceable." She explained that Marianne was hospitalized for operations on varicose veins, and that as her condition would not allow her to return to "housemaiding" at Claydon, a more suitable position was found for her elsewhere, and she concluded this part of her letter with irony about Edmund's "wonderful little sermon." Such passages explain Edmund's apprehensive remarks in letters to his father that his stepmother would "bully him" (July 20 1862) or "scarify him" (April 13 1865) if his father divulged to her certain things in his letters. While Edmund was commander of his own ship, he was quite accustomed to having his personal shortcomings pointed out to him by members of his family, and he seems to have taken their criticism in good part, although it is perhaps understandable that he once complained half humorously that his younger brother George wrote to him in a highly patronizing manner (February 16 1863).

Sir Harry Verney's letters suggest a good and close relation between father and son, and they show that the father gave the son every encouragement to write full and informative letters from Vancouver Island. Sir Harry declared to Edmund on January 27, 1863:

> Your accounts of your life are very interesting to me, though I fear that you may find it rather monotonous. I believe that you will look back on it some day as a very curious, remarkable & interesting portion of your existence, & I am anxious that the retrospect should be agreeable & valuable to you; & for that purpose that you should see & recollect & note down all sorts of things – what may appear at the time trite & common & uninteresting & tiresome may some day be full of interest & importance to you. I have always thought that our enormous Colonial Empire is a very curious study, & you have the opportunity of observing a Colony in a stage of its existence different from any other Colony.

Edmund was encouraged to maintain a good level in his letters not only by criticism of defects but also by praise when he satisfied his father's standards. On December 19, 1862 Sir Harry wrote to him: "I assure you that you keep us quite au fait of your proceedings. I seem to be able to follow you in all that you do."

The Voyage Out: England to Vancouver Island

Edmund Verney recorded his journey from England to Vancouver Island in nine letters, most of which comprise a number of separately dated instalments. They provide an interesting account of travel to British Columbia by the route via Panama generally followed by Europeans during this period. The voyage took almost six weeks to San Francisco, where Verney remained two further weeks before proceeding to Vancouver Island. Accompanied by a personal servant, Henry Tyler,[23] who was to remain with him during his whole time on Vancouver Island, he embarked at Southampton on March 17, 1862 on the Royal Mail Packet *Shannon* (which by coincidence bore the same name as the naval ship on which he had served in India) and on April 1 reached St. Thomas, Danish West Indies, where he transferred to RMS *Tamar* for the voyage to Colon. He arrived there on April 6, and from Panama he continued his journey on the American SS *Sonora*, reaching Acapulco on April 17 and San Francisco on April 26.

The voyage was relatively uneventful but one passenger on the *Shannon* died of smallpox and was buried at sea, the cause of death being concealed, and Henry Tyler subsequently developed a mild case of smallpox. On one occasion the deck of the *Tamar* was damaged by a mysterious violent shock, presumably electrical although no lightning was seen. Verney gave a much less favourable view of conditions on the *Sonora* than on the other two ships. He reported that this vessel was very overcrowded and quite crank, and that a catastrophe might have been difficult to avoid if the sea had not been unusually calm. He commented (April 16): "I believe that a most wicked and dangerous risk is being run in carrying so many passengers: I do not believe that an English captain would dare to do it, or that an English public would submit to it." He declared that he refrains from giving details of "the dirt of the ship, the insolence of the sailors, the rudeness of the waiters, or the manner in which the food is flung on the table to be devoured," but that "it is indeed most pitiable to see the manner in which the third class people are treated." He expressed the wish, frequently to be repeated during the years ahead, that an English line of packets might be established between Panama and Vancouver Island.

To occupy the time on shipboard, Verney reported on the *Shannon* on March 30: "We have the usual 'packet' amusements here: music and dancing and playing of quoits." He chose to spend some of his time in more serious ways. He frequently attended and on occasion conducted divine service. He read government blue books about British Columbia, as he told his father on March 24: "I have read with the greatest possible interest the three volumes of Vancouver parliamentary papers, which you gave me; I wish there were three more: I am now reading the account of the Saskachewan expedition with great interest."[24] He asked his father the next day to send him another book of local interest in his new posting: "Will you be so good as to send out to me overland an eighteen-penny book published by Routledge called the Gold fields of Vancouver's Island and British Columbia, with a map."[25]

On March 30 Verney wrote to his father: "You will like perhaps to hear a little more about some of the passengers," and at various stages of his journey he provided pictures of his fellow travellers. These included a junior officer, George Tomlin, who was en route to join the *Grappler* as second master. Aboard the *Shannon* was Captain Champion, who had commanded the transport *Melbourne* in the Black Sea during the Crimean War: "Miss Nightingale will doubtless remember him: he brought home her dog, and has talked to me about her a great deal" (March 24).[26] In addition to naval persons, Verney took a special interest in clergymen on the various ships, as he was later to do on Vancouver Island.

Verney developed a critical view of English emigrants destined during this gold-rush period for Vancouver Island whom he encountered on shipboard. He wrote about those on the *Tamar* on April 5: "[N]early all are going out without any defined object: one has a promise of 'some appointment'; another a letter to the governor which is to work wonders: two have left the army, and one naturally thinks 'I wonder why they left it'." He was troubled by their attempts to become over-familiar with him, not wishing to give offence to persons going to the same colony but on the other hand not wanting "to find myself saddled with a number of questionable friends on my arrival." His solution to this problem was to adopt chess as his favourite game: "as it is most interesting, and does not admit of conversation." Fortunately the emigrants included some of whose character he could approve. On the *Shannon* as he noted on March 30: "As second class passenger is Mr. Davie, a surgeon, going to the diggings with his four sons: he seems a truly religious man."[27]

On the *Sonora* Verney had what was probably his first meeting with large numbers of Americans. He wrote on April 21: "I dare say you will like to hear my ideas of the American people as they have presented themselves to my view on board this ship." His initial impressions were not very favourable, but he attempted to reach a balanced judgment, taking into account misunderstandings between English and Americans caused both by the currently raging American Civil War and by the common language:

> The manners and language of Americans must not be judged by An English Standard: they do themselves injustice when they ask it: they are a distinct nation, whose excellencies equal those of any other nation, when judged, as those of other nations are, by the standards of their own best men: but they have incorporated into their language expressions which would be considered vulgarisms in ours, and they have entirely changed the meanings of some words: for instance, the

> word 'clever' is the reverse of complimentary: it implies that a person is only one degree removed from idiotcy: the word used to express our idea of clever is 'smart', a word quite offensive to the English ear as applied to individuals.

This was the beginning of Verney's acquaintance with American ways which was to continue amid the large American population of gold-rush British Columbia.

When Verney reached Acapulco he found Royal Navy ships in port. There on April 17 he breakfasted and dined with the officers of HMS *Bacchante*, and had an interview with Rear-Admiral Sir Thomas Maitland, commander-in-chief of the Pacific Station, under whom he was to serve. He reported (April 27) that the admiral was "civil, if not cordial," and that "every-one told me that I was very fortunate in getting command of the Grappler":

> [T]hey say that it is a very interesting appointment; sometimes the Indians are threatening, and orders arrive in the middle of the night for the gunboats to get up steam and be off somewhere: I think I shall like it much as long as there is something to do, and I do not think that I shall be often idle: I hear that, of the two gunboats, the Grappler is in the most efficient condition, and altogether the best worth having.

At their meeting in Acapulco Admiral Maitland granted Verney a week's leave in San Francisco before proceeding to Vancouver Island, which in practice extended to almost two weeks, April 26 to May 8 or 9. Verney spent this time mainly in sightseeing, and social and sporting activities, but he evidently undertook some mission of gathering information for Captain Washington of the Royal Navy's Hydrographic Department. Through the helpfulness of the British consul, William Booker, he was able to stay at the Union Club, and he had a pleasant reunion with the Episcopal Bishop Kip, who had visited the Verneys at Claydon House in 1860.[28] As well as inspecting harbour fortifications and the Mare Island Navy Yard, he made an excursion by steamboat and railway to Sacramento, Folsom, and Lincoln (walking back twenty miles when he missed the train for the return), went snipe shooting, and visited gold diggings. Despite some complaints about broken luggage, the excessive profanity of the inhabitants, and the great cost of everything, Verney clearly enjoyed his stay in San Francisco.

Verney's last letter instalment from San Francisco is dated May 8, when he expected to sail the next day, and his next letter is dated from Esquimalt on May 15. His existing letters do not provide any account of his voyage up the west coast, not even the name of the ship, but in Victoria the *Daily British Colonist* reported on May 13 the arrival at four o'clock that morning at Esquimalt of the steamship *Pacific* from San Francisco, and noted that the passengers included Lieut. E.H. Verney. The *Daily Evening Press* also recorded his arrival on the same day. The next day the *Colonist*, again listing Verney among the passengers, reported complaints that this was a very overloaded ship, especially in the steerage.

Naval Activities

Verney's naval activities as commander of the *Grappler* are documented in the Claydon House archive not only by his letters to his father but also by two letterbooks in which, like his predecessor in command, A.H.P. Helby, he kept copies of official letters on ship's business, addressed to superior officers and to such officials as the Navy's Accountant-General.[29] These sources provide an interesting supplement to other naval records, since it has long been recognized that the *Grappler* and her sister ship, the *Forward*, played an important role in a British Columbia that historians have sometimes termed a "gunboat frontier."[30] These two gunboats, built originally for service in the Baltic and Black seas during the Crimean War, had special utility even during periods when larger vessels were stationed at Esquimalt, because their small size and shallow draught allowed them to penetrate many places on the coast that were beyond the reach of larger ships.[31]

The logbooks of the *Grappler* during Verney's period of command, which are preserved among the Admiralty records in the Public Record Office at Kew,[32] provide the information that the ship was a wooden vessel of 232 tons, with three masts, and draught of 8 feet, or 8 feet 2 inches with two months' provisions. Dimensions are not stated in the log, but other sources give the ship's length as about 106 feet, beam as about 22 feet, and depth of hold as 8 feet. The *Grappler* had a sixty horsepower horizontal Maudsley steam engine and screw propeller.[33] Armament according to the logs was one thirty-two and two twenty-four-pound howitzers. The ship's complement in 1862-63 was forty, including five marines and three boys. Printed *Navy Lists* give the names only of commissioned officers, during Verney's command only Verney himself and for part of 1862 George Tomlin, but the ship's muster books in the Public Record Office list the names and ranks of all those who served under Verney on the *Grappler*.[34]

The *Grappler* and its commander both belong to a period of transition between the old Royal Navy and the new, between sail and steam, between wooden ships and ironclads. Verney was of a generation trained by those who had served under Nelson. In the Crimean War he had taken part, according to a family historian, in what was probably the last attack on land defences by sailing ships and in the first sea fight between steam powered vessels.[35] He had in the *Grappler* a ship which normally proceeded under steam power, and so he records visits to Nanaimo for coaling, and describes the vessel on a long northern voyage as having its decks loaded with coal. But the ship could proceed by sail alone, and Verney tells of his pleasure on finding how well it handled under sail and of his admiration for Lord Gilford's HMS *Tribune* which was famous for its sailing qualities.

In the same month Verney set out for Vancouver Island, March 1862, the duel had taken place between the *Monitor* and the *Merrimack*, apparently demonstrating the superiority of ironclads and rendering older ships obsolete. En route he obtained as much information as he could about USS *Monitor* and forwarded it to the Admiralty from Panama, and on his return journey to England in 1865 he inspected at the Boston Navy Yard the "double-turretted monitor 'Agamenticus,'" upon which he commented (August 27):

> [S]he gives far more the idea of a serviceable sea-going vessel than any monitor I have hitherto seen: her appearance is most formidable, and suggestive of great power, and her arrangements are far superior to any that I have seen before. I wonder how our English iron-clad navy will strike me after what I have seen here.

During his period on Vancouver Island some anxiety was caused when there appeared to be risk of war between England and the United States by reports of the construction of two "monitors" at San Francisco. Verney asked his father on October 14, 1862, "Does the defence of these colonies at all occupy the publick mind at home?" and raised the possibility that the little *Grappler* might be left alone to defend Vancouver Island against American ironclads, while the *Forward* was out of service having new boilers installed.[36]

Fortunately the *Grappler* was never put to this test, but Verney's letters provide accounts of all the main activities in which the ship was engaged during his three years in British Columbia. In the late summer and autumn of 1862 the *Grappler* was involved in the foundation of the new agricultural settlements at Cowichan and Comox, and Verney describes their progress in a number of letters. In the spring of 1863, although suffering from defective boilers, the *Grappler* took part in the search for the Lemalchi Indians believed responsible for a series of murders in the Gulf Islands. Verney was not present at the bombardment by HMS *Forward* of the Lemalchi village on Kuper Island, but he subsequently gives a vivid account of the finding of the body of one of the murdered men at Bedwell Harbour on Pender Island (May 3), and he provides a detailed report of the surrender by the Cowichan Indians of two wanted men (May 5). The principal event of the later part of 1863 recorded in the letters is a northern voyage in October-November to Metlakatla, which includes an extensive account of the missionary work of William Duncan. This voyage in very imperfectly charted waters at a bad time of year proved hazardous, and Verney gives a dramatic description of an occasion when the *Grappler* on the return voyage suffered damage to its bottom and was very nearly lost through striking a rock in Milbanke Sound (November 15). During the Chilcotin uprising in the summer of 1864 naval involvement was somewhat peripheral, since the main scenes of action were inland, but in July Verney wrote from Bella Coola, where the *Grappler* had been stationed to maintain communications with

Governor Seymour, and on September 1 he wrote from Bute Inlet where he had been sent to prevent the Chilcotin Indians from fishing as a means of subduing them and forcing them to give up wanted men. Then in October he made a second voyage to Metlakatla, in a police action resulting from an attack on Duncan's Indian constables by the crew of a trading schooner.

More often than great dramatic episodes, Verney's letters to his father and the *Grappler* letterbooks refer to such activities as visiting settlements, investigating reports of troubles between Indians and settlers, which usually proved exaggerated, and pursuing smugglers and illegal whiskey traders. The letters impress upon one the extent to which the *Grappler* was occupied in peaceful activities which in later times would be the work of such agencies as a coast guard: placing buoys at the mouth of the Fraser, or taking supplies to lighthouses. Verney became secretary of the colonial Lighthouse Board in Victoria, and his separate letterbooks in that capacity have been preserved in the Provincial Archives.[37] In addition to such practical matters, Verney's letters sometimes reveal the *Grappler*'s ceremonial functions: for example, on November 9, 1862 he wrote from Esquimalt that to celebrate the Prince of Wales' coming of age, "tomorrow morning I am going round to Victoria to dress ship, and generally to assist in creating a sensation."

The special value of Verney's letters to his father on naval matters is that they fill out the official records with personal detail, and convey a good sense of what life was like from day to day aboard the *Grappler*, from the viewpoint at least of its commanding officer. Though Verney at first much enjoyed his command, he commented frequently on the special problems he faced, such as navigation on an intricate and still very imperfectly charted coast. Another recurring problem was that of desertions of sailors and marines in a gold-rush colony, where the men could easily obtain several times the rate of naval pay. On July 17, 1862 Verney told his father of his regret that the government had refused double pay to the men of the gunboats. The *Grappler* letterbook reveals that two days later he asked Admiral Maitland for permission to enlist foreigners, as there was no prospect of obtaining British subjects.[38] At times he had serious problems in keeping his ship's financial accounts in order, aggravated by an able but unreliable steward. The grimmer side of life aboard his vessel was impressed upon him when one of his engineers tried to commit suicide (February 18 1864). He records both the personal advantages and disadvantages he found in the fact that the senior officers at Esquimalt came and went at frequent intervals with the movements of their ships, while the admiral until the early 1860s had his base station far away at Valparaiso, and he gives characteristically candid and often critical views of the senior officers. His letters provide such details not found in the official records as the fact that Rear-Admiral Hon. Joseph Denman was generally known throughout the fleet as "Dear Josey" or "Josey Dear" (December 7 1864), because of the effusive endearments of Mrs. Denman, who lived aboard the flagship.

The letters make it clear that for Verney the earlier part of his time in command of the *Grappler* was on the whole happier than the later part. In his early Vancouver Island letters he expresses great pleasure in having command of his own ship and in the life he was leading as its captain, as well as enthusiasm for the coastal scenery and climate. He wrote from Cowichan on August 30, 1862: "I really cannot be too thankful for having got this appointment," and added: "I cannot remember any period of my life when I have been so perfectly happy and contented." His enjoyment of his new command was increased, as he emphasized in a letter of June 1, by the excellent condition in which his predecessor Helby had left the *Grappler*, and the good discipline, training and feeling Helby had established in its crew: "it is a great pleasure, and a great responsibility to command men among whom such good feeling prevails."[39]

Verney's early enjoyment of his command of the *Grappler* had not entirely disappeared by the summer of 1864. On August 22, when his father reported that the First Lord of the Admiralty, the Duke of Somerset, had spoken of the possibility of a posting to the royal yacht, Verney wrote that he had always considered his present command "the best lieutenant's appointment in the service." For various reasons, however, his enthusiasm declined during the later part of his time in British Columbia. Deterioration in the condition of the *Grappler* had become a serious problem by early 1864, partly as a result of damage sustained on the northern voyage during the previous autumn, and this caused much uncertainty and long periods of forced inactivity. In a discouraged moment, Verney wrote on June 4, 1864:

> I am becoming very heartily tired of the "Grappler"; she is very defective: she steams badly: her bottom is all knocked about, and we are so shorthanded that it is one incessant drive to keep the ship in even tolerable order, and it really is impossible to forget all about promotion.

He was faced with special administrative problems as orders had already arrived that the gunboats were to be paid off, and the end of the *Grappler*'s current commission was reached on October 31, 1864, when under the system that still prevailed in the Navy at this period Verney much to his regret lost his best and most experienced men. Although the ship was in service again in November, the admiral recommended that it be sold, because of the cost of repairs, and during his final months in command Verney was awaiting the Admiralty's decision about this. The end of his three-year appointment to the *Grappler* was reached on February 25, 1865, but his letters show that he did not make his farewell to the ship until May 13, when he hauled down its pennant for the last time, three weeks before he began his return journey to England.[40]

During the later part of his time in British Columbia Verney looked forward increasingly to his return to England, and as the letter of June 4, 1864 indicates he became increasingly impatient about his lack of promotion. On February 8, 1865 he complained he had been fourteen years in the Navy and was still a lieutenant. His hope for more rapid promotion was based on his active service in the Crimean War and especially during the Indian Mutiny, when he felt that a virtual promise had been made that remained unfulfilled. His impatience was increased by the fact that on his mother's side he came from a notable naval family. Her brother, whom Verney appropriately refers to in his letters as "Uncle Hope," Admiral Sir James Hope, in 1863 became naval commander-in-chief for North America and the West Indies, but not for the Pacific Station where Verney served. Admiral Hope had written from Shanghai on May 2, 1862 to congratulate Verney on assuming command of the *Grappler* in a place with such a fine climate and such good coal as Vancouver Island, and he subsequently referred favourably to Verney in testimony to a Parliamentary committee, but he showed no inclination to exercise special influence on his nephew's behalf.[41]

The subject of Edmund Verney's claims and hopes for promotion occurs with tedious regularity in his later Vancouver Island letters, and figures prominently also in his father's surviving letters to him; one suspects that Edmund made a special point of preserving the letters he received on this subject. Sir Harry reported several occasions in 1863-64 on which he spoke on Edmund's behalf to the First Lord of the Admiralty, the Duke of Somerset, and his private secretary, Captain Ryder. He always received a cordial reception but the duke impressed upon him the numerous claims he had from other officers, including those serving in unhealthy locations on the coast and rivers of Africa, and he made no promises. Sir Harry wrote to his son after one of these interviews (February 9 1863): "I have done as much as I ought to do," but he was never entirely successful in persuading him to turn his attention instead to other things, although Edmund refers to the subject as "taboed," i.e., tabooed (January 17 1864), and he sometimes seems aware, for example in a letter of November 22, 1864, that his obsession has reached comically absurd levels, almost as if foreshadowing Gilbert and Sullivan on the Victorian Navy. But Edmund Verney was neither the first nor last naval lieutenant to display such an acute concern for promotion. His viewpoint is anticipated by a young naval officer in *Mansfield Park* (1814), by Jane Austen, who had brothers in the Navy: "what can be more unbecoming, or more worthless, than the uniform of a lieutenant, who has been a lieutenant a year or two, and sees others made a commander before him."[42]

Monotonous though this subject becomes in Edmund's letters it has some historical interest as revealing the degree to which family influence was and was not considered appropriate during a period when the Navy's officer class was strongly aristocratic: Edmund refers in one letter to an officer "of no interest," i.e., influence of family or friends, as if that was an exceptional case (November 5 1864). Edmund's letters together with his father's reveal how closely each list of naval promotions was scrutinized by officers and their well placed relatives to ensure that no one got ahead of them or their favoured candidates without clear reason.

The letters are interesting too for the ambiguities both father and son display toward the Navy as a profession. At times both emphasize the importance of complete dedication to the profession, but both also display awareness that, in contrast to the many officers who were younger sons, for Edmund the time in the Navy was a period of preparation and waiting before he succeeded to a great estate and large responsibilities in England.

Viewed from a later perspective, perhaps the most interesting of Verney's naval activities, leaving aside his relations with the Native Indians, which will be considered below, was his involvement in the foundation of the settlements at Cowichan and Comox: this is probably the most enduring work in which the *Grappler* was engaged under his command. The *Colonist* recorded on July 30, 1862 that Verney was present at the meeting called by Attorney-General Cary the previous evening about establishing the Cowichan settlement, and that he proposed votes of thanks to the speakers. Two weeks later he made his first visit to Cowichan, travelling by canoe with Rev. A.C. Garrett, and he wrote to his father on August 16 about missionary work among the Indians there. After the expedition of August 18-21 led by Governor Douglas brought a group of settlers to Cowichan in HMS *Hecate*, Verney remained with the *Grappler* to assist the settlers. He gives his account of the early progress of the settlement as well as the "curious" character of some of the settlers in letters of August 30, September 5, and September 14.

In an editorial on the Cowichan settlement the *Colonist* commented on September 13, 1862: "The uniform kindness and courtesy of Commander Verney of the Grappler, we are happy to hear universally spoken of. His efforts are unceasing to oblige all by every means in his power, and to advance the general interests of the settlement." His private and official letters both show that he continued in subsequent years to take special interest in the Cowichan settlement. In an official letter to Captain Spencer on May 10, 1863 he wrote that he was pleased with the progress of the settlement and "the general contentment of the settlers" but regretted that the Governor's promises to compensate Indians for the loss of lands had not been kept.[43] On June 4, 1864 he wrote his father: "I have just returned from a week's visit to Cowichan which I enjoyed exceedingly, visiting among my friends the settlers, who were most hospitable, and welcomed me very pleasantly."[44]

In the Comox district the *Grappler* is still remembered as having brought the first group of European settlers there early in October 1862.[45] In a letter of October 11 to his stepmother, Parthenope, Lady Verney, Edmund describes this event. In a letter to his father on November 1 he gives an account of another visit to Comox, when he was accompanied by Bishop Hills. The bishop recorded the occasion both in his diary and in a letter of October 30 to Sir Harry Verney which is preserved at Claydon House. In this letter, written aboard the *Grappler* at Deep Bay, Hills stated that at the end of a gathering of settlers for divine worship Edmund offered the settlers the aid and support of his vessel to their temporal prosperity. Edmund's 1862 letters provide descriptions of the rich agricultural land, abundant game, great forests and fine scenery of the Comox valley, and of the enthusiasm of the new settlers, and his later letters show his continued interest in the Comox as well as the Cowichan settlement. On a visit to Comox on May 1, 1863 he recorded a significant mark of the progress of the agricultural settlement: "I had a glass of rich and delicious new milk," and on another visit two weeks later (May 15 1863) he again canoed up the river, and called on settlers in their houses. He read divine service for them on Sunday, and he even brought "juvenile works in verse and prose for distribution among the youthful population of the Comax settlement."[46]

Verney's naval activities and visits to the Cowichan and Comox settlements gave him special opportunities for assessing the future prospects of Vancouver Island. While he was careful to avoid excessive enthusiasm, he consistently reported to his father that Vancouver Island was a good colony for immigrants who possessed reasonable qualifications and expectations, especially if they avoided the gold-rush fever. Thus he wrote on October 14, 1862 that, although he believed the days of making a rapid fortune in land speculation were past, he considered "there can be no colony better suited for a man, whatever his position in life, who intends to make it his home, and never to return to England or go gold-digging."

Other Activities

The letters show that wide-ranging though his activities were as naval officer, Verney quickly and energetically threw himself into many other activities as well. On July 20, 1862 he wrote that, while he was modifying some of his earlier "fanciful ideas" of service, he hoped to do useful work "under the patronage and with the advice of the dear bishop." On September 22 of that year he declared: "I wish no committee to be complete without me, and I wish to be considered as one who has the interests of these colonies most warmly at heart." Four days later he added: "what with being a member of the Immigration Board, of the female Immigration Committee, a magistrate, secretary to the Lighthouse Board, and last but not least, commander of a gunboat, I am always busy." On May 25, 1864 he stated: "I have a good deal of work in hand just now, besides the 'Grappler': I am a member of the 'Exploration Committee', and Chairman of the sub-committee appointed to draw up regulations for and to conclude arrangements with the Exploring party." In the letters of his last months on Vancouver Island he wrote especially of his work for the Victoria Mechanics Institute he had helped to found.

The impression that the letters convey of Verney as one who worked energetically for diverse good causes during his period on Vancouver Island is abundantly confirmed by other sources, such as Victoria's leading newspaper, the *Daily British Colonist*. The immigration scheme which brought the "brideship" *Tynemouth* to the island in September 1862 is a matter in which Verney's father had evidently been interested for some time. On his arrival in the colony Verney himself immediately became involved. On June 9, 1862 the *Colonist* lists him at a meeting presided over by Bishop Hills as one of the committee of the Columbian Immigration Society, formed to encourage the immigration of industrious women and other suitable persons in cooperation with the London Columbia Emigration Society. On August 8 the *Colonist* in its account of a meeting of citizens to form an Immigration Board for the assistance of new arrivals reported in detail a speech by Verney about some of the types of dubious or unsuitable immigrants he had encountered in the colony, persons absurdly ill qualified or unwilling to work.

Verney describes the arrival of the *Tynemouth* in his letters quite fully, no doubt because of his father's special interest. On September 20 he states that he and his men have prepared the Marine Barracks for the reception of the immigrants, and entertained many of them on the *Grappler* at a regatta. He reports that on the whole the scheme was a success, although a few of the immigrants were of bad character, and concludes: "I think the little orphans from East Grinstead took my fancy most: perhaps that is because, being only twelve, they do not expect to get married at once." Subsequently the *Colonist*'s rival newspaper, the *Daily Evening Press*, on September 22 criticized the Immigration Board for failing to make adequate preparations, although it praised the work of Mr. Marshall of the *Grappler* in making ready the Marine Barracks. But John Marshall wrote on the same day to the *Press* stating that he had acted entirely under the direction of Verney as one of the Immigration Committee; and Gilbert Sproat and Robert Burnaby also published in the *Colonist* a refutation of the criticism. When the later "brideship" *Robert Lowe* arrived early in 1863 the *Colonist* (January 13) records that the *Grappler* again accorded naval honours by bringing around the thirty-eight young women from Esquimalt to Victoria: the sailors laid for them a boardwalk from the shore of James Bay to the old Marine Barracks, where more than a thousand spectators gathered. Verney's letters show that he long remained interested in the welfare and marriages of the women who came on the *Tynemouth* and the *Robert Lowe*.

The Vancouver Island Exploration Expedition of 1864 led by Robert Brown was a project of the new governor, Arthur Kennedy.[47] On a visit to the mines at Goldstream in April 1864, which Verney describes in a letter, the governor dined in a tent. There were speeches in which according to the *Colonist* (April 21) Verney responded to the toast to the Navy. Kennedy announced his desire to establish an exploratory expedition to prospect the resources of the island. On April 29 the *Colonist* listed Verney as one of a committee of fifteen appointed at a public meeting to consider ways of raising money and outfitting the expedition. On May 11 the *Colonist* reported that at a large public meeting Verney, who referred to Brown as his friend, moved "amid applause" a motion favouring financial support of the expedition by the community, and on May 20 it reported another meeting, at which he conveyed a communication from the governor, and read a proposed letter of instruction for the expedition. Subsequently when Brown was appointed expedition commander Verney was made one of a committee of five to confer with him and examine credentials of applicants for subordinate positions, and the same subcommittee was later reappointed to draw up rules for the expedition (*Colonist*, May 21, 24).

On the *Grappler* Verney took the members of the expedition to the starting point of its exploration, Cowichan, in June; and in November he brought them back from Nanaimo at the end of their work. Brown acknowledged his assistance in his journal and in the official report on the expedition. On March 20, 1865 the *Colonist* stated that a meeting of the Exploration Committee had approved, after some debate, the introduction to the report, drawn up by Verney and two others. After the publication of the report,[48] as one of Verney's letters reveals (April 23 1865), he sent copies to his father and others in England.

The *Colonist* records that Verney was active from the beginning in the foundation of the Mechanics Literary Institute, generally known as the Mechanics Institute, which gave Victoria its first real library late in 1864. It reported on November 26, 1864 that on the previous night at a large meeting attended by many "mechanics" Verney took part in the debate about founding the Institute and was elected by vote to the committee then set up. On December 15, listing Verney as one of the committee, it reported that the Institute was to open the next day, in a room on Langley Street, with newspapers and both reference and circulating libraries. On January 10, 1865 the *Colonist* stated that the library was flourishing and now contained more than five hundred volumes, thanks to the liberality of citizens "and the energy of several of the committee, among whom Lieut. Verney may be specially mentioned."

Until near the time of his departure Verney continued to donate books, for example Kinglake's *Invasion of the Crimea*, according to the *Colonist* (April 29 1865), while his letters to his father show that he was also soliciting duplicates from the library at Claydon House. Meanwhile in January he had given the second in the Institute's series of lectures, one titled "Ocean's Signposts," on navigation, and determining latitude and longitude at sea. The *Colonist* reported (January 25) that despite rival attractions the Lyceum Hall was completely full and that Verney made his abstruse subject interesting. Late in May, when on the eve of his return to England he resigned from the committee of management, he was given an unanimous vote of thanks. The *Colonist* reported (May 27) that he had been one of the originators of the Institute, and ever since one of the most active and useful supporters, and stated that his departure would be a great loss to the community generally, where he had been foremost in good works.

Numerous other activities of Verney recorded in the *Colonist* confirm his statements in his letters (for example on March 6 1864) that above all things he disliked idleness and inactivity, and demonstrate his zeal in maintaining on Vancouver Island his family's tradition of working for good causes. Among the good works reported in the *Colonist* (February 2 1863), as well as mentioned in the letters, was a meeting in which he took an active part to organize an Esquimalt free school. In 1863 and 1864 the *Colonist* lists him at meetings as a committee member of the Vancouver Island Bible Society, the local branch of the British and Foreign Bible Society (June 6, December 8, 1863; December 6 1864). He is recorded in the press as speaking and responding to toasts on the most diverse occasions, including a speech at a dinner to celebrate the majority of the Prince of Wales on November 10, 1862 (*Colonist*, November 12), which he transcribed and sent to his father. In December 1862 at a St. Andrew's Day dinner he followed Colonel Moody in responding to the toast to the Army and Navy, referring to the close connection of the Navy with Vancouver Island, and giving an anecdote of the seige of Lucknow, to laughter and applause (*Colonist*, December 3). In January 1864 we find him giving an address at the St. John's Church Sunday School Festival (*Colonist*, January 27).[49]

Verney's zeal in involving himself in a wide variety of colonial and civic affairs was so great as sometimes to worry his father that he might be seen as improperly advancing himself or meddling in politics in colonies where nearly everything was affected by party feeling. Sir Harry wrote his son on December 30, 1862 that the speech at the dinner for the Prince of Wales' birthday which Edmund sent him "rather alarms me." He considered that what Edmund said was good, but asked, was it well to say anything? Would Helby have made such a speech, or Uncle Hope when he was a lieutenant? Did the commander of the *Forward* dine there and speak? He urged his son, "so to conduct yourself that no one, & especially no naval officer, may have reason to say that you in any degree improperly officiously or forwardly take part in matters not professional. You know not how important this is." He repeated this warning on February 13, 1863, urging upon his son the special need for discretion, "because many of your duties appear to be more connected with the Colony than with the Navy": under such circumstances, he advised, the best rule is for an officer to "shun notoriety, & not to come prominently forward without necessity." He reported a conversation with W.D. Gossett about the strength of party feeling in British Columbia and Vancouver Island, in which Gossett "said enough to convince me that you had better form intimacies with your Naval comrades than with the Colonial authorities."

In fact, however, only one of Verney's extra-naval activities seems to have caused any significant controversy, his sitting on the bench as a magistrate;[50] and his father's advice may not have proved altogether helpful in this matter, for Sir Harry expressed the hope that his son would learn as much as he could on Vancouver Island that would fit him for his later life as a country gentleman, including the duties of a magistrate. On September 18, 1862 a letter in the *Colonist* signed "Several New Arrivals" criticized Verney for setting up as a magistrate on Vancouver Island, stating that he was not a resident, and that this was contrary to custom. In a letter of November 11, 1862 Verney mentions that his acting as magistrate was also criticized by Captain Richards and other naval officers. However, in an editorial comment on September 18 the *Colonist* defended Verney, declaring that naval officers were *ex officio* magistrates and that he had presumably been appointed by Governor Douglas to exercise this office in remote areas. On December 3 and 6 the *Colonist* again defended Verney against criticism of his role as magistrate that had appeared in the rival paper, the *Victoria Daily Chronicle.* Verney was not the only naval officer to be involved in such a controversy at this period, for Commander J.W. Pike was also criticized by the *Chronicle* for acting as a magistrate, and also defended by the *Colonist* (March 30 1863). On April 30, 1864, however, after Verney had sat in Victoria in a case of illegal whiskey selling, in place of A.F. Pemberton, who was ill, the *Colonist* stated that he acted with ability and impartiality but that he had been appointed magistrate primarily for remote areas, and that other magistrates were needed for Victoria. Verney's attempts to suppress illegal liquor traffic in remoter localities involved him in other problems, including at least one threat of a lawsuit, but these were probably unavoidable for the commander of the *Grappler* carrying out his official duties.

In his late Vancouver Island letters Verney expresses a strong sense of having fallen short of his initial high intentions and expectations of public service in the colony. This sense perhaps resulted from unrealistically high aims and standards, but it may also reflect some personal failings of which he does not write explicitly in letters to his father. In any case, as the *Colonist* recorded, high tribute was paid to Verney for his services to the colony when he was on the point of departure.

The *Colonist* on June 3, 1865 gave a full report of a dinner given in the French Hotel the previous night to honour Verney on his leaving Victoria. Chief Justice Cameron acted as chairman, and the Colonial Secretary, the Attorney General, and many other officials and prominent residents of Victoria were present. In an address signed by "seventy-five of our most respectable citizens," and presented by G.M. Sproat, who acted as vice-chairman of the gathering, Verney was commended not only as naval officer and magistrate who had "contributed to the security and comfort of the outlying settlers in different parts of the island, and to the preservation of peace and friendliness between them and the native tribes," but especially for his work as a citizen in Victoria:

> In almost every important effort for the public good which has been made in Victoria during the last three years, you have taken an active and useful part, particularly as a member of the respective Committees for the care of Female Immigrants, for providing employment for industrious immigrants, for encouraging new settlements, for exploring the Island, and establishing a Mechanics' Institute. The success of these movements was in a great measure due to your practical ability, energy and good judgment, accompanied by a perseverance and public spirit which overcame many difficulties.

That the tribute was a genuine one is confirmed by Sproat's dedication three years later of his book, *Scenes and Studies of Savage Life* (1868):[51] to "Edmund Hope Verney R.N., whose name associated with good works, will long be remembered in Vancouver Island." From a later perspective it can be added that some of the civic enterprises in which Verney involved himself during the formative period he was in the colony had important long-term results. The library of the Mechanics Institute in which he took a special interest later became the foundation collection of the Victoria public library, and the school at Esquimalt he helped initiate was apparently the first free school, open to all without fees, in what is now the province of British Columbia.

People and Politics

In his early Vancouver Island letters Verney expresses great enthusiasm for the scenery and climate, but makes it clear that his opinion of the people he encountered on the island was much more mixed. As has already been noted, his doubts about some of the prospective inhabitants of the island had begun during his voyage on the *Tamar* in the Caribbean, when he found that nearly all the passengers bound for the colony were going out "without any defined object." A few months after his arrival he wrote to his father, on September 22, 1862: "You are right in thinking that this is a very curious place," and he deplored the English practice of sending out those who are "*rather wild*," declaring that unless they are already reformed they "go to the dogs at once." On October 22 he stated: "In this colony I find the country more interesting than the people, nature than art."

Verney belonged to a family known for its support of liberal causes, but the aristocratic Whig and naval traditions in which he had been brought up were far removed from the North American frontier ideas of democracy and equality he encountered on Vancouver Island. On June 1, 1862 he complained: "nobody seems to respect any-body else, but people aim at establishing a most odious fraternity: I hear a grocer address a lieutenant R.N. by his unadorned surname, with every familiarity." An amusing illustration of this state of affairs is provided by an episode he describes on November 15, 1862: while he was waiting his turn at the post office a half-intoxicated miner pushed himself in front of him, and began speaking: "'I say, what a swell we are in our regimentals, ain't we?' Then finding I would take no notice of him he held up some tobacco in my face, and said 'I say governor, have a chaw.'"

On his arrival in Victoria Verney took a severe view of the moral failure of many of its inhabitants, including sexual and marital irregularities, and neglect of sabbath observance, although later in 1862 on October 11 he noted rapid improvement in the state of society: "the bishop says there is a wonderful change since he has been here, and I can detect a change even during the few months that I have been here"; and he added: "Several of the new arrivals have brought *good wives*, a great point." Conscious of his tendency toward harsh judgments, he contrasted two years later, October 27, 1864, his own severity with the greater charity of his friend Tom Howell: "he did me a great deal of good: he is full of charity toward all men, & I am not."

Verney, however, was sociable and good humoured, and despite his severe views – no doubt sometimes because of them – he made a wide range of friends during his period on Vancouver Island, beginning with Bishop Hills, and including the McKenzies of Craigflower, Edmund Coleman the artist, and settlers at outlying points on the coast. His letters are full of praise for his relative Bishop Hills, whom he found on his arrival to be a "most loveable man" and considered needed only a wife to be a perfect bishop (May 25, June 1 1862), a desire he saw fulfilled before leaving the island. He befriended other clergymen, especially Rev. R.J. Dundas. He not only spent his Christmases with the McKenzies at Craigflower but also many Sundays when the *Grappler* was in port. On February 8, 1865 he wrote his father that he had known Coleman for two years and liked him. He stated that the artist was "in some distress here" and attempted to interest his father in him, recommending his book on Mont Blanc. In his speech at the farewell banquet given to him in Victoria on June 2, 1865, Verney, as the *Colonist* reported (June 5), "alluded particularly to the many friendships he had formed among settlers in the outlying districts and with many who are now in the wilds of British Columbia," assuring them of his continued interest in their welfare; the newspaper emphasized this at his particular request just before his departure. When Robert Brown arrived with Verney at Cowichan on the Vancouver Island Exploring Expedition they were received, as Brown recorded in his journal, by M. Jean Compagnon, a "venerable old gentleman, a great friend of Capt. Verney's."[52]

Many of Verney's less favourable judgments were directed at those in official positions. He quickly developed a critical view of the colonial establishment on Vancouver Island, including Governor Douglas. On July 2, 1862 in a letter marked "Private / *Not to be Copied*" he wrote that he thought Douglas should be replaced as soon as possible. He complained that the governor "has no pretension to be a high-minded, superior gentleman,"[53] and gave a picture of him as a pompous and ridiculous figure, parading about Victoria every evening "in uniform with a bombadier [*sic*] of Engineers lashed on to a cavalry sword following in his wake." Verney described a state dinner for the Queen's Birthday as "a preposterously ridiculous farce," and continued: "It is generally stated that all roads are led through the property of the governor or some of his relations, for each of whom he appears to have found a snug berth." He expanded this criticism of Douglas' nepotism on July 20, after attending a "pic-nic" with members of the governor's family.

At the time he wrote, criticism of Douglas' nepotism and of what Amor De Cosmos termed "the family-company-compact"[54] was widespread, but Verney's views are affected by his class biases and his Evangelical religious outlook. He wanted, as he states in the letter of July

20, a governor who will give religious, moral, and social leadership, who will "raise the standard of excellence in religion, in morals, in dinners, servants, gardens, houses, dress, manners, and customs." To counteract democratic American feeling and the immoral influence of the Hudson's Bay Company, he wrote on August 20, 1862, "a refined English gentleman is sadly wanted at the head of affairs." Verney's prejudices appear in their most deplorable form in some of his comments on the governor's wife and daughters, which are snobbish and patronizing, if not worse. The best he can find to say of the wife is: "Mrs. Douglas is a good creature, but utterly ignorant" (July 20). Here Verney appears less perceptive than some contemporary English visitors to Victoria, such as Sophia Cracroft, who showed a sympathetic understanding of the reasons for Douglas' apparent pomposity and a much warmer appreciation of the character of Mrs. Douglas.[55]

Verney, however, was by no means without awareness of the greatness of James Douglas' character and achievements. He considered that the time for Douglas was at an end, but his criticisms are nearly always accompanied by tributes, and he repeatedly describes the governor as a "wonderful man" (for example, July 2 and August 20, 1862). Douglas should be removed with great kindness, he writes on July 20, 1862, "for he has done much for the colonies." Verney emphasizes too that he always found Douglas friendly and kind-hearted, and his own relations with the governor appear always to have been cordial. Indeed the critical remarks about Douglas disappear from his letters after his first few months on Vancouver Island. He records with interest and respect conversations with Douglas in 1863, and in the next year after the arrival of Douglas' successor, Arthur Kennedy, we find him complaining on March 26 that the new governor does not sufficiently appreciate Douglas: "I think Captain Kennedy might be a little more charitable to Sir James Douglas' shortcomings."

In his early Vancouver Island letters Verney is as candid in his views of other colonial officials as of the governor. In the letter of July 20, 1862 he described Douglas' son-in-law, the Speaker of the House of Assembly, "Dr. Helmkin," as "an infidel" and added "but the Governor and he have not spoken to each other for years." He complained that the Colonial Secretary, W.A.G. Young, who was married to Douglas' niece, held too many offices and received too many salaries. On November 23, 1862 he described Douglas' brother-in-law, Chief Justice Cameron, as "an uncertificated bankrupt." He stated he might characterize him as "an inane booby" but he likes him "for he is a harmless old gentleman: he generally wears a benign vacant smile on his countenance." On the other hand, Attorney General Cary is "a clever man, but vulgar, unpopular, and insincere." No doubt such comments as those on Helmcken should be taken as records of the exaggerations of current gossip rather than as strictly literal truths. Verney not only marked the letter of July 20 as "*Private/ Not to be Copied*" but described it to his father as containing "a great deal of scandal, abuse, &c."

Verney continued to make vigorous criticisms of various colonial officials in his letters of 1863 and 1864. He expressed the view that Surveyor General J.D. Pemberton and his assistant B.W. Pearse held more land than persons in their position should; he described the British Columbia judge, Matthew Baillie Begbie, as "hasty and partial" in judgment, and overbearing in his treatment of the legal community (September 4 1863). He characterized the remarks of J.S. Helmcken as "gross, treasonable, and insolent" when the House of Assembly refused to provide financial support and housing for the newly arrived Governor Kennedy (April 6 1864). None of these criticisms is without foundation; all of them, including outrage at Helmcken's remarks, were widely shared. But Verney often made little attempt at a balanced assessment; one could scarcely know from his comments that Begbie, Young, and Pemberton were men of notable ability and achievement. On the other hand, it is interesting to learn from Verney that Begbie sang "in a fine deep base voice" (September 4 1863).

Verney succinctly described the government of Vancouver Island on August 16, 1862 as neither English nor Yankee but Hudson's Bay Company: "mean, petty, slovenly." His first impressions of the British Columbia official establishment and society he found in New Westminster were much more favourable. He wrote his father on July 20, 1862 that although "New Westminster is but a small town of huts in a clearing of the forest" he preferred it to Victoria, for it displayed "more English feeling, more English sabbath-observance, and less American democracy and equality"; there was more courtesy and kindness, and "one can look up to such men as colonel Moody and his officers of Engineers." This judgment, which is repeated on August 8, may seem surprising, since in some circles New Westminster soon came to be seen as a hotbed of immigrant Canadian democracy, but as Verney occasionally emphasized he really knew very little of mainland British Columbia when he reached these conclusions; he had contact only with a small group of officials and officers of the Engineers. He observed later, on February 26, 1865, that "noxious characters" and demagogues existed on the mainland as well as on Vancouver Island, but that the lack of representative government there had prevented them from coming to the surface.

A leading subject of the letters in the earlier part of 1864 is the preparation for the retirement of the recently knighted Sir James Douglas, including the farewell banquet at Victoria, and the reception of his successor as Governor of Vancouver Island, Arthur Kennedy. During this period the *Colonist* records the part that he took in public meetings and committees making arrangements to honour the retiring and receive the new governor (February 22, 23, 26, March 1). There is unfortunately a gap here in Verney's correspondence, and the letter which must have included a description of the farewell banquet to Douglas in Victoria has disappeared, but on March 26 Verney records the arrival of Governor Kennedy, who brought him gifts from his family at Claydon House, and made his official entry to Victoria by coming around from Esquimalt in the *Grappler*.

Verney was at first favourably impressed by Kennedy, but records the manner in which the new governor's cordial reception was quickly followed by problems with his House of Assembly. On September 6, 1864 Kennedy went to the trouble of writing to Sir Harry Verney to explain that Edmund was stationed with the *Grappler* at Bute Inlet outside postal range, and provided this comment on his own current situation: "All goes well, save that I am a good deal embarrassed, and obstructed, by my Predecessors 'belongings', who regard me as an interloper and 'natural enemy'. They are very unappeasable, & keep my 'Rowdy' Parliament in a state of fermentation."[56] During the remainder of his time on Vancouver Island Verney's relations with Kennedy remained cordial, but in his later letters, for example, on February 26, 1865, while he continued to express appreciation of Kennedy's kindness to him he became more critical of him as governor.

Mindful of the fact that his naval appointment was to British Columbia as well as Vancouver Island, Verney made visits to the second new governor, Frederick Seymour, at New Westminster, and he appears to have enjoyed his stays at Government House there, although he complains of the time wasted in sociable idleness and drinking. During his last months on the west coast politics were increasingly dominated by the question of union between the two colonies. In his earlier letters Verney had emphasized the jealousy existing between them. While he declares in a letter of March 26, 1865, "I eschew politics as much as possible here," he makes it clear that he now favours union, preferably under the governorship of Seymour. Verney's letters on this subject gain some interest from the fact that he had engaged in long conversations with the two governors.

In contrast to those who were demanding more representative institutions of government in British Columbia, Verney, when he described accompanying Kennedy on a visit to Seymour, on February 26, 1865, advocated a "firm despotic government," with a mixture of appointed and elected members in the legislature of the united colonies, and on April 4 he wrote that one could not find fifteen men on Vancouver Island who would make good members of parliament or be willing to spare the necessary time from money-making. "We colonists are too young for representative Institutions," he declared on February 8. Such comments come very naturally from an upper-class naval officer. They may suggest that Verney did not always grasp the realities of colonial politics, but they are no doubt influenced by his conversations with the two governors. In his letter of September 6, 1864 to Sir Harry Verney, Kennedy had written: "As is usual in all new colonies, good & sound men, will not go through the ordeal of an election in a very Americanized community." In any case, it is to be noted that the solution favoured by Verney is the one that was eventually adopted: union of the two colonies under Seymour, on the less representative British Columbia model, rather than the more representative Vancouver Island one.

For Verney, as a serving naval officer, to write to his father, a prominent Member of Parliament, as candidly as he did about colonial officials and politics might well have caused serious trouble if it had become known, as both father and son were fully aware. Edmund warned his father on June 27, 1862 to be very careful about circulating his letters. Sir Harry Verney cautioned his son on December 30, 1862: "I cannot too much urge on you discretion & silence both as to your writing to me about Govr Douglas or any one else, & as to any thing that may happen in the colony."

Sir Harry Verney was well aware of his still relatively youthful son's limitations in experience and judgment, and the possible influence of Edmund's letters on the father and his political circles in England should not be exaggerated. But he solicited his son's opinion of Hon. Malcolm Cameron, for example, when the latter came to England as a delegate to express colonial viewpoints and grievances. And on one occasion he used his son's letters as the basis for a speech in the House of Commons and a letter in *The Times*.[57] Since Sir Harry was well connected, at times in almost daily contact with the Prime Minister, Palmerston, his son's letters are interesting as the illustration of an informal channel of communication between the two remote colonies and the imperial centre, particularly if they are considered in conjunction with the various visitors from Vancouver Island Edmund's presence there brought to Claydon House.

Native Indians

Verney's earlier letters and other writings at the time of the Indian Mutiny would lead one to expect a sympathetic attitude toward native races. Even during the period of fierce English reaction to atrocities, he held that the Mutiny had been caused by the contempt displayed by the English for the native races of India, and that reports of atrocities had been much exaggerated.[58] In his Vancouver Island letters a similarly enlightened attitude appears, for example, when he deplores on March 1, 1864 the racial prejudice through which the "coloured" volunteer rifle brigade in Victoria had been excluded by the committee of management from the procession to welcome Governor Kennedy. He expresses the hope that "by a little wholesome agitation on their part they will obtain some recognition," and declares: "I have been surprised and disappointed at the narrow-mindedness that has lately showed itself in connexion with the change of Governors."

Verney's first impression of the Native Indians of Vancouver Island,[59] however, was unfavourable, as he made clear in his letter of May 15, 1862, and he drew contrasts in his early letters between the beauty of the landscape and the ugliness of the Indians. His negative view may be accounted for partly by the facts that his first contact took place in an area in the vicinity of gold-rush Victoria and the port of Esquimalt that had long been a notorious centre of vice and degradation,[60] and that the time was that most terrible moment of coastal Indian history, the height of the great smallpox epidemic. His initial impressions of the Indians at Fort

Rupert (September 22 1863) and Bella Coola (October 15 1863) were also quite negative, but he was much more favourably struck by the appearance of the Indians he saw on his journey into the interior in July 1863, and by the end of his time in British Columbia he seems to have viewed the Indians as picturesque rather than ugly. On May 21, 1865, as he prepared to make his final visit to New Westminster, he wrote that he was looking forward to the great assembly of Indians gathered there for the Queen's Birthday, which would be "a fine sight." His earlier view of the Indians as ugly is in fact refuted by a photograph taken on this occasion at Government House, New Westminster, by Charles Gentile of Verney with Governor Seymour, other colonial and naval officials, and a group of Indians, for it shows among the Indians finer looking specimens of humanity than the officials.[61]

Verney's father in a letter of February 9, 1863 urged him to acquire all the scientific knowledge he could about "the Indian races," as well as other aspects of the colonies, and to communicate it to Admiral Fitzroy, Admiral Washington, or the Geographical Society. But Verney had recognized when he arrived on Vancouver Island that "it will take some little time to get thoroughly up to the Native character" (June 3 1862); and he never had the opportunity to make the close study of any group of Indians that his friend Gilbert M. Sproat had during the several years he lived at Alberni. In the book he dedicated to Verney, *Scenes and Studies of Savage Life* (1868), Sproat described how his initial aversion changed to curiosity and interest; he concluded that the Indians possessed many virtues and he attacked stereotypes of them as dirty and lazy.[62] Verney made collections of Indian artefacts, but otherwise in his letters it is only on rare occasions that he displays special interest and close observation of Indian culture, as in his detailed description of Native fishing methods at Bella Coola on July 9, 1864, which is not apparently linked with the mission he was later given to blockade Indians from fishing at Bute Inlet but is provided as a matter of interest in its own right.

As one might anticipate from his family background, Verney's view of the Native Indians is very much that of missionaries in the Protestant evangelical tradition. He shows a distinctly Protestant bias in his criticism of Roman Catholic influence on the Cowichans on September 7, 1862, although he takes a more favourable view of it a few months later when he credits Bishop Demers, on May 5, 1863, with bringing about the peaceable surrender by the Cowichans of fugitives wanted in connection with the Gulf Islands murders. He was most impressed by William Duncan's work at Metlakatla, and gave an extensive account of it in his letters late in 1863, which survives also in a copy in the Claydon House archive made by a second hand, no doubt for circulation in England.[63]

Verney first encountered Duncan's Indian converts on his mission's schooner, the *Carolena*, and found them "a very attractive set of fellows," although he seems a little worried that they may have been excessively deferential; he writes that one was "almost absurd in his extreme politeness" (October 10 1863). After inspecting Metlakatla he concluded that, while Duncan had not accomplished the miracles some of his admirers claimed, he had "brought some hundreds of the natives from a state of the most degraded barbarism and the blackest heathendom to a state of civilization and outward christianity which may be quite placed on a par with that of an ordinary English village" (October 24 1863). On an occasion when Duncan's converts were given European names on baptism, he contributed such names as Edmund Verney and Frederic Calvert (November 2 1863). It is interesting to note that Sir Harry Verney felt some doubts about this deprivation of the Native heritage. When Edmund forwarded to him notes written by Indian girls from Metlakatla with such names as "Elisa Paley" and "Catherine Marsden," Sir Harry asked, on December 15, 1864: "Do I trace your suggestion in the names of the Indian girls?" And he commented: "the second names ought to have been Indian."

According to William Duncan's journal, Verney was very well received by the Indian converts at Metlakatla. In his quite full account in 1864 of the second visit Duncan includes such details as Verney's participation in a "singing meeting" of the converts on October 9: "He seemed greatly to enjoy it & played an instrument for us." At the end of this visit, on October 11, Verney invited all the villagers to a feast, where Duncan states they enjoyed "a delightful four hours." Several Indians made speeches to Verney, "taking encouragement from his kindness to them," and Verney "responded very wisely & I interpreted his speech to the Indians who seemed much impressed." Duncan wrote out in his journal the speeches given by Verney and the Indians. While Verney complimented the Indians on their progress, and hoped to be held "in your kind remembrance" when the smoke of the *Grappler* had disappeared from view, the Indians paid such tributes to him as Ed Bickersteth's: "As long as I have lived I never saw such a person so kind to us."[64]

Verney's official report to Admiral Denman on his 1864 visit to Metlakatla and Fort Simpson contains interesting information not given in the letters, including an account of a meeting with the Tsimshian chiefs at Fort Simpson on October 7. He states that when he arrived there he invited the chiefs to come aboard to receive the admiral's message, arising out of the attack on the Indian constables: "they were however in a very bad temper and refused to come." He then went on shore with Duncan and arranged to meet them in a chief's lodge, where he and Duncan "found a Blanket spread for us on a slightly raised platform: we sat down with two Chiefs below us and about a hundred Indians ranged round in a Semicircle." Verney then brought out Denman's orders, with the attached depositions relating to the attack on the constables:

> [W]hen I drew forth the thirty-four pages of foolscap they produced a very marked impression: during a dead silence I read out such portions as concerned the Indians, which were interpreted and liberally paraphrased by Mr. Duncan in a speech lasting about an hour: at the end of that time the Indians showed a much more friendly spirit, and intimated that if we would salute the Camp they would return Gun for Gun: we

> returned on board and as we steamed out fired a salute of two guns which was honorably returned.[65]

Like Duncan, Bishop Hills credited Verney with a properly Christian attitude toward the Indians. In his journal he describes an encounter he and Verney had at Qualicum with "the U-kul-tah Indians – a marauding tribe" on October 31, 1862:

> The Indians were saucy, and, after selling a canoe, and taking the money, they wished it back. On being refused they took up stones; but good for evil was returned by the captain [i.e., Verney], who gratified them by some extra payment, and then offered them the stone they had taken up to cast at us, at which they were ashamed.[66]

The letters make it clear that both Edmund Verney and his father advocated the humane treatment of the Native Indians, by the standards of their time, and the avoidance of unnecessary bloodshed. When he learned of the bombardment of the Lemalchi village on Kuper Island, Verney commented that he was "thankful that the responsibility of firing the first shot has not fallen to me" (April 26 1863). When the news of Admiral Denman's attack on Ahousat in November 1864 reached England, Sir Harry Verney wrote to Edmund: "the Illustrated News of this day contains the account of the fray with the Ahousats Indians.[67] I hope that we do not engage in conflict with these poor savages without right clearly on our side," and he added: "I anticipate that Captain Kennedy's loyal manly character will secure justice for the natives" (December 31 1864). This last comment was no doubt prompted by the concern Governor Kennedy had displayed in his letter to Sir Harry on September 6, when, following his account of his troubles with the House of Assembly, he had written: "The Indian population have been neglected and demoralized, to a lamentable extent, and a representative government, is not the best machinery for remedying the evil." In response to his father's enquiry about the attack on Ahousat Edmund wrote that he was not qualified to give an opinion as he was absent in the north at the time: "but all who understand these Indians agree that if treated properly by those who do understand them, it is seldom necessary to resort to violence" (March 10 1865).

In the case of the major crisis that occurred during his period in British Columbia, the Chilcotin uprising, Edmund Verney seems to have concluded that some of the white men who were killed were at least partly responsible for bringing the catastrophe on themselves. This can be inferred from Sir Harry's comment in a letter of November 30, 1864 to his son, which was prompted by a letter on this subject that Edmund had enclosed for Captain Hardinge. Sir Harry wrote:

> I am too well aware of the conduct of our countrymen, relieved from any restraint, to be astonished at the real cause of the quarrel with the

> Indians. When I hear of such a quarrel terminating in blood, I always enquire whether our abuse of their women is not at the bottom of it – for I have too often found that to be the case. If you have reason to believe that that was so, I hope you have said so to Admiral Denman, or the Governor, or to whomever it may be your duty to report on the subject.

On occasions when Verney was involved in controversy, the criticism always seems to have been that he was too lenient, never that he was too harsh, in his treatment of Indians. As he tells his father, when he was called into Bella Coola on account of thefts by Indians from settlers he refrained from taking punitive action once the stolen goods had been returned (October 15 1863). In April 1864 his friend Ernest Walker, who had barely survived an Indian attack at Bentinck Arm in which a companion had been killed, criticized him in the *Colonist* for his failure to arrest Indians following earlier murders.[68] Others in the *Colonist* in June of that year appear to associate him with a pro-Indian policy of Governor Douglas. There is some evidence too that he incurred the disapproval of his commanding officer, Captain J.W.S. Spencer, for criticizing in a letter to Spencer himself the colonial government's failure to settle Indian land claims at Cowichan by making payments that had been promised.[69] Certainly he liked to think he was well regarded by Indians as well as settlers at Cowichan: he wrote after a day spent in visits there on May 6 1863: "I was much pleased with the recognition and welcome which I met with from both Indians and white men."[70]

During his period in British Columbia Verney built up a notable collection of Indian artefacts, which he shipped back in several instalments to Claydon House.[71] On February 20, 1863 he enclosed in a letter to his father a lengthy list of artefacts that he was sending to England on the Hudson's Bay Company ship *Princess Royal*. On February 7, 1864 he again wrote to his father that he was preparing a box of curiosities to send home by the *Princess Royal*, and he subsequently enclosed a second long list of articles sent by this ship in March 1864.[72] On December 11, 1864 he wrote that HMS *Charybdis*, which took home ten men from the *Grappler*, also carried Indian mats and other objects for him, in custody of the chaplain. An entry in the 1863 list sheds some light on the trading methods through which he acquired artefacts:

> One charm, composed to the unbelieving eye only of red cord and weasel skins, but which is really very valuable, and cost a nearly new uniform frock-coat. No bullet can harm the wearer: any one doubting its efficacy is recommended to try it.

In a comment on the artefacts shipped in March 1864, Verney stated he believed that with what he had already sent in the *Princess Royal* and a few articles he retained this was one of the best collections of curiosities of the country ever sent to England, and that, as these things ever grew more rare, probably such a collection could not again be formed, except at great expense. After its arrival in England the collection was displayed for many years in a private museum at Claydon House. It is now dispersed, but photographs that can still be seen at Claydon and other records confirm Verney's claim that it was an outstanding collection. It was rich in Haida and Tsimshian artefacts, among others, and along with many smaller objects included two big Salish house-posts from Comox, described in the 1863 list as "Two large carvings from the mouth of the Courtenay River in the Comux district," which Verney suggested "will do for garden gate-posts"; he repeated this suggestion on September 19, 1864, but proposed also that they might be given to a museum. In a letter from Claydon House on November 30, 1864, his father suggested another possibility:

> If I can ever afford to build a Portico on the N side of this house at the Entrance Hall, & under which carriages can drive to the Door, your beautiful Carvings, like Gog & Magog, may stand on each side to test the Courage of Visitors, as Mrs Pinfold used to hold up her Stick (now in my room, her Legacy to me) to terrify naughty children.[73]

Fortunately these carvings were preserved in the private museum at Claydon House. With many other artefacts from Verney's collection the house-posts are now held by the Museum of Mankind in London, the ethnographical division of the British Museum, where they are displayed in the room that serves as the general introduction to the collection.[74]

As the commander of a gunboat in British Columbia in the 1860s, Verney inevitably appears as the embodiment of nineteenth-century British imperialism: he engaged in "police actions" against Native Indians, he fostered European settlements on Indian lands, he collected and sent home Indian artefacts, he placed his own names not only on the geographical features but even on the Native inhabitants of the coast. In many respects, however, he represents a late and relatively liberal phase of imperialism: he disliked unnecessary severity and bloodshed; he seems never to have fired the guns of his ship except in gunnery exercises and ceremonial salutes; and he criticized the colonial government of Vancouver Island for its failure to keep promises to pay Indians for land. During his political career after his return to England he advocated the abolition of capital punishment, and was aligned with those Gladstonian Liberals who were increasingly critical of the whole imperial enterprise.[75]

Coastal Scenes and Scenery

One of the most attractive features of Verney's letters is the appreciation he displays for the scenery of Vancouver Island and British Columbia. He writes constantly of the coastal setting and the changing seasons. His early letters show that he immediately developed great enthusiasm for the setting of Esquimalt and Victoria. In the first of his Vancouver Island letters on May 15, 1862 he described the "exquisite little harbour" of Esquimalt. On May 27 he wrote of the walks near his rented cottage through scenes with "lovely wild flowers of every hue," great trees, picturesque rock outcrops, and views of the sea and snow-capped mountains. On June 16 he declared: "I am delighted with the country": "there are all sorts of scenery; quiet little woodland dells; open park-land, rugged cliffs, thick jungle, and noble mountains, and with all a charming climate."[76]

Verney wrote with similar appreciation of the "lovely scenery and delicious weather" he enjoyed while the *Grappler* lay in the land-locked harbour at Cowichan on August 30, 1862, and of the fine scenery as well as the abundant natural resources he saw in the Comox Valley when he took the early settlers there (October 11, November 1 1862). In later years too the scenery, flora, and changing seasons of Vancouver Island continued to give him much pleasure, as appears in his description of the beauty of the view from the trail to Goldstream when he rode there with Governor Kennedy to inspect the new gold diggings (April 21 1864). From time to time he described to his father the great trees of the coastal forest, and the beauty of the wild flowers of southern Vancouver Island. On April 8, 1863 he wrote that although he knows he "raved" about the beauty of the flowers last spring, he cannot refrain from doing so again, and he declared on April 27: "I cannot believe that any part of the world can show a greater variety and number of wild flowers than this."

As a result of his appreciation of the flora, on a number of occasions he gathered seeds of plants and trees and sent them back to Claydon. In this he had the assistance of Robert Brown of the Vancouver Island Exploring Expedition, who was a trained botanist. In his letters Verney sometimes complains that his family rarely let him know whether the seeds have reached them or whether they have grown, but when he was about to return to England he received this encouragement from his stepmother, who wrote to him on March 4, 1865: "Your seeds are excellent – just what we wanted – the Colony is celebrated for its Pines & Cypresses – The Bishop says bulbs too. If so perhaps you can bring some with you – all lilies are valuable."

The scenery of the northern coast impressed Verney by its grandeur, rather than appearing desolate as it had to some early explorers. He wrote enthusiastically of the magnificent scenery of the Inland Passage during his northern voyage in the autumn of 1863, and on October 14 he suggested that Captain Vancouver would not have found the area around Bella Coola so desolate as he did if he had been there during duck-hunting season. Eight days later as he sailed toward Metlakatla he wrote: "Our course continues to lie through the most beautiful inland navigation, presenting fresh points of beauty every hour." He became more familiar with this coastal scenery at the time of the Chilcotin uprising in 1864: on July 13 he again described Bella Coola with its "picturesque waterfalls" and on September 1 the area, "wild and rugged in the extreme," at the head of Bute Inlet. So great was the impact of the British Columbia coastal scenery on him that, as will be noted below, when he visited Yosemite on his return journey to England he was inclined to think the scenery there inferior in grandeur.

Verney displays the constant interest in climate and weather of a countryman and a sailor. While in his earlier letters he celebrated the glorious spring and summer of 1862 – "this delicious summer" (August 3), on December 15, 1862 he wrote that he had experienced "a downpour of rain, such as I have not seen surpassed even in the tropics," and commented in this and some subsequent letters on the discomfort of being confined to a small gunboat in wet weather.[77] On March 1, 1863 he concluded that the climate at that time of year was "the most changeable in the world," but on March 30 he wrote: "Day after day the cloudless sun pours its rays upon this favoured island." On February 11, 1864 he declared: "few climates in this latitude can show such glorious days in February." He experienced the coastal weather at its most severe in January 1864, when he wrote of the Fraser being frozen over, so that little communication was possible with British Columbia. He found enjoyment in severe seasons as well as mild ones, and wrote of planning to skate at Esquimalt on February 12, 1863, and of sleighing for the first time in his life on January 28, 1865. But he always made a special point of recording the earliest signs of spring: the first wild flowers, the first hummingbirds, the first peas from his garden.

Verney's letters record many different kinds of scenes, captured at particular moments of time. These include not only remote coastal settings but the "urban" setting of Victoria, described with the aid of a panoramic photograph. As well as physical settings they include social scenes, such as the report of Verney's first Vancouver Island Christmas, spent partly on shipboard and partly with the McKenzies at Craigflower. They include numerous incidents and scenes of action: the finding of the body of Brady at Bedwell Harbour on Pender Island, the surrender by the Cowichans of those wanted for Gulf Island murders, the *Grappler* on the rock in Milbanke Sound. He was stimulated to take special trouble with his descriptions of scenes by his awareness that his family maintained good standards in such aspects of letter writing and that his stepmother in particular was critical when he fell below those standards: as he remarked to his father when he embarked on a description of Yosemite during his return journey to England on June 27, 1865: "you know Mama says I am the worst hand possible at descriptions."

At best Verney's descriptions of scenes convey a strong sense of immediacy. He writes at the time of the Chilcotin uprising from Low Camp, Bute Inlet, on September 1, 1864, in the evening as he lies "under a rude shelter made of cedar bark, with a fire burning before the opening," beside the muddy Homathko River, under tall cedars and spruce, "among which the bayonet of the sentry gleams from time to time." His descriptions often combine aural with visual elements. For example, on January 15, 1863 he writes that the English Camp at Garrison Bay on San Juan Island is "one of the most lovely views in this part of the world," and describes not only its situation "in a deep bay" "completely land-locked and sheltered," surrounded by dense forests; and "the white and yellow houses for the troops" built around three sides of a square facing the water, with the tall flag pole displaying the Union Jack; but he also includes such details as the red coats of the sentries, the pet dogs sleeping in front of the officers' quarters, the sound of bugles calling the men to dinner, the striking of the hours "on a suspended crow-bar which emits a very soft and musical sound," and the curling puff of white steam occasionally let out by the *Grappler* lying at anchor.

Verney uses his ears as much as his eyes in his description of a cold winter scene at Esquimalt Harbour on February 8, 1863:

> [T]onight is most lovely: not a breath of wind stirs the frozen air, and the stars flash like diamonds set in jet; the atmosphere is so clear that every sound is heard with wonderful distinctness, as the tramp of the sentry aboard the Topaze, or every half-hour, as the bell strikes, his cheering cry of "all's well."

In addition to the snow-laden trees and rock surrounding the harbour, he includes in his evocation of the scene "the steady red light of Fisgard Island Lighthouse, and low ceaseless moan of the swells heaving and sullenly breaking on the rocks at its base." The aural element is even more prominent in his description of a paddle-wheel mail steamer entering Esquimalt Harbour on June 21, 1863. Verney hears as he begins to write, "the flapping noise of a steamer" and goes to his door and listens:

> [A] sentry hails a passing boat, there is a flash, a report, a gun, the mail steamer: the echoes roll about the quiet inlets of this bay, now soft, now loud, now dying away altogether; I hear the boatswains mates on board the ships call boats away; the steamer stops, and again I hear the slow dull splashing as she turns astern, and secures to the wharf: lights are glancing in every direction: boats are moving, and the air so silent ten minutes ago, resounds with the clatter of horses hoofs, the rattle of waggons, the barking of dogs, the shouting of men, and, loudest of all, the rush of the escaping steam.

Verney provides on September 3, 1863 a description of a typical morning scene at his cottage, "The Small Bower" on Esquimalt Harbour, with such details as the behaviour of his chickens, ducks, and dogs, the arrival of the milkman by boat, and the excitement again caused by the sudden appearance of the mail steamer. Such descriptions were sometimes written to fill out letters when he could think of nothing else to write about, but they show he heeded his father's advice on January 27, 1863 to "recollect & note down all sorts of things," because what might at the time appear "trite & common & uninteresting" might at some later time be "full of interest." Verney's letters are interesting today because he sometimes did record things no one else thought worth recording.

The Return Journey: Vancouver Island to England

As he states in the later Vancouver Island letters, Verney decided to return to England by the overland route from San Francisco across the

Rocky Mountains and the Great Plains. During this journey he continued to write regularly to his father, in letters which sometimes reached many instalments, since there were few opportunities for mailing. Although these letters have not been included in the present edition, like those written on the voyage from England they are interesting not only in themselves but also in relation to the period on Vancouver Island. They provide a record of travel by one of the more adventurous routes between British Columbia and the Atlantic coast and Europe.

Verney left Esquimalt on June 3 on the *Brother Jonathan,* and after a pleasant voyage arrived in San Francisco on June 7. There he met Governor Low and had an interesting conversation with General Irvin McDowell, who had led the Union Army in the first Battle of Bull Run, and he made an excursion to see the "big trees," giant sequoias, with "two Victoria friends, Gardiner and Young" (June 11). Then, after sending his servant, Henry Tyler, with his luggage to England via Panama, he set off on his overland trip on June 23, carrying saddle bags, and travelling through the west mainly by stagecoach. He spent a week sightseeing at Yosemite, and then crossed the Sierra Nevada, reaching Virginia City on July 7, where he visited a silver mine, and Salt Lake City on July 14, where he remained over a week. Setting out again by stage on July 23 he reached Laramie on July 30 and Denver on July 31, and the railhead at Atchison, Kansas, on August 7. He then travelled by rail via Chicago, arriving in New York on August 12. He next visited Washington, Niagara, and Boston. From Boston he travelled by steamer and rail via Portland and St. John to Halifax. On August 31 he sailed from Halifax on the Cunard liner *China,* reaching Queenstown (Cobh), Ireland, on September 9, and Liverpool on September 10.

The most enjoyable part of the journey for Verney seems to have been the week he spent at Yosemite (or Yo Semite, as he terms it). He wrote appreciatively of the grandeur of the scenery, but made some qualification as a result of comparison with British Columbia (June 28):

> I should not be surprised if waterfalls surpassing the Yo Semite falls should some day be discovered on the coasts of British Columbia: I have in some of those inlets seen scenery more impressive than this, and mountains much higher, but I do not remember to have seen perpendicular precipices of equal height.

His enjoyment of the week at Yosemite was greatly increased by congenial company, especially the companionship of two attractive and sociable young women "in Bloomer costume," a novel form of dress which Verney judged much superior to petticoats for travel (June 27).

Verney's relatively long stay in Salt Lake City was prompted by the intense current curiosity about the religion and way of life of the Mormons. As he wrote to his father on July 16: "There is so much to be related about this extraordinary place and its inhabitants that I quite despair of satisfying either myself or you." He inspected the great temple and tabernacle then under construction; he had meetings with Brigham Young and Heber Kimball, and attended a Mormon service, but did not form a very favourable view of Mormon religion, although he praised the biblical knowledge and the choral singing of the adherents. He was greatly impressed, however, by the attractiveness of the city created in a few years from the desert, and by the achievements of the Mormons in irrigation and agriculture. While satisfying his curiosity about the Mormons, he was able to satisfy that of some residents of Salt Lake city about the colonies where he had recently been stationed. During his stay a Young Men's Literary Association of the "Gentiles" made him an honorary member: "then without the slightest premonitory hint, they called upon me for a speech about V.I. and B.C." (July 18).

When he left Salt Lake City Verney reflected upon recent reports of murders, stagecoach robberies, and Indian attacks, and commented: "truly this is a wild country" (July 22). He found that the stage agent was actually discouraging travellers from continuing eastward under current conditions, and the parting remarks of his friends there were "not encouraging," as he later reported (July 30). They made such comments as: "I hope you'll get safe through," and "I hope you'll get your scalp safe to Denver." In approaching Salt Lake City he had already seen evidence of recent murders and of the prevalence of Lynch law, and on arrival he learned that a stage from Virginia City had just been robbed and the passengers killed. This prompted a recollection from his service as a magistrate in Victoria (July 15):

> [T]his same stage was robbed last summer, the passengers being murdered: the robbers escaped to V.I. and I remember their being brought before me and remanded, and being ultimately given up to the U.S. authorities.[78]

Soon after leaving Salt Lake City he encountered other signs of the hazards of travel, as he passed more than a hundred wagons of westbound emigrants. He noted (July 24) that while the emigrants appeared in good health, their animals were often in poor condition, and "in some places the road is literally lined with the bones of beasts who have died either from cold, starvation, drought, or overwork."

The journey from Salt Lake City to Denver was through "disturbed country" considered dangerous because of hostile Indians, especially in the later part. Verney managed to travel most of the way in a coach with the superintendent of the stage line, Reynolds, which provided advantages both of speed and military escort, first by four and later by eleven soldiers of the 11th Kansas Volunteers. Nevertheless the sense of hazard remained strong, and on July 27 at Ferry House, Platte River, he wrote:

> [I]n this troubled country the Indians have run off the stock, so we are obliged to take the same team through and to travel slowly: it is wise however to sleep with my revolver buckled on, and my rifle by my side.

In Denver they learned that near Fort Laramie, seventy miles from the road they took, many soldiers had just been killed in an attack by a very large number of Indians. After they left Denver, with an escort reduced again to four soldiers, they found much apprehension at Julesburg because of recent killings by Indians in that area. When he reached Atchison, Verney wrote on August 7 of an incident four days earlier:

> On thursday morning one of the stage horses had a fit and died: we at once put in one of the escort horses, and moved our fingers pretty quickly too, I assure you, as we were in a narrow pass where Indians might have had us at a great disadvantage: these Indians are no mean antagonists, very different from those in British Columbia and Vancouver Island: they are provided with good telescopes, and carefully scrutinize all that passes along the road: they also signalize to each other from one hill to another by reflecting the sun in looking-glasses: there is no doubt that they have white men among them, probably who were guerillas during the rebellion.

Verney reached the railhead at Atchison, however, without suffering any dangerous incident. His letters show that he took much interest in the changing character of the country he passed through, its landscape, vegetation, and wild life. He was interested in frontier conditions and in the potential for the future of places that did not yet offer anything of interest in themselves. He wrote to his father on July 31 from St. Vareins, Colorado:

> These places that I name to you consist, in most instances, of but the stage house and stables, and at the best there are but one or two houses besides: the places are of no interest, but they are the only landmarks across a great continent, and may someday give names to cities and districts.

At Atchison Verney felt much relieved to reach the end of staging. He had more than enough of the weariness and dirt of travel by stage, often continuously by day and night, and of the badness of the food at many of the wayside houses. He had often found some relief from the jolting of the stage by exchanging places with soldiers of the cavalry escort, and wrote on July 29: "I have had a jolly day, riding escort horses all the way," but the next day he was weary, after riding over seventy miles in twenty-four hours, and on July 31 he stated:

> I was heartily tired with much riding; riding with a rifle, revolver, & thirty rounds of ammunition, on a rough cavalry horse over wild country, is not like riding one of your horses in Rotten Row with Emily. – or any one else.

The discomforts of the journey were such that he wrote this same day: "I do not think anything would induce me to undergo them again."

During his two or three weeks on the eastern part of the continent Verney enjoyed a variety of pleasurable activities. He dined twice at the British Embassy in Washington; he appreciated the grandeur of Niagara Falls, despite the touristy nature of the place, and he attended a fine organ recital in Boston, as well as inspecting the Navy Yard there. From New York he wrote on August 12 that he would like to return to the United States for a "lengthened visit": "it is *the* school for an English Statesman; pardon my 'highfiluting.'"[79]

Toward the end, however, Verney had become quite weary of the idle life and lack of real occupation; he felt lonely, and after his long absence naturally became very impatient for the return to Claydon and reunion with his family. He suffered some disappointments too. He learned that Captain Mayne, whose book he had admired, was in New York, and hoped to arrange a meeting with him there to give him "the latest news from V.I. and B.C." (August 20), but did not succeed in this. In Halifax he had hoped to see his uncle, Sir James Hope, but found when he arrived that the admiral was at Quebec, where he had recently welcomed the visiting General Ulysses S. Grant.[80] However, Verney was hospitably received by the senior officer present at Halifax, and introduced to the Lieutenant Governor of Nova Scotia, Sir Richard MacDonnell. When he boarded the Cunard liner *China* for the Atlantic passage he found that the passengers included "Mr. Wood, late banker of Victoria, with his wife and two children," whom he had last seen at Yosemite. In his final shipboard letter instalment written on September 8 (Friday) Verney looked forward to arriving at Claydon on Monday afternoon (September 11); and he confirmed this with a telegram to his father from Roche's Point, Ireland, as the ship approached Queenstown on September 9, and a letter after his landing at Liverpool on September 10.

Later Life

Two of the ambitions Verney had expressed in his Vancouver Island letters were fulfilled soon after his return to England: the desire for promotion and the desire to marry.[81] In 1866 while in command of HMS *Oberon* in West Africa he was promoted to commander. He lost a leg in a shooting accident at Claydon in 1869, but he was able to continue in active service, and commanded HMS *Growler* in West Africa and the Mediterranean in 1871-73. In his final period of naval service he was in charge of the Liverpool division of the Coast Guard in 1875-77 and was promoted to captain in 1877. In 1868 Verney married Margaret Maria Hay Williams, co-heiress of a prominent Welsh family, who did notable work for improvements in education and the position of women, but who is now best remembered for her publication of volumes based on the seventeenth- and eighteenth-century Verney papers, continuing a project begun by Parthenope, Lady Verney.[82] A son and three daughters were born to the marriage.

Much of Edmund Verney's later life was devoted to the management of family estates of about nine thousand acres, and to local administration in Buckinghamshire and in North Wales, where he served as Chairman of the Quarter Sessions of Anglesey, but he involved himself also in social and political causes at the national level. Among the causes he supported was Home Rule for Ireland, and his publications included *Four Years of Protest in the Transvaal. A Poem from the South African Blue Books* (1881). In this work, which is actually a prose pamphlet, it is interesting to find the former commander of the *Grappler* as the opponent of British imperial expansion.

Verney served on the first London County Council in the 1880s and sat as Liberal Member of Parliament for Buckingham North in 1885-86 and 1889-91, but in 1891 his career in public life was cut short by a sexual scandal, ironic as this appears in the light of moralistic passages in the Vancouver Island letters. Reports of his being charged with and convicted of attempting to procure a young woman for immoral purposes reached Victoria, and were carried by *The Daily Colonist* (April 14, 17, May 2, 7) under the headings: "A London Scandal," "The Verney Scandal," and "Captain Verney in Court." While some in Victoria who remembered Verney as the conspicuously pious young naval officer thirty years earlier reflected on the ironic nature of his downfall, in other quarters the rumour developed that he had been sacrificed to protect the reputation of the Prince of Wales (who as King Edward VII was to die within a day or two of Verney himself in May 1910).[83] Alternatively one might wonder whether some special sense of weakness in the face of temptation lay behind his regrets about "sad shortcomings and failings" during the period on Vancouver Island which he expressed in a letter to his father on May 9, 1865. When he prepared to leave Metlakatla on October 12, 1864, Verney, reflecting that he was unlikely to see that place or William Duncan again, wrote aboard the *Grappler* a farewell letter, asking Duncan: "Remember me sometimes in your prayers, for I am more easily tempted and more of a state to sin, than, perhaps you would suppose."[84]

In 1894 Verney became Sir Edmund upon inheriting the family baronetcy, together with the Claydon estate, on the death of his father. His great-nephew G.L. Verney in *The Devil's Wind* gives a picture of him in his last years as a kindly figure, loved by the young. When he died in 1910 the Rector of Middle Claydon, Rev. Arthur Gordon, described him as a man who held strong and sometimes controversial views but was without malice, and commended him for qualities that are certainly conspicuous in the Vancouver Island letters: great energy and attention to detail, and a concern for betterment at all levels, from household management to local and national affairs.[85]

In the years after his return to England Verney continued to take an interest in the affairs of Vancouver Island and British Columbia. When the union of the two colonies was at last definitely resolved, he was one of the first to send the news to Victoria. Several months before the act of union was passed by the British Parliament, the *Colonist* reported on

February 28, 1866: "A letter from Lieut. Verney, R.N., who has been ordered on service to the west coast of Africa, to a friend in this city, states that the union may be considered as a *fait accompli.*"

In his later years and even to the end of his life Verney remained in contact with some of the people he had come to know on Vancouver Island, as appears from various letters he preserved. In 1869, for example, he received letters from Gilbert Sproat and Edmund Coleman. On April 27 Sproat, then also in England, wrote that he expected the Northwest Territories recently acquired by Canada to be immediately made a new province called Saskatchewan, that he was sure British Columbia would soon join Canada, and was convinced that a strong Canada was the only way to prevent British North America from being absorbed by the United States. He asked Verney's opinion about the ambition he had developed for himself of becoming either the last governor of British Columbia or the first lieutenant governor of Saskatchewan. Four months later in August Coleman wrote from Olympia about articles and illustrations he was preparing in Washington Territory, and brought Verney up to date on the progress of the Mechanics Institute in Victoria, which had recently moved to large new premises at the corner of Fort and Government Streets. He expressed his gratitude to Verney for using "your interest to gain for me" his position as librarian of the Institute. When Verney lost his leg in the shooting accident in October of this year his family received notes of sympathy not only from Bishop Hills but also from Sir Arthur Kennedy, now knighted and Governor of the West African Settlements, who was temporarily in England.

In the last years of the century Verney still occasionally received letters from Vancouver Island. On November 15, 1897 Senator William J. Macdonald wrote soliciting a contribution to a fund for Bishop Cridge, who was eighty and unprovided for.[86] He addressed Verney as "an old acquaintance" and as "one who knew Vancouver Island in the early days" and who took an interest in church affairs. He recalled the time when Verney was there, "a young man liked by everybody," and described the progress Victoria had more recently made, including such improvements as electric light and electric railways, and water supply from Elk Lake, but reported that apart from the expansion of the dockyard the village of Esquimalt was little changed, and "the 'Small Bower' is much the same as when you left it." Until the end of his life Verney remained in touch with the McKenzies of Craigflower; on April 6, 1909 a surviving daughter of the family, Goodie (Wilhelmina Ann) McKenzie, sent him a postcard of Esquimalt harbour with her greetings on his birthday.

In later times the three years Edmund Verney spent in British Columbia seem to have been less remembered within his family than the youthful courage and ability he had displayed during the Crimean War and the Indian Mutiny, and his command of the little *Grappler* was overshadowed by his later command of the larger *Growler*. When G.L. Verney provided a sketch of his life in 1956 in *The Devil's Wind* he did not mention the period in British Columbia at all. Yet that period left a number of marks, as well as the achievements mentioned at the farewell banquet to Verney in Victoria in 1865.

In a letter from Esquimalt on October 27, 1864 Verney asked his father whether the seeds of "Wellingtonea Gigantea" (or sequoia) he had sent back to Claydon had thriven. A hundred and thirty years later it can be answered that they have thriven greatly and grown to a mighty size, although the seeds actually originating in British Columbia have not left such conspicuous marks on the landscape at Claydon. While the Indian artefacts Verney collected in British Columbia are no longer to be seen at Claydon House, some of them are to be found in the collections of the British Museum. In British Columbia the consequences of Verney's period there include the presence on coastal maps and charts of the large cluster of names associated with him and his family. Perhaps, however, it is the letters he wrote from Vancouver Island that now best commemorate the three years Edmund Verney spent there.

Notes

1 Dorothy Blakey Smith, ed., *The Reminiscences of Doctor John Sebastian Helmcken* (Vancouver: University of British Columbia Press, 1975), 115-16.

2 In British Columbia the existence of these letters appears to have remained unknown until I published the first accounts of them in the articles, "Letters of a Victorian Naval Officer: Edmund Verney in British Columbia, 1862-65," and "More Letters of Edmund Verney," *BC Studies* 86 (Summer 1990):28-56, and 96 (Winter 1992-93):100-03.

3 For example, in the letter of December 2, 1863 Verney wrote "a great to the profession": "loss" has been inserted after "great," between the lines; and in that of December 12, 1863 "by letters" has been emended to "my letters." Some of these corrections were no doubt made by Sir Harry Verney as he read the letters, but it is not always possible to distinguish such minor emendations made by the father from those previously made by the son.

4 For the following letters, for example, Sir Harry Verney marked the dates of receipt placed here in brackets: September 8, 1864 (November 30), October 6, 1864 (December 14), May 20, 1864 (July 15), February 26, 1865 (May 1), May 7, 1865 (July 8).

5 Quoted from the *London Gazette*, May 25, 1858, 2587, by Edmund Verney in *The Shannon's Brigade in India* (London: Saunders, Otley & Co., 1862), 153. Information about Verney's earlier life as well as the period in India is given by G.L. Verney in *The Devil's Wind* (London: Hutchinson, 1956). See the next paragraph for fuller titles of these two books.

6 See the article on Sir Harry Verney by Margaret, Lady Verney, in the *DNB*,XX, 263-64.

7 Ibid.

8 On Sir James Hope (1808-81) see the *DNB*.

9 Sir Harry Verney, *The Verneys of Claydon* (London: Robert Maxwell, 1968), 258.

10 See the list of the members of Verney's family in Sir Bernard Burke, *A Genealogical and Heraldic Dictionary of the Peerage and Baronetage* (London: Harrison & Son, 1900), 1512-13; but the archive at Claydon House is the principal source for information here.

11 Florence Nightingale's great sense of loss and grief when Emily Verney finally succumbed to consumption in 1872 is described by Cecil Woodham-Smith, *Florence Nightingale 1820-1910* (London: Constable, 1950), 530.

12 Various place names were identified by John T. Walbran in his *British Columbia Coast Names* (Ottawa: Government Printing Bureau, 1909) as connected with Verney and his family, but such names are more numerous than even the well informed Captain Walbran could have realized.

13 Walbran, who also lists Mount Verney and Verney Passage, notes that Verney Cone on Cunningham Island is named for Edmund Verney (p. 511). He gives a completely unrelated derivation for Cunningham Island itself (pp. 124-5), but one may suspect a Verney connection in this case too. In addition there is Verney Falls at the head of Lowe Inlet, and Hope Island, Queen Charlotte Sound, is named for Verney's uncle, Admiral Sir James Hope.

14 On Bishop Hills (1816-95), who belonged to a naval family, see Jean Friesen in the *DCB*. The Claydon House archive includes Hills' extensive correspondence with Frederic Calvert as well as with Sir Harry Verney. Several families closely related to the Verneys were also early supporters of the Columbia Mission, including Hammersleys, Abel Smiths, Hanburys, and Kinnairds.

15 Although neither Edmund's extensive Vancouver Island correspondence with his sister Emily nor (with insignificant exceptions) his Vancouver Island letters to his brothers, aunts, and uncles have survived, the Claydon archive includes some letters written to him on Vancouver Island by his brother George, his uncle and aunt Fremantle, and his uncles Frederic Calvert and Admiral Hope.

16 Discussions of confederation which culminated in the British North America Act in 1867 took place at the Charlottetown Conference, September 1-9, 1864, and the Quebec Conference, October 10-27, 1864. Sir Edmund Walker Head (1805-68) worked for confederation as Lieutenant Governor of New Brunswick in 1848-54 and Governor General of Canada in 1854-61.

17 Edward Henry Stanley (1826-93), later fifteenth Earl of Derby, had as Lord Stanley served as Secretary of State for India and presided over a commission on the sanitary state of the Indian army. Sir John Lawrence (1811-79), later Lord Lawrence, had held a series of prominent positions as administrator in India, and subsequently became Viceroy. William Massey (1809-81) while Member of Parliament held several governmental offices in England before going to India as Minister of Finance in January 1865. Charles Pelham Villiers (1802-98), Member of Parliament for over sixty years, was President of the Poor Law Board, 1859-66. Although Florence Nightingale usually refused visits from those unconnected with her work, she made an exception for Garibaldi who came on April 27, 1864 in Sir Harry Verney's carriage to avoid notice. See Woodham-Smith, *Florence Nightingale*, 430.

18 The Claydon archive reveals at least one occasion on which Florence Nightingale's assistance was solicited on a British Columbia matter. In a letter to her from Victoria, January 22, 1862, Archdeacon H.P. Wright, stating she wrote him before he left England enquiring how she might aid the military settlement at New Westminster, asked her contribution toward the cost of a large collection of books that had become available locally for the library of the Royal Engineers.

19 Derbyshire was familiar to Parthenope Verney because her family, the Nightingales, spent part of the year at their Lea Hurst estate in that county.

20 William Driscoll Gossett, an officer of the Royal Engineers, had served as Treasurer of British Columbia but proved incompetent and was replaced in

September 1862. Among the manuscripts at Claydon House is a copy of a "Minute on British Columbia" by him, undated but presumably 1863, in which he criticizes James Douglas' government of the mainland colony, and urges the appointment of a separate governor and the establishment of a more representative and responsible government for British Columbia.

21 Henry Thomas Pelham, third Earl of Chichester (1804-86), was "deeply interested in religious, social, and educational questions," and served for half a century as president of the Church Missionary Society: see G. Norgate's article on him in the *DNB*, XV, 692-93.

22 Parthenope Verney was afflicted with severe arthritis. G.L. Verney in *The Devil's Wind* describes her as "cross, over-bearing and bad tempered" (p. 14), and she appears as a difficult character in the biographies of her sister, Florence Nightingale.

23 Tyler, who had previously been with Verney on HMS *Emerald*, is subsequently listed as commander's servant in the muster book of HMS *Grappler* (PRO, ADM 38 8204), which gives the place and date of his birth: Chatham, Kent, 1842.

24 Sessional Papers concerned with Vancouver Island itself were few and slight in this period but Verney probably refers to the substantial ones prompted by the gold rushes in the mainland colony, issued as *Papers Relating to the Affairs of British Columbia*, two volumes (1859), and *Further Papers*, one volume (1860). The reports of the exploratory expedition led by John Palliser were not fully published until 1865, but Verney no doubt had one or both of the two preliminary publications: *Papers Relative to the Exploration by Captain Palliser of that Portion of British North America which lies between the Northern Branch of the River Saskatchewan and the Frontier of the United States; and between the Red River and the Rocky Mountains* (1859), and *Further Papers* (1860).

25 Several books and pamphlets with similar titles were published during this period, but Verney probably refers to William Carew Hazlitt's *The Great Gold Fields of Cariboo; with an Authentic Description, Brought Down to the Latest Period, of British Columbia and Vancouver Island* (London: Routledge, Warne, and Routledge, 1862). The price listed on the cover is only one shilling, but it has a reasonably good map. Verney had presumably seen an advertisement in advance of publication, as the preface is dated April 20, 1862.

26 *The Illustrated London News* in 1854 provided illustrations of the *Melbourne* (December 23, p. 640), as well as of two ships on which Verney served, HMS *Britannia* and HMS *Terrible* (October 7, p. 352).

27 John Chapman Davie (1811-69). One of the four sons who accompanied him in 1862, Alexander (1847-89), became premier of the province of British Columbia, 1887-89, and another son Theodore (1852-98), who arrived on Vancouver Island later, also became premier, 1892-95.

28 For Bishop Kip see the notes to Verney's letter of July 2, 1862.

29 The first letterbook, which is mainly the work of Helby but includes letters by Verney at the end, extends from October 8, 1861 to July 12, 1862. The second, containing Verney's letters exclusively, extends from July 17, 1862 to April 6, 1865. The letters are concerned mainly with routine matters – finances, victualling, clothing, personnel: promotions, qualifications, discharges – but they shed light on such problems as desertions and they sometimes contain information about special missions and activities, for example reports on Verney's northern voyages in the autumn of 1863 and the autumn of 1864.

30 See especially Barry M. Gough, *Gunboat Frontier: British Maritime Authority and Northwest Coast Indians, 1846-90* (Vancouver: University of British Columbia Press, 1984).

31 See G.A. Osbon, "The Crimean Gunboats," *The Mariner's Mirror*, 51 (1965), 104-15, 211-20, and A. Preston and J. Major, *Send a Gunboat! A Study of the Gunboat and its Role in British Policy, 1854-1904* (London: Longmans, 1967). The *Grappler* and the *Forward* were both *Albacore* class gunboats. The *Grappler* was launched at Blackwall in March 1856, and after some refitting arrived at Vancouver Island in July 1860.

32 The logs are classified as follows: ADM 53 8157 (October 1861-July 1862), 8158 (July 1862-May 1863), 8159 (May 1863-February 1864), 8160 (February-October 1864), 8385 (November 1864-May 1865).

33 The *Grappler*'s full speed was 8½ knots, according to information assembled by Admiral Patrick W. Brock, "Ships' Dossiers," BCARS, ADD MS 265.

34 ADM 38 8204 (1859-64) and 8205 (1864-65).

35 G.L. Verney, *The Devil's Wind*, 21; but it should perhaps be noted that the author was a major-general rather than a naval historian.

36 When Edmund decided to return to England by way of the United States in 1865, Sir Harry Verney was a little apprehensive that war might yet break out between that country and Britain, and his son might be made an American prisoner, as his own father serving in the British army during the war of the American Revolution had been an American prisoner for several years after the surrender at Yorktown.

37 C/AA/30.73 j 1, 2.

38 In a letter to Arthur Mills, August 30, 1862, which is preserved in a file relating to HMS *Grappler* among the Colonial Correspondence in BCARS, F1214, Verney states that there had been nine desertions from the ship since he announced in the middle of June that pay would not be doubled.

39 In his unpublished reminiscences of his ministry in Nanaimo, Rev. John B. Good testifies that under Helby's command the *Grappler* had already acquired a reputation for the piety and good conduct of the crew: he states that Helby "by his personal example and interest in his men had the most devout and sober crew that ever came under our observation. For years his vessel was remembered for the high and exceptional character both of its officers and men." ("The Utmost Bounds of the West," BCARS, E/B/G 59, p. 26.)

40 On the later fate of the *Grappler* see the note to the letter of May 7, 1865.

41 See the letters of May 29 and August 3, 1863 and notes below.

42 Edmund Bertram's comment on William Price's promotion to second lieutenant, Ch. 37 (New York: Dell, 1959), 350.

43 See the copy of this letter enclosed by Verney with his letter to his father on June 27, 1864.

44 The *Colonist* on May 31, 1864 reported that Verney in the *Grappler* was visiting Cowichan in his capacity as magistrate, and that he conveyed there the former bailiff of Constance Cove Farm, Thomas Skinner and family, who were now obliged to leave Esquimalt. Among the papers at Claydon House is a petition addressed to Verney, evidently as magistrate, c. 1863, by fourteen Cowichan settlers, expressing concern about the sale of liquor to Indians and urging the appointment of an Indian constable.

45 The jacket of *Land of Plenty: A History of the Comox District* by D.E. Isenor, W.N. McInnis, E.G. Stephens, and D.E. Watson (Campbell River: Ptarmigan Press, 1987) reproduces a painting by Bill Maximick which recreates the scene of the *Grappler*'s arrival with the settlers at Comox in October 1862.

46 Verney's interest in the Comox settlement is further recorded in his shorthand diary at Claydon House. Later in 1863, for example, he writes that on September 15 he took the two Robb daughters (members of a family that had come

out on the *Tynemouth*) on a visit to their parents at Comox, and that on October 2 he joined Rev. R.J. Dundas in divine service with a congregation of ten at the Robbs' house.

47 See *Robert Brown and the Vancouver Island Exploring Expedition*, ed. John Hayman (Vancouver: University of British Columbia Press, 1989). Brown acknowledges Verney's zealousness in offering help to the expedition, in his journal, August 27, 1864, p. 117 in this edition.

48 *Vancouver Island. Exploration. 1864* (Victoria: Printed by Authority of the Government by Harries and Company, 1864).

49 For Verney's involvement in Anglican church affairs, his letters can be supplemented by Bishop Hills' diary (Archives of the British Columbia Provincial Synod of the Anglican Church of Canada, Vancouver School of Theology; microfilm BCARS, A796). For example, Hills records that Verney accompanied him on June 3, 1862 to the opening of Saanich Church, and rode out with him the next day to mark the site of the church at Cedar Plains. While Verney writes in a letter of June 6 of taking Hills to the dedication of a new church at Nanaimo, the bishop writes in his diary of riding to Mount Douglas with Verney and Archdeacon Wright on June 10.

50 Verney's commissions as Justice of the Peace for Vancouver Island, dated August 25, 1862, and for British Columbia, dated September 25, 1863, are preserved at Claydon House. Each bears the signatures of James Douglas and Colonial Secretary W.A.G. Young, with the seal of the relevant colony.

51 London: Smith, Elder & Co. Sproat (1834-1913) arrived on Vancouver Island in 1860, managed the A.C. Anderson & Co. sawmill at Alberni, and was active in other commercial and civic affairs. After Confederation he became agent-general for British Columbia in London and a member of the Indian Land Commission. See T.A. Rickard, "Gilbert Malcolm Sproat," *British Columbia Historical Quarterly*, I (1937), 21-32.

52 June 8, 1864, in *Robert Brown*, ed. Hayman, 42.

53 Verney's view of Douglas and the "fur trade elite" is similar to that of his relative, Bishop Hills. See Hills' comment on Douglas quoted by Jean Friesen in her article on Hills in the *DCB*, XII, 441: "He does not know the tone of the upright and high minded gentleman." In 1860, however, Hills wrote that his congregation in Victoria "contains a larger proportion of shrewd, thinking, intelligent, educated gentlemen than any in England out of London" (Columbia Mission, *Occasional Paper, June 1860*, 7).

54 See De Cosmos in the *Colonist*, February 12, 1859.

55 See *Lady Franklin Visits the Northwest: Being Extracts from the Letters of Miss Sophia Cracroft, Sir John Franklin's Niece*, ed. Dorothy Blakey Smith (Victoria: Provincial Archives of British Columbia, Memoir No. XI, 1974), 22-24, 64. Verney's view of the Douglas daughters, however, is similar to that of an officer of the Royal Engineers in 1858: see *Mapping the Frontier: Charles Wilson's Diary of the Survey of the 49th Parallel, 1858-62*, ed. G.F. Stanley (Toronto: Macmillan, 1970), 28.

56 The opening shows that this was not the first of Kennedy's letters to Sir Harry Verney, but earlier letters have not been preserved.

57 See the letter of August 7, 1862 and note.

58 See *The Shannon's Brigade in India*, especially pp. 41-42, 79. Verney here appears freer of assumptions of European superiority than many of his contemporaries: he writes that dreadful scenes have taken place, "but I have heard of great cruelties being perpetrated by our own people during some of the sieges in Spain and elsewhere, yet we claim to be the most

enlightened nation in the world," and that while the current war is generally regarded as one of extermination, "I feel nothing but compassion for our enemy" (p. 79).

59 I recognize the modern objections to the use of "Indian" for Aboriginal or First Nations inhabitants of British Columbia but employ it here as the term generally used in Verney's period.

60 Other naval officers appear to have viewed the Indians of this area as negatively as Verney. See for example G.P.V. and Helen Akrigg, *H.M.S. Virago in the Pacific 1851-55* (Victoria: Sono Nis Press, 1992), 106.

61 A copy of this photograph is preserved at Claydon House and reproduced in the present edition.

62 See especially pp. 19, 52, 151.

63 A copy Verney made in his own hand of a long letter by Duncan to Bishop Hills, August 13, 1862, about his problems and progress following his move from Fort Simpson to Metlakatla is also preserved at Claydon House.

64 Duncan MSS, microfilm BCARS, ADD MS 2758.

65 Copy of report dated October 21, 1864, BCARS, Colonial Correspondence, F1223.

66 Quoted from an extract from Hills' diary as published in the *Fourth Annual Report of the Columbia Mission for the Year 1862* (London: Rivingtons, 1863), 50. The manuscript original of the diary shows that the extra payment was in the form of powder and shot. Cf. Edmund Verney's letter to his father, November 1, 1862 and note.

67 *Illustrated London News*, Dec. 31 1864, p. 664.

68 See the letter of April 6, 1864 and note below.

69 Verney was not sure exactly what Spencer had taken exception to, but this is the only passage in the relevant letters, copies of which he enclosed to his father with his own letter of June 27, 1864, that could have proved controversial.

70 That Verney was not inclined to take action rashly against Indians is confirmed by his response to an alarm about the threat of Indian attack raised by a settler named Thomas Smith at Maple Bay. After investigation, Verney reported on June 12, 1864 to Admiral Kingcome that the complaint was groundless (BCARS, Colonial Correspondence, F1223).

71 Verney, who had made earlier collections in India and Hong Kong, is thus to be added to the collectors whose activities are described by Douglas Cole in his *Captured Heritage: The Scramble for Northwest Coast Artifacts* (Vancouver and Toronto: Douglas & McIntyre, 1985).

72 This list which is dated only by the month and year has been placed at the end of the March 1864 letters in the present edition.

73 Mrs. Pinfold, mentioned also in Edmund Verney's letters of June 6 and December 5, 1863, is listed in the 1861 census (PRO) as Elizabeth Pinfold, widow, aged 75, resident in the Alms Houses at Middle Claydon, to which she had presumably retired from a domestic post at Claydon House.

74 Verney's collection of British Columbia Indian artefacts seems to have remained intact at Claydon House until 1931, when part of it was acquired by Harry G. Beasley. This passed with Beasley's large ethnographical collection to the British Museum in 1944. Information about Verney's collection is to be found under the year 1931 in volume III of Beasley's manuscript catalogue, now held by the Museum of Mankind, as well as in the museum's other records. I am indebted to the staff of the Museum of Mankind for allowing me to examine these records.

75 Rev. Arthur Gordon in his *In Memoriam Edmund Hope Verney* (privately printed, 1910) records that among the letters of condolence received by the family following Verney's death was one from the Society for the Abolition of Capital Punishment.

76 Verney shared this enthusiasm for the scenery with his relative Bishop Hills, who wrote on his arrival in January 1860: "*Victoria* must be, I think, the most lovely and beautifully situated place in the world. I never saw anything before like it (Columbia Mission, *Occasional Paper, June 1860*, 5).

77 In a letter of May 28, 1864 to Admiral Kingcome in the *Grappler* letterbook Verney requested rain awnings for the whole length of the ship because of the almost ceaseless rain in winter, stating that several of his crew were laid up with colds and rheumatism.

78 The extradition proceedings in Victoria are reported at some length under the heading "The Idaho Stage Robbery" in the *Colonist*, December 16 and 17, 1864.

79 In a publication of his later years, *American Methods* (London and Edinburgh: W. & R. Chambers, 1904), Verney suggested that Britain had much to learn from the United States in such fields as education and industrial methods.

80 A newspaper report about Admiral Hope's meeting with General Grant dated August 7, apparently from the *Boston Journal*, is enclosed with Verney's letters.

81 Materials for Edmund Verney's later life are abundant in the archive at Claydon House. Among the printed sources are the *Navy Lists*, late nineteenth- and early twentieth-century editions of *Debrett's Baronetage, Knightage and Companionage*, the obituary in *The Times*, May 10, 1910, p. 13, and the biographical account in G.L. Verney's *The Devil's Wind*.

82 As well as being the author of the *DNB* articles on her father-in-law, Sir Harry Verney, and earlier members of the Verney family, Margaret Verney (1844-1930) is herself the subject of a *DNB* article (by H.E.D. Blakiston), a distinction her husband did not achieve. See also the privately printed *In Memory of Margaret Maria Lady Verney* [1930], a copy of which is held by the British Library.

83 The ironic aspects of the downfall are fully developed by David W. Higgins in a chapter, "Two Celebrated Cases," in his *The Passing of a Race* (Toronto: William Briggs, 1904), 74-90, where Verney appears as Lieutenant Blank of the *Snapper*. The view that Verney was sacrificed to save the reputation of the Prince of Wales has most recently been stated by Peter Murray in *The Devil and Mr. Duncan* (Victoria: Sono Nis, 1985), 232.

84 Duncan MSS, microfilm BCARS, ADD MS 2758.

85 A copy of Gordon's privately printed *In Memoriam Edmund Hope Verney* (1910) is held by the British Library.

86 W.J. Macdonald (1829-1916) came to Vancouver Island in the service of the Hudson's Bay Company in 1851, was a member of the House of Assembly there in 1860-63, and became a Canadian senator on Confederation in 1871. For Bishop Cridge see the note to Verney's letter of April 26, 1863, and the letter of July 3, 1863.

Letters

The Palace. Esquimalt. May. 15. 1862.

My dear Father,

I date from the house in which I found Captain Helby living, and in which I am allowed to remain rent free for a week or ten days: the rent demanded for it is £50 a year, but it has been tenantless for two years, and it is just possible that I may get it for £20, or £25: it is called the palace in distinction to Lascelles' house, which is called the cottage: if I should be so fortunate as to get it at the low rent, you may be sure that I shall inflict on you a very elaborate description of it.[1]

I made my first cruize this morning, from Esquimalt to Victoria and back; I was naturally a little nervous on entering the harbour for the first time, as there are many rocks in it; thanks however to Helby's careful instructions on Tuesday, I managed successfully: I went about some boilers for the Forward, and have the same trip to make tomorrow afternoon.

You will want to know what I think of the place, and how I like my appointment: well, at present everything promises to be very delightful: the gun-boat's cabin is terribly small for two people, but by having a room or a small hut on shore in which to keep my books, meteorological instruments &c, where I can live when I desire to do so, I shall get on very well: I have been looking at several horses to-day, with a view to buying one: they are all so very expensive that I think I shall defer the purchase until the Autumn: horses are now of nearly double the value they were three months ago, as so many are bought for Cariboo: a good strong pony is £40., and I dare say I shall be a good deal away in the summer.[2]

The only other man of war here is the Charybdis: the Forward went to San Juan and New Westminster yesterday: in a few days the Grappler will be caulked and painted: then I shall have my cabin put to rights, and see how much of my gear can be stowed there. Helby has behaved very handsomely to me, having left me matting, chairs &c which would certainly not sell for much, but which it would have cost me a round sum to have bought.

The bishop has gone to New Westminster: he has most kindly put a room in his house at my disposal whenever I have occasion to go to Victoria.[3] I think the scenery here is beautiful: this exquisite little harbour is surrounded by little hills and bushes and pine trees growing down to the water's edge: those who have been here some time think the pine trees very ugly, and they certain give the land a ragged and quite unique character: they [*sic*] pictures in Vancouver's book are very good: the natives are hideously ugly and atrociously dirty: their customs are beastly, manners they have none: there has been a compulsory exodus of them which is still going on, on account of the small-pox which is raging fearfully among them; as soon as they clear out their houses are burnt down: the bishop and one or two of his clergy have been working most assiduously among the wretched dead and dying of this loathsome disease, which shows itself among these poor wretches in its most malignant form.[4]

A great effort is made to keep Victoria as the principal port: I have no doubt however that Esquimalt must eventually supersede it. I suppose you will have seen Helby by the time you receive this: he has promised to Call on Aunt Fanny: Henry is well and flourishing.[5]

May. 19. This house has been bought by a very worthy farmer who lives about a mile off, called Mackenzie: he will let it to me for £25. a year until he can get a tenant who can afford to pay the full rent: I shall only occupy a couple of rooms, and the others will be very useful to lend to Naval officers who want to live on shore while their cabins are being painted &c. I have the house rent free until the 25th of June; then it is lent to Mr. Wood the clergyman until the 4th of August, and after that I enter on my lease: in the mean time I have full possession of the garden, which my landlord will improve and extend into a little shrubbery, and I have free permission to cut down trees, make walks and cut views. Mr. Mackenzie only bought the house the day before yesterday, and has a right to have it thoroughly put in order on purchase. A small room has been set apart for a meteorological observatory, on the North side, and when the Hecate comes in, I shall ask one or two of the surveying officers to come and live here, and so I shall learn a good deal: In a few days the Grappler will be beached and overhauled, and then caulked and painted: then I shall have my cabin thoroughly put to rights, and go and live on board.[6]

Everything promises to be very prosperous and pleasant: tomorrow, or the next day, I intend to go outside the harbour, and practise shell firing at a target: the men appear to be very efficient in their drills, and the ship is in good order; on our way round to Victoria on Friday, we exercised at fire stations, and by getting the steam to work the pumps, were able to throw a very fine column of water.

The Forward has returned from New Westminster and San Juan, but brings no news of any importance[.]

Yesterday, I read service on board in the morning, and was surprised to hear how well the men sung, led by one of the engineers. I enclose a letter for Emily.

(May 22.) Yesterday afternoon the mail steamer arrived and took us all by surprise: she was not expected until tomorrow. I have finished my memorandum, but doubt whether I shall be able to despatch it until next mail.

Now I will close this letter; we were all terribly disappointed that the steamer brought no English letters; I cannot think how it is, for I am beginning to long for a letter.

Every-thing here is very comfortable, and we are having a succession of lovely days: with love to Mamma, believe me,

Your affectionate Son,
Edmund Hope Verney

H.M.S. Grappler. Esquimalt.
May. 25. 1862.

My dear Father,

I am much charmed with the great beauty of this country: the pines would be very ornamental if it were not for the fires which have at various times passed through these forests: these have killed the trees, but left them standing, in some places entire, in others but short stumps, and these dead trees and blackened stumps are often a great eye-sore: the living trees generally, grow to a much greater size than we are accustomed to in England, for I think we usually consider the pine to be a light stemmed, brittle tree, but here they grow to a gigantic size, both of height and of circumference: when I am a little more at home here, I will send you the girths of some of the largest, and in Autumn I will look out to collect some cones. The forest is in most places pretty thick, but here and there it opens into park-like enclosures, and large masses of rock crop out, bare of all but moss, a little soft turf in the hollows, and the most exquisite wild flowers, among which one recognizes in great abundance the calcilaria, the violet, the sweet-briar, and the strawberry: indeed the forest is as full of wild strawberries as possible, and it abounds with other fruit-bearing shrubs: last summer, the officers of the "Grappler" made enough preserve from the wild berries to last them all through the winter.[1]

It is very easy to lose oneself here, so I have transferred Freddy's little compass from Miss Hardinge's penwiper to my purse:[2] Last night I dined with the Governor,[3] and on my way home lost myself twice in the bush within a few hundred yards of my own house: it was a pitch dark night and the horse found the way home: when we were lost the first time, I dismounted and tried to pick up the path again, but it was too dark to distinguish any-thing; I remounted and rode a few yards each way as far as the bush would permit, and at last the horse struck the trail again: I was one hour going the last quarter of a mile, and I am sure I should have had to sleep in the woods if I had been on foot: on both occasions the horse deserved all the credit of finding the way.

Small-tooth-combs are at a premium out here, and I am sorry to say I have not got one; when you see Arthur Mills, pray reproach him for me.[4]

The various little odds and ends you have given me are here worth their weight in gold: those candlesticks that shut up, and the little leather drinking cup: I am told that I could sell the large knife you gave me in India for almost any price I chose to ask: indeed no little nic-nac you have given me could be more valued in any part of the world than here: on the whole I have done remarkably well in the things I have brought out: had I quite known where I was coming, I should have brought out things to give away or to sell to friends at cost price: I think the bishop's house is the most complete in Victoria, and the one best furnished in refined good taste: being wifeless he is but half a bishop, and I mean no joke when I say that his friends ought to marry him to some good creature as soon as he revisits England: several people have told me that both in his Episcopal and private character, to be well married would be the best thing in the world for him: he would have the best house in Victoria to bring his wife to, and she would be the first lady in the two colonies[.][5]

The mail is expected tomorrow, and if no letters come for me I shall be indeed disappointed: will you be so kind as to send the enclosed scrap of paper to Admiral Fitzroy: I wrote to him by the last steamer and forgot to put it in the envelope.[6]

May. 27. This afternoon I went out with Lascelles to the Race Rocks, in the "Forward": it is not a very inviting rock, but covered with beautiful wild flowers: there are three paid light-men and women, one of whom is wife to the chief: they have imported children and rabbits of their own, and with a few fowls, make a thriving little colony: I am sorry to say, however, that the little boy and girl are terribly ugly.[7] The "Forward" is in very good order, and Lascelles has got a comfortable little cabin: certainly, having a second master does interfere with one's comfort in that respect, but it also has its advantages.[8]

Some of the walks in the immediate neighbourhood of the Palace are very lovely: how I long for the "old folks at home" to be with me to enjoy them:[9] in the middle of thick bush, up crops a large rock covered with moss and lovely wild flowers of every hue, with the gray stone showing out in the prominent places; you can imagine how lovely this is, overshadowed by the magnificent pines, and through an opening in the forest one sees the harbour, the men of war, the light-house, and in the distance the lofty snow-capped mountains of the Washington Territory, and perhaps one or two ships sailing up the straits: certainly this "Palace" is by far the best suited to my taste of any house near: it is perhaps fifty yards from the beach, but concealed by Maple trees which yet do not spoil the view: it is surrounded by bush, and with no house nearer than three quarters of a mile or a mile.

May 28. How refreshing and delightful for my poor eyes, to see once more your handwriting; rumour says that the American steamers have refused to convey any more the English mails, at any-rate I am almost the only one in the colony who has received letters, and this because they came in the bag with the despatches: indeed I deserve a letter; ten weeks the day before yesterday since we parted, and no news of any of you until this blessed evening: there is nothing in your letter requiring immediate answer, so I will look over it tomorrow after the steamer has sailed.

I saw the Bishop to-day; he returned on Monday; he looked far better and jollier than when I saw him before: he says that a good "outing" always does him good, and he will have plenty of that all the summer: poor man, he sadly wants a wife to cheer him up and comfort him, for he has his troubles.

Your affectionate Son,
Edmund Hope Verney

Private

The Palace. Esquimalt.
June. 1. 1862.

My dear Father,

I just mark this "private" because I do not wish it be publick.

If you see Lord Clarence or any influential person at the Admiralty, do tell them what I say about the "Grappler":[1] I never saw Helby before I came out here, and we were not here for four and twenty hours together, so if I praise him it can be from no motive of personal regard: on the contrary, if I praise him, I throw myself in the shade, for if things do not go on smoothly in the ship, I cannot say or hint that Helby left her in a poor state of discipline: then surely if one has any pride in one's profession it is a duty to let the heads of it know who are their best servants; now I consider that Helby left the Grappler in a most creditable state of discipline, and that with little or no punishment: few officers succeed in getting men into good discipline without some severe punishment, and those who do ought to be known: I venture to predict that any ship Helby commands will be very efficient and very comfortable: can the Admiralty say that of many men on the commander's list? they know best: at any rate I think it is only right and fair to him to ask you to mention what I say, to some one at the head of affairs: I have now been nearly three weeks on board, and there has been no complaint of the most trivial description: certainly the men drill very well: of course this is all in a great measure owing to the gunner, Mr. Marshall,[2] but still the credit or discredit of a ship must rest mainly with the Captain: if I wish to remark on the conduct of any officer of the ship, I have ample official means of doing so, but with regard to Helby I do not see how it can be done except through a private Channel: it is a great pleasure, and a great responsibility to command men among whom such good feeling prevails.

I dare say you will like to hear my opinion of the Governor: well, I think he is a well-meaning man, really anxious to do right, but not knowing what to do: if the Bishop would go to England and fetch out a good wife, and if you would send us out a good Governor with a good wife I believe the whole tone of the Colony would be immensely raised: nobody seems to respect any-body else, but people aim at establishing a most odious fraternity: I hear a grocer address a lieutenant R.N. by his unadorned surname, with every familiarity:

I have already shewn that I will not tolerate that, so one or two have effected a compromise by calling me "Captain." The Navy has great influence here; I wish they were more sensible of their responsibility: the Bishop is a most loveable man: after the experience of another year or two, if he marries he will get on well: I fancy I see you making a little face at my dwelling as much on the importance of his marriage, but it is most important: his servants are very fond of him and take good care of him: indeed touching creature comforts he is not to be pitied: you or his other friends may send him any little presents and be sure they will be prized more than you are inclined to believe: I would suggest such things as two or three good chairs of some new design: some good paper to paper a room: some stuff for covering chairs; tasteful drawing-room table-cloths: in fact any little nick-nacks, not necessarily expensive, but selected with care and good taste: I have no doubt that his is the only home-ly furnished house in Victoria: almost anything may be bought for money but the patterns are few and it is difficult to get things in good taste.

Your affectionate Son,
Edmund Hope Verney

You will of course tell me what Captain Washington thinks of my confidential memorandum: it went home by last mail, and I am naturally rather anxious about it.[3]

The Palace. Esquimalt.
June 1. 1862.

My dear Father,

When I was at San Francisco a story was going the rounds of the papers, which appeared so absurd that I simply laughed at it; I have just heard the same story from an eye-witness, Mr. Fielder, who came out with me from England; I know him well and am sure that he would not exagerrate, and I deem the story so remarkable that I write it for you: it appears that three weeks before we arrived, a woman set to work to kill a cock for dinner, so she cut its head off: observing signs of vitality beyond what her previous experience would have led her to expect, she cauterized the neck all round, and to her astonishment the bird recovered; it is still, I believe, to be seen living at San Francisco: one pays a shilling to see it, and it is kept in a cardboard box to prevent its walking about, as of course it cannot see where it is going; the head is kept by its side in a phial of spirits: Mr. Fielder saw the bird, handled it, and saw its head: he tells me that the head is severed just below the skull, so that all the bone is off: the top of the neck is quite squarely cut off, and there is just a blue scar all round, where it was cauterized: Mr. Fielder saw it fed, which was thus done: at the top of the gullet was placed a very small piece of raw beef, which it made a convulsive effort to swallow; failing in this, it was washed down with a small squirt containing milk and water: when it fairly had disappeared, the cock gave a sort of crow, which was not on the whole very successful: this sounds very much like a Yankee story, but coming from Mr. Fielder, I cannot doubt a word of what he says he himself witnessed.

I heard also to-day a story told of the Bishop: it is said that last year, when visiting the mines with some of his clergy, five I believe, he was suddenly called on by a miner to baptize a child: feeling in his pocket he found that he had no prayer-book, so he turned to his clergy and asked one after another to lend him one, but not one of them had one: however, by a little prompting, between the six of them they managed to get through the service from memory, and the child was duly baptized: the miner now produced a bottle of wine, and insisted that the bishop should drink the infant's health, but, alas! he had no corkscrew; instantly each of the five clergy, headed by the Bishop, put his hand into his pocket and produced a corkscrew: I did not hear this from the Bishop himself, but I know he did visit the mines last year.

You can perhaps imagine how delighted I was to get your note from March 18. to April 1. by last mail: but I only got it owing to its being sent through the Admiralty: I send all my letters to you through the Admiralty bag, so I hope you have nothing to pay for them.

I was very sorry to miss my tin box, and wrote to Stone about it to blow him up: I suppose I shall get it in October: many thanks for the trouble you took to have it forwarded: you say that you think of filling up the box with Isaiahs: I have talked to the Bishop about it, but I fear there will be little chance of selling them here: gold is plentiful at times, but I suspect that then religion is scarce: at present there is very little gold here.[1]

I am afraid that you will complain that I have given you no interesting descriptions of the place: certainly I saw little here but what I had been led to expect from the Bishop's letters, and from Vancouver's account: I dare say that you will glean my experiences of the country from future letters written when I am on cruizes better than from more formal accounts: the wild flowers and wild fruits are perhaps among the most remarkable features of the country: the people who are wanted here are not diggers, but settlers with eight or ten children aged from four to twenty-four: in the absence of servants children with an able-bodied mother are indispensable: it is cruel to send out bad people here in the hope that they will reform; they will simply die like dogs in the streets; but it is a true kindness to send out a poor, steady, hard-working, industrious man, with a large family to support, struggling in vain to make both ends meet; kindness both to the man and to the colony; he will probably make his fortune, his daughters will marry well, and his sons will have the blessings foretold by an older pen than mine; happy the man who has his quiver full of them:[2] women ought to be sent out: pray do not send bad women; there are plenty of them here, and the curse of the place: you mention this subject in your letter: I will talk to the Governor and to the Bishop about it.

Many thanks for the news you give me of my being elected to the Geographical: I suppose I need not pay anything until my return home: if I can find any-thing worth writing a paper about, I will send it to you first: I am anxious to hear my fate about the St. James' Club: I have a very kind note about it from Alan Herbert; he has met the De Granceys.[3]

Pray do not seal your letters: yours arrived in a very tattered condition, the seal having stuck to some other letter, and the cover having been torn in the separation: foreign note-paper need not be used for letters sent through the Admiralty. If you have ever anything very important to tell me, you can telegraph in three weeks or at most a month viâ New York and San Francisco: I do not hear that the charge is very exhorbitant all things considered: for instance if ever their Lordships should see fit to promote me, it might make a great difference to me to know it a fortnight or three weeks before it could arrive officially; it might prevent my being sent on some distant cruize: if you were to telegraph through Mr. Booker our Consul at San Francisco, he would take care it was quickly forwarded for he is an excellent fellow.[4]

Henry is very well, and getting on very well: he grows more sensible as he grows older: he whistles and sings from morning till night, so he cannot be very miserable: do tell me what he writes to his sister.

I think I have mentioned on more than one occasion, a surgeon Dr. Davie, a fellow-passenger: he intended going to Cariboo, but has now settled down into a comfortable little practice: being a really worthy good man, he is already making £20. a week: there is no great want of doctors, but in all classes there is a want of worthy men who inspire confidence: I do not imagine that Mr. Davie is a very remarkably good surgeon, but he is married and has brought out four sons and an old maidservant: he has written home for his wife and the rest of his family, and moreover he doesn't get drunk.[5]

June. 3. 1863 [*sic*]. Last night, to my great joy, came another letter from you: I am very sorry to hear of Mr. Western's death, he is a great loss: I will again talk over the question of the Isaiahs with the Bishop, but you must not be too sanguine: I am quite sure that there will be little chance of selling them at present, as there is hardly any gold on the Island: when the miners come down in the Autumn, there may be more money flying about.

Jno. Norman's address is 5. Brunswick Villas, Hill Road, St. John's Wood: he and his wife are very worthy people.[6]

I have heard nothing of any row with the Indians lately; the Grappler is being caulked and painted, but will be ready for service at the end of this week: I hope however to have a day or two longer in harbour, to let the paint dry: after that I hope for plenty of cruizing and to get myself well up in the topography of the neighbouring coasts: I suppose it will take some little time to get thoroughly up to the Native character.

What you tell me about Freddy is most pleasant to hear, and the brightest part of your letter: I enclose a short-hand scrap for him. Many thanks for the review of our book which you sent me: pray send any more that may appear: but for your wise pruning, it would not have met with so much leniency as it has, from every publication that has noticed it.[7]

June 6. Tomorrow I go to Nanaimo with the Bishop, to consecrate a church there, and do not return until Monday:[8] as the mail will probably arrive and depart before my return, I close my letter now: all is well, and all promises to be well: during my absence, my traps will all be removed to the ship, as next week I shall live on board: we are still in the middle of painting ship, which is a very great bore: however, if we are not disturbed until the paint has set well and become quite hardened, she will look very tolerable, though to make a 60-horse-power gun-boat look well, is almost an impossibility.

Some gentlemen meet this morning to endeavour to form a committee with a view to encouraging emigration from home: the Bishop is one, and will try to get me on it in time: I have supplied him with an extract from your letter to me on the subject, and I think something will be done.

Your affectionate Son,
Edmund Hope Verney

I enclose a thin note for our "littel bodye."

H.M.S. Grappler. June 16. 1862.
Esquimalt Harbour.

My dear Father,

On Friday morning I went to the Island of San Juan, and returned here on Saturday evening: the entrance to the harbour, Camp Creek, where our troops are, is very narrow and dangerous, and I was very glad to get safely in and out the first time. The Island is very beautiful, and much of it is fertile, so that besides its importance to England as a military post, it is valuable as an agricultural district: it is to be hoped that nothing will ever induce us to give it up: now that the rest of the boundary has been settled, we ought to insist on San Juan being given up to us.[1]

I continue to like my appointment very much: I think Tomlin will leave me shortly: he wishes to go, and I think he is right: I shall try to get him appointed to some comfortable ship: he is a very good young fellow, and sure to get on wherever he goes: the Admiral will be here in a week or two, and then we shall see about it.[2]

I find plenty to do here, and am never idle: there is so much interesting country to see that one does not easily tire of it. The bishop started for Cariboo this morning, I wish I could have gone with him: he will not be back for three or four months.

Will you send out to me, for the use of our emigration committee, some of the parliamentary blue-books on male and female emigration: I was particularly requested to ask you to send them out.[3]

I am delighted with the country, and am sure that it is the place of all others to send emigrants to: the woods are full of roses, sweetbriars and other flowers, and strawberries and other varieties of fruit: there are all sorts of scenery; quiet little woodland dells; open park-land, rugged cliffs, thick jungle, and noble mountains, and with all a charming climate.

The mail steamer has arrived this morning and will sail tomorrow. (Evening.) Alas! no letters for poor me; I cannot understand the postal arrangements: since I have been here I have received two letters and one "Army and Navy Gazette," the latter dated April 26: what has become of the previous Gazettes, and the Navy List all which have doubtless been sent?[4] I ought to have had more than two letters in the five weeks I have been here, and doubtless my letters to you are equally erratic: and if some communications are sadly slow, others are very quick: thus we have to-day papers of the first of April, and we can get telegraphic news sometimes in thirteen days: the result is that this is a great place for vague rumours, but we are badly off for authentic news.

Shiploads of oranges, diggers, and cocoa-nuts arrive from New Zealand, and depart with timber and diggers from Cariboo: the Cariboo diggers are rushing down to Salmon river: the Stickeen diggers are tearing away to Cariboo, and the Salmon-river diggers are mad to get up to the Stickeen: numbers of the diggers are coming down the country and settling to work at Victoria, and numbers of the Victoria workmen are going up the country to turn diggers: so we are all like the boiling water in a kettle, and no end of bubbles.[5]

Your affectionate Son,
Edmund Hope Verney

H.M.S. Grappler. Esquimalt.
June 27. 1862.

My dear Father,

I must own that I feel ashamed of myself that the mail has come in, and I have not a letter ready to send; but I must beg of you to regard it as a good sign: it shows that I am busy, well, and happy, and taking a great interest in all my work: when I am more settled, and get sent on some long cruize, I shall have more spare time, and will get up my arrears of correspondance.

I have been a second time to San Juan, and tonight I start for New Westminster, to assist in laying down buoys at the entrance to the river: there I shall probably have more time at my disposal: the Admiral is here, and I think I shall get on well with him, but it will not be easy to fill Helby's shoes.

So Emily is likely to remain abroad during the summer; I am very glad of that; it was my parting advice to her. I have your intimation of Uncle Hammersley's death; I hardly expected ever to see him again in this world.[1]

There has not yet been a second meeting of the immigration committee; when there is one, I shall be careful to forward your views, and to let you know the result.

Tomlin has left me, and gone to the Charybdis, where he is very comfortable: she is likely to go to Valparaiso, where he has a sister.

So busy am I to-day, that I have not yet found time to read my letters, and have only glanced over yours. My horse is a delightful one, and the Admiration of the whole colony. I think I may say on the whole, that I am much pleased with my appointment: you must let me know what Captain Washington thinks of my memorandum.

An immense deal of mischief has been done here in more than one instance, by people's letters from this place being shown about and copied in England: I do beg you to be most careful of mine: I am on my guard as to what I write, but I will send you some letters written more freely bye and bye.

I should be ashamed to send this scrap, were it not that it goes home for nothing in the Admiral's bag, so Adieu; with love to Mamma.

Believe me, your affectionate Son,
Edmund Hope Verney

Not to be copied

Private

H.M.S. Grappler. At Sea.
July 2. 1862.

My dear Father,

For the first time since I have joined this ship, I feel inclined to write you; (as Bishop Kip would say.) and as I have marked this "private", I will talk to you about "people".[1]

I am on my way from New Westminster to Esquimalt: I left the latter place on Saturday morning, arriving at New Westminster that same evening: on Monday and Tuesday I was employed laying down buoys at the harbour's mouth, at the Sand Heads and now I am on my way to San Juan to get some lime and timber for the use of the Fleet, and return to Esquimalt tomorrow.

Having been out here nearly two months, I may venture to give an opinion on matters in the Colonies. I think that the sooner the governor is relieved, the better; with every good intention, he is I think a great drag on the place: I am also very much inclined to think that there ought to be a separate governor for British Columbia. Considering his great disadvantages governor Douglas is a wonderful man, but he has no pretension to be a high-minded, superior gentleman; he is very pompous and ridiculous, and always cruizes about in uniform, with a bombadier [*sic*] of Engineers lashed on to a cavalry sword following in his wake: this solemn procession of two may be seen parading Victoria every evening: on the Queen's birthday he gave a state dinner, and put on all the gold lace he could muster: he proposed the Queen's health in a penny-a-liner speech, with three times three: you may guess what a preposterously ridiculous farce it was, when I tell you that we were only eleven at table, and all burst out laughing when we ought to have cheered: the two servants at this state dinner were dressed in morning dress, not even in decent black: the governor is much led by his niece and her husband Mr. Young: the latter is anything but popular.[2]

It is generally stated that all roads are led through the property of the governor or some of his relations, for each of whom he appears to have found a snug berth: I think that when he goes it will be a relief to the colony: what this place wants above all things is to have its morale, and its whole tone raised: this the bishop does but little towards because he is unmarried, and the governors influence for it is nil.

British Columbia is very jealous of Vancouver Island, and very naturally so: the former finds nearly all the revenue, while the latter has the Fleet and the legislature. I cannot quite venture to offer an opinion of Colonel Moody: perhaps he would make a first-rate governor with more power: the very little I have seen of the people of British Columbia has impressed me more favourably than the sister colony: I am inclined to attribute this to Colonel Moody's influence: he is a great visionary, but perhaps this is not such a bad thing after all.[3]

Now as to climate: since I have been here the weather has been most delicious, but then this is the best time of the year; it will not be quite such good fun in winter. From the opposite reports I hear, I cannot make out whether there is really much good land that may be cultivated or not: I suspect however, that there is a very fair proportion in each colony: I only hear of one man who has found farming a very lucrative affair, but that will doubtless mend as the farmers acquire more experience annually, and as there is more capital: it does not seem at all difficult to make a fortune here by shopkeeping or steady manual labour, but gold-digging is very hazardous: the best diggings are upwards of a month's journey from New Westminster, and the road is dangerous. People will some day regret the delay in settling the San Juan affair; no good can come of it, but much evil doubtless will: it should be settled at once: it is rumoured that the Russians would not be unwilling to give up their three-hundred miles of sea-board[;] *you* know of what vital importance this is; if the governor were a superior man, he ought to be employed to negociate it out here: numbers of miners have gone to the Stickeen river, which empties itself in Russian territory: this might give rise to most serious complications.

If you should hear that the Grappler has touched on a rock in Victoria Harbour, I tell you that Tomlin put her there:[4] I dare say you will hear nothing of it, in which case it is better to say nothing: I am sure *you* will believe me when I tell you that his leaving this ship was in every way a most right thing: but do not suspect that we had any quarrel: we were throughout the best friends, and both agreed that it was better for him to go: I have a very high opinion of him, and shall ask him to sail with me again if ever I get a larger ship. (July 3.) This morning we have anchored in Esquimalt, where we find a mail: I just send this off to assure you that I am well and generally jolly.

Your affectionate Son,
Edmund Hope Verney

I find letters up to May 15.

H.M.S. Grappler. Esquimalt.
July. 17. 1862.

My dear Father,

Our verse to-day is Matt. viii. 26.: for tomorrow it will be short enough, but even then a significant one.

I enclose a number of seeds from the Island of San Juan; I am sorry to say that I can give you the names of none; one only is marked: they were collected for me by an officer of the marines.

As the summer advances, I will get more seeds. The news from the diggings are very good: the gold is rich and abundant, but the difficulties of reaching the gold-fields are so great that many are discouraged, and turn back when only half-way there.

The gold mania has brought out some extraordinary people: one man was introduced to me, bearing the honorary title of Captain, in virtue of having once served with a Turkish regiment; he stated himself to be a relation to Lord Galway, and said that he had come out because his father-in-law said he had no energy, and now having proved his energy, would I lend him, or stand surety for him for £60, to go home again; or failing that, would I introduce him to the Governor and ask him to lend it? He went on board the Bacchante, and amused the mess by handing round his marriage lines to prove his identity: he may be seen any-day swaggering down Government street, with a generally horse-y Appearance, and a little cavalry forage-cap stuck on one side of his head. I believe he is going to the diggings after all, so his father-in-law will be delighted with his energy: I think he may very likely turn out to be a groom out of place: he certainly [is] out of place here.[1]

The mail has this morning come in, but we have not yet got our letters: Sir Thomas Maitland, we hear, is made rear-admiral of the red, and will shift his flag this evening: I am sorry for it, because the white is such a pretty ensign. I must say, I like the Admiral much: he is very civil, and listens to all I have to say, and does everything I ask him.[2]

In consequence of the great number of people who are gone to the Stickeen river, I think it highly probable that I shall be sent there: the Stickeen river is in Russian territory, in nearly the same latitude as Sitka, and it would be a most interesting journey.

I cannot say a good word for the Young Man who brought out that letter of introduction to me: 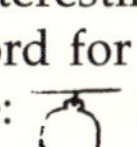 he is not my style at all: I was of course civil to him, and took him out for a little excursion one day to the Race Rocks Lighthouse; but now, having done my duty, his conduct here is not such as to make me desire to have him known as my friend: it was he that introduced me to the Turkish Captain, the energetic.

I am sorry to say that the government has refused double-pay to the crews of the gun-boats; it is, I think, a mistake, as you cannot expect men to resist the temptations of gold diggings unless they have higher pay on board: besides, the prices here are very extravagant, and a man's pay will not go far. Having to keep a separate mess, and having sundry extra expenses connected with the ship, I find myself a far poorer man than I was in England: I even contemplate having to sell my horse, as the price of food is so high.

Good bye, my dear Father; I trust that all is well with you, and I think of you, probably enjoying this delightful summer; with love to Mamma believe me,

Your affectionate Son,
Edmund Hope Verney

I have only received three newspapers since I have been here: the "Army and Navy Gazette" used to be published every Saturday.

July. 17. 1862. H.M.S. Grappler.
Esquimalt.

My dear Father,

I add a line to thank you for your letter of May 30. arrived this morning, with the last part of it dated May 31.

I am very sorry indeed to hear of Uncle Hope's being wounded again: it must be a great drain on his constitution.[3]

I am delighted to hear that Emily is to spend the winter abroad; I am sure it is the best thing for her.

Your scraps of political intelligence are very acceptable; just what one wants out here; to know what is engaging public attention.

You write as merrily as a grig: it is very pleasant that all should be so prosperous with us Verneys; let us not forget to thank the Giver.

Your affectionate Son,
Edmund Hope Verney

Private
Not to be copied

H.M.S. Grappler. Esquimalt.
July. 20. 1862.

My dear Father,

I want to give you some idea of the necessity for a new Governor here, and drag-downwards that the present Governor is. Yesterday there was a pic-nic in a bay on the harbour here, and I went thereto. The first thing that struck me was how entirely the Governor has provided for his family: when he first came here, about a dozen years ago, he brought a niece with him to instruct him and his wife and daughters in the ways of the fashionable world, of which she was supposed to be a habituée: this niece, of whose praises I cannot sing, acquired a great influence over him, and doubtless polished him a little: as the daughters grew up, and their mother learnt to be "fashionable", she by degrees subsided, and at last married Mr. Young; in virtue of Mrs. Douglas being a half-breed, and her daughters quarter-breeds, Mrs. Young considers herself, and is considered by many, the leading lady in the island: how she fills a post which might be one of great usefulness and influence, I need not say; she still retains great influence over the governor, and obtains various good things for her husband, viz; secretary of British Columbia, secretary of Vancouver Island, and secretary to the Boundary commission, all of which he receives pay for, in addition to his full pay as a paymaster in the Navy; by his conduct he has made himself very unpopular with the Navy, and, I think, with every-one except his superiors: the pic-nic, which was on a hill near Mrs. Young's little country cottage, was one at which every one was expected to assist by bringing their own share of victuals.[1]

The governor's eldest daughter, a fine squaw, is married to the speaker of the House of Commons, Dr. Helmkin, an infidel, but the Governor and he have not spoken to each other for years: Mrs. Helmkin however, was there.[2]

The governor's second daughter eloped to Washington territory with Mr. Goode, a laddy-da government clerk; she is always correcting her sisters for not being sufficiently lady-like, but they can hardly be worse than herself: Mr. Goode was at the pic-nic, but not his wife:[3]

The governors third daughter is perhaps the best of the lot; she is a fat squaw, but without any pretence to being anything else; very good-natured and affectionate, but not affected: she married a Mr. Bushy, who is, I think, Recorder of British Columbia: thus you see, the colonies provide for the Governor, his three daughters and his niece: in addition to this the Attorney-General's wife is more distantly related to him: now, can you wonder that people complain that the colonies are governed by a family clique, who know that in these civilized day[s] their reign cannot last long, and are feathering their nests as fast as they can?[4]

Of the governor, I can only say that he is a wonderful man; considering that he has had no education, and knows nothing of the world, he deserves great credit for all he has done for the colony; he is thoroughly kind-hearted and pompous, but the colonies have now reached a stage so much beyond him, that he is a great drag on them: for instance, yesterday afternoon, he conversed chiefly with a man who is living in open adultery with an Australian woman, and who ought not to be admitted to decent society: this was all very well in the days of the Hudson's Bay company, when they encouraged their servants to co-habit with native women to keep up trade, but now it shocks refined people, and turns the balance the wrong way, with those who are not very decided.

Mrs. Douglas is a good creature, but utterly ignorant: she has no language, but jabbers french or english or Indian, as she is half Indian, half English, and a French Canadian by birth.

Have I not depicted a sad state of society? It would be a great stride for the colony to get a new governor, who might come out with enlightened feelings and ideas, and a lady for his wife, but Governor Douglas should be removed with great kindness: it would not be right to hurt his feelings, for he has done much for the colonies: Colonel Moody is far from a perfect being, but he has done much towards raising the tone of British Columbia, which is much more English in feeling: New Westminster is but a small town of huts in a clearing of the forest, but I would far sooner live there than in Victoria, for there are more English feeling, more English sabbath-observance, and less American democracy and equality: among that very small society reigns good-feeling, gentlemanly-kindness, and courtesy, and one can look up to such men as colonel Moody and his officers of Engineers.

There is a great deal of animosity among people here, and the ladies fight like cats. The salary of the Governor here should be high, and I cannot see why it should not be one of the best governorships, held by the best stamp of man: it has none of the discomforts of India, or a West Indian Island, and no discomforts except the lack of servants, which a high salary would make up for; it is not isolated, it may become very politically important, and offers a boundless field for the botanist, the geologist, the mineralogist, or any scientific man.

The people here are not pressingly civil or polite to me, and I hardly know any-one; but perhaps that is a good thing as I think I have no enemies, and if there is any stuff in me, they will find it out sooner or later: I came out with fanciful ideas that I would devote myself to the colony and make myself known, respected, and liked; perhaps I may achieve that yet, some day, but I am subsiding into a quieter way of going to work: perhaps you had better not shew this bit to Mamma, she will bully me: I am going the road to distinction by working at the lighthouses, to bring them up to high order and efficiency, and on the committee of immigration I will try to be of use, and under the patronage and with the advice of the dear bishop, I may leave a worthy footstep behind me. An old and not over-refined proverb says that the way to a woman's heart is through her children, to a man's heart, through his belly; so when I get any visitors on board I feed them up, always avoiding spirits and champagne.

This letter contains a great deal of scandal, abuse, &c, but I have long wanted to throw it off, as I think you may help us to get a better governor; we want a man who will raise the standard of excellence in religion, in morals, in dinners, servants, gardens, houses, dress, manners and customs; the poor batchelor bishop fights hard for it, but does little alone.

When these colonies are peopled with sensible, highminded men they will appreciate and revere the memory of George, first Bishop of Columbia.

For the present, my dear Father, Adieu; I see little bits of character in many people here which I think would shine out if judiciously and competently worked; but the man at the head is not competent to make the most of his materials.

Your affectionate Son,
Edmund Hope Verney

In addition to the before-mentioned political offences, Mr. Cameron, the Governor's brother in law, is judge of the Supreme Court, an office which he cannot legally hold, not being a lawyer.[5]

July. 28. 1862.
H.M.S. Grappler, Esquimalt.

My dear Father,

I intended to have sent this letter in the Admiralty bag, but I am sorry to say that it is too late, so I fear it will cost a power of money.

This morning the Admiral told me to stand by for a trip to Nanaimo: this afternoon I met the Governor to whom I said that I was going to Nanaimo: he replied that he thought I was going further, and asked me if I had charts of Sitka, and the Stickeen river: I afterwards heard that he and the Admiral had been having a long confab together; if I really go there, it will be the most delightful and interesting trip possible; but the mail goes in an hour, and I can only leave you in the same state of uncertainty that I am in myself.

I am as well as possible, and full of occupation: with much love to all, believe me,

Your affectionate Son,
Edmund Hope Verney

H.M.S. Grappler. Esquimalt.
August. 3. 1862.

My dear Father,

I will indite to you a little epistle of my hopes and fears.

Last Friday it was arranged that I was to go to Nanaimo, wait there some days and then go on to Sitka with the Devastation:[1] I was overjoyed at this prospect, than which nothing could be more delightful: yesterday however it was all altered and I am now ordered to be ready to go with a party of fifty or a hundred settlers to the Cowitchin river, in a week or ten days time: the fact is that anything in the way of activity pleases me, but I should have liked an expedition to Sitka and Stickeen: it is just possible that I may go on from Cowitchin to Sitka, but I am afraid it is not probable.

I am extremely happy and contented: I cannot remember when I have been so perfectly contented, except when I was tented in India: this extraordinary sort of peaceful happiness may in a great measure be the result of climate, and this delicious summer; so I dare say in the winter I shall be cross and irritable enough. Day succeeds day, without a cloud; the sun shines, and the birds sing, and everything is as jolly as jolly can be: the scenery too is so beautiful, and the Indians are so ugly, and the breezes are so cool, and the sun is so hot, and the wild berries in the woods are so good that I cannot help thinking I am a very lucky dog: I cannot help thinking that a uniform coat looks better with three stripes on the cuff than with only one, but that may be a matter of opinion after all.

Freddy's chum, Bevan, is a midshipman in the Bacchante, and I often see him: he says he has written to Fred: I like the looks of him very much.[2]

I get on capitally with the Admiral and on board my ship, so I have much to be thankful for: letters and newspapers arrive in erratic and unexpected ways: a steamer arrives from San Francisco, without having seen the steamer from Panama, yet brings me a newspaper or two, and perhaps a letter: I dare say they have been left behind from a former mail, but letters here are notoriously uncertain.

I am busy collecting seeds, but find drying them a troublesome business: they are very apt to mildew, or sprout, or do anything except dry.

I made a little short speech at a public meeting the other day which was well received: the meeting assembled to discuss the question of "settling up" the Cowitchin valley, and I proposed a vote of thanks to all who had spoken for or against: this was a happy hit for my first appearance, as of course everybody was pleased, and you know that is not always an easy thing to do.[3]

Now Adieu, my dear Father; I hope that you will feel that you could not possibly have had a more satisfactory letter from me; I trust that the next letters I receive will be equally happy: with love to mamma and any of your chickens that may happen to be under your wing, believe me,

Your affectionate Son,
Edmund Hope Verney

H.M.S. Grappler. Esquimalt.
August. 7. 1862.

My dear Father,

I will tell you a subject that is exciting some interest and discussion in these parts: it is the subject of belligerent ships entering neutral ports: a few days ago, an American man-of-war steamer arrived here, and was immediately warned by the Admiral that she must depart in twenty-four hours: she got under weigh and went out at once: on the other hand our corvette, the Mutine, is lying at San Francisco, having gone there to be docked: now if we cannot afford hospitality to American ships for more than twenty-four hours, how can we claim to send our ships to their ports to be docked, and to lay there for weeks: it is an anomaly, and will, I think, lead to bad feeling. The question does however strongly point out the necessity of establishing a large dockyard here, a step which, in my opinion, ought to be taken at once.

I am very glad to see that you have been speaking in the House, and writing in the "Times", about these colonies: I have no doubt that the letter, from which you read extracts, was mine: but I feel that since I left England, all my letters have been miserably bare and uninteresting, far more so than during any previous absence: of course your moving in Columbia matters in England is a great help to me out here.[1]

August. 8. Yesterday afternoon we had a meeting of the female immigrant committee: I think that the committee is composed of the very best ten persons that could be got together for the purpose, and so far that is very satisfactory: I read an extract from your letter to me dated March. 18.: although it was received with every courtesy the very natural question was asked, "is your father a member of the Committee in England?": I was obliged to answer no: then I was asked, "do you think that your father expresses the views of the Committee in England?" I answered that I believed you expressed the views of the committee at that time, but I could not deny that those do not appear to be the views of the committee at the present time, as we gather from the letters we have received: and now I will notice the points in your letter to which exception may be taken.[2]

You start by saying "I wish the British Columbians to know": now there is an expression which shews how little idea you people in England have of the attitude of these two colonies: Columbia hates Vancouver Island, and there is great animosity and difference of sentiment between them: Columbia is thinly populated, rich, and aristocratic: Vancouver has all its population at Victoria in a lump, with just a few outsiders at Nanaimo & other places, is very poor and comparatively democratic: the Victorians monopolize the Fleet, the Government, the Bishop, commerce: the Columbians have taxes, and custom-house and are rich: New Westminster is thoroughly English, Victoria is half American: Colonel Moody and the Engineers have introduced an upper class, as well defined as in England; here the Governor and his poor wife are nowhere: Victoria is really a very respectable town, doing a very respectable deal of business; New Westminster is a few huts, comparatively, standing in half-cleared forest: it would have been rather absurd for Miss Coutts to have sent her peal of bells to the Cathedral at Victoria, but her having sent them to New Westminster would be intensely ludicrous, were not one more overpowered by the contemplation of her generosity: yet to New Westminster they must go, on account of the inscription cast on them:[3] well then you send emigrants to British Columbia: why, I doubt if there is house-room for them: at the outside, half a dozen may go there, but not more: this would not do perhaps to state at a public meeting, but I think you will like to know the truth: the New Westminsterians deserve the greatest credit for having established their little town at all, in the face of great difficulties, but in giving them this credit, we must not expect too much: from this I should recommend that to prevent misunderstanding and ill feeling, all communication should be addressed to the two colonies, never naming one without the other.

Again you say "in Columbia they have plenty of gold": true, but I have already shewn that I expect not more than half-a-dozen women will go to Columbia: the gold-possessors will come to Victoria, and I earnestly hope will take to themselves wives, but a great many will, I fear, leave these colonies: at present if we were to call for subscriptions, all would be subscribed by the few open-hearted people who subscribe to everything, and the aggregate would not amount to much: it is proposed that everyone who applies to the committee for a servant shall pay a very heavy fee, and perhaps a monthly subscription afterwards, but nothing can be settled until we have official intimations, probably by next mail, of the understanding on which the females come out: there are several things we should like to know: on what basis or authority is your committee founded? is it purely Church of England? does it send emigrants to the colony or to the mission? we have agreed to receive them for the colony, not for the mission. Is your committee essentially religious or only philanthropical? It would for instance be interesting to me to know whether prayer is offered up at every meeting at the Committee.

In a letter from Mr. Sarjeant, the secretary, he says to the effect that any amount of funds are forthcoming: from the tenor of letters we have received, we are inclined to accept these women as a free gift from the people of England, and to believe that they do not expect to be repaid as you say in your letter: if you think it advisable, I hope you will get appointed a member of the committee.[4]

I myself have serious doubts as to the great want of women in these colonies, and have an idea that all the money we can get here, will be absorbed in maintaining for a time those women for whom situations cannot at once be found: in any case I think it would be madness to send out any more women until it has been seen how this experiment answers. I think that you imagine more public spirit, more unanimity than exists here: this may be in some degrees caused by the large number of Americans. I think the English Society ought to change its name so as to embrace both colonies. Other members of the Committee are more sanguine than I am of the facility of finding places for the women, and they have more experience: still I feel sure that the immigrants have been led to expect too much, and you will hear from them that they have been more or less disappointed.

I would further remark that the "Tynemouth" left England on the 10th of June and that it is given out that she is due here from Sept. 15. to Oct. 1.: I think there is no possibility of her arriving before the middle of October, and that this trifling inaccuracy is to be regretted.[5]

Your affectionate Son,
Edmund Hope Verney

H.M.S. Grappler. Port Townsend.
August. 11. 1862.

My dear Father,

On Saturday night, just after I had turned in, the quartermaster came down and reported to me a great row on board the flag-ship; beating to quarters, lowering boats &c: I went on board of her and found that fourteen men had taken the cutter from the boom, and gone away: at daylight yesterday morning, I was sent off to try and recover the boat: first I went to port Angelos, then to New Dungeness, then in to Port Washington, then up to the head of Port Discovery, and then round to this port, where I anchored last night: It was a very curious feeling, and very interesting to follow step by step the route Vancouver took, and to recognize each place I had read the description of in his journal in the library at Woodhall: here I heard that the boat had been seen to pass up the Sound, so this afternoon, having repaired a defect in one of the boilers, I shall go after her up Hood's canal, looking in at Port Ludlow and Port Gamble: of all trips, I know none I could have chosen for myself more pleasant than this, poking into all sorts of little out of the way corners: the weather is not very fine or it would be most delightful.[1]

(August. 13.) Yesterday afternoon, being unable to find the flag-ship's cutter, I returned, looking along the coast to port Angelo: here I found her: the deserters had landed at the mouth of the river Elwha about ten miles to the West of Port Angelo, where they had left the boat in the surf: she was found there by two American fishermen who brought her in to Port Angelo, and will receive salvage for her.

This evening I have come round to Victoria where I shall lie until Monday, and then proceed with the Hecate to Cowitchin to establish that settlement.

Tomorrow I purpose riding to North Saanach, and going by canoe to Cowitchin, returning here on Friday evening: Mr. Garret, the Indian's missionary will accompany me, and as he speaks their language, I hope for a very pleasant trip: the weather is rather shaky, and cowitchin is proverbially damp, but I shall take a tent.[2]

Your affectionate Son,
Edmund Hope Verney

H.M.S. Grappler. Victoria.
August. 16. 1862.

My dear Father,

I am lying in Victoria to assist the police in apprehending any men who may try to desert.

Next week I go with a hundred settlers to the Cowitchin valley, and I am to remain there for a month or six weeks to assist in establishing the settlement: altogether, I like the prospect of this, although it is not so brilliant and exciting as would be a trip to Sitka or the Stickeen river: it will be interesting to watch the first development of a community, and may give me the means of being of considerable use.

But I am sorry to say that all does not promise very well about this settlement; the best pieces of the land have been bought up by speculators, and I fear that this will cause some dissatisfaction, as there is not much of it.

Last thursday, at noon, I started from this place on horseback, with Mr. Garret the clergyman: we reached the house of Mr. Low, the clergyman of South Saanach at about 3.30. where we had lunch, and the house of a Dutch farmer, Mr. Axener, at about 6.30:[1] here we left our horses (at North Saanach.) and got a canoe with one Indian: Garret and I had to paddle of course, and starting from Union Bay, were heartily tired when we got to a village on the South side of the Cowitchin mouth at 10.30. P.M.: here we hauled our canoe up on the beach, pitched our tent, lighted a fire, and supped off bread and chocolate: then rolling ourselves up in our blankets, soon dropped off to sleep.

In the morning, we went to the house of a neighbouring French Canadian settler, where we had by far the nastiest breakfast I ever ate in my life: the piece de resistance was eggs and bacon fried in fish oil: the taste comes back and makes me shudder yet: we then went in a canoe to the North side of the river's mouth, and took a trail for two or three miles through rough country to the Quamitchin village: from here we steered north to Quamichen lake, and generally rambled about; then we took canoe down the river to where we had encamped the previous night, and returned as we had come, reaching Victoria at midnight.

In this trip I saw a little of the land, and certainly came to the conclusion that the land is not as good and as clear as the settlers have been led by the government to expect: it is a sad pity that a government should descend to any subterfuge or disguising of facts, and only shows me what I have for some time observed more clearly, that we do want a new governor, and an infusion of fresh blood: it is too bad that all the officials should be connected by blood, and that they should be so completely apart from the mass of the people: the government here is not Yankee certainly, but it is not English: it is a Hudson Bay government, mean, petty, slovenly: these are harsh sweeping expressions, but you know I am only a sailor and can't know much about it: still I do not prophesy that this will be a success: I fear that this effort to settle the Cowitchin valley will be a failure, and that many poor fellows will lose their little all: the government look to me for help, and they shall get all I can give them for the sake of the settlers: I fear there is some underhand dealing among officials in this matter.

Aug. 18. This morning, the Hecate took the settlers to Cowichan, and towed round the schooner "Explorer", containing their luggage: the Governor, the Surveyor General, the Attorney General, and a lot of other Generals went in the Hecate, and I trust that the settlers will be comfortably established: the Hecate will probably return towards the end of the week, and then I shall go up to remain there for a month or six weeks.[2]

By the last steamer from San Francisco, (abbreviated to "San Fran", or even to "Frisco"), we were much shocked to hear of the loss of the Steamer "Golden Age":[3] she had the same captain and crew as the "Sonora", the steamer in which I left Panama: I am afraid that there will be some difficulty in getting an English line of packets established: one feels thankful that the accident did not occur on board an overcrowded north-going ship: I do not think that there can have been any very important letter from me on board of her: I see that all the mails were lost: there is now no contract for conveying mails to and from these colonies: the old contract expired a week or two ago, and at present we are entirely dependent on the civility of the American captains: a mail is expected in a few days, so I hope to hear from you.

I am the happy owner of *three* dogs: first is Mr. Snap, a sort of Indian mongrel left me by Helby: then I have two puppies of pure blood; the first "Claydon" will grow to be a large white spaniel, the second "Grappler" is a pure scotch terrier: besides these, one of the engineers has a dog called "Watch", a pointer: this is far too great a number of dogs for a little gunboat: when we get to Cowichan, I shall probably live on shore in a tent, and keep them there, and when I live on shore in the winter, they will be a protection to my house: you see it is very easy to give one away, if I find they are a nuisance.

Henry is most valuable to me: I do not know what I should do without him: I hope he writes word to his sister that he is happy and comfortable: he appears to be a good correspondent.[4]

August. 20. By the same mail as you receive this, I hope you will receive a parcel of seeds which I am sending.

This afternoon, the female immigration committee met to receive the report of the Archdeacon from New Westminster:[5] by the wish of the committee here, he tried to form a committee of co-operation there, and a public meeting was held, the upshot of which was that the people of New Westminster saw no reason for forming a committee there, as the immigrants are consigned to the Bishop and governor here: at the meeting however most unpleasant things were said, the people teeming with animosity towards the governor and this colony: the feeling there is very strong, and is hardly to be wondered at: it is said that the revenue of British Columbia will this year amount to £120,000, while that of Vancouver Island will not amount to £20,000: surely this is too large a sum to be left to the control of one individual, and he, Governor Douglas:

In praise of the Governor, personally, too much cannot be said: having been in this country forty years, having never seen a railroad, and having imbibed the not very liberal sentiments of the Hudson Bay Company, he is a wonderful man, but in the present advanced stage of these colonies, he is a terrible drag on them: an event occurred a few days ago which has given great offence: a certain Captain Wells, a great swell in his own way, connected with the English line of packets on the S.W. coast of America, came up here to see about establishing a line of packets from Panama to New Westminster: he went to the Governor to talk the matter over, and see what he had to say, but the Governor, instead of asking him to dinner, and encouraging him, received him coldly, and told him to put his views on paper: there may have been some reason for it, of course, I only state what is said here.

The view that I am inclined to take at present is, that there should be a governor at New Westminster, and a lieutenant-Governor at Victoria; the former should be an energetic, fine fellow; the latter a refined and polished man.

The officials here are a very poor set: I do not know whether they are always so in colonies, but I do not think that the best men here are selected for office.

It is said, and I fear with some truth, that an immense deal of jobbery goes on: even if untrue, it is bad that the Government should be so little esteemed as they are.

Although I feel competent to speak positively on few points, I do venture to say that the Governor is a great drag on the colony, and I can say this the more freely, because he is always extremely friendly to me, and is really a very good, kindhearted sort of man: with the democratic American feeling here, and the general immoral influence of the Hudson's Bay company, a refined English gentleman is sadly wanted at the head of affairs: a man who is perhaps living with a woman who is not his wife may be seen in intimate familiar conversation with the Governor, or even met at his table: then, really, for Mrs. Douglas and her daughters, the less said the better: I do not conceive that I can do any good by recounting instances of their ignorance & barbarism.

I hope soon to hear from you, on what particular subjects you wish to be informed: in the mean time, if I fill my letters with all sorts of rubbish, it is erring on the right side, as I am sure you will be most careful who sees my letters.

The mail will probably be in in a day or two: tomorrow morning I intend to pull round to Esquimalt, when I shall leave this letter in the Admiral's bag: on Friday or Saturday, when the Governor returns from Cowitchin in the Hecate, I shall go there to lie for a month or six weeks.

Now I think I have told you all that you will care to know: I dare say that you are now enjoying a happy time abroad with Emily, and doubtless the next mail will bring me intimation of your plans.

Our verse to-day, is Matt. 10.20: the number of the verse, agreeing with the day of the month: every morning, when the day is bright, I land, and take sights with the artificial horizon, Uncle & Aunt Fremantle gave me: this is to correct my chronometer and to exercise myself in keeping up my nautical astronomy.

I have just finished reading La Case's account of Napoleon at St. Helena: I have been much interested in it, but the chapters on the war in Italy were unintelligible from my ignorance of History and Geography.[6]

I shall now attack "friends in Council": the "Recreations of a country parson" I have read with great delight, and while a good many shots came home to me, I thought I saw one or two that might have smitten you.[7]

Now, dear Father, good bye: believe me with much general love to everybody, your affectionate son,

Edmund Hope Verney

Aug. 20. 1862.

H.M.S. Grappler. Victoria.
August. 22. 1862.

My dear Father,

Spread open on the table before me at this moment is a panoramic photograph of Victoria: although barely two years have elapsed since it was taken, I can already see great changes.[1]

The view is taken from the point marked in the Chart as Songhies point, on the Indian Reserve: on the extreme left of the picture is a bridge which was formerly on the road to Esquimalt, but which is now taken away to encrease the harbour accomodation: a ferry plies there now, and the Esquimalt road crosses two bridges a little further up the Victoria Arm: near the bridge is a large barque, unloading: below the barque are the huts which for the most part constitute an Indian Village.

The spire and tower further to the right belong to a dissenting church which is built entirely of wood, and is a great ornament to the town.

Travelling along further to the right, we come to the large ugly Hudson's Bay Store, probably at that time the only brick building in the town: off the wharf lies the steamer "Cariboo," subsequently blown up: to the right is the stockade of the company's fort, now entirely pulled down: the blank rock astern of the steamer is now all filled up with wharves.

Further to the right, on the hill, is the hideous little wooden cathedral, with its short stumpy spire: a couple of hundred yards beyond which now stands the bishop's palace: there can be no doubt that the site will be very fine for a stone cathedral some day, but money not being too plentiful, I am sorry to say that another wooden wing is now being added.

To the right again is the wooden bridge across James' Bay; the white gable end to the right of the bridge, is the end of the governor's house: directly under this, in the picture is the spot where the Grappler is now at anchor: a photograph was taken of her, the day before yesterday from the water's edge near where the brig is lying a little to the right of the cathedral: of course I shall send you a copy, but I wish you to know, when you get it, what will be the land you will see near her.

To the right of the governor's house are the government buildings, built in a curious, un-English, fantastical, gingerbread style: they are flimsily built of brick and wood: the corner room upstairs, in the nearest angle of the large centre building is my office as secretary to the Lighthouse Board: it has two north windows, looking towards the town, and one side west window.

The low building to the left of the centre one is the land office, the corresponding one on this side, which is not so clearly seen, is the Treasury.

Now I think those are all the particulars I can give you: the picture gives a very good general idea of the town, and the ragged look the fir trees have: but many of the latter have been cut down now, as the town has extended. The wharves are more numerous: to the right of the Hudson's Bay store, in lieu of the stockade has risen up a row of very respectable merchants offices and stores, and brick houses are every day replacing wooden ones.

Your affectionate Son,
Edmund Hope Verney

H.M.S. Grappler. Cowichan.
August. 30. 1862.

My dear Father,

I arrived here on Monday evening, but most of the settlers had returned to Victoria for implements and provisions, so hitherto I have only been exploring the country with a gun on my shoulder: this place is renowned for its game, but the surveyors and settlers who have been here lately seem to have frightened it all away, for I have shot nothing: but to leave the subject, I will now answer your letters received last saturday.

I was much delighted to receive such a big package, and it made my heart very happy, as the Indians say; how well you seem to have got on with the bazaar: I made ladies silk watch-guards on board the "Sonora," and sold them for a dollar a piece for the benefit of the bazzaar; I will make it up to £5: which please deduct from my next quarter's allowance: you will also perhaps let me know for what amount you filled in the blank cheque I gave you for the bootmaker in Mount Street.

I am sorry to say that the chronometer-watch is a decided failure at present: it cost £4. to have it looked over at San Francisco, and then it was returned to me losing five seconds a day: since then, about five weeks ago, the rate has increased to seven seconds an hour: I shall not spend any more money upon it, but try if I can get it to settle into some regular rate, by attending to the regulator: at any rate, as it is quite useless for any practical purposes now, I cannot make it worse.

All your news are very satisfactory: I have two notes from Uncle Hope dated, April. 18. and May. 2., but containing no very startling intelligence. You tell me that you are sending me a parcel by *"Elliott"*: who is Elliott, and what is he coming here for? the only Elliott that I can think of is the late captain R.M. of the Emerald, but I should never expect to hear of his coming out here.[1]

I really cannot be too thankful for having got this appointment: it seems quite strange to me to rise in the morning and feel that I have not a care or anxiety: full liesure of mind and body to read, or to do a little nautical astronomy: so much to do that I can never reproach myself with being idle, so little to do that I am free to choose my own employments: I cannot remember any period of my life when I have been so perfectly happy and contented: of course it will not be quite so jolly when I am sent to cruize about these intricate waters in fogs, sleet and snow, but at present I am lying in a land-locked harbour enjoying lovely scenery and delicious weather: of all lucky dogs, surely I am the luckiest: of course there are some little roughnesses, but they are not very rugged.

September 5. Things are promising very well here: some of the settlers seem men of good solid determination, and of the right sort to overcome obstacles and not easily be daunted: I have hardly yet had time to make acquaintance with them all, but I have instructed them to communicate with me frequently, and to let me know how I can be of use to them. There is certainly more good land here than I had expected to find, and land that can be cleared with comparatively little trouble, and now some of the settlers have brought up their wives and children which looks as if they were in earnest.

September. 7. This morning, Mr. Garret, the Indian missionary held service on board here, and I afterwards went on shore to hear him deliver a sermon to the natives in their language: it was a very interesting sight to see some thirty or forty gathered round him, with their dark eyes fixed intently on his face, as he explained to them in simple childish sentences a highly coloured picture of Adam and Eve being driven out of the garden of Eden.

A Roman Catholic Priest has been among these Indians for some years, but he has extorted money from them, and got them to build a church, in return for which he has taught them to chaunt a horrible jargon of French, Chinook, and Latin about the Virgin Mary &c, not one word of which do they understand: it is at first very pleasing to hear their chaunt wafted over the calm evening air, but one can not derive pleasure from the sound when one reflects on the mockery of religion which produces it: I think that the poor creatures were a good deal struck to-day by the comparative simplicity of the truths pointed out by Mr. Garret.[2]

Sept. 9. Adieu, my dear Father: you may suppose that towards the end of this year, I shall begin to think about promotion, but until it arrives, I am not much to be pitied.

Your affectionate Son,
Edmund Hope Verney

H.M.S. Grappler. Cowichan.
September 14. 1862.

My dear Father,

Tomorrow at 5. A.M. I leave this place for Victoria, but I dare say I shall come back again towards the end of the week: I think that it requires somewhat of what Napoleon called "two-o'clock-in-the-morning courage" to turn out and navigate a ship through intricate waters at 5. A.M. on a raw chilly morning:[1] there is to be a meeting of the Female Emigration Committee, and I wish to arrive in time for that, at 2. P.M. The mail is expected in tomorrow, and I hope to send this letter and to receive others from you.

The "Mutine" is at Esquimalt, having arrived there a few days ago. On Tuesday or Wednesday the Admiral will sail for Valparaiso: on the whole I am sorry for this: it is much more satisfactory to get one's orders direct from him, than from some Captain who is afraid of responsibility: in every respect I have got on very well with the Admiral, and find him a most agreable man to serve under. For the present I suppose I shall be under the orders of Captain Graham of the "Mutine" until Captain Richards arrives in the "Hecate".[2]

I still think that this settlement will prove a success, but I am sorry to say that one of the best of the settlers has given it up, and will return with me tomorrow morning. Some of the settlers are most curious characters:

a man and his wife have taken [*sic*], both well-educated people: they have rigged up a sort of wigwam of boughs and a tent under which they have established a four post bedstead: the gentleman shoots and looks over his property, the lady washes, cooks, and does needlework: this is tolerable fun now, but in a week or two the rains will come, and they will both be laid up, and perhaps lose their lives: I have today been urging them to set about building their log-house; to take advantage of the fine weather and not to fritter away their time: "oh," they say, "it won't take long when we once get to work." The gentleman's future, he says, is a brewery, and a large farm: the lady's a good vegetable-garden and poultry yard: you may guess how stable their wigwam is when I tell you that a few nights ago, in a dead calm, the roof fell down on their noses in the four-post beadstead [*sic*].

Having now been here for three weeks, I am quite out of Victoria gossip, but shall perhaps pick up a little to finish my letter with tomorrow. I will tell you my experience of the climate since I arrived here in the middle of May: at first the days and nights became regularly warmer and warmer as in England, up to the end of July: then the days became considerably hotter, and the sun was quite scorching, burning up the grass, and the nights began to grow steadily cooler until a week ago: now the nights are positively cold, and are sometimes accompanied by hoar frost, while the heat of the sun in the day-time is more moderate: strange to say, these alternations of heat and cold do not seem to affect people's health.

Victoria. September 20. We arrived here on Monday morning last, and the intervening days have been rather eventful: the most interesting event to you perhaps is the arrival of the "Tynemouth": she anchored off Esquimalt on wednesday night: yesterday the women were all landed, and nearly half were received into people's houses at once; the remaining half were placed in a building that had been prepared for them by the Committee: before entering into particulars I will say my general opinion: I should think that on the whole, the female immigration in the Tynemouth, may be considered a success and to rank among the best of efforts that have been made for female immigration: but if other efforts have been worse, I am nevertheless sure that this might have been better: among the females are good, but also bad: some of the arrangements have been suitable, others, the reverse, and while the decided success of this is a cause for thankfulness, it is anything but a cause for self-congratulation and pride.

Some of the little ones are very pretty, and attractive: I do not know whether this is quite grammar, but I am talking of the immigrants: I think the little orphans from East Grinstead took my fancy most: perhaps that is because, being only twelve, they do not expect to get married at once.

September 22. 1862. Yesterday the ship "Cyclone" arrived, bringing me six cases of Wine and Brandy from Basil Woodd, which I shall probably receive in a few days.[3] This afternoon I have come round from Victoria to Esquimalt, towing the ship "Somass" which has arrived from England with our new boilers.

The accounts you send of Emily are very delightful, and a cause for much thankfulness. We expect the Bishop back in a few days now: although I did not see so very much of him before he started, I have already conceived a great affection for him, and I look forward anxiously to his return.

September 26. This letter must end some day, so I will conclude at once: what with being a member of the Immigration Board, of the female Immigration Committee, a magistrate, secretary to the Lighthouse Board, and last, but not least, commander of a gunboat, I am always busy.[4]

Your affectionate Son,
Edmund Hope Verney

H.M.S. Grappler. Victoria.
September 20. 1862.

My dear Father,

On the whole I think it better to turn to a fresh sheet of paper to continue my say about the arrival of the Tynemouth.[1]

Until three days before she came in, no preparations had been made for the reception of the females beyond plenty of discussion at committee meetings: we concluded that we could do nothing because, as a committee, we had received no information that such a ship as the "Tynemouth" was on her way out, nor did we know, as a committee, on what terms she was bringing out female emigrants: so when ladies came to us to engage servants we could not answer what wages they would expect, nor whether they had made any agreement to accept such situations as the committee should procure from them: in addition to this, we could procure no official recognition of our existence as a committee from the governor or any one else: I must observe that with regard to the first difficulties, we have received no particulars concerning the women up to this moment, except a semi-official list sent to the Archdeacon, which two members of the committee were fortunately allowed to copy privately: an official recognition of our existence as a committee, was sent to us by the Colonial Secretary *after* the women were landed: add to this that the Bishop is at Cariboo, the Governer in British Columbia, and the Archdeacon at New Westminster, and you will divine how aghast the Committee looked, when they were told that their sixty young ladies might be expected in two days or less.

I think the committee deserve great credit for the way in which they all (with the exception of one who went into the country; and has not come back since, another who was obliged to be at the police court, and a third who had "important business["]) went to work to meet the emergency: I landed nearly all my men to scrub, clean &c, and tradesmen were called in to provide everything needful, so that by noon on Friday all was complete: the ladies too came forward *man*fully, and without a murmur waited three or four hours to receive the immigrants:

At three yesterday afternoon the Forward brought them round from the Tynemouth at Esquimalt, as the Admiral had granted her at my request, and to the great delight of a considerable crowd the ladies landed safely and marched up in a body a few hundred yards to the "Marine Barracks" the building that had been prepared for them. And now as I am stating facts you must take the unpleasant with the pleasant: one female was carried up helplessly intoxicated, and two or three more were *evidently* the worse for liquor.

You must take into consideration the great excitement under which all laboured, and the irregularity in meal hours that necessarily attended the disembarkation, and not think this so very serious after all: of course, these little failings were not paraded before the crowd, nor, I hope, generally known.

Nearly half the females slept out of barracks that night, having either gone into situations at once, or having been kindly received into people's houses as a temporary arrangement: a fence had been put up round the building inside which none but the committee were admitted: a few straggled away, but were brought back by the vigilant police, and although the night was very dark I believe that no harm took place: the committee did not separate until half-past eight, when they were not sorry to go to bed.

Today we have had a grand regatta, and the question arose, what was to be done with the immigrants; so it was settled that they should come on board the "Grappler", where they have been all day, regaled with buns, sherry, tea &c: the committee were, ex officio, entitled to a more recherchè [*sic*] repast a la fore sheet in the captain's cabin: the Grappler's boats won three prizes, sixty-five dollars, and lost two, value ten dollars; clear profit on the transaction, fifty-five dollars, equal circum £11.00.00.[2] Having landed the ladies, turned off two or three more of them, and settled a few murmurings, I sit down to write this letter: thus exits the historical part of my account.

But having premised that on the whole, the experiment may so far be considered satisfactory, and believing that any expression from the committee of opinion on the subject will be rather formal and entirely complimentary, I must say that I had expected the affair would have been more carefully attended to in England: there is not a shadow of doubt in my mind or in the minds of at least one more of the committee with whom I have spoken, that at least one or two of the women are *thoroughly bad* and must have been so before leaving England, and there must be unpardonable neglect somewhere that they were ever allowed on board: the system, which prevails with some people, of giving undeserved recommendations, is a great sin the frightful consequences of which are not appreciated:

Mr. Scott is not popular with some of the females: how far he is the best person that could have been procured, I do not feel competent to say because I do not know how difficult it may have been to procure any one to undertake such a task. I believe that Mr. Scott and the Captain have not been on speaking terms since the ship was at the Falkland Islands:[3] personally, I think the Captain seems a good sort of man and earnestly anxious for the welfare of the females, but unsatisfactory accounts of the cleanliness and discipline of his ship are rumoured abroad: many of the other passengers, or perhaps only a few ought never to have been allowed to go in a ship with female emigrants: it is said that no actual harm has taken place on the voyage, but I do not feel sure of this. I am quite sure that people who ought to have known better have spoken most foolishly and improperly to these women before leaving England to the effect that they would soon have rich husbands: all have been more or less misled with regard to the position they would occupy here but not so much as I had expected: the following were two answers given to the committee, selected from others equally extraordinary: "I don't care where I goes or what I does so long as I gets plenty of money": then, "I really cannot undertake anything like hard work; I should like an American family where I should be on a footing of equality": yet the Committee are working hard and finding situations for even such as these: the average wages are 15 dollars a month, £3, or £36. a year. I think we have found places for but two governesses, a class really not wanted. As much as thirty dollars has been offered, but the committee has in no case hitherto allowed more than twenty. No attempt to repay the society in England for sending out these women is being made.

Your affec. Son,

Edmund Hope Verney

Private. H.M.S. Grappler. Esquimalt. Sept. 22. 1862.

My dear Father,

You are right in thinking that this is a very curious place: some newspaper paragraphs I send you will doubtless amuse you, as curious specimens of our local press.[1] The want of a public opinion in favour of right and morality is a great want to these colonies. In all your letters you talk of British Columbia: I must ask you to remember that I know little or nothing about that colony: I have only been in one town belonging to it, and that for but a few hours: all my experiences have been of Vancouver Island.

I assure you I am not very miserable: I get a little bullied sometimes, but I feel that I am sensibly getting on towards the goal I have been aiming at: I wish no committee to be complete without me, and I wish to be considered as one who has the interests of these colonies most warmly at heart, and I do find that I am getting on in that direction, and that the leading influential people of Victoria are disposed to receive me into their ranks: in a late case when I was on the bench, a merchant captain was fined £145., and with costs he will have lost about £300: yet I was much gratified to hear that he had spoken of me behind my back in a most complimentary manner, and said that although he believed I was wrong, he was sure I had acted conscientiously.

I have not yet been able to get hold of the "Times" in which you inserted a portion of my letter to you, but I dare say I shall get it.

Decidedly more females should not be sent to this country until the committee at Victoria sends home its report of this batch, and its suggestions for future guidance. I do not think it would be practicable to have the expenses of female emigration paid by these colonies: If you were to hear the notions of high wages expressed by some of the female emigrants from the Tynemouth, you would see how impossible it would be to get back from any of them the money it has cost to send them out here, unless they had been bound by law to repay it, before leaving England, but I do not think that such a course would be wise: many of them quite changed their tone after being here a few hours, and hearing the enormous wages they might command: one said to me, "I ain't a-going below my value, you know:" but really the excitement of landing &c quite turned some of their heads for a short time. Very impressive addresses were delivered to them yesterday, and some were deeply affected.

You anticipate that I shall find strong parties here: that is true, but not quite in the form that you appear to anticipate: the two parties are the government and the people: this is a most unfortunate division, and I do not see how it is to be helped: a mayor and town council have lately been appointed, which is a step in the right direction: there are no parties of different officials as you suggest.

There are two points on which I look forward for enlightenment by next mail: what you said or did with regard to asking Captain Washington for travelling expenses, and whether I have got in to the St. James' Club or not.

You say that you are sending a letter to me by Mr. Hastings: you will understand that I am making for myself a character here, I do not yet stand on a secure and proved character: one point on which I am obliged to be most particular is who I choose for associates: you sent me a letter by Mr. Bell: I was civil and kind, but a few days after his arrival I saw him walking in a public part of the town in the afternoon with a woman of improper character: of course, since that I have seen as little of him as possible: I do not ask you not to send people with letters to me; on the contrary, the more you send, the better: but do not be surprised if they write to their friends and say that I was civil to them for a day or two, and then dropped their acquaintance: you may be quite sure that any one bringing a letter from you shall have a fair chance of retaining my acquaintance and even friendship, and the more you send the better, as perhaps one may come to whom I really can be of use. You say you hear that Mr. Hastings has been "*rather wild*:"; how cruel then of his friends to send him here: unless he is already a reformed character he will just go the dogs at once: I could go out into the streets and pick up half a dozen such any day, all born gentlemen, now drunkards and reprobates.

September 25. It is surely time for me to close this desultory letter. I have been again troubled by my left knee, and have had it blistered: at Cowichan I had not my horse, and by walking about a great deal, I brought back the old complaint, but it is now much better: the left knee is considerably larger than the right, and the doctor says it may perhaps trouble me, as I grow older. Your observations as to the causes of success or failure as an M.P. are after my own heart: I like them exceedingly. I wonder what you will think of my attempts at establishing myself on shore here: I think you will approve, but say "be very careful": well, so I am, but you see how the wretched newspapers of this place bully me.[2]

Your affec. Son,
Edmund Hope Verney

H.M.S. Grappler. Victoria.
October 11. 1862.

My dear Father,

One reason that letters fail to arrive punctually is that those sent through the post office are often insufficiently stamped, and no matter how trifling may be the overweight, or short payment, they are then detained until there happen to be a ship going round the Horn, Sailer or Steamer.

I fear there is something radically wrong with the chronometer: I paid upwards of £4. at San Francisco to have it put in order, and it is now as bad as ever again.

Emily is very good and writes to me often, so I am pretty well informed of all her movements: I do hope that the next mail will bring intelligence that she has quite got over her cold. I hope that you will press to have the San Juan question settled.

I received safely the box you sent by Elliott: it cost 18^s: I mention this in order that you may be able to estimate the cost of sending a box out here at any future time: many many thanks for all the beautiful things you sent me: the thermometers arrived quite safe and unbroken; they are a most useful pair: the little box contained just the things most acceptable out here, such as really good pencils; then the pamphlets are very interesting, as one wants to know all that people are talking of and thinking of at home.

I dare say you will have heard that the Bishop returned last Wednesday week: it is a great pleasure to have him here again: I have no doubt that I shall be ordered to take him for a trip somewhere soon.

Your very affectionate Son,
Edmund Hope Verney

Lighthouse Board Office. Victoria.
October 11. 1862.

Dear Mama,

Your pleasant letter of August 15. was very acceptable and interesting: I do above all things like to know such little details of your life at Claydon: from what you say, I conclude that Captain Helby has been staying at Claydon, but no one else alludes to it: it was very kind to ask him: from an acquaintance of twelve hours, and from all I have heard of him since, I have a very high esteem for him: I hope he will soon get some good appointment.

I wonder whether it will ever be possible to get Mme. Goldschmidtt to Claydon again, when more of Papa's brats will be there: I should think that she always volunteers to sing wherever she goes, as she must know that there are some people virtuous enough not to ask her.[1]

You remind me of sending you pine cones: if only half the seeds I have sent you arrive safely, you cannot grumble at me: I have got no cones yet: I suppose that now is the time of year to look out for them: I think I have sent you two detachments of seeds, and I have another ready.

I am very glad that you have been happy in the garden, and that this year has been generally satisfactory: I know that when I come back, you will have all sorts of changes and improvements to astonish me with, and I shall be prepared to praise you for all except the gravel walk down the middle of the lawn, all idea of which I hope has been given up.

And now to tell you a little about myself: I think I have said in almost every letter that I like my appointment very much indeed, and believe it is the best that a lieutenant can hold, so there is no need to repeat that. About ten days ago I started from this port with about five and thirty men, to go and look at the Comucks country, about 54. miles north of Nanaimo: we started from the Hudson Bay Company's wharf at nine A.M., and anchored at sunset about ten miles below Nanaimo: the next morning we started at six, and at about 3 P.M. landed at the mouth of the Courtney River: I had to return to Nanaimo for coal so saw but little of the country, but when I returned a few days afterwards to take the intending settlers back, I found them all in ecstacies with the country: they said that there was most excellent land, and praries over which a man might walk for days in one direction: I suspect that the open land is to be found North, as far as Cape Mudge, South, nearly to Nanaimo, and West to the head of the Alberni canal: game was extremely plentiful; elk, bear, deer, grouse, and wild duck in abundance: all the time that I was there the weather was very bad, or I should doubtless have shot my cock hare and pheasant.[2]

In this colony I find the country more interesting than the people, nature than art: still the improvement and cultivation of the former must depend upon the amount of improvement and cultivation bestowed on the latter, and there is every prospect of a great improvement in the state of society here before very long: the bishop says there is a wonderful change since he has been here, and I can detect a change during even the few months that I have been here:

Several of the new arrivals have brought *good wives*, a great point: now a good bishop's wife, and a good governor's wife would work wonders if they did not fight.

Your affectionate stepson,
Edmund Hope Verney

H.M.S. Grappler. Esquimalt.
October 13. 1862.

My dear Father,

Sitting alongside of me at this moment is a young man of the name of Everard, a great-nephew of Lord Berners: I have often heard you speak with great admiration of Lord Berners, so I thought you would like me to be civil to his great nephew: I picked him up at luncheon with the Bishop yesterday: he seems a very sensible sort of young man, really worth something: he is at present earning his living as a carpenter, and works at building wooden houses: he knows Mr. Upsher very well, who is also a great-nephew of Lord Berners: Mr. E. was for some time in the Royal Mail Steam Packet Company's service, but was obliged to leave it on account of ill health: he is the sort of immigrant who is wanted in this colony: not to go about telling people who are their relations in England, but to settle down manfully to whatever work they can get: I hope to see more of him, and to try and get something for him.[1]

I am trying what I can do towards establishing an "Immigrant's Home": I think I shall succeed.

If you see Kerr, tell him that Everard was at school at Radley with him: he had a brother a midshipman in the Firebrand in the Black Sea, whom I knew very well, but who has since died.[2]

I am very glad that Aunt Fanny received my letter: there was some mistake about its not being prepaid, but I am glad that Aunt F. got it after all.

Everard was cutting up some wood for a lemonade-manufacturer a few days ago, who has a servant who came out in the Teignmouth:[3] she was very civil to him until last saturday when some of the passengers by the Teignmouth came to see her and indulge in a little flirtation: then she thought she would like to show off, so she turned to Everard and said "now young man, take care what you are about; you know master said you were not to drive the axe into the ground"; to which Everard replied, "oh I intend to charge him for digging his garden." He said that was the only uncivil speech that had been addressed to him since he arrived in the colony.

Your affectionate Son,
Edmund Hope Verney

Private

H.M.S. Grappler. Victoria.
October 14. 1862.

My dear Father,

Does the defence of these colonies at all occupy the publick mind at home? I believe that there is no doubt that one, and probably two "Monitors" are being constructed at San Francisco; in the event of war with America, we are not likely to have sufficient warning of it to construct "Monitors" to meet an enemy: and in case of War we have no docks in which to repair our ships: I believe that the only dock on the West Coast of America is the floating dock at San Francisco, and even if there is one at Valparaiso, which I doubt, it is too far to think of sending damaged ships from here: The only plan would be to send them across to China, where I believe there are merchants' docks.[1]

I believe that Captain Richards and others have urged on the Admiralty the importance of having a dockyard here, and have represented how admirably Esquimalt harbour is by nature adapted for a dockyard, and I cannot think why the works are not at once undertaken.

If iron-clad vessels are really in course of construction at San Francisco, our government must be aware of it, and it will not be fair to ask the "Grappler" to give an account of two "Monitors" within the next three months: for the Forward would not be available in case of war, as she is having new boilers put in.

Iron-clad vessels might be built here without any difficulty: if two are being built at San Francisco, two should be built here, and put under the command of the commanders of the Forward and Grappler, whose crews should be trained to man them and work their guns in case of war.

Victoria has much advanced during the short time I have been here: four clubs are being established: 1. an Immigrant's Home: 2. a young men's society: 3. a commercial reading room: 4. a general club: a company is being talked of to make a railroad between Esquimalt and Victoria: the gas-company is just making a start with lighting the town: and various companies having a tendency to open up and civilize the country are starting into life: I believe that more progress has been made within the last three months than during any previous six months:[2] many people that have come out expecting to realize a rapid fortune have, of course, been disappointed, and many have gone home again decrying both colonies; but they are both very thriving, and they must thrive: rapid fortunes might have been realized here a few years ago, when land might be bought for next to nothing, but now those days are past: I consider, however, that there can be no colony better suited for a man, whatever his position in life, who intends to make it his home, and never to return to England or go gold-digging: the price of skilled labour is as high as ever, notwithstanding the great immigration this summer: any fair carpenter can earn 18^{s} *a day*: which will keep him and his family, and leave a margin: Everard can only earn from 8^{s} to 10^{s} a day at present as a carpenter.

Unskilled labour may be had as low as 2^{s} a day with board & lodging, or even less: it is now a drug in the market.

Your affectionate Son,
Edmund Hope Verney

H.M.S. Grappler. Victoria. Oct. 15. 1862.

My dear Father,

I must tell you an incident that occurred at the Sunday-school here last Sabbath: the fifteenth chapter of judges was under discussion, and the teacher asked a very small boy, with reference to the 2nd verse, where Samson got his wife from: the child hesitated a long time and, after being duly encouraged, stammered "Out of the Teignmouth, Sir."

Mr. Dundas, rector of St. Johns, breakfasted with me yesterday morning: he has been up the country with the bishop, and decidedly thinks that the bishop takes too bright a view of these colonies: unbeknown to him, however, I took down in shorthand this sentence from his own lips; now I come to look for it, I find it is on shore, but I will enclose it: it was to this effect: "I should never call British Columbia a good agricultural country, but it is one where for several years to come the agriculturist may realize, not a competence, but a fortune": but capital is sadly wanted here, and a class of people who come out to settle, not merely to make a fortune and go home again: I should consider Dundas a very good authority: he seems to have had a most interesting time with the miners.[1]

Mr. and Mrs. Davies are the keepers of the Race Rocks Lighthouse: they have a little boy in England at Mr. Warner's, basket-maker, No. 7. Langley Court, Long Acre, London: his name is George Davies, and he is about seven years old: his parents could afford to pay perhaps £20. towards bringing him out; could you persuade any society in England to pay the rest, and to send him out in some immigrant ship? I have promised the parents to ask you to see if anything can be done in the matter; but I have not led them to expect any result.[2]

October 17. An inn-keeper stopped me in the street to-day; "do you know the Hon. Malcolm Cameron?" "No", said I: "then I will introduce you to him": "thank you", I said, "I was introduced to him about six weeks ago": "oh, but he wants a passage to Nanaimo": "well", I said, "I shall not take him": "Why"? said the inn-keeper: I said "I only give my particular friends a passage in my ship, and I expect them to consider it a very great favour": "oh! but he is going home to represent our grievances, and he will be able to do you a good turn": and I really had difficulty in persuading my friend that I had a right to select my own guests: I believe this Mr. Cameron is a good sort of man, and I should like to make his acquaintance but I can admit no one's right to quarter himself on me for even a few hours.[3]

October 20. The Tynemouth sails for San Francisco to-day at noon, so I take that opportunity of sending this letter.

Of myself I have little to say: I am very jolly, but not likely to be sent to Fort Simpson or any distant place, I am afraid: I dare say that I shall have the pleasure of carrying the Bishop to Nanaimo or Cowichan one of these days, but I should like to get a longer trip.

One of my engineers is a Mr. Bencke, a German: he is a very good young fellow: his father lives on Lord Elgin's property, and I believe looks after some machinery of his: he says he knows Mr. Cumming Bruce very well.[4]

I am sorry to say that I have not yet collected any cones for you: they are scarce this year, and I have not yet seen one: Captain Richards told me he wanted some, but had not yet seen any this year: I shall make a point of getting some now.

The Victoria and Esquimalt railway is a matter much talked of now: I understand that a company has been formed, and that the line will probably be commenced very shortly.

The "Topaze" is expected shortly, and as she will have communicated with the "Tribune", I hope she will bring up my box.[5]

Your affectionate Son,
Edmund Hope Verney

H.M.S. Grappler. Esquimalt.
October. 18. 1862.

My dear Father,

I beg to submit to you the following solution of the San Juan question.[1]

Article 1. of the treaty is, I believe, the only one on which any question has arisen: it runs thus,

- - - - - the line of boundary - - - - shall be continued westward along the said forty-ninth parallel of north latitude to the middle of the channel which separates the continent from Vancouver's Island; and thence southerly, through the middle of the said channel, and of Fuca's Straits, to the Pacific Ocean.

With all due deference to the wise men who have been puzzled before, I cannot see any difficulty in deciding exactly where the boundary line must run: it must start from that point on the forty-ninth parallel which is in the middle of the channel which separates the continent from Vancouver Island: to find this point, bisect a straight line joining the point on the 49th parallel cut by the westermost continental coast line with that on the 49th parallel cut by the eastermost island coast line: it is clearly immaterial whether this point falls on an island or in the sea, in either case it is that from which the boundary line commences its southerly course: it so happens it falls in the sea.

On the same principle the boundary line must proceed southward in mid channel between Vancouver Is. and the main land: the course of the boundary line can only be affected by the shape of the coast lines of Vancouver Island and the main land, and not in any way by islands that may intervene.

The treaty expressly provides that the boundary line is to be in the middle of a channel, which channel is to be determined by Vancouver Island on the one hand, and the main land on the other: I conceive that nothing could be clearer.

The accompanying chart, which is tolerably accurate, will appear more distinct if pasted on to a sheet of white paper: there I have drawn, in red, various lines from prominent points on the one boundary of the channel, to the nearest points on the opposite shore, and have bisected them for mid-channel: the boundary line connecting the points of bisection is drawn in blue: this gives us the whole of San Juan Island and of Smith's Island: on the latter, the Americans have erected a lighthouse: it would therefore be fair for them to make us a present of Point Roberts and the whole of Saturna Is., on condition of our presenting to them all other islands cut by the boundary line, and Smith Is.: in all other respects the boundary defined so accurately by the treaty should be adhered to.

Of course, in a more accurate chart, on a larger scale, the boundary line might not be exactly as I have placed it, but I am satisfied that there could be no very material differences.

I hope that I have made my meaning plain, and that by the help of the chart, you will see that my solution of the question is both law and equity.

Your affectionate Son,
Edmund Hope Verney

H.M.S. Grappler. Nanaimo.
November 1. 1862.

My dear Father,

Last monday I was ordered to pay another visit to the settlements on the East Coast of the Island, so I invited the bishop to accompany me: we anchored on Monday night in Reid's harbour, in Stewarts Island, and on Tuesday night, in Port Augusta at the mouth of the Courtney River. On wednesday morning, the Bishop and I pulled up the river about three miles, in my gig, to an Indian village: here we got a canoe, and went about a mile further up: then we landed, and visited about twenty settlers, who were all busy finishing their log-houses.[1]

I was surprised to see so much clear land: I had often heard the fertility of the Komux country spoken of but it exceeded my expectations: the open land runs in belts, stretching for miles, and separated from each other by other belts of timber, not so thick however but what it might be easily cleared: the land is undulating and well watered, and the snow-capped mountains in the interior makes the scenery very attractive: game of all sorts is abundant: grouse, deer, ducks, elk, geese, bears and jackals: trout, salmon, and salmon-trout are in all the streams: the settlers live principally on game, which they can buy from the natives at a very low rate.

North of Nanaimo, in the neighbourhood of Nanoose Harbour, lives the Nanoose tribe of Indians: further north again on the Qualicum river, the Qualicum tribe: between the Qualicum and Courtney rivers, the Pundtlutch tribe, and North of Cape Lazo, the Komux Indians: still the whole range of coast from the South entrance of Baines Sound to Cape Mudge, is usually spoken of as the Komux Country.

We had altogether a very long and delightful walk on wednesday, and I think that no colony can offer so great temptation to the agriculturist as this, and when the island is further explored I have no doubt that much more good and clear land will be found: the soil in the neighbourhood of the Courtney river is what I suppose would be called a rich sandy loam.

On Thursday morning I went out shooting alone in the woods, and there came upon what I have not previously met with in the colony, namely, clear forest without underwood: the effect was very fine, the enormous trunks rising to a great height without throwing out any branches, and then forming a thick canopy overhead, but yet each tree being sufficiently far from its neighbours to allow of its spreading out above to its utmost powers: standing in this clear forest one could see around one for perhaps 80 or 100 yards in a circle: I got some cones from this forest, which you will receive some day.

At two, the bishop held a service on shore, which was attended by about twenty settlers: there would have been more, but the notice was so short: at 4. P.M. we got under weigh, and steamed down to Deep Bay, at the entrance of Baines Sound, where we anchored for the night.[2]

Yesterday morning we steamed down to the mouth of the Qualicum river, where we anchored, and the bishop and I went on shore: we did not find much open land, or make any very important discoveries, but it is an interesting spot, as being only fifteen miles from the head of Barclay Sound: I have no doubt that some day, there will be a good road across, and in years to come, a railroad. There is a remarkable dip in the mountains here, rendered the more conspicuous by the jagged snow-capped peaks of Mount Arrowsmith on the South; at the Qualicum river, we found a party of the Yuclata tribe, a very impudent set, whose appearance we did not like: this tribe is much feared by the other Indians, as they are the marauders of the coast.[3]

A remarkable feature in this country is the great steepness of the banks of some of the sandy spits, which in most parts of the world are a sign of very shallow water: thus in Deep Bay, the ship hardly moving through the water, the leadsmen heaving the lead as quickly as possible, the soundings were, no bottom at thirteen, eight fathoms, four, and a half one; all in a space of not more than the ship's length certainly: I have noticed this in Port Augusta, and several other places.

On Friday night, that is last night, the Bishop went on shore to stay with Mr. Goode, the clergyman here, until tomorrow night, as I intend to start for Cowichin on Monday morning at daylight.[4]

November 3. 1862. When you write, pray tell me whether I have got into the St. James' Club, or not: I wonder why you have not answered this question in any of your letters. We do not sail for Cowichan until tomorrow morning: the bishop asked me to stay here another day, as he has some business he is anxious to finish.

You will like to know what sort of weather there is in Vancouver Island at this time of year: well, today is a fine clear day, cold, with a bright fresh N.W. Wind: yesterday was mild, and it poured the whole day: saturday was gloomy and heavy with a light S.E. breeze: before that we had northerly winds with most delicious weather: cold at night, with the sun quite hot by day; this climate, so far as I have had experience of it, is very delightful, and one never suffers from that indescribably [*sic*] feeling of oppression which accompanies an English East wind.

Esquimalt. November 9. Tomorrow there is to be a grand public dinner in honour of the Prince of Wales' coming of age, and on the following day, the Governor will give a ball: tomorrow morning I am going round to Victoria to dress ship, and generally to assist in creating a sensation: the day has been wet and gloomy, but it has cleared off this evening, and I hope that we shall have a fine day for tomorrow's festivities[.]

November. 15. I posted a letter to you yesterday morning, and unaccountably forgot this sheet, which I now forward. While waiting my turn at the post office, a half intoxicated miner came up, and stared me in the face: I took no notice of him, and he then very rudely elbowed himself in front of me: still I took no notice, and he began speaking to the by-standers: "I say, what a swell we are in our regimentals, ain't we?" Then finding I would take no notice of him he held up some tobacco in my face, and said "I say governor, have a chaw?"; "No thank you", I said, "I think it is like your impertinence speaking to me at all"; "ah, come," he said, "I'm glad to find you're a good-tempered fellow": by this time I had got to the window, and the clerk told me I had six bits to pay for my letter: "oh, do you want six bits" said the miner "here are six bits": "oh, thank you" I said; then to the clerk "this gentleman will pay my letter", and I slipped away in the middle of a general laugh against the miner: when I came back an hour afterwards however I found he had not carried out his generous intentions.

Your affect. Edmund Hope Verney

Private

H.M.S. Grappler. Victoria.
November. 11. 1862.

My dear Father,

Yesterday we had a grand public dinner in honour of the Prince of Wales' birthday: races in the morning, salutes and dressing ship during the day, eating and drinking in the evening.[1]

Last week I was assured that I had made myself very unpopular with Captain Richards, and other Naval people, by sitting on the bench as a magistrate, and otherwise identifying myself with the interests &c of the colony, and I was strongly advised not to speak at yesterday's dinner: I was told that if my speech was poor, I should be most unmercifully cut up and ridiculed, and if good, it would only excite ill-feeling and jealousy against me.

After no slight consideration I came to the conclusion that I *would* speak, for surely if it was right to speak at all, the fear of ridicule should be no impediment: the toast assigned to me was "the bar" coupled with the name of the Attorney-General, probably the most unpopular toast of the evening:[2] you will imagine how carefully and anxiously I prepared my speech, and how restless I became as the time drew near: nevertheless my speech was an entire success, and my friend who had croaked about it before, said he thought I had been quite right not to take his advice, and that it would do me good and not harm: fortunately Captain Richards, who is clever and sometimes sarcastic, had left the table before my turn came, so he can only judge of my speech by what he hears, and it was so well received that I think he will only hear good of it: I think you will like to hear these particulars, and will feel interested in them, but I have marked this letter, "private", because all the world will not care to hear my effusions about myself.

I begin to think a good deal about my promotion now: if Uncle Hope is at home by this time, as I suppose he is, I should hear of my promotion about new-year's day: I try to persuade myself that I shall not be in the least disappointed if it does not arrive: I make all my calculations with that view: I am going to sell my horse by auction: If I were to keep him till May next, I could get what I gave for him, £50, but it would be very expensive to keep him through the winter: I should do this if I thought I should be here next may: now I shall perhaps not get £30 for him, as feed is so very expensive during the winter. I have no doubt that every-thing will be done about my promotion that is possible, and so I must just be content to wait.

The "East Lothian" has arrived to-day from England, bringing me some things from Chambers, on the Hard.

There was no good speaking at the dinner yesterday: the Governor and the Bishop were wanting[,] the former in matter, the latter in delivery: some drunken rows and breakages terminated the "*festivities*".

November 13. This letter shall be closed tonight, ready to be sent by the mail that is expected tomorrow. The rains have set in drearily: I have sold for £35, the horse I bought for £50, and consider that on the whole I have not lost by the transaction: I keep all the "belongings" in case I buy another horse some day, but if I do, it will be some wretched old hack, or a donkey: a good horse gives me too much anxiety[,] expense and trouble; I am quite lighthearted at being so well rid of my former one.

Your affectionate Son,
Edmund Hope Verney

Private.

H.M.S. Grappler. Nanaimo.
November 1. 1862.

My dear Father,

I enclose a copy of some shorthand found in Mamma's bible: probably her last meditations on earth: I am sure you will value them very much, and agree with me that they should be kept very sacred; and shewn to *no one* except perhaps your and her children.[1]

The following are the exact words made use of to me by Mr. Dundas, the other day, when speaking of British Columbia,

"I cannot ever call it an agricultural country, but it is one in which, for several years to come, an agriculturist will make not a competence, but a fortune."

Your &c
E.H.V.

My funny report of my own speech is not pro bono publico, as you may suppose: I have tried to write what I *did* say, and not what I *meant* to say, but the temptation to the latter was very strong. The good people of Buckingham have always received my attempts at speechifying so kindly that I was not prepared for a sneer, and was only too glad to have carried it off entirely at the expense of some other matter I had intended to say. I spoke so late in the evening that more than one drunken atheist would have been glad to have put me down: I got the feeling of the people so entirely with me in the end, however, that when one did try to speak, he made no allusion to what I had said.[2]

E.H.V.

Prince of Wales' Dinner.
Victoria. Nov. 10. 1862.
Speech of Lieut. Com[r] Verney,
R.N. reported by himself.

Gentlemen,

After all that has been said this evening of Her Majesty, both in her capacity as a sovereign and a Mother, little remains to be added: but with the expression of such feelings of loyalty, we must not forget the sentiment from which that loyalty springs, and by which it is nourished: (Hear, hear,)

A few days ago, a settler at Cowichan said to me, we will have nothing foreign here, every thing here shall be English, thoroughly English, and first of all we must have our church; all were ready to unite in building the church. (a laugh & a sneer.) Gentlemen, I trust you will not consider these remarks out of place: the sentiments of religion to which I allude is the noblest characteristic of the English nation, and one in which our country is unique: (cheers) this was the sentiment that reigned in the trenches before Sebastopol, & in the beleaguered residency of Lucknow, that animated the noble Havelock and sustained him to the last:[3] (hear, hear,) and though revolutions may rage near us, though convulsions may rend neighbouring nations, still wherever the flag of England waves, where the first sod is turned before the plough of the settler, or the first tree falls before the axe of the emigrant, there Englishmen are united by the double bond of union, religion and loyalty, God and our Queen. (Loud cheers, & cries of "that's the sentiment")

And after our loyalty, perhaps the next object of our national pride is our laws: - - - - - - - - - - - - - - -, and shall we not be proud of those gentlemen of the bar who have made these laws their study!

&c &c

H.M.S. Grappler. Esquimalt.
November 21. 1862.

My dear Father,

I send you a bit of the British Columbian, but you know all the newspapers both in this and the sister colony are very inferior.[1] I have received your letters of September 7 and 27 this afternoon: how quickly the time does fly: in a few weeks I shall begin to look forward to hearing something about my promotion, and I try to make up my mind that I will not be disappointed if it does not arrive.

We have had beautiful weather hitherto: but few rainy days, and the thermometer never very low: I hear that the worst weather may be expected after Christmas. You seem tolerably satisfied with my letters, but the continual interests and occupations of my command have made me a poor correspondent. I used at one time to think that when I am promoted I shall not come straight home: now I begin to think differently, and that I shall linger very little, if at all on my return: travelling is very expensive.

Your accounts of Emily are on the whole very satisfactory, and the darling child writes to me in good spirits: I hope that some day I may travel in Switzerland with you. You mention your intention to try and see the De Granceys: I am afraid that there is no chance of your having accomplished that, as they live a long way from Dijon, but if you are able to manage it, I am sure they will be delighted to see you, and you would enjoy your visit.[2]

What a triumph it would be, if you were to learn shorthand: but I fear that when you get home, you will have so much to do that you will not persevere with it.

I am sure that you will wish to hear a little about myself, but I have nothing to say: my time is employed in comparatively uninteresting cruises to San Juan, to the Race Rocks Lighthouse &c: and just at present I am employed on very unromantic duty: a ship full of ammunition is in Victoria, and I am bringing it round to Esquimalt, making one trip a day: at present I have thirty tons of shot and shell on the decks, which is very dirty and in every way a great nuisance.

My employments are consequently very much on shore, and as each day comes round, so also something useful and desirable to do: to-day I have been squaring up all the lighthouse accounts, which I take a great pride in[.]

When I come home, I suppose you will want to know a great deal about British Columbia; but the fact is I have only been there once for a few hours: I saw Colonel Moody this evening, who was very kind, and expressed his regret that I had not been at New Westminster more frequently.

Henry behaves very well on the whole, and is invaluable out here: sometimes he gets an odd fit of the dumps, and I cannot make out whether he is in love, or homesick: about three months ago he had a very severe attack, and I really thought for a few days that he was a little out of his mind, but lately he has been much better and more cheerful.

I want to hear about the St. James' Club: Alan Herbert kindly tried to help me to get in: how is Lady G.? I heard from Lady C. some weeks ago, but did not write again, as her letter was in answer to mine.[3]

Good bye, my dear Father: I trust that the day of our meeting is not very far distant now.

Your affectionate Son,
Edmund Hope Verney

Will you let Ridgways know that all newspapers for this place should have a two penny stamp: I do not know why, but he only puts a penny stamp on: and occasionally they come all right by Panama, but generally they come round Cape Horn in a sailing ship marked "insufficiently stamped": by the last mails I received three May newspapers, marked insufficiently stamped, and one September one, all carrying a penny stamp.[4]

Private

H.M.S. Grappler. Victoria. V.I.
November 23. 1862.

My dear Father,

I am encouraged to write to you again on the subject of the government of these colonies: my experience since I last wrote to you on the subject has only confirmed the opinions I had then formed: I am convinced that the sooner a new governor is sent out the better: certainly half of the officials ought to be changed, perhaps even a greater proportion, and a new governor, with fresh independent ideas would, I believe, put things to rights. Yet I think Governor Douglas deserves great praise for all he has done, and he is certainly a wonderful man in some respects: I think no one likes Mr. Young, the colonial secretary: he can write a very good letter, but no one speaks well of his honesty of purpose, or sincerity: he is disliked by Naval Men as much as by others. The Governor likes to know everything, and to keep everything in his own hands: he has in the Council only men who are willing to be his tools, or perhaps one or even two who make a tool of him: I have no doubt in my own mind that he keeps up a system of espionage which is unworthy of the Governor of two English colonies. I used at one time to think that I should like to get some appointment out here when I am promoted, and remain for a year or eighteen months: now, I am sure that I could never get on with men I do not respect: the Chief Justice here is, I am told, an uncertificated bankrupt: my authority (let me remind you of the heading "private") is the Attorney General, who I fancy knows something of his previous character: but he is the governor's brother in law, so although he knows nothing of law, he is made Chief Justice: I should characterize him as an inane booby; but I like him for he is a harmless old gentlemen: he generally wears a benign vacant smile on his countenance: the Attorney General, Cary, is a clever man, but vulgar, unpopular, and insincere: the Surveyor General Pemberton, openly says that he does not care a fig for the colony: the Treasurer is a good sort of man, Watson by name, but too young to have any influence; ditto the Registrar General Alston, yet these two last are in the Legislative Council, ex officio.[1] When I talk to any of the officials about the incapacity or unsuitablness of other officials, they quite agree with me, but say that there is such difficulty in getting good men; but that is only what the Americans call "bunkum". Alas! these poor colonies; the only chance I see for them is to send them a really first rate governor, who will soon learn far better than I can suggest which *are* the worthless officials, and weed them out. Your affectionate Son,

Edmund Hope Verney

If you like to read the enclosed letters before forwarding them, pray do so.

H.M.S. Grappler. Victoria. V.I.
November 29. 1862.

My dear Father,

Will you be so good as to send the enclosed letter to Uncle Frederic. (December 4.) I send you a couple of newspaper extracts which may amuse you.[1] How long this wonderful weather is to last, I know not: day after day we have of bright clear sunshine: it is pretty cold, and sometimes foggy, but most healthy bracing weather.

I have nothing particular to tell you, but the mail steamer is expected in tonight, and I go to San Juan with stores tomorrow morning, so I think it is as well to leave a letter behind me just to say that I am, up to this date, all right and tight.

The world wags smoothly enough with me, and if I had not a bad cold, I should be quite at a loss for an Englishman's priviledge, a grumble: by the way, I suppose I shall soon have a right to grumble if my promotion does not arrive: it might come any day this month or next, but in the meantime I have plenty of interesting work on hand.

Now, pray give my kind love to Mama and Freddy, and believe me,

Your affectionate Son,
Edmund Hope Verney

H.M.S. Grappler. Esquimalt.
December. 7. 1862.

My dear Father,

Will you be so kind as to forward the enclosed to Lord Walter Kerr: if the Emerald is paid off, I dare say you can find out his address.

As this month draws on, I begin to think more and more about my promotion: I am afraid it will almost break my stupid old heart if it does not arrive by the 31st of January.

Your affectionate Son,
Edmund Hope Verney

H.M.S. Grappler. Esquimalt.
December 8. 1862.

My dear Father,

On Saturday I left for sale on commission at the principal bookseller's shop in Victoria twenty nine copies of Isaiah, and sixteen copies of the tracts: the former are to be sold at a dollar and a half a piece, and the latter at half a dollar, and the commission will be ten per cent. Thus, if all are sold, and the commission paid you ought to receive forty-six dollars, thirty-five cents – about £9.5^{s}.[1]

The tin box arrived safely by the Topaze a few days ago: perhaps after all the most precious contents of the box were the odd numbers of the Leisure Hour, Sunday at Home, and Good Words: it is a real pleasure to me to send them forward on the lower deck to my men: I wish I had a pile of them to distribute to the settlers I visit along the coast. I think the Leisure Hour and Good Words are the most attractive.[2]

We continue to have most remarkable weather: to-day, although cloudy, has been quite mild and almost sultry. A note received yesterday from Admiral Washington says he has seen you, so you must have returned home a day or two sooner than Mama expected you: I hope you spoke to him about the delicate pecuniary subject I mentioned some time back.

When I leave this colony, if that event takes place in January or February, I shall have hardly a shilling after everything is squared up: my passage home and Henry's, will come to about £100; the Admiralty will pay two-thirds of my passage, and I hope of Henry's too: the Admiralty will also owe me about £50 or £60 which they will not pay until certain accounts are passed: thus, you see I shall have to draw a bill on Ommaney in advance, and I shall write and explain it to him, and say that I have acquainted you with the facts of the case.[3] The sooner my promotion comes, the greater pauper shall I be and vice versâ.

I suppose the Emerald is being paid off about this time: had I remained in her I should have paid off as first lieutenant, which I should have liked very much: I do not know though that I should have been any nearer my promotion than I am now, and in any case it is a comfort to know that I did not seek this appointment, but had that I had [*sic*] no choice but to accept it.

(December 10.) I enclose a paragraph from a San Francisco paper sent to me by Bishop Kip, and written by his son: it seems to me to be interesting and well written.[4] The Mutine sailed this morning for the coast of Mexico.

Dec. 13. The mail is expected to arrive tomorrow: it is sad that there is no law here to prevent the mail steamer sailing on Sunday, which is illegal both in California and the Washington Territory. The Hecate will sail for England in a few days viâ San Francisco, Sandwich Is. Australia, &c: she leaves behind a small party to continue the survey of British Columbia under the command of Pender, master of the Hecate: he will command an old paddle-wheel steamer, the Beaver, which will be hired from the Hudson's Bay Company: he is an old shipmate of mine in the Havannah and in the Britannia: he is a first-rate surveyor, and I like him very much: my second engineer, Mr. Bonwich, has volunteered to go with Pender, in charge of the Beaver's engines, and I have approved of his application; so he will probably be appointed: this arrangement will leave me with only two engineers, but they think they will be able to do the work: I think I have mentioned them to you before, Mr. Fitzgerald, and Mr. Bencke.[5]

I shall be with you in thought, my dear Father, on Christmas day, and I know that the toast of "the absent ones" will be drunk thoughtfully and affectionately by you, as you and I, and Freddy, and Uncle and Aunt Fremantle drank it together last Christmas day: when you receive this letter you will say, "ah I wrote and told Edmund we had done so": do you not remember telling me to let George know that we had drunk his health on Christmas day, and how pleased he was when he heard of it: well! wherever I may dine on that day I shall drink "absent friends". and Aunt Fremantle whispered to me, "Now we must contrive to make Papa merry this evening", and I remember that we did succeed very fairly: by the way, I must not forget that Uncle Frederic was there too, and will most likely be there next time, adding not a little to the universal jollity. But Christmas will not be quite the jolly time it ought to be at Claydon until you have some little grandchildren to help you out with it.

I shall be anxious to hear about your health; I think that just this time of year is generally critical with you, so I trust that you are particularly careful of yourself.

December. 15. I have nothing of particular interest to tell you to-day: both yesterday and to-day, and last night have witnessed one steady continuous downpour of rain, such as I have not seen surpassed even in the tropics: you will understand that in my very small craft a wet day is very particularly unpleasant: this morning I had to go to Victoria to tow the Beaver round, and although it was so very wet, I was glad of anything to break the monotony of the day: if I had half a score of messmates to bully and be bullied by, I should consider it a great improvement. The Beaver is the first paddle-wheel steamer that ever flapped the Pacific Ocean: hence she is quite out of date, and devoid of any pretension to beauty of model, yet not antique enough to be a curiosity: with that keen appreciation of artistic effect which so eminently characterizes their Company, the Hudson Bay Traders have painted windows and red curtains looped up with yellow cords and tassels all across the stern. Pender is, of course, delighted with her, although I am afraid that the highly decorated stern is too much even for him: by a judicious application of black paint, I have no doubt she will be made tolerably respectable ere long.

Your affectionate Son,
Edmund Hope Verney

H.M.S. Grappler. Esquimalt. V.I.
December 20. 1862.

My dear Father,

it is half-past eight in the evening, and the mail steamer has just arrived: in half an hour I may perhaps get any letters that have come through the Admiralty, and tomorrow morning we shall get the mail.

I have sent a letter so recently, that there really is nothing to add now, but as this letter may perhaps not reach you for a fortnight after the one sent the day before yesterday, I just write a few lines: if I am in Esquimalt on Christmas day, I have engaged to eat my Xmas dinner with the Mackenzies.

I hope that all the seeds I have sent have arrived safely, and seem disposed to grow. The Hecate will probably sail for England tomorrow.

9.30. P.M. The last mail brought us no letters from the West India packet, and now I find that some have arrived this evening: you may suppose that to go without letters for two mails is a pretty considerable disappointment. Still it is just possible that there may be some letters, viâ New York, in the morning. It is said that the Federals have had another licking at Rappahannock: their loss is variously stated as six and at twenty thousand.[1]

Two of my men are going to be confirmed tomorrow: the bishop will only consent to confirm those who intend to become communicants, and I am very glad of it.

Your affectionate Son,
Edmund Hope Verney

December 21. Your note of the first of last month arrived this morning, enclosing a view of Steeple Claydon Spire: it seems very nice as far as one can judge from a drawing, but it seems also to have entirely altered the character of the church. I am glad you have received a packet of seeds at last; they probably came through the Admiralty.

I wonder when Uncle Hope will come home; I should have thought he would have been in England ere this.

E.H.V.

H.M.S. Grappler. Esquimalt. V.I.
December 24. 1862.

My dear Father,

The last mail went on Sunday, and now we cannot expect letters for another week or ten days. Between this and San Francisco lies the town of Portland on the Columbia River; the mail steamers touch their [*sic*] either on the northward or southward journey, taking it alternately: thus, last thursday the mail arrived viâ Portland, but the last mail, having come direct, arrived three days afterwards: letters to England were not sent by Sunday's mail, because she would touch at Portland, but by the "Hecate" which was going to San Francisco direct.

The mail steamers are very inconvenient for this place: they are arranged to communicate with the New York boats, three times a month, and so they often just miss the West India mail boats, twice a month: thus the most expeditious, but not always the most certain, way of writing to me is by New York.

Another source of annoyance is that the steamer constantly comes in and goes out again on the Sunday: is it not extraordinary that although this is illegal in territory belonging to the United States, it is not illegal in this British colony: in a colony, "mail-day" is always the busiest and most exciting of all days, and when this falls on a Sunday it is truly lamentable.

December 26. This is a legitimate day for writing letters, and I do not doubt that more than one letter will reach me in a few weeks, dated on this day. I will give you the details of my Christmas day, although perhaps there will be nothing very new to you, or varying from what is usual on such an occasion.

Our morning was passed in the ordinary routine of a man of war up to ten o'clock: then we went to divisions and general inspection: the lower deck was brilliantly illuminated, and one or two chandeliers had been made on board, and decorated with coloured paper, ribbons &c: a portion of the christmas dinners was laid out in the messes, and cold turkeys, half-a-dozen, one to each mess, having been presented by the man who ought to be their best friend: (the word "*their*" refers to the messes, not to the turkeys.) Of course the lower deck of a little gunboat cannot pretend to make a very grand show, but I think the most was made of it. After inspection came divine service, and a very short sermon read from the usual Christmas text "Glory to God in the Highest and on earth, peace, goodwill toward men". After church I went on board the Topaze, and went round her lower deck, with Captain Spencer and his officers:[1] everything was very tastefully got up, and as we were expected to taste a piece of the duff from every mess, it was rather embarassing: of course Captain Spencer's progress was cheered round the messes: after performing this ceremony, we all sat down to lunch in the Topaze's wardroom. After this I came back to the Grappler, and by this time the men had finished their dinner, so now every officer had to submit to be carried forward on one side of the deck, to go below, and eat six pieces of duff, one from each mess, to come up again and be carried aft the other side, and to be cheered the whole way, and to be told that he was a jolly good fellow, and to that they were all agreed: the men too had attired themselves in unwonted garments, one boy acting as boatswain's mate, and another as quarter master, while a few appeared in Indian head gear ornamented with beads and skins and furs. At 5. P.M. I went up to dine with the McKenzies of Craig Flower: here was assembled a large party; dinner was followed by toasts, not forgetting "*absent friends*", toasts were followed by songs, songs by tea, tea by charades, charades, by dancing, dancing by blind-man's-buff, and blind-man's-buff was *the* entertainment followed by all. The amusements of the evening were sprinkled with negus, and the crannies were stopped with Scotch cake and bun:

then being warmed with hospitality and genial heartiness, a cement of friendship was run in, which at once took a natural polish. The first yawn was observed on the countenance of the smallest child at about 12.25., and at 1.15. I was in bed on board the "Grappler": there were no signs of breaking up when I left, and for all I know, they may be dancing yet.[2]

It did hold up for a good part of yesterday, but it is raining like one-o'clock today to make up for it.

Whenever I enclose open letters to be forwarded, I am very glad that *you* should read them, but not all the world.

December 27. I remember Uncle Frederick saying one day that when you hear nothing at all about a man, you may be quite sure that he is going on very well: taking this view of the case, I have a painful consciousness that I must be going on dreadfully well: it must be difficult to hear less about anybody than about a lieutenant stowed away in a small gunboat in a bay in Vancouver Island: I only hope that when the Duke of S. is making out his list of promotions he will take my insignificance into his favourable consideration.[3]

Not one of my men was the worse for liquor on Christmas day: I question whether it would be easy to pick out at hazard thirty:five men in any other ship of whom the same could be said: and yet I believe that Christmas day was as jovially and merrily kept up as possible.

I am afraid that George Price is not promoted yet: do you know any one who would speak a good word for him?[4]

Dec. 28. Mr. Woods, a clergyman here, who always used to preach on board the Hecate, has now transferred his services to the Grappler, and performed Divine service on board for the first time this morning: he used to preach on board very frequently in Helby's time. After church, to my great astonishment, one of the petty officers came forward, and said that he had been requested by the ship's company to offer for his acceptance a small present, as a slight mark of their regard, esteem, &c &c, and then produced a very tasteful *meerchaum pipe*, with an amber mouth-piece: the pipe was one of the prettiest I have ever seen, being an eagle's claw, grasping an egg: it would be difficult to say who was most pleased, Woods or myself. It seemed rather queer though, to present it just as we rose from our knees: how amazed one would be if Mr. Cross stepped forward after morning service at East Claydon, and presented Uncle Fremantle with a clay pipe as he descended the steps of the pulpit, as a mark of esteem from his congregation: yet on the whole I do not know that I ever heard of a more genuine present: it came purely from the men, who had evidently studied what Mr. Woods would like, had found out that he really enjoyed a pipe sometimes, and had shewn great taste in their selection. Altogether it was very funny, but very gratifying.[5]

December 30. Last night the barometer fell very low, and it came on to blow very hard: the glass till keeps very low, and we have heavy showers of rain: I have no doubt that it is blowing a gale of wind outside.

I have made the acquaintance of a youngster on board the Topaze, of the name of Hope: his father lives near Romford in Essex, about fifteen miles from London: he says he is a relation of Captain Sackett Hope, and of the Hopetouns:[6] do you know who he can be? I told him that until he could prove the contrary he must consider himself my cousin. We expect the mail in tomorrow or the next day, when this letter will be despatched with its enclosures.

January 1. 1863. I do not like to let this day pass without a line to you: one cannot take leave of 1862, and enter the unknown future of 1863 without a solemn thought or two, and rarely a congratulatory one: we cannot however look back upon the past year without much thankfulness for many mercies, and we can trust the future to our Father as we have done before. I feel quite sure that you are this day writing to me, and that I shall get your letter in six or seven weeks: a happy new year to you my very dear Father.

Jan. 5. The mail arrived this afternoon and will sail this evening: no private news of any importance. Captain Spencer hoists his broad pendant as senior officer in command of the station tomorrow morning[.] On Saturday we had the first fall of snow, ten inches deep, but fine weather has succeeded it. As there is nothing in your letters requiring immediate answer, I can answer them better at my leisure. With love to Mamma and Freddy, believe me,

Your affectionate Son,
Edmund Hope Verney

Private.

H.M.S. Grappler. Esquimalt. V.I.
January 6. 1863.

My dear Father,

I certainly should not have written a jolly letter to you if I had known how awfully I was to be blown up, and harrowed up, and chawed up, and jumped on for being in a good humour: do not believe, my very dear Father, that I can ever be seriously injured by an excess of happiness and prosperity when I am so far separated from you and Emily and those I love: I have my troubles, and to alleviate your anxiety on that score, I will give you an account of one, but what I do feel to be such a blessing and such a comfort is that my ship is really, for the time being, my home: however the senior officer may snub me, the papers cut me up, the Teignmouth young ladies perplex me, the ladies committee vex me, the fast young men chaff at me, or the regular rowdies laugh at me, on board the Grappler there is peace, here I have at least one or two who, I know, are true as steel; and among my books, my letters, and my duties (duties ought to have come first, I suppose) I can shut out my troubles for a time, and write to you about my happiness and prosperity.

Now I really must treat you to a lucubration, as follows; — Lascelles, the commander of the Forward, always lives on shore, and since the arrival of the Topaze, her paymaster, Scaife, and captain of marines, Shute, have also lived there: now this party belongs to a set with which I have no sympathy, the horse-racing, fast set, the set with which I have merely an acquaintance, the set which was always very hot against poor Helby, and which has no great love for me: of course I am always most courteous and civil to them whenever I do meet them.[1] Now, when the Topaze first arrived, Captain Spencer was civil, asked after you &c, and I looked forward to getting on very well with him, but the very next time I saw him his behaviour was entirely altered, and has been so ever since; he frequently goes to "the cottage", (Lascelles' house) is very intimate there, dines and spends the evening there, and there can be no doubt that through him, the cottage influence is being brought to bear upon me: Captain S. is very much led by Scaife, who was once an Admiral's Secretary, and knows the service thoroughly, and although I have hardly ever spoken to him he has twice been rude to me in a most marked manner: now that Capt. S. is made commodore, Scaife will virtually be commander-in-chief of the station, and I assure you that I view the future with some apprehension: I have been told by other people, also, that Captain Spencer's want of courtesy to me, undoubtedly originates at the "cottage": however, as I have got to know Captain S. better, I have got on better, and I must just go steadily on with my duty and *trust*.

Now, I dare say I could rake up one or two more difficulties if I tried, but, even at the risk of your severe displeasure, I will not: I fear, do you know, that hilarity is in some degree the consequence of this climate. I cannot remember when I have been so free from petty vexations as I am now, and I cannot help thinking that so far from its being hurtful to me, it is doing me good, and raising me to higher enjoyments, and worthier aspirations: I wonder whether you will see any change in me when I come home; perhaps you will think I have only grown into a selfish old ruffian; quien sabe?

But whatever you may think, I can see one or two decided improvements in myself lately: I am getting into a habit of regular private morning and evening prayer, which has always hitherto been fitful and irregular, I am regulating my accounts, and writing a small scrap of daily journal, and entering more deeply into questions of lighthouse organization and detail.[2] I asked some one whether he thought many of my men would desert in the spring; he said no, that they had got into such an old-fashioned way now: I like that old-fashion.

You say that Uncle Hope is not expected till the spring: well, I must be content to wait: I shall have been five years a lieutenant on the twenty-second of March: I have always thought it a great thing to be able to say that I passed for a mate the day I was nineteen, and that I was a lieutenant at nineteen, and I *should* like to be able to say I was a commander at four-and-twenty: I have heard it said of other people, and fancied it sounded well.

You say you have heard a good account or high character of the Mr. Garrett here: if you were to see him you would think you had heard aright; I thought much of him at first, and can see now what he might have been, but he has a most unsuitable wife; and his house and children are always dirty: so his domestic arrangements are a terrible drag on him, poor fellow.

How very odd that you will not answer my constant question as to whether or not I have been elected to the St. James' Club: I can only conclude that I have had a shower of only black-balls, and that you hesitate to say so.

January 12. 1863. On Friday the "Robert Lowe" arrived from England with 38 female emigrants under the care of the Rev. Mr. Reece. This afternoon I took them all round to Victoria in the ship, and landed them there: they are evidently of a lower class than those who came in the "Tynemouth"; and perhaps better suited for the colony on the whole.[3]

Jan. 15. On Tuesday I started for San Juan, whence I am now returning. Yesterday I rode over to the American camp at the other end of the island, distant thirteen miles: the English end of the island consists principally of rocks and thick forest, which will all be available for settlers some day, but will require a good deal of clearing and labour; the southern end is much more lightly timbered and better watered, and has a good deal of open country just ready for the plough to be put in: there are swamps also, which might easily be drained and would then be very fertile: there are several houses about, belonging to settlers who in a small way farm and breed stock, but the uncertain ownership of the land is of course a great bar to improvement: the Americans have done little or nothing to improve their camp: they began building a redoubt which was put a stop to by the treaty, but could be soon finished.

The English camp presents one of the most lovely views in this part of the world: it is situated in a deep bay, approached from another bay, entered from a narrow channel between San Juan and Henry Island: thus it is completely landlocked and sheltered: the white and yellow houses for the troops are built on the three sides of a square facing the water and levelled for a parade ground, and in the centre of the remaining side is a guard-room in front of which rises a long flag-staff made from one of the tallest pines: on all sides rises the dense forest varied with gray crags and the gnarled distorted trunks of trees determined to grow under difficulties: a short distance up the hill on the right, are four pretty little cottages surrounded by verandahs, and with some attempt at ornament, with a winding path leading up to them among the rocks: these are the officers' quarters and mess-room; on the little plot of level earth in front of them, which has been made artificially are half a dozen favourite dogs dozing in the sun, and perched about are beautiful tame pigeons.

On the whole, I pronounce the little scene *perfect*: then it is enlivened by the bugles calling the men to dinner, the red coats of the sentries, or of the whole detachment on parade: the hours are struck on a suspended crow-bar which emits a very soft and musical sound, and to crown all the union jack waves from the top of that tall straight staff, and the ensign staff of the Grappler at anchor: a little curling puff of white steam from the steam-pipe every now and again indicates a latent power within, and although at present she may merely greatly enhance the loveliness of the scene, she is not such a fool as she looks[.]

Well you see, I have much to be thankful for in the duties which occupy me, and which are often so extremely delightful: but I often sigh for you or some dear one to share it with me; I wish I could recommend Emily to come here next winter.

January 17. The mail arrived and departed again during my absence at San Juan: we anchored in Esquimalt Harbour on Thursday afternoon: in the evening, minute guns were heard, and supposing them to proceed from a vessel in distress, I was ordered to get up steam, and two boats were sent out from the Topaze; I went out to the entrance of Victoria Harbour but could see nothing particular and returned: we afterwards found that the guns were part of a joyous demonstration made by the coloured population on account of the American emancipation proclamation.[4]

I used to hear, in the summer, a great deal about the terribly bad winters: as far as my experience has gone hitherto I do not think that this winter has been as cold or dreary as an English winter; but we may have worse weather in store.

A Tynemouth girl, "Sophia Shaw," was married a day or two ago to a Mr. Poineer, a Cariboo miner: she was a smart flashy girl, but not without some good in her: every thing was ordered to be carried out in tip-top style: the milliner was instructed that the bridal dress was not to cost less than £400; the breakfast not less than £200: a ball took place in the evening, at which the bridegroom became tipsy: the next morning he came back to the ball-room to see if his wife was still there, as he had not seen her since supper: I have not yet heard whether she has turned up or not, but of course everybody is talking about the wonderful wedding.[5]

Jan. 20. The mail is expected in tomorrow, so I must give you news up to the latest date. As for myself, I am quite well and jolly, and as for the world in general, it can boast of nothing very startling. I have been busy for the last few weeks in reading up matters connected with lighthouses, and am now trying to persuade the government to place these lighthouses on a different footing: at present, lighthouse and harbour dues are thrown into the general revenue of the colony, and then of course all expenses under those heads have to be passed in the estimates: now this is manifestly unfair: on the one hand, if lighthouse dues yield a revenue *greater* than lighthouse expenses, it is unfair to use the surplus for other colonial purposes and ask shipping to construct roads &c: on the other hand, it is not fair to take taxes paid by people on shore to support lighthouses they never see, if lighthouse dues yield an *insufficient* revenue: nor is it fair that the poverty of the colony should be pleaded as an excuse for not expending money on the lighthouses, or making that department as efficient as possible, or extending it.

I want to see Lighthouse dues, collected by officers under that department, paid in to the Treasury to the credit of that department, without interference from any other department, and subject only to the control of the Governor himself.

Then I want to see all harbours, buoys, beacons, and pilots placed under the Lighthouse Board, and its name changed to *Trinity Board*. But I do not expect to see many of my suggestions carried into execution in my day: I shall leave all written memoranda in the office when I go away, and perhaps a few years hence they may be improved and acted upon: I have the more faith in them because they are not my own ideas but derived from the report of the Royal Commission on Lighthouses.[6]

You ask if the emigration blue-books have arrived: not yet, but parcels perform the journey here in a slow and erratic manner at the best of times.

I enclose two more letters from Bishop Kip's son at Japan; I think they are interesting.[7]

Jan. 21. 30. minutes P.M. Your letter of Nov. 15. has just arrived. I should be glad if you would see Ridgways when you are in town some day, and tell him that my newspapers arrive most irregularly, most of them bearing the words "insufficiently stamped:" and yet those that arrive all right have a penny stamp the same as the others.

You have told me before that you expect to see a Western Californian republic some day: I do not hear it talked of as likely at present: although there are many southern people in California, I think that the chief part of the property is owned by Northerners, and there is such a want of stability among the people, and they have such lawless unsettled tendencies that I do not anticipate any combined action from them. It is not impossible that when the South is established as an independent nation, & the Western States have become more peopled & settled, they may secede and receive countenance and assistance from the Southerners: secession once established will be an easier thing in future.

I *do* take care, in your own words, that no one should be led to suppose that change or alteration of any kind is in consequence of what I may tell you: if I did not observe discretion on this point I should soon be surrounded by a host of enemies, and indeed moreover I have not the slightest ground for supposing that such is the fact: it is far better that I should not.

Our verse today is Matt. 16.2 You ask if I know Mrs. Peter Wallace: yes, very well: she is one of the jolliest little parties here, and awfully Scotch: but *he* is one of the greatest donkeys it is easy to meet: it is said, falsely of course, that he tried to get two or three people here to marry him, but failing that was obliged to send home for the girl he had been engaged to before he came out: I hope I shall have the luck some day to get a wife as much too good for me as she is for him: not a very difficult matter that, Mama would say.[8]

Now, my dear Father, I have answered your letter, and must just seal up and despatch this, this afternoon. I suppose that without being too sanguine, I may expect to be promoted this spring, and indeed, apart from any influence Uncle Hope may exert, I *ought* to be so: then the question arises, how am I to come home: I might go in a ship to Japan, and home by China and India, or across the Rocky Mountains, or across the prairie due East from San Francisco, or down to Valparaiso and across the Andes. I must own I should infinitely prefer the first, but even travelling as economically as possible, it would cost a large sum of money. Perhaps I may get a word of advice from you as to route, when the auspicious day arrives.

Now with love to Mama, believe me

Your affectionate Son,
Edmund Hope Verney

Aunt Fremantle's letter of November 14. has arrived to-day.

H.M.S. Grappler. Esquimalt. V.I.
January 26. 1863.

My dear Father,

This afternoon we had a public meeting at Victoria on the subject of the Lancashire distresses: at the conclusion the governor put his name down for £40, which was certainly very handsome: we had no very eloquent speeches.[1]

Being winter time, there is nothing much going on; I am more particularly giving my attention to the lighthouses, and studying to make them in every respect as efficient as possible. The bishop talks of going home in a few weeks, probably about the middle of next month: it will make a great difference to me when he is gone, and I hope I may soon follow.

I wonder what you think of the Duke's new secretary, Captain Ryder: I knew him a little when he had the "Hero", and he was always very civil to me then: I suppose you know him too: I should think he would be a capital man to succeed Captain Moore: I remember Lord Harrowby and the Misses Fortescue came up from Boconnoc to see him, and were caught in a gale of wind, and had to sleep on board the "Hero" in Plymouth harbour. Captain Ryder was on the Royal Commission for Lighthouses, whose report, in the form of a blue-book, I have been reading with much interest.[2]

How does your short-hand get on: I do hope you are not losing courage about it.

January 30. The Robert Lowe will sail for San Francisco on Sunday morning, and take a mail: since I commenced this, I have not been under weigh at all: I have been spending three days with the Bishop, and generally indulging in a little dissipation at Victoria, dining out &c: the weather is variable, as it always is in winter, but yet so as to allow the climate to compare very favourably with England. People are already beginning to move up towards the mines, but I suspect that they make a mistake in going too early: the bishop expects to start for England in a few weeks, and his loss will be much felt: he does not talk of being absent more than a year, but I fear it will be 18 months. I am sitting here with my pen, not knowing what on earth to say, so I shall give up the attempt and see if an inspiration comes tomorrow.

Little birds flit over here and tell me that you are learning short-hand, and that you have really made some progress in it: do send me a specimen of your skill. I dare say you have heard that the letters of the names, "Florence Nightingale," make up the sentence, "flit on cheering angel."

January 31. At present we are busy trying to establish a Free School at Esquimalt, and I think we are likely to succeed:[3] the Lancashire relief fund has been a great tax just lately, and it is not so easy to collect subscriptions for any other object.

The bishop works too hard, especially now that he is trying to get through business and go to England: I fancy his work presses upon him rather hard, and cannot be good for him: it is quite sad to see him living alone, with only Mr. & Mrs. Bridgeman to look after him.[4]

Had I been told, when I left England, that on the 31st of January I should still be a lieutenant, I should have been grievously disappointed: now, however, I do not think much about it, and am extremely contented in the interesting life that I lead: a mail will be here on Tuesday or Wednesday, by which I suppose I shall hear something of Uncle Hope's movements.

I have been regulating my chronometer-watch myself, and think I have improved its going, yet do not feel sure that I appreciate it other than as your gift: I do not think Mr. Dent has treated you well: you said you would put it into a gold case for me when I come home, if it is worth it: I am not inclined to think that it will be worth it: at present the sun is too low for me to take many observations, but I shall use it more as the days grow longer.[5]

With kindest love to Mama & Freddy, believe me,

Your affectionate Son,
Edmund Hope Verney

H.M.S. Grappler. Esquimalt. V.I.
February 5. 1863.

My dear Father,

How delightful to sit down to my little table, in my little cabin, cabin and table that you, alas!, are never likely to see, and answer the pleasant and loving letters scattered about, which arrived this morning.

Yes, other people are suffering and in distress while with us all is prospering: let these mercies fill our poor luke-warm hearts with zeal and gratitude to show forth our Redeemer's praise not only with our lips but in our lives. I have so much to be thankful for here, so many objects of interest, that I can well afford to wait for my promotion; I do think however that if I am to stick to the Navy, it must be as a *young* officer: mediocrity would not satisfy me in a profession which I am becoming really attached to.

Your kind advice concerning the tact and judgement necessary in colonial affairs not immediately connected with the Navy, is most just, and these qualities are those of which perhaps I have no superfluity; but they may be increased and strengthened.

I hope the walk down the centre of the lawn will be finished by the time I return, and may it never catch my eye from my bedroom window without impressing on me the lesson it will bring, and in time to come may my path through life, whether through gardens or deserts be full of many such gravel walks.

Helby's conduct and character were admirable, but not in every respect what I could follow now: his life was passive while mine is active: and, as you say, there have been incredible changes during that short time: then you add "you can certainly speak confidentially on such matters to Captain Richards or some other judicious friendly naval officer." It is no use entering into a long story, but Captain Richards was neither friendly nor judicious: I did not love him one bit, and I am sure he did not love me.

Neither do I get on very well with Captain Spencer: at this distance, and the interval that must elapse before you receive my letter, it is not worth while to trouble you with all my little grievances: you will not, of course, tell all the world what I have just written, and as I *did* get on with Sir. Thos. Maitland, you will not believe that the fault is all on my side: the position of Captain of my own ship makes it comparatively immaterial whether the senior officer likes me or not, so long as I do my own duty strictly, and I dare say it is not bad for me to have to mind my Ps and Qs. In a few weeks the Grappler will be laid up to have her new boilers put in: this operation will occupy six or eight weeks, and will, I fear, be rather dull work: I shall have to live on shore, and if possible shall make a little excursion to British Columbia, and see what is to be seen.

I expect that the Bishop will go home this next mail, leaving here about the middle of this month: I shall feel his loss very much, but I am sure his visit to England will do him good if his friends will receive him affectionately, and really look after him and take care he does not overwork himself which he is fond of doing. In all that he may tell you about these parts of the world I warn you that I think he is a little bit of an enthusiast; I mean just what I say, really only a *little* bit, and after all that is quite natural: I have before said that I feel sure he would be happier if he were a married man, and the more I see of him the more convinced I am of that fact: but I am afraid that he will desire to judge for himself on that point.

Admiral Washington writes me word that the L.C.A. allow me £13. for the expenses of which I wrote to you: rather a small proportion out of £50, which is the exact sum I spent in that ten days, everything included, but then I had a great deal of pleasure into the bargain.[1]

Farewell, my dear Father: with kind love to Mamma, believe me

Your affectionate Son,
Edmund Hope Verney

Henry is well and hearty: he does not like the "Grappler": she is too small, and has not got proper accomodation for the Captain's steward: he requests that you will ask the D. of S. to promote me and give a larger ship.

H.M.S. Grappler. Esquimalt. V.I.
February 8. 1863.

My dear Father,

This is Sunday evening, and it is pleasant to send a few thoughts to wind there [*sic*] way to you round nearly half of this big ball: my Sunday has been spent with the McKenzies, as has been spent every other Sunday since I arrived here, when the Grappler has not been away on a cruise: and I have just dismissed my bible-class which I began about five or six weeks ago: we were in all six, and considered Romans viii, a well worn but not therefore threadbare chapter.

The mail left on Thursday, and it then began to snow, and continued almost without intermission until this morning, so now it is bitterly cold and everything is covered with snow: yet this afternoon, the sun came out bright and clear, and it was quite hot, and the light from the snow most dazzling and painful to the eyes: tonight is most lovely: not a breath of wind stirs the frozen air; and the stars flash like diamonds set in jet; the atmosphere is so clear that every sound is heard with wonderful distinctness, as the tramp of the sentry on board the Topaze, or every half-hour, as the bell strikes, his cheering cry of "all's well". The snow-laden boughs of the pine trees fringe the harbour, relieved by large masses of rock, and here and there a break in the forest shows the tall spectral poles of dead trees blackened by fire, like ghosts of the Indian chiefs who lived, hunted, and died here before gunboats were. Add the steady red light of Fisgard Island Lighthouse, and low ceaseless moan of the swells heaving and sullenly breaking on the rocks at its base, and you have as vivid a picture of this lovely scene as I can portray with my poor pen.

I fear that my romantic admiration of this sight is not entirely shared by the quartermaster of the watch whom I overhear saying that he will be glad when it is twelve o'clock; but then he is a coloured man, and cannot be expected to prefer walking on deck with this faery scene to going to bed.

Mr Reece, who came out as chaplain of the Robert Lowe, preached on board here this morning; he is rather a queer fish in the pulpit: I wish clergymen would read and preach in as rational a tone of voice as they ask for another slice of beef: on the whole I certainly liked Mr. Reece, but he looked uncommonly comical with a long black dressing-gown down to his heels, a black sash round his waist, and – – – a bearskin cap: quite one of the Noah's Ark men, of doubtful sex.[1]

(Feb. 12.) The last few days have been very cold, but fine: there has been skating, and on Monday a large portion of this harbour was frozen over, so that boats could with difficulty make their way: I have not yet put my skates on, but purpose doing so the first opportunity: to-day it is snowing hard and it snowed hard all night, so the ice will be spoilt for skating: it is strange that this very cold weather should only have come on late in the winter, but I am glad of it as we shall soon have the spring.

The day before yesterday I dined with the bishop, and met at dinner a young man of the name of Packe, son of Colonel Packe whom you will

Edmund Hope Verney, about 1860.
BCARS 71122

Sir Harry Verney, 1867. A portrait by W.B. Richmond.
CLAYDON HOUSE TRUST AND COURTAULD INSTITUTE OF ART

Parthenope, Lady Verney, her sister, Florence Nightingale,
and Sir Harry Verney at Claydon, about 1890.
CLAYDON HOUSE TRUST

The west front of Claydon House. NATIONAL TRUST

HMS *Grappler*: Two pictures of the ship preserved with Verney's papers. The one above is probably the photograph Verney mentions in his letter of August 22, 1862 as taken two days earlier in Victoria harbour. To the right is a photograph in one of Verney's albums of an otherwise unknown painting, also dated 1862.
CLAYDON HOUSE TRUST

HMS *Forward*. This photograph by Charles Gentile serves to show the appearance of the *Grappler* as well as the *Forward*, since the two sister ships were almost identical. BCARS 27404

Panoramic view of Victoria from Songhees Point, 1860. Verney describes this linked series of photographs in his letter of August 22, 1862. Read from left to right across the top and bottom of the facing pages. CLAYDON HOUSE TRUST

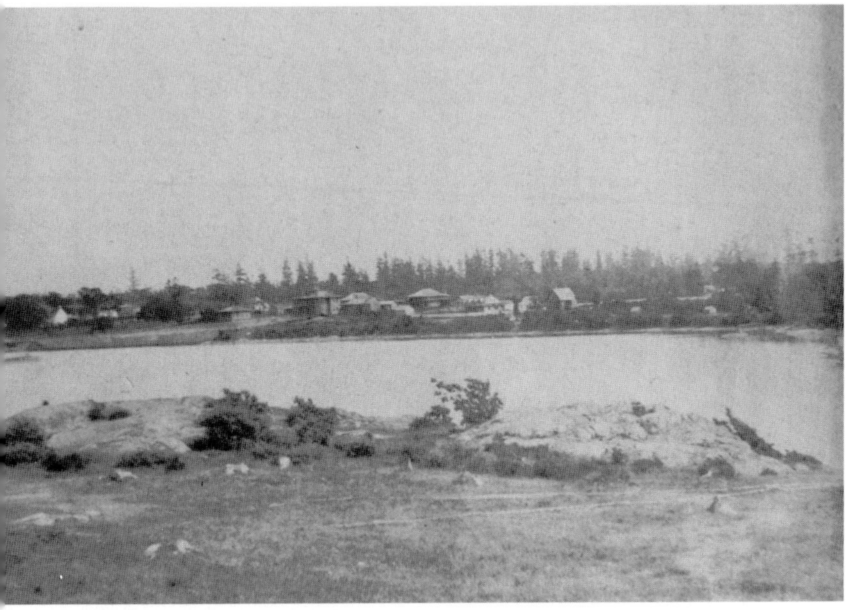

The McKenzies' Craigflower farmhouse, where Verney spent three Christmases and many Sundays, photographed by Charles Gentile about 1865. BCARS 3351

"The Small Bower," Verney's second Esquimalt cottage. John Russell, coxswain of HMS *Grappler*, is to the right in the photograph. See the letter of February 22, 1865. CLAYDON HOUSE TRUST

"A Chief of the Eucletaw Tribe. V.I.," a photograph with this inscription in Verney's hand attached to his letter of March 15, 1865. CLAYDON HOUSE TRUST

Group photograph taken by Charles Gentile on the grounds of Government House, New Westminster, May 24, 1865. In his annotation Verney identifies those seated in the front: from the left, Assistant-Surveyor Daniel Pender, Colonial Secretary Arthur Birch, Commander T. Morton Jones, Governor Frederick Seymour, and Verney himself. He states that standing at the left of the back row is an Indian from Fort Rupert who served as an interpreter on the *Beaver*, and that the others are Indian chiefs (the one in the fur cap being a man of influence), but he does not give their names. CLAYDON HOUSE TRUST

Verney in the American West, summer 1865. This photograph is titled "Crossing the Rocky Mountains" in an album at Claydon House. CLAYDON HOUSE TRUST

The Museum at Claydon House in 1902, showing the two Salish houseposts from Comox and other Indian artefacts collected by Verney. NATIONAL TRUST, CLAYDON HOUSE

remember to have met in Switzerland with his family years & years ago. he dined with me yesterday, slept on board, and has gone back to Victoria this afternoon: I am inclined to like him: his name is Edward and he has been in the Indian Army: he arrived at Lucknow a day or two before I left it, and served with the 23rd: but his health would not stand India, and he resigned his commission: then he tried being a clerk in the India office, but that was too sedentary, and the prospects of promotion too remote, so now he has come out here with £1000 in his pocket to make his fortune, and I regard him as on the whole a hopeful colonist: he tells me that his father is dead, and that Fanny Packe has never married.[2]

February. 16. The snow is fast melting away, and the air is quite warm and mild: we should have liked a few more days skating, but I suppose that we shall not have much more winter now. We are hourly expecting the mail: this steamer will probably not bring Panama letters viâ St. Thomas', but only viâ New York: although we do not get many letters that way, yet we hear tolerably late news.

Things generally are very quiet in the colony: people have not yet begun to start for the mines, nor are many immigrants arriving from England. The bishop hopes to get away early in March, but is at present up to his eyes in business. I enclose a note for the Casa Anfonso. 8. P.M. The mail has just arrived bringing principally intelligence of spiral doings at Claydon,[3] and Freddy's departure from Harrow: the last I regret much, but suppose it was absolutely necessary. I have the funniest note in the world from George: I am convinced that he was intended to be your eldest son; he assumes such a jolly air of superiority over me that I feel quite small, like a poor bullied younger brother: he writes as if the whole world lay at his feet and as if he possessed the most unlimited control over the future: he is a dear old fellow, and writes most affectionately, although I must add, patronizingly.

You mention not having written to me by some opportunity: I think I have always heard when other people have but when I do not hear, I must confess that it is a disappointment. Your last date is Dec 30. I am very glad to hear that I have been elected a member of the St. James' Club: I must say that as I never heard, I feared I had not been elected. You mention nothing about Uncle Hope or his movements, but I suppose he is at home by this time.

I will not trouble you about my knee: it is an old offender, as I think you will remember, and I was told years ago that the only thing to be done for it is to rest it when it is painful: it only hurts me when I walk too much, and then a couple of days rest sets it right again. If I sent an account of it to Paget he would only charge guineas, and tell us what Ceely told us when I was a youngster: if I was by your side, I could bring it all back to your memory.[4]

The steamer goes out again tonight, so I must say adieu: she has brought me many pleasant letters from all sorts of people, but yours is the only one to be answered by return of post: however long my promotion may be delayed, I am quite sure that as a lieutenant I could not be better off than where I am, and that were the reverse the case, this appointment came as a duty, and not of my own seeking. With love to Mama,

believe me your affectionate Son,

Edmund Hope Verney

When you see Sir Thomas Fremantle, will you thank him for his kind letter to me?[5]

H.M.S. Grappler. Esquimalt. V.I.
February 20. 1863.

My dear Father,

I send you a list of articles that will leave this in a few days for England by the Hudson's Bay Company Ship Princess Royal: there is nothing *very* valuable, but quite enough so to make it worth while to employ an agent to look out for them: they are adressed to you in South Street, but of course an agent will take care to have them carefully sent wherever you may desire.[1]

Three days ago, on the 17th, I had been twelve years at sea: I feel quite an old fellow now in my thirteenth year: would twelve years be long in the army to attain field-officer's rank? you, I know, were nothing like so long.

February 21. Yesterday evening we had a concert for the benefit of the Lancashire distress: every-body, whether amateur or professional gave their services gratuitously, and the whole thing was a great success: there was not perhaps much good music, but both audience and performers came prepared to be amused and to amuse, and they thoroughly succeeded.

Yesterday was bleak, cloudy, and wintry; now I write from my office at Victoria, with the sun shining brilliantly, the window wide open, the air soft and sweet, and the delightful exhilarating sensation of a cool bright summer's day in England: if there were not a few clouds about, the day would be positively hot.

I am at present very inactive and secretly longing for a ship to get wrecked, or the Indians to kick up a row, or for something to give me a little work: lying at Esquimalt is very dull. If you could see what a lovely day this is you would not wish me to stay indoors inventing something to say, instead of enjoying the Saturday half-holiday: even though the mail steamer *is* expected hourly.

8. P.M. The mail steamer has arrived: Dr. Forbes of the Topaze has looked at my knee: he says nothing can be done for it, except that when it hurts me I must give it rest, and if it is very painful it must be blistered, and painted with iodine: in knowing language he says there has been a fracture of the patella, and a thickening of the bone which cannot hurt unless it grows, which I think it is not.[2]

No news whatever has come by the steamer, as she did not connect with the St. Thomas' steamer, but it is possible that we may hear something bye and bye that has come viâ New York. The "Princess Royal["] will probably sail about the 25th.

Feb. 22. 10. A.M. I have just received orders to go to the assistance of a ship about three or four miles off, anchored too near the shore, so I shall send the letters to the mail steamer at once, although she will not sail before the afternoon: it is a pity to have one's Sunday broken into thus, but I am glad of any excuse to get something to do.

I received a letter last night from Captain Carter of the Emerald: he does not expect that she will be paid off for some time.[3]

Adieu my dear Father: the next mail will bring the usual English letters about ten days or a fortnight hence: with love to Mama believe me,

Your affectionate Son,
Edmund Hope Verney

List of Articles sent to England in the Princess Royal.

Two large carvings from the mouth of the Courtenay River in the Comux district: they will do for garden gate-posts.

One bundle of walking sticks.

One pair of elk-horns from the Comux district.

One box, containing the following articles,

A muck-muck box, a carved wooden dish or tureen from which the natives eat their food: this came from some Indians on the Qualicum River.

Two canoes from Sitka. (Models.)

One model of a Cape Flattery canoe: this contains some cones, and also some South American nuts; and the leaves of a plant that grows in the swamps at Cowichan, used by the natives to make a sort of tea: also the wings of a heron and of a kingfisher, shot at Cowichan.

A little bundle containing arrows: needles used for making rush mats, and a piece of wood for smoothing the seams.

Four small pairs of deer's horns, principally from Nanaimo.

One ladies bonnet of the latest Indian fashion, formerly the property of Her Majesty Queen Freezy. (Freesy.)[4]

One spoon from Fort Simpson.

One charm, composed to the unbelieving eye only of red cord and weasel skins, but which is really very valuable, and cost a nearly new uniform frock-coat. No bullet can harm the wearer: any one doubting its efficacy is recommended to try it.

One semicircular rug of dog's hair with a broad fringe: these rugs, made by the Northern Indians are becoming more scarce every year, and are considered valuable.

One rug made of the skins of four mountain sheep from British Columbia.

One bearskin from Nanaimo.[5]

Edmund Hope Verney

February 20. 1863.
Victoria. V.I.

H.M.S. Grappler. Esquimalt.
February. 24. 1863.

My dear Father.

The above-written noble little vessel is at present lying on the beach to enable the engineer to do something to one of the valves: we intended to have floated off this morning, but the tide did not rise high enough, so we hope to get off tomorrow: we are having delightful spring weather, which I hope is going to last.

March 1. On wednesday last we hauled off the beach: there was a slashing sou'-westerly breeze at the time, so we made sail and ran across the harbour in grand style, picking up our berth with a running moor under the stern of the Topaze: I had no idea that a little gunboat would have sailed so well.

Yesterday I had a dinner party, which was a great bore: we sat down to table to the vast number of five, which is the most I can accomodate comfortably: one of my guests was young Hastings who brought out a letter of introduction from you, I suppose, but I never received it, because he lost his writing case: I am disposed to like him, but I dare say he thought me terribly slow.

Tomorrow will be twelve years since I sailed from Plymouth Sound in the Calliope. I went to sea in March, I joined the Navy in February, I passed all my examinations between the middle of February and the beginning of April, I became a mate in the beginning of April and a lieutenant in the middle of March, so I hope this is to be always in future a fortunate time of year.

As to the climate at this time of year I can only call it the most changeable in the world: in summer it is the most certain, in winter the most uncertain: the night before last was, to everybody's astonishment, a hard frost: yesterday was a hot spring day: last night it drizzled; to-day it has poured without ceasing, and I am convinced that tomorrow will be lovely: and yet for the last three days the barometer has kept steadily up.

I think of you as probably in town by this time, and spending your days in those amusements which busy men delight to complain of as "business", and your nights among the collected wisdom of the "House", the club that I pay income tax to support for you: however, I must say you are always very hospitable when I come to see you there.

You always growl about the way I write the letter "y" in the middle of a word so I have been looking over some letters to see how other people manage, and I find that the correct thing is to turn the tail up the right as if it was a "q" thus: "  " even the model letter you sent me in Evelyn Ashley's handwriting does this, so I shall try and get into that way.[1]

We shall get another mail about this day week, so I hope that before then I may have something interesting to add to this insipid letter. I dare say you will like to read the two enclosed letters before forwarding them: I think I can guess the little lecture I should get about the one of the date March. 2. if you were alongside of me.

March 5. Tomorrow we may expect the mail, but at this time of year she is often a day or two late: the bishop is not ready to start yet: I help him with his work what little I can, and in reward he praises my handwriting, and we both agree that it is a capital hand and that you must be mistaken when you abuse it.

I see no prospect of my being sent anywhere on an agreable yachting cruize, and I find it very dull lying here: very strong symptoms of spring are beginning to appear, but we must not expect to be safe from wintry weather until the end of this month. I hope that you read all letters that I send open in longhand: they will interest you sometimes I have no doubt. How do you get on with shorthand? I am longing to receive a shorthand letter from you, and to hear that I may write to you in like fashion. I enclose an extract from a Californian paper.[2]

March 6. The mail has arrived this morning, but unfortunately she did not connect with the steamer from Panama, so we have no letters: I saw my friends who had returned today from San Francisco: the roads were almost impassable in the interior of California, and they had not been able to get me any seeds of the Wellingtonia.

I have no news to send you: I am well, thank God, and very quiet, wishing for a cruize. I am afraid you will grumble at this envelope containing so little for yourself, but I hope you will read all the open letters, and believe me that they are also addressed to you.

Your affectionate Son,
Edmund Hope Verney

H.M.S. Grappler. Esquimalt. V.I.
March 8. 1863.

My dear Father,

Spring weather is coming on apace, and most of the trees and bushes are budding: yet a few flakes of snow fell this morning, and it froze hard for an hour or two during last night: I believe that this is considered the most changeable month in the year.

March 9. This morning we went out to the Race Rocks Lighthouse to pay salaries: on our return we had a little target practice, which was certainly good: a trip to the Race Rocks Lighthouse is generally a very pleasant thing; there is a good view from the top in fine weather, in all directions, and we were much disappointed that to-day was dull, and inclined to be misty and foggy. An opposition steamer, the Herman, was expected to-day from Frisco, and we had looked forward to getting letters, but as she has not made her appearance we suppose that she has been again bought off, as she was at the beginning of last summer. I enclose a bill of lading for some Indian curiosities &c, sent home by the Princess Royal: I will send another by some future mail, and keep the third for myself: I was recommended *not* to pay the freight beforehand.

March 12. My friend has returned from San Francisco, bringing seeds of the Wellingtonia Gigantea, which I send you: may their shadow never be less: and I dare say that you will be able to spare one to the Fremantles, Admiral Washington or other friends. Every-thing is very quiet here: the Forward went to New Westminster this morning to lay down buoys at the Sand Heads, the job I had last year. The weather calm, mild, dull, and dry, like myself.

The news from Cariboo are good: many claims have been worked more or less every day through the winter, and miners are beginning to throng up the country: experienced people say that it is a mistake to crowd up to the mines so early in the season, and I expect to hear that it leads to much suffering as it did last year: the roads are improving and so provisions will not be again at quite such famine prices as they were. It is astonishing how blind gold makes some people: I know several young men who say they are going up this spring, who are no more fit to encounter the hardships of a miner's life than Emily is, and who will certainly return in a few weeks broken down in health, purse, and spirits, and who might get on very fairly by plodding along in Victoria, making a few dollars, putting them out to safe investment, and turning them over[.]

March 21. The day before yesterday I went over to San Juan, returning last night; we had two charming days and found the spring even more advanced there than here; we took a large party over and enjoyed ourselves much, shooting, walking and boating, and in the evening we had guitars and singing: at night we exercised at quarters when the echoes among the hills were very fine.

This morning the steamer has arrived from San Francisco, bringing however no English Mail I am sorry to say: it is always a great disappointment when the steamer brings no mail; especially as we never know beforehand, and always expect one: the telegraphs from Europe appear unimportant: sometimes I get a letter through New York and so perchance I may get one this afternoon when the mails have been sorted.

I have a San Francisco paper of the 17th which states that there are serious insurrections in Poland, and that France forbids Prussia to interfere; but really one never can believe what an American paper says, and certainly not a Californian one.[1]

Then we hear that the Americans are protesting against our sending merchant ships to run the blockade; and that they are triumphing over a ship captured from Mr. Lindsay: but their tone is generally bitter against England although we are meek and enduring.[2]

It is pleasant to hear of the arrival of cotton ships, and that the distress in Lancashire is rather diminishing: I wish it may give an impetus to the tide of emigration to these colonies.[3]

H.M.S. Grappler. Esquimalt. V.I.
March 14. 1863.

My dear Father,

It is very sad to have to sit down to write to you, with the consciousness of having nothing to say: the mail steamer was expected in this morning, so now I suppose she will arrive some time during the night: we are all feeling quite starved for want of letters.

On Sunday last I met a gentlemen who said he had had a dream about me the previous night: the next day, monday, I met a lady who said she had dreamed about me the night before; on the third day, tuesday I met another gentleman, who also told me he had dreamt of me the previous night: on the fourth day, wednesday, I picked up a knife in the street, which proved to belong to a government clerk of the name of Young; on the fifth day, thursday, I picked up another knife in the street, which I found belonged to a boy at the school, called Young: now putting these coincidences together, do not you think I have a right to be superstitious, and regard them as omens of some event of which I shall probably receive intelligence tomorrow? but I cannot divine whether they are to be accepted as propitious omens or not.

Probably the arrival of the mail will furnish me with some sensible material wherewith to conclude my letter. My tum-tum is happy tonight because Dr. Ash, a gentleman who came out in the Robert Lowe, has presented to me a curious, dirty, ugly, old, German glass claret jug, worth at least a £5. note to a connoisseur: I hope I shall get it safely to England some day: captain Cumming had a great taste for old glass: this was given to Mrs. Ash by some old woman she had been very kind to, and who had nothing else to give but this old bottle, and Dr. Ash only found out accidentally that it was a valuable curiosity.[1]

I have told you that the chronometer watch has not come up to our expectations: I occasionally altered the regulator myself whereby I have somewhat improved it, but it is not at all to be relied upon as the following results will show. The regulator was last touched on the 25th of January; since then its daily rates losing have been, Feb. 1. 14″.6; Feb. 2. 8″.6; Feb. 4. 4″4.1.; Feb. 5. 12″.6.; Feb. 6. 15″.6.; Feb. 8. 3″.1.; Feb. 9. 3″.6.; Feb. 10. 0″0.1.; Feb. 13. 0″0.4. gaining; Feb. 15. 5″.6. losing; Feb. 16. 7″.6.; Feb. 17 1″.6.; Feb. 19. 11″.6.; Feb. 22. 7″.3.; Feb. 23. 8″.4; Feb. 24. 0″0.4.; Feb. 26. 2″.6.; March. 2. 9″.3.; March 5. 9″.5; March 6. 3″.1.; March. 8. 0″0.5.; I am sure that if you show the above to Dent he will acknowledge that a chronometer bearing his name should do better things than that, and he will be willing to take the watch back when I go home.

March 16. All saturday, all sunday, and all this morning we have been waiting for the mail steamer, and very weary work this waiting is: in the meantime to-day is a lovely bright summer's day, quite hot in the sun, with a light cool breeze from the S.E.

Your affectionate Son,
Edmund Hope Verney

March 17. This morning the mail arrived, and this day year I left Southampton. I slept last night at Victoria, and this morning walked down to the Grappler: in the mean-time my letters have been sent up to me in town, so I have just missed them: I am now going to walk up to town, so if there is anything that requires to be answered, I shall yet have time to answer them: I send you another ugly phiz, which I dare say you will nevertheless be glad to have: at any rate you can see the waistcoat made by Miss Hardinge and Emily, and the Lucknow pin.[2]

Your very affectionate Son,
Edmund Hope Verney

H.M.S. Grappler. Esquimalt.
March. 30. 1863.

My dear Father,

On Saturday afternoon I saw the bishop, and told him that the Devastation was going to Fort Simpson: he said he was sorry he had not known of it in time, as he would have liked to have sent one of his clergy up in her: on Sunday forenoon I heard to my utter astonishment that he had himself gone up in her that morning; this will delay his journey to England for at least a month. He will have a most delightful and interesting cruize, and it is an expedition that he has long been most anxious to undertake: his account of the work Mr. Duncan is doing will be deeply interesting.[1]

Our real bonâ fide summer commenced upwards of a fortnight ago, to the great surprise of the oldest inhabitants: the air has not yet had time to become warm, but day after day the cloudless sun pours its rays upon this favoured island, forcing every bud and shoot to expand: each succeeding day finds the forests more green, and shows more wildflowers springing into blossom under one's feet: such weather in March seems quite unaccountable.

I enclose a photograph of a person with whom you are doubtless acquainted. I was very much pleased with the photograph you sent me of the Prince and Princess of Wales: it represents her as a most lovely person, and comes to me as a mark of your kind thoughtfulness of your absent son.[2]

We expect the mail steamer to arrive on Saturday next, six long days, and I hope it may bring some good news.

April 3. The mail steamer arrived here early this morning bringing your letter of January 27. All the good news are very pleasant. You ask me to tell you what I think of Mr. Cameron, and whether he is a trustworthy man: I will tell you candidly my private opinion.[3]

I never took a great fancy to Mr. Cameron, and when he once asked me to give him a passage to Nanaimo I declined: he was a different man in different houses: at a batchelors house his conversation was loose, vulgar, and slightly amusingly immoral: at the bishop's it was sensible, grave, and propriety itself: at a doctors it was vague and longwinded, and I heard that at a dissenting minister's it was very democratic: he was a man who could be all things to all men: a man who habitually at all times uses the little arts and artifices which in England we sometimes allow ourselves to use at elections: hardly a trustworthy man I should say, but not a dishonest man: a vulgar and coarse-minded man to a refined person, but not so bad as he seems: a clever shrewd man, with an eye to the main chance, but doubtless an affectionate husband and father: such a man whom one would rather have as an acquaintance than as a friend: I suspect that the people of New Westminster who paid his passage home begin to fear they have been gulled: the Governor and some others treated him with great consideration while he was here.

I am very glad to hear that Fred met Uncle Hope on the pier at Southampton: when he left home I intended to have met him on his return had I been at home.[4]

I had quite made up my mind that I was to receive my promotion by this mail; I should be much more contented and quiet if I knew definitely that it was not coming yet, and in your letter you do not refer to the one subject which, whether I will or not, occupies much of my thoughts.

I have written very plainly about Mr. Cameron, more plainly than I should like to see published to the world, but I know you are very careful who sees my letters.

The Colonial Surveyor General, Mr. Pemberton, goes to England by this mail: he is a good sort of man in a general way, but I do not think the Thames need fear conflagration in consequence of his visit.

Your affectionate Son,
Edmund Hope Verney

My Newspapers are arriving a little more regularly.

Private. H.M.S. Grappler. Esquimalt. V.I.
April 8. 1863.

My dear Father,

You will read with interest and pleasure the enclosed note from the Revd. C.T. Woods which accompanied a silver cup, a birthday present from Vancouver Island friends: far away from home and those on whose affection I have a hereditary claim, I thank God that he has given me friends not less true, with hearts not less warm. I send you also my answer.[1]

I have been playing at cricket this afternoon, and you will be delighted to hear that I got one run in my first innings and two in my second. In our walk to and from the cricket field we passed the most exquisite wild flowers: I believe I raved about the wild flowers last summer; I see every prospect of having another attack this year.

1.30. A.M. April 9. I have just been on deck: yesterday was cloudless, now the night is cloudless; the moon is rising, the stars are piercingly brilliant, while a magnificent Aurora Borealis occupies the northern heavens: it is a trouble to me that by night and by day I see so much that is exquisitely lovely without you or Emily or any that I love to share in my delight, but I myself a solitary hermit in a gunboat.

11. A.M. Dundas breakfasted with me this morning: he told me that Hastings has gone to Callao: I dare say you will remember that you gave

him a letter of introduction to me, and at the same time wrote to me about him: I was not able to see much of him, but he dined on board with me one day; he never presented your letter as he said he had lost it: he has now swindled several people, Dundas amongst the number, and gone off leaving a number of unpaid debts: I am, of course, always very careful whose acquaintance I make, but I thought Hastings was a safe character both because he brought a letter from you and because Dundas thought very well of him and asked me to be civil to him: his manners were certainly engaging and gentlemanlike.

April 12. I am sure you will be extremely gratified to hear that when playing cricket yesterday I got three runs, so I am steadily improving: the astonishing thing is that I am always caught out, and whenever I strike the ball it will fly up into the air.

Almost every day brings out some new wild flower that I have not seen before while some of the earliest ones are already going off: the first humming-bird was seen this year on the 29th of March.

April 14. I will tell you a little incident that will show you that the management of public affairs here is not as it should be: about three weeks ago it was loudly whispered that a defalcation to the extent of £100 had been discovered in the department of the Registrar to the Supreme court, an official receiving a salary of £300 a year: the circumstances were not made public, although very generally known: one of the gentlemen appointed to inquire into the matter, a lawyer, assured me that there could be no doubt of dishonesty somewhere, and that the affair must come into a court of justice: the appointment was offered to him with an increase of £100 a year, but declined although pressed by the Governor personally: since then it has all rather blown over, and I hear that the Registrar is to retain his appointment: at any rate there is to be no public enquiry, and the reason confidentially assigned is because the chief Justice, said, by the way, to be a retired draper, is implicated in the matter; whether fraudulently so or not I know not, but I think very likely because his affairs are a good deal involved, and it would be unpleasant and inconvenient to have them dragged up in court, for he is a foolish benevolent old chap.[2]

Now the Chief Justice is the Governor's brother in law.

Perhaps I had better turn back and write "private" on the first page.

Although a great deal of the above is necessarily hearsay, there can be no doubt of two *facts*: first, that those who were appointed to inquire into the matter considered it a question to be brought into court; secondly, that now it will not be brought into a court.

The mail is now due, and may be expected at any moment; I just exist from mail to mail, and as one steamer does not bring the wished for news, I count the hours to the next: I think that next week, the Grappler will probably be laid up to have new boilers put in, an operation which will probably last a couple of months.

I am reading Mayne's book: I think it capital, and wish I could write one half as well.[3]

April 15. This morning the mail steamer arrived bringing however no English mail: one official letter came from the Admiralty dated February 11.: the next steamer will be here on Tuesday, I hope: she ought to bring me a letter from Uncle Hope.

Notwithstanding the wonderful summer weather we have been enjoying, and which we are enjoying to-day, yesterday was quite cold, and we had a fall of snow: yet this afternoon is like June.

The Forward has just started on a trip up the East Coast, to try and catch some Indians that have been murdering white people: she will have a most delightful trip from settlement to settlement, and one which I should have enjoyed extremely, but it is not likely that I shall be sent away before my new boilers have been put in.[4]

Good bye my dear Father, believe me, Your affectionate Son,

Edmund Hope Verney

H.M.S. Grappler. Esquimalt. V.I.
April 20. 1863.

My dear Father,

By the steamer that arrived here on wednesday last, we received news up to the 23rd of February, viâ New York: tomorrow, another steamer is due, and if by her I do not hear that I may shortly expect my promotion, I shall hire a house on shore to live in while our new boilers are being put in, and generally prepare for a longer stay out here: I wish I had known, when I left England that I was likely to be kept even as long as this, and I would have had many things sent round the Horn.

The good bishop has not yet returned from Fort Simpson, but the Devastation is expected daily. I wrote a short time ago to Mrs. Kinnaird telling her about a very nice girl from her school, who came out in the Tynemouth, Jane Ann Saunders: she was married a few days ago to a Mr. Nesbitt, in Victoria, a well-to-do baker: I went to see her to-day, and was quite charmed with her simple, modest, happy appearance, and also amused with the little matronly air she put on: she has always been a great favourite of mine: Mrs. Kinnaird's other girl, Emily Berry, has not been well during the winter; she is now better however, and engaged to be married to Mr. Cave, catechist at Nanaimo: she is a good girl, but I have not known her as well as Mrs. Nesbitt: there can be no doubt that Mrs. Kinnaird's two girls were quite among the best of the consignment: it would have been well if other people had been a little more particular whom they recommended for the Tynemouth.[1]

April. 22. The steamer arrived this afternoon, bringing no West India Mail: every one is much disappointed; and this is the second mail that has brought me no letters.

I have now taken a house on shore for three months, just a little cottage, and shall set to work tomorrow to prepare it for habitation, while the Grappler's new boilers are being put in: it is a picturesque little shanty at the head of Constance cove, that Helby once inhabited for a short time: I have named it the "Small Bower": I shall probably not go into it for at least a fortnight.

It is a great disappointment to have received no letter today; I think that it would be a good thing if you were always to send my letters by New York, as I should thus hear from you by every mail, and get a week's later news.

The Bishop is still away in the Devastation, and the Forward is on a cruize among the islands on the East Coast; the surveying vessel Beaver sails northwards tomorrow morning: the Camelion is daily expected from the South:[2] we shall not get another mail until next month, perhaps on the fourth or fifth: hope deferred maketh the heart faint.[3]

Your affectionate Son,
Edmund Hope Verney

H.M.S. Grappler. Esquimalt. V.I.
April 26. 1863.

My dear Father,

On Friday evening letters arrived from the Forward: she went up to Admiral Island a few days ago to arrest some Indians who had murdered some white people: it appears that two of the murderers were arrested, but that others were harboured by a tribe on Kuper Island who refused to give them up: these poor Indians had sent their women and children away, and thrown up a stockade: Lascelles fired upon them, and killed several, his own loss being one killed and one wounded, but we have not yet heard all particulars; in the mean time I think it is not improbable that I may be sent up to that neighbourhood: opinion is divided here as to whether this little brush will prove a wholesome lesson to these wretched savages, or whether it will lead to a general row and desire for retaliation.[1]

It is most unfortunate that the Grappler's new boilers have not yet been put in, as it will be a reason for my being kept in the background: the old boilers however are not so bad but what they could be made to work for another six months: at any rate if this little affair leads to further hostilities I cannot but be thankful that the responsibility of firing the first shot has not fallen to me, and I must be content quietly to do my duty from day to day in the background or any where else.

With the very scanty information that has reached me, I do not know what view to take of the matter: I hear that the commodore thinks more lightly of it than the colonial government: it is not said that Lascelles acted either hastily or injudiciously.

Mr. Cridge has a letter from the bishop; the Devastation left Fort Rupert on her way north on the 8th instant, so we must not expect him back just yet.[2] He said that the extensive sale of liquor among the Indians had made great ravages among them: also that they had expressed a desire to have missionaries sent to them.

The weather is most delightful: it was so hot in the middle of the day that one could only walk quite slowly after an early dinner: I think the oak is the only tree not yet out: new-comers are enchanted with the climate.

April 27. I am about to proceed up the coast tomorrow morning to put myself under Lascelles' orders: from what the Commodore says he evidently expects that there will be no more fighting: I have taken on board an assistant surgeon, Dr. Turnbull, and filled up with ammunition: it is not unlikely that I shall go to New Westminster before I return here: I am most heartily glad to have something to do, as you may suppose.

A lieutenant of the Topaze, Wilson, goes up with me on leave: it will be a glorious trip if the present fine weather continues: every day some new wild flower comes out, delighting the eye with its rich colour: I cannot believe that any part of the world can show a greater variety and number of wild flowers than this.[3]

I shall leave this letter behind tonight, as it is possible that the mail may arrive and depart before I return.

Good bye, my dear Father, believe me,

Your affectionate Son,
Edmund Hope Verney

H.M.S. Grappler. Nanaimo. V.I.
May 1. 1863.

My dear Father,

On Tuesday morning we left Esquimalt at 4. A.M. and reached Cowitchin at 9.30: there we remained for an hour and then started for Nanaimo, which we reached in the afternoon: there we found the Devastation with the bishop on board: on wednesday morning we started at six for Port Augusta, where we arrived at about two and found the Forward.[1]

I spent the afternoon in visiting the settlers who had much advanced since I was last there: land was being ploughed up; trees felled, and gardens cultivated, and I had a glass of rich and delicious new milk: the Comax promises to be a most thriving settlement, and it is not improbable that before long it will even surpass Cowitchin: much mischief is done by illegal whiskey trading with the Indians.

Yesterday morning at eight, the two gunboats started for this place where we arrived at about half-past three.

Last night I wished our dear bishop good-bye, as he hopes to go home by the next mail, so he will bring you very late accounts of me: he went down this morning in the Devastation.

Tomorrow morning at about two, the two gunboats will probably start for Kuper Island, to look after the Indians who have been troublesome: we shall have a bright moon, and reach the Indian village at about daybreak, which is a good time for a surprise.

May 3. Yesterday at 2.A.M. we started from Nanaimo, and reached Kuper Island at about five: we found that the Indians had abandoned their village taking with them all their traps, so a party landed and burned it: the Forward got on shore, and did not get off until about

2.P.M., so we anchored and waited for her: we steamed into the little bay in front of the village in the morning, at quarters, with all our hammocks and bags stowed round the gunwale as protection against musketry, fully expecting that the Indians would have made some resistance.[2]

Two murders have been committed, and the Kuper Island Indians, the Lemanchets, harbour the murderers: this is a piratical tribe numbering fifty or sixty men, a band of ruffians from which, some six or eight, have been carrying on a system of murdering isolated white men for the last two years: two murders have been committed lately: one near Plumper pass, where a man was shot for the sake of plunder: his wife, a young girl of sixteen, ran screaming away when an Indian ran after her, caught her by her waist-belt, while a squaw stabbed her in the breast till she was dead: they then stripped her, and threw her into deep water with a piece of an iron stove tied to her hair to sink the body.[3]

The other murder was committed at Pender Island; two men were out in a whale boat for the double purpose of shooting and cutting grass: their names were Brady and Henlee: after they had encamped for the night, three Indian men and two women arrived in a canoe: the white men cooked their supper and gave a good share to the Indians, after which they all went to sleep, the Indians lying by the fire in the door of the tent: presently the Indians fired into the tent, wounding Brady and Henlee; they awoke and discharged their rifles, upon which the natives ran to their canoe and made off: three days later, Brady died, and Henlee, wounded in three places, succeeded in making his way to Victoria.

Yesterday our boilers gave out, and it is only this evening that they are repaired, so this morning I went in the Forward to search for Brady's body: two suspected Indians were on board, one of whom was doubtless one of the murderers: he pointed out to us the spot: we first steamed up a beautiful inlet called Bedwell Harbour, and then landed in a little cove at the head of it: we walked a few yards by the side of a murmuring rill, and in the most retired, secluded, romantic spot, under a spreading cedar lay the putrified body of poor Brady: it was a sight to make the most careless look grave: nothing had been touched since Henlee had left: the corpse was covered over with blankets, the caps of two Indians were lying near, where they had dropped them in their hurry to escape, and it was the sort of lovely retired spot that one would select for quiet meditation and never suspect would be the scene of violence: we brought away a few articles where-by to identify the murderers and their victim, and the Forward returned with me to Ganges harbour, whence I now write: she has gone to meet the Devastation in Cowichan Bay, where I shall join them tomorrow morning.

May. 4. 1863. I close this letter this evening to send it down to Victoria by Lascelles tomorrow morning.

Your affectionate Son,
Edmund Hope Verney

Cowichan. May. 4. 1863.

H.M.S. Grappler. Cowichan. V.I.
May 5. 1863.

My dear Father,

Yesterday morning we left Ganges Harbour, and steamed to this place where we found the Devastation and Forward. The Roman Catholic Bishop Demers had been here for a week, and I believe that it was owing to his endeavours that these Indians were willing to give up two murderers whom we came in search of: all the morning was spent in saying masses for them, and it was agreed that a flag should be hoisted as soon as the two men were ready, that a boat might be sent for them.[1]

At about two o'clock, Captain Pike pulled away towards the river in his boat, with the inspector of police, and a lady, Mrs. Macnamara, who was on board for a cruize: shortly afterwards the flag was hoisted, and Lascelles and I started off in my gig: when we reached the priest's house, we found a large body of Indians assembled, perhaps a couple of hundred: through the interpreter they asked all sorts of questions, and seemed desirous of prolonging the discussion as much as possible: what particularly puzzled them was, that they could not understand why four Indians were to be hung when only one white man had been killed: the oldest men said that ever since they could remember it had been considered fair and just that if they killed a man of another tribe, one of their own must suffer, but we were not content with that. At last Captain Pike was tired of waiting: the Indians wanted to deliver up the prisoners the next day, so he walked down to his boat with Mrs. Macnamara, telling the Indians that as they would not give up the murderers they would bring trouble on the whole tribe.[2]

Lascelles remained behind with the inspector of police, two of the Devastation's men with revolvers under their frocks, and myself, and my boat's crew were armed with stretchers, waiting behind some bushes at the foot of the hill, in case I called them.

In the mean time we explained to the chiefs that we *must* have the murderers at once, and while we were making hasty arrangements to take them by force, of a sudden the assembly opened, and down a lane formed in their midst, marched the two villains, with every possible sign of majestic, dignified, sel[f]-importance, charmed at the sensation and excitement they were producing.

First they adjourned to their lodge where each was fitted out with a new blanket, and a new pair of socks, and many of their friends emptied out their little collections of treasures to give them parting presents, and at last amid the howling of the women, the sobbing of their friends, and the farewell salutations of whole tribe they embarked in my boat and we took them on board the Forward.

Their chief request was that they might be hung on the marshes at the river's mouth, in presence of all the neighbouring tribes, and not at Victoria. The whole scene was a wonderful and interesting sight which I am very glad not to have missed.

We are very much indebted to the Roman Catholic Bishop for his efforts to persuade the Indians to give up the culprits: I do not think we should have got them but for him: he has been in these parts all his life, and has had a great experience of the natives; he is an agreable man to talk to, with a good deal of information: I think he is a French Canadian.

This morning the Forward started for Victoria, having on board the prisoners and Bishop Demers.

May 6. 1863. I have had an extremely pleasant day, spent in visiting the settlers: I may say that I have been astonished at the progress and improvements made by all: this is very much owing to the fact that none but men in earnest would have remained here hitherto: several have thrown up their preemption claims, or sold them, and this has been for the benefit of those that remained, as the former were obliged to sell off their provisions, implements &c for whatever they would fetch.

The Cowichan Indians are, on the whole, very peaceable, and well disposed towards the settlers, who treat them with kindness and consideration: it is a long time since I have been here, and I was much pleased with the recognition and welcome which I met with from both Indians and white men: I even regret that I must not expect my lot to be cast in these parts for much longer.

We expected the Forward to have returned with orders to-day: however, as she has not yet arrived, she will probably be here tomorrow, and bring the mail up.

May 9. Yesterday Morning Captain Pike, being tired of waiting for the Forward, went to Esquimalt leaving orders for me to remain here until Monday, and then proceed to New Westminster.

When walking through the woods a short time ago I saw the very curious sight of a snake eating a toad: the toad seemed a good deal bigger than the snake's throat, but the snake had got the two hind legs and the lower half of the toad's body already down and had squeezed and elongated them; the toad was alive, and apparently quite reconciled to his novel position, but as the snake takes a long time to swallow anything, perhaps it had become numbed; we killed the poor toad with a rap over the head, when the snake disgorged it and escaped. When the toad was killed all his internal arrangments escaped through [h]is head, owing to the great pressure the snake had brought to bear upon his body, so perhaps by this means the pressure upon the brain had taken away consciousness: if not, it must be a cruel lingering death.

There are many toads about now, probably emerging from their torpid winter condition: they delight to scrape away a little round plot of herbage, and lie down with their bellies on the warm earth, with their mouths open: flies come and settle on their tongues, but they do not devour each separately; no, the lazy ruffians wait till they have a good mouthful, and then eat them all together: it is while they are thus entrapping the poor little flies that the snakes prey on them, and the snakes in their turn have to look out for hawks.

A mail must have arrived at Esquimalt a few days ago, but I have as yet heard nothing of it: however I do not grudge the waiting for my letters, so that I am not left doing nothing at Esquimalt. The lying idle for so long a time tries my patience beyond endurance, and with my present orders I see no prospect of returning there for a fortnight.

I suppose it is superfluous to say that the weather is like the middle of summer, and that the wild flowers of every hue are innumerable. As I said good-bye to the bishop at Nanaimo, I suppose he has at last started for England.[3]

May 15. 1863. On Monday we left Cowichan for New Westminster, where we arrived the same afternoon: the object of our visit was to lay down, paint, and generally inspect the buoys at the mouth of the Frazer river: Tuesday was employed in rigging purchases and getting on board a buoy and mooring stone: I rode "out" to Burrards Inlet with Dr. Seddall of the Engineers:[4] Col. Moody has cut a road to Burrards inlet, running due north: when the Frazer was frozen over last year, communication was kept up through this road, and had it not been in existence the scarcity of provisions might have been very serious: the Colonel deserves the greatest credit for his foresight, for the river opposite the town was frozen over for seven weeks: during this ride I saw the largest trees I have ever seen in my life, much larger, I should think than any in Vancouver Island.

Wednesday was occupied in attending to the buoys, and yesterday we left New Westminster for Nanaimo, where we arrived in the afternoon: this morning we left Nanaimo, and are now on our way to the Comax settlement, and hope to arrive at Port Augusta at about four this afternoon.

I have on board, on a visit, Mr. Nicholl, manager of the Nanaimo coal Company, and his wife, rather nice people: they will probably remain with me until my return to Nanaimo on Monday: Mrs. Nicholl is working her passage by sitting under the awning mending my gloves, while I read aloud that celebrated poem, "the Prince and the Outlaw", which I am taking up with other juvenile works in verse and prose for distribution among the youthful population of the Comax settlement.[5]

I am very glad to be kept employed instead of laying at Esquimalt doing nothing: while I have other things to think of, I can afford to dismiss from my mind all anxieties for letters, or news, mail or female: although I have not received my letters from the last mail; and today a second has probably arrived: so I look forward to a stunning batch of letters on my return about a week hence.

May 18. On Saturday I went up the Courtney river in a canoe, with my two visitors, and we visited several of the settlers in their houses; this settlement is going on well, but not making quite so much progress as Cowichan: what amount of prairie there may be about here is not yet ascertained: the best land is heavily timbered and free from underwood.

Yesterday morning I read the service twice, first on board the ship, and then to some settlers on shore who had intended to come off to the ship but were too late: they seemed very glad to have it read to them, and they appeared grateful for some tracts I left with them: today, we hope to reach Nanaimo.

May 24. Since I last wrote I have had no time for letters: we have been busy searching the coasts and Islands in the neighbourhood of Kuper Island for the Lemalchey Indians, and for the murderers of Marks and his daughter: we have destroyed about a dozen of their canoes and have been partially successful in obtaining the men; on Friday last I commanded a party of blue-jackets and marines, marched about ten miles into the country near Cowitchin, to meet another party marched from another point on the coast; we bivouaced on Friday night and reached the rendezvous the next morning where our party consisted of fifty men: we returned on board last night: today we have discovered a cave which we thought would have contained their plunder, but it was empty: the continual work is rather harrassing and fatiguing, but I never had better health in my life.[6]

Your affectionate Son,
Edmund Hope Verney

H.M.S. Grappler. May 29. 1863.
Esquimalt.

My dear Father,

On wednesday we returned from our operations against the Lemalcha Indians, and at last I have some spare time to answer a large batch of letters received a few days ago: my dear Father, I was almost sorry to see so much of your handwriting, as I know how many people have claims upon your pen. Your letters were dated Feb. 9, and March 16 and 30.

Now with regard to what you say about my promotion: a body of officers serving under Peel met with the approbation of the Admiralty; to mark their approval, their Lordships gave to each officer one step of rank; this was a great boon to every officer except two, the senior lieutenant and the senior mate, who might each have expected their promotion from their seniority, independently of their services: each of them was mentioned honourably in despatches, and they were the only two officers captain Peel recommended for promotion: recognizing these claims in the case of the first lieutenant, he was promoted to the rank of captain as soon as he had served one year in the rank of commander, and he received the C.B., an honour never before accorded to a commander: in the case of the senior mate these claims were not recognized, but he received his one step of promotion like every one else, at a time when he would probably have received it on account of the Russian war and Crimean services, had he then been serving in Portsmouth harbour: he has now the mortification of seeing those who were much junior to him, catching him up, as every midshipman was promoted as soon as he passed; and of seeing those senior to him going far ahead, as I see by the last papers that one who was a lieutenant in the Shannon, Wilson, is now a post captain: thus every officer who served in the Shannon now sees his name in the Navy list considerably above those of his cotemporaries, while my name stands among those who were midshipmen of my own standing: if my next promotion is not given to me soon, it will be no more of a boon than was the last.[1]

At the same time I must say that I have an appointment which I thoroughly like, and the duties of which I endeavour to perform zealously and to the best of my ability. I earnestly desire my promotion with a view to the future more than the present: if I am not very shortly promoted, the chances of my serving afloat until I reach the higher ranks are diminished, although my present wish is always to remain intimately associated with my profession: I am quite content to know that you see all this, and will press my claims as far as is right, and it is a relief to know that I am to wait yet longer, as I felt so very unsettled before. I have now taken a house on shore, and only want a wife to be complete: you may send me one out by the next consignment of the Emigration Society.

This afternoon, the Grappler has gone alongside the wharf to prepare for having the boilers taken out, and new ones put in, so we shall have no more cruizing for the next two or three months: I hope for a month's leave to go to British Columbia. Probably the small Bower will be ready for me on Monday or Tuesday, and I am anxious to get out of the ship before all the hammering begins[.]

The information you ask for about what lieutenants have been promoted during the last two or three years could be best obtained at the Admiralty itself, perhaps from Mr. Noel who was Admiral Pelham's secretary and has always shewed a kindly disposition towards me:[2] it might also be obtained from Ommaney with a little trouble, by comparing Navy Lists, and he would be very likely to know about officers personal characters, and what service they have seen; I consider him to be an excellent trustworthy man.

Pray do not ignore the New York way of sending letters: it is much the quickest, and if you have really any little item of news to send, or if a letter to be forwarded arrives late, it is a great treat to get a letter viâ New York sometimes when there is no mail viâ St. Thomas' and every-one else looks blank: besides it is a much quicker way, and many people here never hear from home any other way: if it were not for the expense of letters, I should ask you always to write viâ New York.

The news of the death of Captain McCleverty are very sad: he is a most serious loss to the service: Sir James Outram's death was not so unexpected, I suppose.[3]

I get on better with the Commodore than I did: being thrown into contact with various commanding officers teaches one tact, but, between you and me, I fear that Commodore Spencer is rather an empty-headed individual.

The Bishop is a great loss, and is missed by many here who never called themselves his supporters; to me the loss is perhaps the heaviest, as I knew him best and could appreciate him. Many thanks for what you tell me about public opinion with regard to the United States: in war or in peace I rejoice in my appointment although I cannot but regret that it must be some time before the Grappler is fit for sea again.

If the Admiralty has any intention of promoting a commander on this station, and I know that one or two are expecting it, it would be a very great boon not only to promote me but give me the vacant command: this would save them the expense of sending out another commander, but it would be a very great favour which I dare not expect: I mention it however, that you may know what to ask for if the Duke of S. intimates that he would esteem it a great favour if you would name a wish.

I see that you are on the Committee for considering the grievances of Naval Officers:[4] you have a difficult task before you, but there is no doubt, I think, that the Navy as a service is in a dissatisfied condition: I have not formed any decided opinion as to what ought to be done, but I think that every officer who has not committed himself in any way ought to be able to claim as a right two things; first, active service, for a certain proportion of his time; secondly promotion, sooner or later.

On one point I am quite clear: every lieutenant who has served under Peel in India and is at present commanding a gunboat in *any* of Her Majesty's colonies ought to be promoted forthwith: of this I think there can be no doubt, and I think you should mention it to Lord Clarence, and at the same time casually observe that in the event of his disagreeing with you you shall recommend that every officer's pay throughout the service shall be doubled, unless he is serving in the Admiralty, when it shall be stopped and divided among lieutenants of five years standing.

There can be no doubt that the Bishop has done an immense deal for the colony, and that it is difficult to say what state it would have been in, but for him; but the crying evil is the want of a high honorable tone among the colonial officials; a really first-rate governor is wanted *Now*, to put things in a proper train, and it would not matter so much who his successor might be five years hence.

You ask about the Archdeacon: personally, I like him, but do not know enough of him to say that he is a religious and good man for his post, which is your question: I should *not* like to see him made bishop:[5] I should not think that our dear cousin has ever had the slightest intention of resigning his bishopric: I never heard it whispered before.

We do not agree in our verses: we differ in two verses, and I think you must be wrong as I mark mine with a pencil, but you can easily mark them up and see: Mine for today is Matt. 21-38. But when the husbandmen saw the son they said among themselves, "This is the heir; come, let us kill him, and let us seize on his inheritance."[6] Many thanks for the large parcel of "Leisure Hours" you sent me: they are most acceptable, and shall be distributed among the settlers.

Dear Sarah Medlycott is to be married at last; she writes me such a happy letter.[7]

June 6. What will you think of such a long interregnum in my letter? The reason of it is that I have been busy turning over from the "Grappler" to the "Small Bower" whence I now write: to-day for the first time I can say that I am settled, but I have had a great deal of trouble as you may suppose: I have made arrangements to keep this house as long as I am in the colony, and I pay a rent of £1. a month: if I hear by letters in the Autumn that there is no chance of my promotion, I shall have to go to some little expense in making it habitable for the winter: it is situated in a damp shady place, but on a tolerably dry soil.

June 14. The mail arrived this morning, bringing your letters of April 10. and 15. On Friday last the Sutlej arrived with Admiral Kingcombe: it is a great joy to me, for Commodore Spencer was not a pleasant senior officer to be under, although personally I liked him: the Admiral's secretary, Browne, was in the Britannia with me, and is disposed to be very cordial and kind: I have no doubt, too, that I shall like the flag-captain, Conolly: I knew him slightly before: he is a widower; his wife was the sister of Carter in the Emerald. I have also met the Admiral before, although I have not yet reminded him of it: I have no doubt I shall like him: he is a thorough sailor; every hair of his head is a rope-yarn, and every drop of blood, the best Stockholm tar: one must beware of forming too hasty an opinion, but the Sutlej appears to be in capital order and very comfortable.[8]

Pray remember me most kindly to old Mrs. Pinfold: she can look forward to very shortly joining those whom we have loved so dearly:[9] I expect to find great changes at the House when I come home, you seem to be doing a great deal.

You say you have been again speaking about my promotion at the Admiralty: I honestly think that I shall be hardly used if I am not promoted at once; but on the other hand I am far happier serving here than I should be as an idle man at home waiting for employment: the delay of my promotion now is a sad drawback, and much to be regretted with reference to the future, but as far as the present is concerned I never expect to be happier or more contented than I am now: I can heartily thank God that my lines have fallen in such pleasant places, and will trust Him for the future.[10]

We hear nothing here of hostile intentions on the part of the Americans, but I cannot conceive why the Admiralty do not at once establish a large Naval depot and dockyard here: I believe it has been recommended and urged by every successive Admiral and senior officer: I have not the least doubt that a dock, a patent slip, or a floating dock would pay even as a private speculation.

I have letters by this mail from Emily, from Aunt Fremantle and from Uncle Frederic, but they must be answered bye and bye. I am very well, and a richer man since I sold my horse. Although I do not write my miseries and woes, you need not imagine that I have no troubles: only the blessings far outnumber them.

Your affectionate Son,
Edmund Hope Verney

I am very anxious to know whether any of the seeds or berries I have sent home, have come up, and if so, which.

The Small Bower. Esquimalt. V.I.
June 21. 1863.

My dear Father

As I begin my letter this evening I hear through the still night air the flapping noise of a steamer entering the harbour: I go to my door, I open it and listen; yes! there is no mistake, a paddle-wheel steamer is coming in; I see her lights; up go the position lights on board the men of war; a sentry hails a passing boat, there is a flash, a report, a gun, the mail steamer: the echoes roll about the quiet inlets of this bay, now soft, now loud, now dying away altogether; I hear the boatswains mates on board the ships call boats away; the steamer stops, and again I hear the slow dull splashing as she turns astern, and secures to the wharf: lights are glancing in every direction: boats are moving, and the air, so silent ten minutes ago, resounds with the clatter of horses hoofs, the rattle of waggons, the barking of dogs, the shouting of men, and, loudest of all, the rush of the escaping steam.

In an hour or two I shall hear if there are any news of importance; some mails seem to come quite barren, others full of all sorts of news. How curiously the arrival of the mail has altered this harbour; my bower is at the head of a snug little nook, but even here I hear the little waves washing up against the shore, disturbed by the steamer: ten short minutes ago the water was like glass, reflecting every brilliant star above, now it is ruffled and troubled, but we know that the stars are safely anchored in Heaven, and it is only their reflection that is a little moved: see the collect for the fourth Sunday after Easter.[1]

June 22. This morning I have your letters of April 26. and May 1.: you say you have received my letters up to March 17., so I receive an answer in three months and five days.

I imagine that Americans in this colony are very fairly balanced as regards North and South, but I do not think that either party bears us much good-will: they are very quiet and give no trouble. I have as yet heard no particular news by this steamer: I have a letter of course from my persevering correspondent Mr. Beeby: I must really make his acquaintance when I go home: it is so very kind of him to take such a warm interest in my pecuniary affairs: I do not think he has missed a mail since I came out here: if you do not already know him, I dare say any Naval friend would introduce you: he writes a capital hand:[2]

Admiral Kingcombe is a most active man, and I expect that he will do a great deal for this colony: he is very popular, so far: I think he is alive to the importance of making this a great naval depot: it is to be hoped that friends in England will back up any representations he may make on this subject. I dare say that by this time you have made the acquaintance of Lord Lauderdale: the papers say that he was in town ready to be examined before the Naval Promotion Committee: I hear that he has an only daughter to whom he is devotedly attached.[3]

I find that you had as mild a winter as we had: I hope that no late frosts will have destroyed this years promise: our cloudless days are in full swing, but the afternoons are almost too warm: it is worthy of remark that the first humming-bird and the first wild rose appeared this year on the 28th of March.

The Grappler will not be ready for sea for the next eight weeks, and as soon as I have made all things straight with the Admiral I hope to go up to New Westminster and the Fraser river for two or three weeks.

Now, my dear Father, Adieu: with love to Emily, Freddy, and Mamma, believe me,

Your affectionate Son,
Edmund Hope Verney

Private.

The Small Bower. Esquimalt. V.I.
June 29. 1863.

My dear Father,

It is indeed strange that I should ever be at a loss for matter to fill a letter to you, and yet I often am because I do not know anything that is likely to interest you: you often seem to think that I am *too* happy here, so I will now tell you a grievance to prove to you that although this is a first-rate appointment, it is not altogether devoid of anxieties:

When I joined the Grappler, I found on board a ship's steward of the name of Haddy, a man in whom Helby placed implicit trust, and whose duty it was to look after the ship's accounts: I found him thoroughly well up to his work, which all lay in the department which is under the paymaster in a larger ship, and work of which I knew absolutely nothing: I became, of course, responsible for these accounts, but never interfered with them in any way, as he so well knew the work, and I knew nothing.[1]

By degrees this man's conduct has become worse and worse, until about six weeks ago it became necessary to disrate him, and he went to hospital where he has been ever since.

On his departure I got the clerk of the stores on shore here to look over my accounts, and it was then discovered that some things had been neglected since January last, and everything since April: moreover Haddy was very angry at being disrated, and feigned to be worse than he was, and refused to render any assistance in getting up the accounts, on the plea of illness.

When the Sutlej arrived, the secretary was so kind as to lend me a clerk to get the accounts up, but had he not been a friend of mine; or had the Admiral been a very sharp hand, this might have led to my losing my command: I have known for some time that the accounts were in a shaky state, but only a few days ago did I know how very bad they were; so you see I have some anxieties: of course it was my own fault as I ought to have taken the accounts regularly in hand myself, but I only did as Lascelles does now: Helby overlooked the accounts a good deal, and I cannot help thinking he did not altogether trust Haddy: Haddy has been a regular villain, for he used to tell me that things were up, which now prove to have been a long way behind: he has been accused of theft on shore, which he has so far admitted as to make good the stolen property.

When you consider how any exaggeration of this story would injure me, you will not wonder that I have marked this letter "private": I [am] happy to say that although some of the accounts are still very complicated, we have today made the cash account all square: the secretary is very friendly towards me, having been with me in the Britannia: had he been animated by the feelings which I fear were borne towards me by Scaife of the Topaze, I might have had a very different tale to tell.

Nevertheless, I maintain that however careful the Commander of a gun-boat may be in the matter of his accounts, he must always be to a great extent at the mercy of his ship's steward: my horizon is by no means clear yet, for although in a week or two I trust that all my accounts will be square, I doubt if I shall be able to get even a second rate ship's steward out here, and I can foresee nothing but botheration on that score until his grace of Somerset earns for himself everlasting immortality by sending me my promotion.

I have a sick midshipman spending a few days with me; he cut his foot when bathing: his name is Woodd: his father is the member for Knaresborough: he is a quiet boy, and I should think likely to do very well.[2]

July 3. 1863. The summers here generally dry up at about this time, and every thing that ought to be green takes it into its head to turn brown: to the surprise of the oldest inhabitants, we have had four days of almost continual rain, which has freshened up everything in a wonderful manner, and seemed to give all vegetation a fresh impulse, as it were: so probably this will be even a more delicious summer than the last.

July 3. 1863. My servant has just brought in to me a humming-bird's nest with two little humming birds therein: it was quite painful to see the poor little bright-eyed half-fledged things, and to hear their feeble chirp: as they could not be replaced, I thought the kindest thing I could do was just to pop them into a bottle of alcohol, where they now are, and I hope to be able to bring the nest safely home.

The Admiral has caught a cold, and been rather unwell lately, but today he is better. The one draw-back of my little bower, this charming climate, and the lovely view from my window, is the absence of those I love, to enjoy it with me: with one of you by my side now, how happy should I be: my dog Claydon lies asleep under the yew tree: my cock and hens are dozing in the bush near at hand, and my pigeon winks lazily in its cage: I hear one of my men at work completing the pigeon house, when I shall get a couple more pigeons, and set them at liberty: my rabbits also are thriving: my kitten is becoming more companionable: my garden looks much fresher after the rain and the peas have sprouted visibly.

Mr. Cridge, the rector of Christ-church, is spending a day or two with me: he has not been very well, and he revels in the thorough change of air and scene.

Miss June Bird's application for my vote in the Royal Naval Female School arrived too late for my answer to have been in time for the election, or Miss Clarke should certainly have had my vote.[3] I am very glad to hear of De Grancey's marriage: I hope it is a good one in every way.

July 4. This is the great day with the Americans, when they celebrate their independance: it is rather a wet evening for the fireworks in which they generally delight to indulge. The mail is expected in tonight or tomorrow morning, but I am by no means confident that we shall have any English mail.

July 5. 1863. The steamer arrived this morning, so I must say adieu: believe me,

Your affectionate Son,
Edmund Hope Verney

The Small Bower. Esquimalt. V.I.
July 11. 1863.

My dear Father,

Today the Admiral has given me a fortnight's leave, and I hope to start for British Columbia on Tuesday: there are many reasons why I should not have chosen this time to take my leave, but it is the only time I can expect to have while I command the Grappler, as my services may at any time be suddenly required when the ship is fit to go to sea: the engineer of the Sutlej says that he hopes to have us ready by the end of this month, but I do not expect to steam out of the harbour before the beginning or middle of August.

We are now fairly launched into summer, and the heat of the mid-days are [*sic*] quite oppressive: the berries are beginning to ripen, and also some of the wild-flower seeds, of which I am making another collection: I should very much like to know whether any of the seeds I sent to you last year have thriven: I do not know of any reason why they should not all flourish.

I have a hen sitting on nine ducks eggs, and my stock of animals generally are in a very flourishing and satisfactory condition: but I cannot succeed with my pigeons: they are wilful and easily beguiled to fly to any habitation rather than the one prepared for them: I must get a pair of very young ones, and endeavour to attach them to this place.

I can really send you no news from this place: we hope for a mail tomorrow.

July. 13. Tomorrow morning I leave Victoria for British Columbia, so I leave this little scrap of a letter to be sent, after I have gone.

Your affectionate Son,
Edmund Hope Verney

The Camp New Westminster. B.C.
July 14. 1863.

My dear Father,

This morning at eleven I left Victoria for my fortnight's leave in the H.B.C. steamer "Otter", arriving at New Westminster at about 7.30. P.M. We had a very hot passage across, in a dead calm, and there was a good deal of haze which prevented our enjoying the beautiful view: tomorrow I hope to start for the Harrison Lake and Douglas, and to have something worth reading to write.[1]

July 16. Yesterday was spent at New Westminster as the steamer Governor Douglas did not leave until 7 P.M. In the morning while I was sitting at lunch with Parsons of the Engineers in came the Archdeacon with the very kind offer of his horse to take with me. P. and I consulted a little and came to the conclusion to accept it, which I did with much gratitude. At 7 P.M. we got away in the steamer in a drizzling rain which was very disappointing. Even had it been fine we should not have seen very much as it soon became dark. I was very fortunate in having for fellow passengers Mr and Mrs Reece of Victoria who are just going round in the steamer for a little pleasure trip. During the night there was a good deal of thunder and lightning and rain, but I slept like a top. We only stopped during the night for an hour or 2 when it was very dark and the channel was intricate. A little before sunset I asked the mate if we should anchor that night and he answered, "Wall, I guess we shall tie up bye and bye." However, we only tied up to a tree for an hour or 2.[2]

This morning I was up soon after 4 A.M. to enjoy the view but it was very monotonous. Every now and then it rained and heavy clouds hung over the low hills and nothing was to be seen. When we entered the Harrison River soon after 7 A.M. the water changed colour very suddenly, from a yellowish mud colour to a clear green, but even that was not as bright and clear as usual owing to the recent rains. At length, at about 9 A.M. it began to clear up a little from time to time as we steamed through the Harrison Lake, but at no time did the clouds lift very much, and we had no view of the mountains, which are celebrated for their great beauty. We were much pleased, however, with what we did see, the shores of the lake being in many places quite precipitous, and beautiful cataracts were dashing down them. We saw also places where silver mines had been worked, but they have never been found to pay. Douglas is situated at the head of a very little lake at the top of Harrison Lake. To enter it we had to pass through a very narrow slue where we brushed against bushes as we passed, now on this side and now on that. Presently Douglas came in sight. It is a very small place, struggling into existence, and like most other places entirely depending upon the success of the mines. I went at once to the house of the magistrate, Mr Gaggin, whence I now write, and there I put up my horse. Then I went to see a waterfall near the town. It was very fine, but I suppose it is impossible to describe a waterfall, for there is not much variety in them. In this there was no sheer descent but the water rushed down a very steep decline, and the rocks all round were covered with thick soft moss and beautiful shrubs. After this I called on the parson, Mr Gammidge, and his wife. They seemed very nice people but are going home soon. They spoke rather despondingly of their work here, their average number to church being only 5 or 6 every Sunday, and they seem to have no congenial companions.[3]

I think we have now done with the wet weather, so this afternoon at 5 I hope to start on the way to the next lake, called Lake Anderson. Mr Gaggin, the magistrate, goes with me, which will be so much better than travelling alone. We intend to sleep at the 16 mile House, which is about ½ way or less, and then to go on to catch the steamer in the morning. Among the passengers who came with me this morning was a young man from Canada going to the mines, the son of the man after whom the Frazer River was named.[4] It was a curious coincidence to meet him on that river. The Harrison and Frazer Rivers are very different in every respect. The latter is very swift and muddy. It is continually depositing mud at its mouth and forming fresh banks, and its course is incidentally full of floating trees. The Harrison is not nearly so rapid and its colour is usually a bright green or blue, reflecting the mountains at the side. In many places it is of great depth and the bottom is always of gravel or rock. I believe that the lake has never been sounded, although many attempts have been made. I should think that the lake must be most lovely on a fine day. This dull day has been rather a disappointment. All the hills are covered with pine as elsewhere, but on the banks of the Frazer we saw many other trees. The water is now at its highest and some houses are under water. In a few months it will have fallen 10 or 15 feet. The Governor Douglas is a large stern wheel steamer drawing only 3 feet of water when loaded, and at one time she used to go 15 knots. Now all she goes is 12 or 13. There were not many passengers on board, and they say that things are rather dull this year. My luggage consists of only a knapsack and a little roll containing a mosquito curtain and a Scotch plaid. I have also my opera glasses. So you see I am travelling very light.

July 16. 1863. The 16 mile House. 10.30 P.M.

6.15 P.M. I started from Douglas on horseback with Gaggin the magistrate, and arrived at this place, 16 miles from Douglas, at 9.30. Our road was good and lay through beautiful ravines and glens, among cataracts and mountain torrents, and occasionally along the Lilloet River which is, I think, the most rapid river I have ever seen.

The general appearance of the country reminded me much of Jamaica and of the Organ Mountains, although of course the foliage is very different. There are several Houses along the road, all distinguished by their number of miles from Douglas. At the 10 mile House, which is kept by a coloured man, we were recommended to ride on quickly, to get past that part of the road which was overflowed, before dark. When we arrived there it was nearly dark and the water for several 100 yds was above our horses' girths. Gaggin told me after we had got through that had he been alone he would have turned back, but that he was ashamed to do so before me. It certainly was very dangerous as the water was an overflow of the river and was rushing along very fast. Had the horse made one false step his legs would have been swept from under him and we should both have been thoroughly wetted if nothing worse. Tomorrow we intend to start for Anderson Lake.

Friday. July 17. This morning at 7.50 we started again on horse-back for the 29 mile House on the Little Lilloet Lake, whence I now write. At noon we go on in the steamer to Pemberton. We arrived here at about 10.30. The road lay through a beautiful ravine by the side of the Lilloet River. Its rapidity was quite wonderful. Travelling continually by it one did not notice always the speed with which the water was rushing by. But every now and then a large log or block of wood would come tearing by, rolling over and over in the boiling water. Then it would come against a boulder or sunken rock, give a twirl, a start into the air and then a dive and presently reappear, rolling along as before. There were no great waterfalls except from the tributary brooks and streams we continually crossed and these were very fine, and even a little fall of a few feet had a magnificent effect with such a large body of water. The recent rains had rendered it of a thick milky colour, but the streams which joined it were of a bright green. One part of the road was very much under water like what we passed last night, and I had to unsling my knapsack, etc., to prevent their getting wet, as the water was above the horses' girths. But there was not so much danger as it was day time. There are a good many clouds even today, although it is not as dull as yesterday, so I have not yet seen the distant mountains. But it has the advantage of making the air so much cooler for travelling. Many of the hills we passed were very high and covered with fir, with here and there a large abrupt cliff of some bright coloured rock and a cataract dashing over it. The forest was very romantic, abounding in wild flowers and various coloured berries, many of the latter very good to eat. We passed a number of Chinamen on the road on their way to the mines. They are a wonderful race, generally keeping very much together and patient and enduring. I never saw a Chinaman looking otherwise than contented, and I never saw one the worse for drink. And there they were today, toiling and plodding along, but withal cheerful. 2 or 3 times we passed a broken-down miner, broken-down perhaps in purse, spirits and health, and a most melancholy-looking spectacle, and one who perhaps had landed in this country but a few weeks ago, full of life and hope.

At the 20 mile House are hot springs and baths which are very good for rheumatism and are much used by travellers. I saw the water bubbling out from a stone, and close by was a stream of cold water. I could taste nothing particular in the hot water, but it is said that horses are very fond of drinking it. Some people say it contains sulphur. The spring is situated in a very pretty spot on the banks of the river, and will doubtless be a valuable property some day.

9.20 P.M. The mosquitoes are so terribly bad that I can hardly manage to write. We left the 29 mile House in the steamer at 1 P.M. and steamed up the little Lilloet Lake. The clouds on the tops of the mountains rather added to the beauty of the scene and made the weather cooler. The scenery was beautiful. Between the little and big Lilloet Lake are the rapids, not passable when the water is low. The steamer could not get through without the help of a rope although she steams 12 or 13 knots. Her name is the Prince of Wales. She was built on the lake, and made her first trip last May. She is very creditable to her owners. She is of course a stern wheel steamer. The captain was very civil to me and gave me a free passage. The trees and bushes of this country appear very much the same as those of Vancouver I., but as a rule the country seems better watered. We reached Pemberton at 4.20, and came on 14 miles to the ½ way House which we reached at 7.20 P.M. The mosquitoes are perfectly frightful, and I really cannot write more now.

July 18. 1863. 8 A.M. Last night the mosquitoes were very bad indeed. They must be quite different from ordinary ones. It requires considerable skill to catch one generally, but these seem confident in their numbers and allow you to kill them as much as you like, and when you have killed one, another takes his place. We rose this morning at 3.30 A.M. after a rather sleepless night and started at 4.10. The road lay among mountains pretty much as before, abounding in brooks and streams. At 6.30 we reached Anderson Lake House and here I had a bathe in the lake. The water was decidedly cool. Then we breakfasted and at 7.50 started in the steamer, whence I now write. This lake is like the others, very long for its breadth and embedded among high mountains. There was rain last night and the clouds have not quite lifted off the hill tops yet. The hill sides are covered with the everlasting pine. The steamer is called the Lady of the Lake. She is a side wheel boat but very small and dirty.

After leaving Pemberton yesterday we saw a hare, and a pair of birds they call partridges, but they appeared to me more like small pheasants; they were very graceful birds, which the partridge is not. This morning we saw a pair of large owls, sitting together on one small tree and very tame.

July 19. 1863. We reached the end of Anderson Lake yesterday morning at 9.50. There I landed and rode across about 1½ miles to the steamer on Seaton Lake. These lakes are all connected by very rapid streams which are not navigable. We left Seaton Lake at the West end at 10.50 and arrived at the town of Seaton at 12.30. The town of Seaton is a thriving and populous place containing at least 4 houses and inhabited by several Indians besides the whites. It boasts an hotel which is said to be well kept but which I did not stay to examine but rode off at once to Lilloet, a distance of 3½ miles, where I arrived at 1.20 P.M. On emerging from the long valley or ravine between Douglas and Lilloet, one is pleased and surprised to open out into the comparatively open valley of the Frazer River. The view of the mountains round Lilloet is certainly pleasing, although after all it is merely a larger hill and broader valley. Before arriving at Anderson yesterday morning we passed Summit Lake whence the waters flow to the Fraser both by Douglas and Lilloet. From the window of the hotel whence I now write, I can see the blue water from Seaton Lake flowing into the muddy Frazer, keeping on its right bank and not mixing with it as far as I can see, but preserving its bright contrast of colour. The former river is very rapid just here.

When we left New Westminster we passed first through thick forest and jungle down to the water's edge. Then we came to the lake scenery, where the forest was frequently less thick, and bare open places were to be seen on the sides of the mountains. Then when we got to Seaton, at this end of the lake, the mountains became much more precipitous and less covered with trees. And now, at this place, is the most remarkable scenery that I ever remember to have seen. From the banks of the Frazer rise 3 or 4 tiers of high terraces and flats of brown sandy dust or small gravel, with hardly a tree or shrub of any sort on them, and wearing a most desolate, arid look. What freak of nature can have made them it is difficult to conceive. Here and there run little streams whose courses have been diverted for irrigation, and whose neighbourhood are marked by little bright green patches of cultivation. These terraces look low in comparison to the mountains which surround them, but in any other situation they would be high hills. Their brown dust colour has an air of dreariness it is impossible to describe. The reflected sun from them makes this place extremely hot on a bright day. The air is dry and parched. It is, in fact, a desert. No wonder the river is so rapid here: the water must be in a hurry to get away from such an uncongenial spot. The town itself consists of one street with very fair shops, although of course all prices are very high. When I mention this as my opinion I am told that it is nothing to what I shall find a few miles further up the country. There is a nice little church here, disfigured, however, by an ugly white cross on the top. The parson Brown is now up the country. I believe he does very well here from what I hear, and is much liked.[5]

July 20. This morning I rose and breakfasted at reasonable hours and at 11.30 A.M. started from Lilloet. As soon as the horse was saddled he was found to be quite lame. I was very unhappy, as you may suppose, and could not conceive what was the matter. At last, a large iron nail was discovered 1¼ in. into his foot. It was pulled out and hot resin poured into the wound, and then I started on my journey, in company with Mr. Fraser, the son of the man who discovered Fraser River. He proved a very agreeable companion, having previously been a Canadian farmer. He is on his way to the mines to make his fortune, like everyone else. We first rode to a place called Fountain, 8 miles from Lilloet. There we saw a good deal of land, perhaps 150 acres, under cultivation. All this land can only be cultivated by irrigation, and it is wonderful to see from what distances water has been brought. We rested at Fountain 4 upwards of an hour, and fed both ourselves and our horses. We crossed the Fraser at Lilloet by a ferry – a flat bottomed boat hauled over by a rope. We arrived at the water's edge just as the boat had arrived, and asked how soon it would be going back again. The ferry man said about 20 minutes. We waited upwards of ½ an hour and then asked how soon he would go. He said, "Well, I guess my dinner is nearly ready, and I shall not go until I have had that." So there we had to wait till his dinner was ready, and then until he had leisurely eaten it. After crossing the ferry we fell in with a man called Dodge who proved an agreeable companion. He was owner of several roadside inns and also of several drays and teams of mules. He came out here in 1858 with a little property, which he soon lost and then commenced again without a cent. He is now very prosperous and well-to-do. He gave us much interesting information about the early days of the colony before there were roads and houses. After a good rest at Fountain we started again, and at the 17 mile House, more generally known as the Big Frenchman's, we stopped again for refreshment. On our way we saw several little farms and gardens, looking very flourishing but all kept alive by irrigation. At the Big Frenchman's, I fell in with Captain Martley, the man to whose House I was going. Captain M. has been a captain in the army but he sold out. He has now a flourishing farm, and the Bishop knows him well and thinks highly of him. I introduced myself to him and told him I was coming to his House, so he asked me to come and stay there, which I joyfully accepted. So we rode on together. Captain M. owns a road side inn known as Martley's. We passed this first at 22 miles from Lilloet and then rode off the main road to his private house 2 miles further. Here I was introduced to Mrs M. and his 3 little children. From his house I write now, after a capital supper of toast, cream and fresh butter, etc. Our road today has been through the valley of the Frazer, with high mountains on either side and the road running along or winding round some of the same ugly mud and gravel flats that disfigure Lilloet. This house is at the foot of Pavillion Mountain where the pretty scenery begins.[6] The natives we have passed today have been decidedly better looking, not so flat in the face, and much more intelligent looking. We passed many on the road coming from the valleys in the interior, to fish for the salmon on the river. On my way across the Lilloet ferry I was asked by an Indian if I was la plate,[7] that is, the priest. I indignantly spurned the accusation. Subsequently, several Indians in passing me crossed themselves, and I was again asked the question. I could not imagine why I was treated with all this respect, but I afterwards learnt that the Indians recognised the Bishop's horse. They are always in the habit of seeing it ridden by some great episcopal swell such as a bishop or an archdeacon, so they thought I must be some such swell. It is remarkable that they should be so observant, as this horse cannot have passed up and down more than ½ a dozen times. I also had the sides of my large wide-awake hat looped up, which may also have given me an ecclesiastical appearance in their eyes, and I wear no moustache, which may also have impressed them.

July 21. 1863. I have just got up after a delicious night's rest, lulled to sleep by the gurgling of a little stream close to the house last night. It is as lovely a morning as it is easy to conceive. This happy valley presents a beautiful appearance. But I am summoned to my toilet.

Let me try and describe to you this house. In the first place it is called the Grange. It is but one storey high and built entirely of the logs. The sides are of large squared logs, and the roof is of small round logs covered with earth and having barley, etc., growing on the top. It is a rambling house of no particular shape, having had a room added here and another there just as it was wanted. There's no attempt at furniture yet; Captain M. has not yet made enough money to be able to afford that sort of thing. I write now from the largest room in the house. It is about 20 ft. by 22 and 10 feet high. It is to be a sitting room some day, but I fancy is not much used at present. The interstices between the logs are filled up with mud, neatly plastered on. At present the kitchen seems to be the room most used. Captain M. has 3 children; one little girl of about 5 years of age, a sweet little thing. He has also a small baby and a boy of about 7. The little girl has just come in to say good morning, and put her arms round my neck and gave me a sweet little kiss.

Compared with the aridity of the country we have passed through, this is a charming spot, quite a happy valley. And from the windows we can see the bright green crops of barley, just turning yellow, and quantities of land covered with light bushes, that will soon be cleared and cultivated. It would be quite hopeless for me to attempt to make even a Chinese sketch of these lovely mountains and of the surrounding scenery. I shall send this letter to you just as it is, but I feel sure that every page contains the words lovely, charming, and beautiful, at least a dozen times. A great deal of this country has been formed by slides; that is, a mountain has crumbled away and is still crumbling away, and has slidden down to the valley and is still sliding down into that valley in the shape of gravel, pebbles and loose angular stones. A slide is the most difficult obstacle the road makers have to overcome.

1.45 P.M. I started from Captain Martley's house with him this morning soon after 10, and we rode together up the Pavillion Mountain to what is called the 29 mile House. As soon as we began to ascend the mountain, the scenery entirely changed and became quite park like, the ground undulating and trees standing in grass. I had been led to expect that it would be very pretty, and I was not disappointed. At the 29 mile House Captain M. left me to pursue my way alone, and through such delightful country one does not feel lonely. Moreover, we passed many travellers, going both ways, who were glad to exchange a hearty good day. The road up and down the mountain is a great work and does the contractors much credit. In many places the ground is beautifully carpeted with wild flowers. The mosquitoes begin to be troublesome, so I cannot write much more. My horse is picking up some delicate bits of grass while I write. The weather is lovely and fine, and nothing could be more enjoyable than an excursion like this. Frequently I come to a little lake bosomed among the mountains, like a mirror, and of a deep blue colour. But I think I must pack up my letter again and continue my journey.

9.30 P.M. After my rest at the foot of Pavillion Mountain, which lasted a little better than ½ an hour, I rode on to Clinton, whence I now write.

July 21. 1863. 9.30 P.M. The last part of my road lay along a valley lightly timbered, with the pine trees standing at a little distance from each other in grass, having a very picturesque effect. At about 43 miles from

Lilloet I met the Gold Escort, among whom were many friends.[8] They were much astonished to see me, as you may suppose, and I was much pleased to see them en route. They looked pretty dusty and fagged, but in good spirits. I reached Clinton at 4 P.M. It consists of 4 or 5 houses and a saw mill moved by water power. It is intended that there should be a town here and the town lands are to be sold in a few days. It is very doubtful whether any one will be found to buy them. This is the furthest point I reach. Tomorrow I start for Victoria again, by Lytton and Yale. So far as I have gone I have not found it nearly as hard travelling nor have I had to rough it nearly as much as I had been led to expect. The food here is the worst I have met with as yet, but for tea I had ham, lettuces and milk and bread, so I am not much to be pitied. Tonight I am going to sleep on the floor for the first time, and save a dollar by it.

July 22. This morning I felt unwell when I got up but this evening am rather better; but I have been quite uncomfortable all day. I have taken plenty of quinine which perhaps has done me good. At 10.10 A.M. I left Clinton and at 1.10 had gone 14 miles to a House called Scotty's. There I stopped for 20 minutes to lunch off bread, butter and milk, and started again. At 2.30 having passed the 18 mile House from Clinton known as McCleans and feeling very seedy I tied up the horse and lay down by the road side under a tree; at 3.20 the mosquitoes drove me on again. At 4.30 I reached a House called The Mountain Inn 5 miles from Cornwall's which I reached at 5.30. This House is kept by 2 brothers who are farmers and to whom I brought a letter of introduction, but they were both absent. After leaving Clinton this morning the first 10 miles lay through beautiful country abounding in water, grass, and trees standing singly. But afterwards the country became pretty only as a distant view, the soil being very dry, arid and barren. My road today has extended over a distance of 30 miles.[9]

July 23. I started this morning from Cornwalls at 8.30 A.M. The weather was very fine, indeed quite hot and sultry. The trail lay over a hill where was very pretty scenery, and even grass among the trees. After riding for about 10 miles parallel to the Buonaparte River, from the top of the hill I had a splendid view of the Thompson River. Then descending the hill I came to the R.E. camp on the river, 18 miles from Cornwall's. Here are about 60 men employed making the road under command of Lieut. Palmer R.E. With him is Doctor Oliver, and here I shall sleep tonight.[10] It is quite refreshing to come upon this piece of civilisation in this rugged country. The officers' tents are pitched in a lovely little thicket through which murmurs a little brook which supplies them with water for every purpose; while in another place the branches are cut away and twined over head to make a sitting room impervious to the sun's rays. It is a lovely and romantic spot. After I had been there about an hour, namely at 2 P.M., a thunder storm came down with wind and rain, which cooled the air most pleasantly. The men have a tough bit of road making to do here where the road is to wind round a steep bluff on the side of the river. On my journey today I passed several green patches where vegetables had been persuaded to grow by dint of much irrigation; and I think that by this means much more of this now dry parched up land might be brought under cultivation.

July 24. This morning after breakfast, at about 8 o'clock, I left with regret the R.E. camp. I rode 6 miles to the ferry across the Thompson River, where a large flat bottomed boat runs across on a rope. The river was rapid and it would have been unpleasant if the rope had broken, which it sometimes does. From the ferry I rode to a House on the Nincomin River called the Nincomin House, distant from the ferry 12 miles. There I stopped to rest my horse and take some lunch. There I was joined by a Mr Wilson, a butcher living at the ferry, who rode into Lytton with me, making altogether 29 miles.[11] The last part of our ride was through a very pretty ravine; the road winding along near the top while the river was foaming and roaring beneath. The road is a remarkable piece of engineering but I hardly expect that it will last long without needing repairs. It crosses many slides which will probably give way next spring and the road will always be a great expense. O! I forgot to mention that the day I left Clinton I passed a few camels in a field grazing.[12] I believe that they have not been found to be a good speculation. My horse was much terrified at them, and could hardly be persuaded to pass them. Lytton is situated on the Fraser just where it is joined by the Thompson. It is much the same sort of looking place as Lilloet but smaller and more confined in appearance. I think it is rather a gainer in this respect, for the large expanse of the Lilloet flats is any thing but pleasant to the eye. A Mr Ball, the magistrate here, has received me very kindly.[13] I arrived here at about 3 P.M. Mr Wilson proved a most entertaining companion. His father and mother were both English but he says he is a Yankee. He was born and brought up in New Jersey. He says that his father was an austere man and that when he was a little boy he used to feel it mighty hard to be wailed by a foreigner.[14] He is a northerner but has no sympathy for black folk. Little can be said to describe Lytton. It just consists of a few wooden houses in the valley of the Fraser where it opens out a little into dry arid flats and is surrounded by high mountains. Within a couple of miles of the town, however, are some small farms and large gardens which are very productive because well watered by irrigation. Otherwise this is a terribly dry place. It is very healthy and there are no mosquitoes. The only trees are the pine trees; a sort of white pine with a red bark and prickly leaves – little spikes, in fact.

July 25. This morning at 10 I started from Lytton and rode 15 miles to the ½ way House, which I reached at 1.10 P.M. There I unsaddled my horse and gave him a feed of hay and also fed myself and took 40 winks. There I met Mr. Robson, the Wesleyan parson stationed at Yale, on his way to follow the route by which I had come down.[15] We were able to inform each other mutually of the roads before us. I believe him to be a good man. When he was stationed at Nanaimo he took a trip with me in the gun boat to Comax. I started again from the ½ way House at 4.10 P.M., and after journeying 2 or 3 miles the whole aspect of the country suddenly changed. With the exception of Pavillion Mountain and the neighbourhood of Clinton, the air since I left Lilloet has been hot and dry like the air at the top of the grand staircase at Claydon on a very cold winter's day – so dry indeed that it became necessary to keep my mouth entirely shut and in- and exhale through the other organ provided by nature. But soon after leaving the ½ way House the hill sides became covered with bushes and shrubs, etc., and the air became cool and moist. I passed gardens and fields of wheat which did not appear to require irrigation and were thriving. Indeed I had been told at Lytton to expect this and it was very remarkable. I attribute it to the neighbourhood of mountains whose summits are perpetually covered with snow all the year round which probably attract and condense moisture. I passed many diggings, principally worked by Chinamen. The abundance of water in every part of this country through which I have travelled is a remarkable feature in its favour. I reached the small village of Boston Bar after a further journey of 11 miles, making a total run for today of 32 miles. On approaching the houses I saw gardens. "Good," said I; "this looks well for vegetables for supper." Presently I saw cows. "Good for milk," said I. Shortly afterwards, bullocks. "Good for beef," said I. And all these delightful anticipations to a hungry traveller were borne out by results. I put up at the House of a Frenchman. As soon as I arrived I explained to him that I knew the character of his country men for good cooking, and I expected him to keep it up. Not only was it a national characteristic, I said, but his House stood pre-eminent on this road. He looked immensely flattered. I said I was not difficult to please, provided every thing was clean. He promised it should be, and nobly kept his word. Did I speak French? he asked. "But a few words," I replied. He was ravished. Had I ever been in France? "A few days," I said. He was enchanted. Had he any eggs? I asked. "None!" He became desolated. To arouse him from his despair, I asked for a glass of water. He flew to get it, and the whole evening has diverted me with his amusing French exaggerations. He has a sparkling little black eyed daughter whose name as nearly as I can make out is Aniseed pronounced in French. Altogether I find that I have fallen into good but not splendid quarters.

July 26. Yesterday when about 10 miles from Boston Bar, 3 or 4 natives came running past me calling out, shouting at the top of their voices, while abreast of them a canoe was paddling down the most rapid portions of the river, containing 4 men gesticulating violently and working most energetically. Presently the men on the bank came to a village where 3 of them got into a canoe and pushed off in pursuit of the first comers. Presently a turning of the river hid them from my sight, and I have heard nothing since except that the first canoe contained an Indian who had just committed a murder and was trying to escape. I could not but admire the courage and dexterity with which they shot through the whirling eddies and boiling rapids of the river when every moment their little canoe seemed on the point of being swamped. I left my quarters at Boston Bar this morning at 4.30 A.M. and rode about 3½ miles to a place where the road is not yet completed. There it became necessary to unload my horse and carry my traps along the unfinished road while an Indian led the horse over a very rugged mountain. This operation took me about 10 minutes and the horse nearly an hour, and when we met he was very much done up and had evidently had hard travelling. This spot is called the Chinaman's Bluff and is a very difficult piece of engineering. Here there was a clear descent of upwards of 1000 feet down to the river. The mountains here are very contracted on each side of the river, those to the W. being topped with perpetual snow. After leaving the bluff the road lay for a few miles along good ground by really remarkable instances of engineering skill. I noticed here, as in many other places, trees growing out of the solid rock; and I carefully examined them and can say positively that there was no earth round their roots. Also where the rock had been blasted away in making the road, I saw roots of the trees above, growing in the solid rock, and forcing it asunder. Presently I came to another place where the road was unfinished and had a toilsome bit of climbing for both horse and man over a rugged mountain. At 8.50 I reached the camp of the Messrs Trutch, the road contractors, at a distance from Boston Bar of 11½ miles by the newer road, but 15 by the way the horse had come.[16] I passed several places where mining for gold is still carried on by Chinamen and the natives. They average from 4 to 10 dollars a day and yet such diggings have no attraction for white men. They must go to Cariboo through much hardship and suffering with the hope of quickly making their fortune. I saw 2 decrepit old native women digging and learned that they easily washed out 3 and 4 dollars a day each. This was where the Nincomin River runs into the Thompson. One of the most picturesque sights I have seen has been the natives fishing for salmon. You are perhaps struck by some very romantic gorge or cañon on the river where the mountains close in like 2 massive stone walls on either side and the water dashes through with increased rapidity, furiously lashing the grey water-worn rocks and throwing up sheets of spray, perhaps a place almost fearful to behold, when the eye is caught by a few frail sticks projecting over the river and the bright colour of the Indian's blanket as he sits with a landing net in his hand catching salmon. The immensity of the scale on which the rest of the picture is represented makes the man appear like a Lilliputian imp perched on a few frail twigs, although doubtless they are strong poles and the man is of ordinary stature. There he will patiently sit hour after hour with no view but the whirling and eddying waters, no sound but the roaring and foaming of the stream and no occupation but the monotonous one of plying his landing net at the end of a long pole. The most romantic gorges are the best suited for their purposes as the fish have a narrower channel through which they must pass. Nature works on a grand scale in these parts. The eye easily becomes deceived as to size. A pebbly beach turns out when approached to be a mass of huge boulders, a few young firs a forest of full-grown pines, a heap of stones for mending the road becomes a gigantic slide, a brook becomes a river, a little waterfall a glorious cascade. I spend this day in the Trutch's camp. A suspension bridge is about to be thrown across the Frazer at this place. The piers are completed and the wires will probably be thrown across towards the end of this week. This bridge and the road to Boston Bar will always be a sight worth coming to see; but in its present unfinished state it has been the worst piece of travelling I have met with, and although the distance was so short it has quite knocked me up for the day.

Monday. July 27. 1863. At 4.50 A.M. I left the Trutch's camp and rode 3 miles to the ferry opposite Spuzzum. The trail lay through bush and natural shrubberies which were fresh and pleasant in the early morning air. After ½ an hour I got across the ferry and continued my ride towards Yale, a distance of 11 miles, where I arrived a few minutes before 9. These last 11 miles by the river side showed certainly the most remarkable river scenery I have yet beheld. The Frazer here narrows very much, and the mountains close in on either side, frequently their bases being abrupt precipices, and almost give one the idea that they are about to fall in. Large masses of rock and small islands bar the progress of the river, upon which the water lashes itself with great fury. And where the stream is the most turbid and its rushing noise is the loudest, there sits the Indian with his landing-net, patiently catching salmon. The cañons between Yale and Spuzzum are certainly very striking. Some of these rocks appear like stupendous boulders that have been hurled in by some giant hand. Others appear to have always stood where they now are, and as if the stream had forced its way on either side of them. Some are covered with pine trees and verdure; others are but bare rock. Generally the water heaps up on one side of them and a bank of sand and shingle accumulates on the other. By riding along the banks of rivers for so long at this time of year, I have had an excellent opportunity of judging of the Indian races, for they now come from many miles to the nearest rivers for their fishing. I have within the last few days seen finer specimens of the Indian than I ever saw before; many of the men with eagle eyes and aquiline noses and a few women fairly entitled to be called beautiful. I have been disappointed in the mounted Indians I have seen. I had pictured to myself that they would have had among them some sort of rude chivalry. But no! Their horses were miserably wretched and poor because they begin to work them as colts and consequently they die at an early age and are never allowed to reach their full size and strength. Yale is a small place, with, however, more signs of activity and life in it than either Douglas, Lilloet or Lytton. As the head of steam boat navigation on this route to the mines it will doubtless increase rapidly in importance as soon as this road is completed, which will not be before next spring unless more energy is shown in the matter.

July 29. 1863. Monday was spent at Yale in considerable anxiety lest no steamer should arrive to take me to N. W. In the evening, however, the Hope arrived, much to my satisfaction. I drank tea with the magistrate, Mr Saunders who married a Miss Moresby, niece of Admiral M. The clergyman, Mr Reeves, was at Shang-hae for some time, and has stayed at the Rectory in 1857 when you came to talk to him about Chinese matters.[17] I saw near Yale some very good specimens of the Indian winter houses. They consist of deep round holes dug in the ground, the earth being thrown up all round as an embankment. They are then roofed over with poles and earth, a little square hole being left in the top to let the inhabitants in and the smoke out. The river from Yale to Hope and to about 10 miles below it, runs through mountains of great height and very close to each other. After that, the hills are lower and the river is not so confined. Hope is a desolate and deserted place, generally now known as Forlorn Hope. When Hope was the head of navigation, it was a place of some importance, but now grass grows in the streets. I think, however, that it is a place likely to increase again.

We reached N. W. at 3 P.M. on Tuesday, yesterday, having started that morning at 6 A.M. Here I found the mosquitoes rather bad. We left New Westminster in the Otter this morning at 11, and are now on our way to Victoria. The mosquitoes were such a plague last night that I hardly got any sleep.[18]

July 30. 1863. I reached Victoria in the Otter last night soon after seven, and reached home before nine: thus ends a very pleasant and instructive trip, which I have endeavoured faithfully to portray to you day by day: great allowance must be made for errors in grammar or style, as much as been written when I have been very tired, or writing under considerable difficulties.

Believe me, my dear Father,

Your affectionate Son,
Edmund Hope Verney

H.M.S. Grappler. August 3. 1863. Esquimalt. The Small Bower

My dear Father, The mail arrived last night, bringing letters up to the first of June. After the adventures of my trip in British Columbia, I am not sorry to be again comfortable settled in my bower, a wiser but a poorer man: my journeyings cost $10. (£2.) a day; near £30. in all, but at any rate I know now something of the neighbouring colony, and its inhabitants. With reference to Freddy, you describe his whereabouts by reference to Bradshaw's railway map: I regret to say that we have not yet arrived at that high state of civilization indicated by a "Bradshaw".

If you have an opportunity of sending me a Dietrischen's almanac for this year, and one for next, the cost to yourself will be one shilling, and the delight of your sun and air, beyond price. I am reading Kinglake's book on the Crimea, and am more interested in it than I have been in any book for a long time; Lascelles has lent it to me: he has a sister who sends him every new book that comes out of any importance. It must be worth anything to have a sister of that sort.[1]

Acland has been spending a couple of days with me, and returned to the Sutlej this morning: I like him.[2]

I will make a point of endeavouring to obtain for you all the information I can about the Russians obtaining possession of the strip of land below Sitka. We have a report here that the Governor has resigned, but do not know whether to place any reliance on it or not. You recommend me to read Uncle Hope's evidence on naval promotion, but I do not know where it is to be seen: perhaps you have sent me an account of it:[3] the only papers I see regularly are the Army and Navy Gazette, the United Service Gazette, and sometimes the weekly despatch:[4] what you tell me about his reference to me is very pleasant indeed to hear, and rejoices me much.

I do not trouble about my promotion now: I do not expect it yet, and can be quite philosophical in attending to the duties of to-day: it was when I was in a state of uncertainty that I was vexed and bothered. As you say you did, so did I: I used to look to the newspapers for my promotion as soon as they arrived: now I am in a much calmer frame of mind, and quite at ease. You know Uncle Hope got his own promotion through being a flag-lieutenant, to a relation.

Colonel Moody is much distressed at Sir Culling Eardley's death; I suppose it was very unexpected.[5]

I am glad you have seen Kerr: he is a good fellow and will get on, I have no doubt. I do not know that I have anything particular to say about the naval promotion committee: without having looked into the subject much, am I not justified in saying that the greater number of our celebrated Naval Heroes have been men pushed forward through private family interest: do you not think that to be a post-captain, and to command a frigate at nineteen would make a hero of any man? I must own that I am inclined to think so, and if I must now give up for myself the hope of being very rapidly advanced, I would not see our glorious Navy without its very young men starting up from time to time, and astonishing the sober old chaps: family interest is no great evil after all, if it is moderated wisely to hinder the advancement of positive fools, and to help on those who have seen service: I do not grudge advancement to Maxse, Seymour, and Erskine, although the latter took a flying leap over my head.[6]

Good bye, my dear Father: I fear it will be a month yet before the Grappler is ready for sea again: believe me;

Your affectionate Son,
Edmund Hope Verney

The Small Bower. Esquimalt. V.I.
August 8. 1863.

My dear Father,

I dined with His Excellency last night, and he was so good as to tell me something about the Stekin Territory and the Russian sea-board. He evidently has a very good opinion of that portion of the continent, and of its climate: he described a plain near the mouth of a river a little north of the Stekin river as a place of surpassing beauty, and he named it Eden: it is well watered by the constant melting of neighbouring glaciers; he visited it in the month of June, and when he had left Fort Simpson a short time before, he had left it cold and dismal: at Eden he found meadows covered with grass two feet in height, watered by streams flowing over pebbly bottoms, and wild-flowers of lovely hues abounding in every part, while the view was bounded by perpetually snow-capped mountains.

The coast is generally of a grand aspect, but monotonous, uninviting and of that sombre character imparted by the unfailing dark green pine: the shores are bold and rocky, and when carefully surveyed will doubtless be found to contain many good anchorages.

The Governor appears to believe that both for gold mining, mineral wealth, and agricultural capabilities, the Stekin Territory can well compare with British Columbia and that if ever it is colonized there will be no difficulty in getting back the Russian sea-board; but that at present the latter colony ought to absorb all the immigration and European interest that is directed to this part of the world. He believes that at the time the seaboard was signed away to the Russians, it was believed to be worthless, except for fur trading, as one of the French Kings is said to have signed away Canada, under the impression that he was only parting with seven hundred miles of snow.

The Governor does not seem to think that the Home Government care very much about this line of seaboard, or that it would be very advisable to open the question.

I am in great glee just now, because my eggs are being hatched: all my ducks appeared in one day, nine, and today I have nine chickens and three not yet born. All my attempts to establish pigeons have heretofore proved a failure: I expect two pair from New Westminster this evening.

August 14. Having just arisen from my downy couch; the hour of the day being Ca 6.30. A.M., I do perceive from my chamber window the mail steamer Brother Jonathan, lying alongside the wharf at Esquimalt. When the steamer brings English letters, she generally flies an English ensign forward, which the Brother Jonathan does not display today: when the mail steamer does not bring letters, we yet hear a good deal of news, and sometimes receive letters that have come round by New York.

Yesterday afternoon, I hired a horse to go to Victoria: I dropped a small parcel and had to dismount to pick it up, when the horse broke away from me: I tried unsuccessfully to catch him, and after three hours was obliged to give up the chase, and as soon as I did so, the horse went quietly back to his own stables.

When I look round for news to send you from this part of the world, I am nonplussed: we are receivers of news rather than dispensers: I dined last night with the Admiral, where I met the Governor, and words he spoke certainly favoured the idea that he expects to be superseded shortly: it is reported that he has resigned, which I dare say is true.[1]

No letters from you by the mail.

Your affectionate Son,
Edmund Hope Verney

H.M.S. Grappler. Esquimalt. V.I.
August. 18. 1863.

My dear Father,

A Good deal is said and thought here about the debate in the House of Lords on the second of July: two things particularly strike me: in the first place Lord Donoughmore states that a ship cannot go from Esquimalt to Victoria without passing within cannon-shot of San Juan: this shows that he can not even have glanced at the map.

The second point is that the Duke of Newcastle tells their Lordships that there is no American armed force at San Juan; that it has been withdrawn: I am surprised that he has not received better information on this point: you doubtless know that there are sixty or seventy soldiers. I suppose that in a mail or two, we shall hear what is really going to be done about these colonies.[1]

August. 20. The mail steamer arrived this evening bringing letters from you of June. 14. and June. 30., to my great delight. How charmed and happy you must be with our littel bodye at home: your accounts of her do not give one the idea of a very stalwart damsel, but we can trust all that to Our Father, I am sure.

I sent you some cones and pine seeds, but you shall have some more as you desire: I am anxious to hear whether any of the seeds I sent home last year have appeared this year. Many thanks for the bright extract from Mama's letter, and for Mr. Pritchard's letter:[2] you write to me long, long letters, and I read them with avidity and delight, but I fear that if you write so much to me other people lose their rightful share of your correspondence.

There seems at length to be some prospect of the repairs of the Grappler being brought to a close: steam was raised in the boilers this afternoon, to see where there might be any leaks, and there were found to be very few, and the trial was considered satisfactory. On Saturday, we shall get up steam again and go out for two or three hours run to see that the engines work satisfactorily: after this, it will take a week or two to cover the boilers in, and to lay down the deck, after which the "Grappler" will be again a sea-going ship. You may be sure that I shall be delighted when all our repairs are concluded: I believe that the Admiral has a trip to Fort Rupert in store for us.

When you write again, please tell me something about Mrs. Robert Webb: you have not mentioned her in any letters latterly: how are her children? I think I remember that you gave her a piano: I hope her little ones are prospering on it.[3]

I am aware that my letters lately have been short and empty: I can only ascribe it to the very monotonous life I have been leading, and I hope that my British Columbian journal will have atoned for it in some small degree. I was much pleased today to receive a letter from Randal Plunkett:[4] it shall be answered very soon with others in shorthand which have gladdened my heart this evening: but I cannot undertake to answer many letters by the same steamer as they arrive: a considerable portion of the few hours the steamer remains in Esquimalt is taken up in official correspondence with friend Beeby and others.

Aug. 21. Today I begin bringing some of my things back to the Grappler, and when she is ready for sea, I shall live on board some time while a chimney is built in my house to make it habitable in winter without danger of fire. My twelve chickens are beginning to fly, and give their mamma considerable uneasiness.

Your affectionate Son,
Edmund Hope Verney

H.M.S. Grappler. Esquimalt. V.I.
September. 2. 1863.

My dear Father,

As the steamer will probably arrive tomorrow from San Francisco, I think it is time to prepare a letter, although I fear it will be as uninteresting as most of its predecessors. The Grappler is at present the only ship in port, as the Admiral has gone on a cruize in the Sutlej, taking with him the Forward and Cameleon: his intention was to go first to Nanaimo, then to Burrard's Inlet, and then to anchor off the mouth of the Frazer river: he was seen steaming into Burrard's Inlet on Saturday, so I expect his return every hour: artificers from the Sutlej were left behind to complete all repairs, and I hope that next week, the Grappler will be again a sea-going ship.

As soon as the ship is ready I intend to go and live on board, while a chimney is built in the Small Bower to make it habitable in winter: I have just completed a verandah and a porch: one of my own men built it, and my landlord allowed me five months rent to buy the materials, but that did not quite cover it: I expect that the chimney will cost about as much again, £5. I hope that a chimney will keep the house so warm, that I shall not have to paper the rooms.

I have reason to hope that when the Admiral comes back, I shall take him up to Fort Rupert: it is a place I have long wished to see, and I think he would be a pleasant companion.

I think of you at home; probably to-day you have a few friends come down for a day or two's shooting, and Freddy is making great havoc among the cock hares, not to mention the pheasants: it must be a wapping opportunity for him. I shall doubtless get a little shooting if I go up the coast.

(September 3.) In the absence of any more interesting subject to write about, I think you are always interested to know exactly what I am doing. The time is 7. A.M.: I have just finished my morning cup of coffee which Henry has brought me, and I hear him at his breakfast in the kitchen: I write from my sitting room which has not yet been swept and dusted, and I must make haste, or Henry will be here to turn me out: the door and window are wide open, and when I turn my head I see the glassy waters of the harbour, and the more distant pine clad hills bathed in the glorious early sunlight: the white buildings on Thetis Island, are whiter than ever,[1] and along-side the wharf lies the Grappler: nearer to me is a small boat pulling up to the house, while in front of the window march three turkeys in review; then comes a hen with a light squadron of a dozen chickens in the greatest disorder: then another hen, with very little tail at all to speak of, and that crooked, with a stately array of nine young ducks: then a white cock flaps his wings, gives a loud crow, and, apparently by way of a joke, makes a dive among the ducks, scattering them in all directions; in their confusion some fly to the first hen, for refuge, but get well pecked for their pains, and run back to the crooked-tailed lady; by this time I have heard the keel of the little boat grating on the beach, and the milkman appears at the gate: as soon as the little click of the latch is heard, out fly my dogs Claydon and Jacky, barking furiously as if he were a theif or a tax-gatherer, but he is not alarmed, as he knows it is only their fun: the morning is very cool, and *fresh*: for my house has so many trees to the eastward, that it does not catch the early sun: I shall probably cut some of them down in the winter. And now, even while the pen is in my hand, behold the mail steamer coming round the point: the little column of white smoke darts out from her bulwarks, and the ring of her gun announces to our world the arrival of the mail[.]

And now follows another event, very characteristic of these parts: scarcely has the steamer secured to the wharf, when a dense white wall of fog rolls in at the harbours mouth: whether it will remain there, or whether it will spread over the whole view: whether it will last for a short time, and then be dissipated by the sun, or whether it will dull our whole day, it is impossible to predict: the fogs here are the most capricious, and the most partial that I have ever seen: this fog, half an hour earlier, might have delayed the mail for a long time, and even now may very much embarrass the ships the admiral has with him.

The steamer carries no English ensign, so I fear that she does not bring the Southampton mail, but I may receive a letter from you viâ New York.

Noon. As I expected, the steamer has brought no letter for me, unless there be one in the Admiral's bag which I have in my cabin, but must not open: this is rather tantalizing, as you will understand: an officer of the Bacchante has arrived, to go to the hospital: he reports that that ship has been severely visited by fever, and that there have been several deaths.

The Admiral may be expected tomorrow or the next day from Burrard's inlet.

Good bye, my dear Father, with love to all at home, believe me,

Your affectionate Son,
Edmund Hope Verney

Private.

The Small Bower. Esquimalt. V.I.
September 4. 1863.

My dear Father,

Yesterday I dispatched an epistle to you, and today the Admiral has not arrived: in my cabin lie the unopened despatch bags, containing doubtless a letter from you. However, I have no doubt that the Chief will be here tomorrow.

Perhaps the most interesting intelligence that has arrived is Mr. Fortescue's speech in the House, about these colonies: he has seen the way in which Mr. McClure wrote out about the Governor, possibly you helped him to it, and he has given an opinion on it which will have a good effect here: had he spoken still more strongly, it would have done no harm. From the tone of his speech, I fear that he has chiefly gained his knowledge of these parts by conversation or letters with a *few* people: doubtless he has consulted the *best*, but he does not appear to have the subject at his finger's ends: I suppose that really the fact is, when a man has *all* the colonies to look after, he cannot have them *all* at his finger's ends: in short, he has not fingers enough,[1]

From what I can hear of Mr. Langford, I think he must be a good sort of man. I hear that the Hudson's Bay Company treated him very badly, glutted the market when he had corn to sell, so that he could make no profit, and succeeded in nearly ruining him: but then I also hear that he was not judicious, that he made virulent attacks upon the Company, and declared open war, so of course the end of it was that the weaker went to the wall: he was hospitable, popular with the navy, and of refined tastes and habits: whatever right he may have had on his side seems to have been thrown away by his want of tact and judgment. But, of course, this is all hearsay, as I never saw him.[2]

It seems almost a pity that Mr. Fortescue is willing to grant the papers required: why stir up mud? You, in England, cannot sit in judgment on the officials out here: neither your acquittal, nor your condemnation would have much weight, indeed, the former certainly none: and suppose that the papers required to be produced should appear to prove all the officials here to be rogues, you cannot supersede them without a fair trial, and you only produce an immense deal of ill-feeling here, and place these presumed rogues in an unfair and awkward position.

That there are more than one or two officials in these colonies who ought to be superseded immediately, I firmly believe, but the person to judge of that, and of the way that it ought to be brought about must be on the spot. As I have said in former letters, the governors who are sent out now, ought to be very first-rate men, men of high unblemished character, men of great self-control and firmness, shrewd men, who can see as far into a milestone as most. Many of the salaries ought to be raised, as good men will not come for the present salaries: I can believe that it might be desirable to bring out men from England expressly to hold some appointments, but this would be an extreme measure that a Governor would hardly like to adopt until he had been here a little time, and was sure there were no suitable people in the colony.

Now I will say a few words about individuals, and for the convenience of writing I will speak positively: you, I know, think as well as myself, that it is a dangerous thing to speak positively in terms of disapprobation of anybody, but especially do I feel it in the present case, so pray understand that if I were speaking I should use many more words, and merely hint what in writing privately to you there is no harm in saying outright.[3]

Mr. Cameron, of course, ought to be superseded at once: he is a good man in many ways, but a very inferior man, and utterly unfit to be a chief-justice.

Mr. Cary ought to be superseded, but I doubt if there is any-one here fit to be Attorney-General: he is a vulgar man, and a superficially sharp fellow; he may be honest and honourable in private life, but he really seems to think that honesty and honour may be dispensed with in a public character. I am also of opinion that the amount of private property he has may fairly be considered a disqualification, although such a sentiment must seem strange to your ears.

Mr. Pemberton, the Surveyor General, and Mr. Pearse, his assistant, have both more property than they ought to have in those positions: if they do decide fairly in vexed land questions which affect themselves, they will never get the credit of it.

Mr. Watson, the Treasurer is a sterling fellow, and scrupulously honourable and upright; he is far too young for his appointment, but even if he could be superseded I do not know where a better man could be got.

I do not like the colonial secretary personally, yet I do not know why: perhaps he is a little overbearing, and apt to forget that he is only a paymaster in the navy, after all: one thing I am sure of; if well kept in order he might be a good servant, but he would never make a good master.

Alston, the Registrar General, is a gentleman: he is very quiet, and one never hears anything about him.

Mr. Crease, the Attorney-General for B.C. is an empty fellow, always making the stalest & most stupid jokes.

Mr. Begbie, Chief-justice of B.C, may be clever, but he is a tall blustering man, hasty and partial: not at all the calm impartial judge: he has more than once given very great offence to barristers, by what they have called his overbearing insolence; but he sings a good song, in a fine deep base voice.

In the government of this colony of Vancouver Island, I am sure that the Hudson's Bay element is too strong, and does not exert a beneficial influence. Great changes require to be made in nearly every department, but he who undertakes them will have no light task, and no small responsibility.

Your affectionate Son,
Edmund Hope Verney

H.M.S. Grappler. Esquimalt. V.I.
September 12. 1863.

My dear Father,

This day we have been inspected by the Admiral: he came on board at 9 A.M. and we got under weigh, and went out to the Race Rocks

Lighthouse: afterwards we fired at a target, and performed all sorts of drills &c, which were very edifying: it rained repeatedly during the day, which considerably damped our ardour, and made the whole thing a great bore: the Grappler may at last be said to be fairly fit for service, but we had carpenters working up to a late hour last night, so we were only just ready for inspection.

I am now living altogether on board, and a chimney will be built at the bower, after which I shall lend it to Mr. Palmer of the Engineers and the Archdeacon's daughter: they are to be married on the sixth of next month, and to spend their honeymoon at my house.[1]

On Monday or Tuesday, I am going up to Fort Rupert, to take up twenty of the Cameleon's men to relieve twenty of the Sutlej's men who are lent to the Beaver, surveying vessel: I have never been so far north, and I look forward with great pleasure to this trip, which will probably occupy about ten days: after my return, I shall most likely be sent up still further north to Bentinck Arm, where it is said that the Indians are inclined to be a little troublesome.

This morning the Cameleon sailed for the West Coast, Barclay Sound, and Nootka Sound, where there are Indian difficulties to be arranged: she will probably return in ten days or a fortnight. The Admiral expects to leave this for the South on or about the twenty-fifth.[2]

September 14. This morning the mail steamer arrived, bringing among other letters, yours of July. 13: two months in coming out: now I will send this letter by New York, and you shall see whether or not it will reach you more quickly than usual.

Tomorrow I shall probably start for Comax & Fort Rupert: I hope I may have a pleasant trip, but certainly the weather is not promising at present. We have been having several rainy days, and short fitful gales of wind.

You mention that Adeane has been much longer in the service than I have: that may be, but he is only twenty-five days senior to me as a lieutenant, so I do not think he is so very much to be pitied after all: though of course you were quite right to condole with Miss Adeane on the subject of his promotion: it is so nice to condole with a young lady about her poor dear brother.[3]

When this bad weather is over, we shall have an Indian summer, and then the regular winter will set in: your skates are hanging up in the small Bower, in as good order as when they left England.

With love to all at home, believe me, your affectionate Son,

Edmund Hope Verney

H.M.S. Grappler. Forward Bay.
September 17. 1863.

My dear Father,

On Tuesday morning we left Victoria, and proceeded to San Juan, and on to Nanaimo: yesterday we left Nanaimo and went to the Comax: this morning we left the Comax at five, and anchored here at 5.P.M.

Forward Bay is on Cracroft Island in Johnstone's Straits, about 43 miles from Fort Rupert: we expect to meet the "Beaver" at Fort Rupert tomorrow; when I shall turn over to her an assistant surgeon and twenty men from the "Cameleon" and take back a corresponding number of the "Sutlej's" men to Esquimalt. Since we left Victoria, we have had nothing but the most lovely weather, which was better than I had ventured to hope for at this time of the year; most heartily rejoiced am I to be again cruizing in the "Grappler", instead of being laid up at Esquimalt.

The Comax has hitherto been the most northern point of my cruizing, so all this country is new to me: it is very picturesque: on Vancouver Island, to the Southward of where we are lying, is Mount Palmerston, a fine bold mountain, five thousand feet high, capped with eternal snow: the sun has been very clear for this last day or two, and when entering Baynes Sound yesterday, we saw Mount Baker, a hundred and ten miles off, a very remarkable distance.

We shall probably return to Esquimalt too late to send letters by the next mail, but as I last wrote by New York, and told you I had this cruize in view, you will doubtless not be astonished if you receive no letter.

September 22. On Friday last we reached Fort Rupert, and started again the following day, and this afternoon we anchored in Esquimalt. All things considered, we have had a most successful cruize, fine weather nearly every day: there is not much to be said about Fort Rupert: it was an interesting place to see as it consists of one of the old Hudson Bay Company's forts, and its adjacent Indian village: the premises struck me as being beautifully clean, and the buildings and the stockade were strong creditable pieces of work: indeed it is remarkable that such good buildings should have been erected, when we consider what an out-of-the-way spot on the face of the globe Fort Rupert was ten or twelve years ago: indeed it can hardly be described as a place of fashionable resort now: the natives are very quiet, dirty, tame, and uninteresting.[1]

The coast at the north end of Vancouver Island, and in British Columbia in the corresponding latitudes, is very rugged, and indented with many more and much deeper inlets than are marked in even the best maps. An inlet, now named Kingcome Inlet, has just been discovered, as large, and running as far into the continent as any yet known: it is about in the same latitude as Fort Rupert, but perhaps a little further north.

The Admiral intends to sail in the Sutlej the day after tomorrow, and the Cameleon will be left as our senior officer: I shall be very sorry to lose the Admiral, as he and his staff have been very civil and kind to me.

September 23. I feel bound to communicate my troubles to you occasionally, or else you are apt to imagine that I have none, and that I lead too happy a life: my ship's steward, who has charge of all my accounts, proved himself a great blackguard some months ago, but during the last two months has been behaving well, so I have been disposed to give him another trial to retrieve his disgrace: he is a capital accountant, writes a first-rate hand, and is thoroughly well up to his work; to-day another hand was offered to me in lieu of him, a dull honest fellow, who would never make a first-rate steward: usually, where two paths present themselves, duty seems to point more particularly to one, but in this case I could see no duty: I chose definitely to retain the bad man, and give him a chance: when I came on board, I found him drunk and had to put him in irons: you can imagine how disappointed I felt, and how anxious I am at this moment lest I should have made the wrong choice. I should feel far more comfortable had I seen that the one course was more my duty than the other.

The Sutlej will sail for the South tomorrow morning, and if there is no wind, she will be towed out by the Grappler: I have been on board dining with the Admiral, and wishing every one "good-bye": I have received much kindness from both the Admiral and his staff: he is exceedingly fortunate in his Secretary.

In a few days we shall start for a long cruize to the North of the Island, visiting Bentinck Arm, and possibly Fort Simpson, and Queen Charlotte's Islands, but the two latter are very uncertain: it will depend in a great measure upon the weather, which at this season of the year is not at all to be relied upon.

September 26. 1863. We bid farewell to the Sutlej on Thursday morning, and then the Grappler sailed across the harbour to a part of the beach where we ground when we want to do anything to the ship's bottom: there we put some packing round the screw shaft, and yesterday we sailed back again, the wind shifting in our favour each day. Our senior officer now is Captain Hardinge of the "Cameleon": it is one of the few disadvantages of my appointment that my senior officer is so frequently changed, without any corresponding change in my duties, so I cannot help drawing comparisons.

We are having a succession of rainy days, which are the reverse of inspiriting, for one is far more dependant upon weather in a new country than in an old one: in a small ship like the "Grappler" I miss the fine large messplace, the cheery messmates, the maindeck promenade, and the band of the "Emerald," especially on a wet day: the majestic solitude of the captain's cabin is but a poor substitute, although I am happy to say there is a sort of satisfaction in a general sense of being on friendly terms with all (3.) the officers, and I think pretty nearly all the men: (although I have not expressed exactly what I mean now.)

September 28. Tomorrow at 6.A.M. I purpose sailing on my northward cruize: if you hear nothing of me for a couple of months, you must not be surprized.

I am delighted to say that Dundas the parson goes with me; I am very glad of this both for the sake of my own men, and of those we are likely to fall in with in out of the way places.[2]

Your affectionate Son,
Edmund Hope Verney

H.M.S. Grappler. Nanaimo. V.I.
October 1. 1863.

My dear Father,

On the twenty-seventh ult. we left Victoria on our northern cruize. At this port we have been taking in coal, of which our usual complement is 24 tons: we have now taken 27 extra tons on deck, making a total of fifty-one tons on board, which ought to take us at least 1200 miles: this great weight of coal brings the ship down in the water a good deal, but does not cover the copper: it is an evil too that will be always decreasing. Tomorrow morning we shall make a start for Comax as our first anchorage. It is pleasure indeed to have Dundas with me, not only because I shall enjoy his society and have a companion, but also because my own men, and those settlers whom we shall visit will have the benefit of his ministry.

October 5. We reached Fort Rupert last night, and this morning started across to the mainland to seek for the "Beaver," to communicate with her and obtain any information we can about the coast: we have not yet succeeded in finding her, and are anchored tonight at the head of the first reach of "Well's pass" which you may see marked in the chart: tomorrow I intend to go round Broughton Is. and out by Fife Sound, when I shall probably pick up the "Beaver" somewhere: the weather has been fine, the sea like glass, and the scenery of surpassing beauty: what is marked in the chart as Broughton Island, is really a group of islands of every size, and covered with trees: in the absence of correct charts the navigation requires considerable care.

October 10. On the sixth we fell in with the Beaver, and proceeded on to Shuchartie Bay, to the north of Fort Rupert, where we fell in with the Carolena, Mr. Duncan's schooner from Metlakatlah: his assistant, Mr. Cunningham was on board, and he came to us, with several of his Christian Indians: they came down into my cabin and were interested in looking at all one's little &cs: afterwards they sang some hymns to us very nicely to-gother [*sic*]; they were a very attractive set of fellows, and when they sang their expression of earnest solemn piety was very touching: they were all very cleanly dressed, and polite in their manners: one was almost absurd in his extreme politeness: and all spoke a few words of English, such as "thank-you, Sir", "good-night" &c: one of them, Robert Hewson, goes with us as pilot and interpreter.[1]

The day after we anchored at Shuchartie, and the next day were wet, and it blew hard, and I had a slight attack of illness, but yesterday we got under weigh again, and with a strong breeze, under sail and steam, passed Cape Caution, entered Fitz-Hugh Sound, and anchored in Safety Cove: this morning we left Safety Cove, and are now under sail in Fitz Hugh Sound: one of the valves in the engine-room broke about an hour ago, but it will soon be all right again, and then we shall go on again right merrilly: the barometer, which has been very low for the last four or five days, is rising, and we have a beautiful day.

October 12. I hardly know whereto I can compare the scenery through which we are steaming: it is very like the Harrison Lake, and the lakes leading to Lilloet, but the mountains on either side are finer, and the cataracts more numerous: this inland navigation is indeed very remarkable: a line-of-battle ship might be brought up here into the interior of the country under the cascade mountains: our weather is wet, I am sorry to say, which somewhat obscures the view, but the glimpses one obtains among the clouds of the snow-capped summits are very fine: the water is deep, in most places fathomless, and there are but few anchorages.

October 14. We anchored off the Bella Coula river the day before yesterday: it is simply the termination of a fiord: a river runs down from the cascade mountains, through perhaps a mile of level country on each side, and beyond that the mountains rise towering up, one behind the other: when we arrived the tops of the more lofty ones had snow on them, but two days bad weather has brought the snow down half-way to the valley: the level land on either side of the river appears to be all deposit from the upper country, and most of it is overflowed from time to time; the river appears to be always undermining, and washing away, in one place, and depositing in another: there is capital shooting on the flats, duck, geese, and teal. Vancouver describes this as the most desolate inhospitable country the most melancholy creature could be desirous of inhabiting: (vol. 1. page 374.): it was even too dreary and lonely for the mussels and cockles they had hitherto met with:[2] can you not picture to yourself the solitary, used-up, misanthropic cockle watching for a fair tide, then slowly detaching himself from his boulder, and shaking the last grain of sand from his pediment, drift down the arm, bidding adieu for ever to this desolate and inhospitable country, and betake himself to join a society of gay and hospitable cockles on Vancouver Island. I dare say Vancouver was not here in the duck season.

There are a few settlers here, who cling to the hope that this may some day be a great route to Cariboo: it is now used a little, and if the country steadily progresses, will perhaps be used more, but I cannot think that it will ever be a great route: wherever one goes, one finds people very enthusiastic about their own settlement, to the exclusion of all others: Alexandria may be reached from here in ten or eleven days, by a foot-traveller: the trail is not good, but is continually being improved: goods are carried up the river in canoes for five-and-twenty-miles, after which they are packed through to Cariboo on horses: last year, one or two pack-trains came down to the river's mouth, but I believe that it is found cheaper, and quicker to send goods up in canoes for the first twenty-five miles.

October 15. 1863. This morning we left Bella Coula, and hope to anchor tonight in Restoration Bay. Yesterday morning, I pulled up the river to the Indian village, in my gig, and having assembled the chiefs, made to them a short oration through the medium of an interpreter: they had stolen a shovel and an axe from one of the settlers, which I required them to give up; this they did, as they were much frightened at the appearance of the gunboat, and the articles were humbly brought to the

Grappler in the afternoon: no punishment was inflicted on the thief, as there had been a regular row, in which some Indian heads had been broken, and the natives had got considerably the worst of it.

The Bella Coula Indians are a very degraded set; they speak a harsh dialect most grating to the ear: we saw them herding together like animals, some quite destitute of clothing.

Today is a dull day, with a leaden sky overhead, through which the brightness of the sun is barely visible: the mountains on each side shew us that these are snow clouds, as high up to the right and left we see that it is snowing hard: it is a regular dull wintry day, but we are very thankful to have it dry down here.

October 18. After leaving Restoration Bay, the chart was found to be so totally incorrect as to be of little or no use, and on the night of the sixteenth we anchored in a narrow channel from which there was no second outlet: yesterday we had to retrace our steps, and, after going much out of our way, found ourselves in Milbank Sound in the afternoon: a canoe came alongside, and an Indian pointed out to us an anchorage: we steamed up to it, and found it to be a very small bay, but affording good shelter from the S.E. wind then blowing, and indeed it became so thick with rain and fog, that I hardly thought it prudent to go out again to look for a better anchorage: the bay was open to the N.W. and at midnight the wind sprang up suddenly, and it blew very hard from West, and W.N.W. for a couple of hours: we dragged our anchor, and drifted alongside the rocks, where we lay till the weather moderated a little, with five fathoms of water on the off side: the corner point of the bay sheltered us just enough to keep the water tolerably smooth: at about three, we hove in our cable, and steamed out in the dark, to my intense relief: we had nearly reached the middle of the East end of the Sound, when we passed a solitary rock to windward: from the darkness of the night, and the plainess with which we could see the white foam breaking over and around the black rock, it must have been less than a ship's length from us: after a night of the greatest anxiety, we anchored this morning at daylight in another bay, three or four miles from the first. I trust I may never spend such a night again.

Beyond having lost a few sheets of copper, the ship does not appear to have suffered in any way: we have lost a small kedge anchor which I dare say we shall pick up tomorrow, if it is fine: from the moment we first dragged our anchor, the glass has been steadily rising. Verily the navigation of these unsurveyed waters calls for the utmost caution and circumspection.

October 22. Yesterday morning we left Milbank Sound, and anchored in Carter's Bay; on Saturday we hope to arrive at Metlakatlah. Our course continues to lie through the most beautiful inland navigation, presenting fresh points of beauty every hour: now it is some grand and lofty snow capped mountain, then some bold cliffs and precipices, then perhaps a sweet little valley, with a torrent rushing down and emptying itself in one broad foaming sheet into the water, or down the steep bare face of the rock comes a slender waterfall, streaming down over the smooth water-worn surface, with many a sheer descent, or slightly glancing off from crag to crag.

And all this is the view from one's own windows, as I may call it, unaccompanied by all the vexations of travelling, bad servants, bad food &c: and it is additionally delightful because I have a charming companion in Parson Dundas.

Some Indians came alongside this morning in a canoe, from whom we bought some beaver, and mountain sheep: I have already eaten beaver, but do not like it much: it is said that the mountain sheep is particularly good.

October 24. 1863. Yesterday morning we arrived at Metlakatlah,[3] and in the afternoon, Dundas and I walked over the village, and heard the children read and sing: fancy fifty Indian children singing "see our oars with feathered spray", and well known catches, pronouncing the words quite as well as English children would, and singing quite as correctly: Mr. Duncan has done nothing incredible at Metlakatlah, as some of his admirers would fain have you believe: he has not converted whole tribes, and miraculously imbued them with a love of eau-de-cologne and kid gloves, but he *has* brought some hundreds of the natives from a state of the most degraded barbarism and the blackest heathendom to a state of civilization and outward christianity which may be quite placed on a par with that of an ordinary English village: the conditions under which a man may become a resident at Metlakatlah are that he must give up all heathen practises, he must obey Mr. Duncan, and he must become a hearer of the Word.

So now there are those people living decently: feeding on nearly the same food as before, with perhaps a few more vegetables; their houses clean; their persons decently clothed, their children educated: superstition banished: the old heathen distrustful scowl vanished, and in its stead a manly open expression of countenance: willing to labour and earn money, and then to spend it wisely: paying taxes, making roads and gardens, building good houses, and forming little trading societies: teatotallers, when they can get tea, strict observers of the sabbath, living in very general harmony.

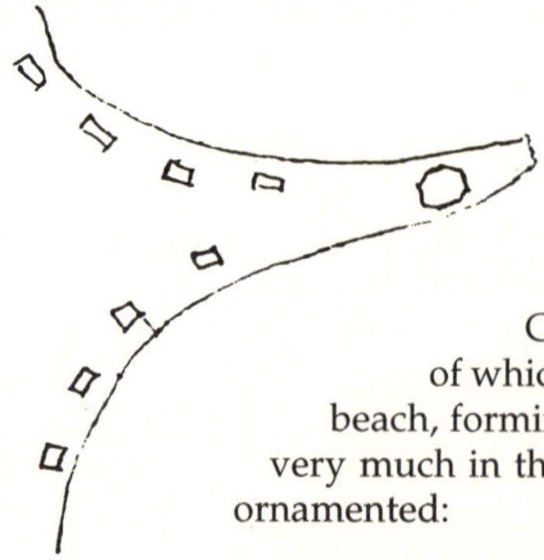

Mr. Duncan is a J.P. for B.C.: two women were brought before him for quarrelling two days ago: both found guilty, and condemned to kiss each other, which was done with great solemnity.

The Mission House, School, or Church, stands on a point, from each side of which sweeps a bay thus with houses on the beach, forming two streets, as it were: they are built very much in the English fashion, and some are neatly ornamented:

October 26. The moment the bells ring for church, every one issues from his house, and they walk up to church in two long lines: there is no waiting for a second bell; none of the thousand and one excuses which we find for staying away from church in England; no one prefers cooking his sunday dinner to going to God's House; no one remains at home because he has no clothes good enough to go to church in; none are too young or too old; all come forth, dressed at least neatly and cleanly, and in two long ranks, march reverently up to the Mission House: it is indeed a very striking sight.

All the houses are, of course, built of logs, which make them warm and comfortable: in the centre of each is some earth and gravel on which are placed the blazing logs, while the smoke ascends through a hole in the roof: some of the houses have regular chimneys, while others have stoves, and some Indians have gardens round their houses: in process of time, every Indian will have a stove in his house, and a bit of garden in front of it, besides a potato-patch elsewhere.

The soil is remarkably good, and the culture of potatoes very renumerative: Mr. Duncan has a schooner flying between Metlakatlah and Victoria, to help the Indian trade. When one sees what Mr. Duncan has succeeded, by God's blessing, in bringing these Indians to, one is filled with indignation at the conduct of the Hudson's Bay Company, who by example and precept have thrust the poor degraded creatures into still lower depths of vice. I ought rather to say the servants of the company, for I know that they have rules about performing Divine Service every sunday, and, establishing schools for the Indians which look fair enough on paper: but I know that even now, it is customary for their steamer, the Labouchere, to trade on Sunday, and neither in fort nor steamer is Divine Service ever performed. I now close this letter: it is going by canoe to Fort Simpson, to go down to be mailed at Victoria by the steamer Labouchere.[4]

Believe me, your affectionate Son,

Edmund Hope Verney

October 26. 1863.

H.M.S. Grappler. Metlakatlah. B.C.
October 29. 1863.

My dear Father,

It is certainly very interesting to see Mr. Duncan's work here: of course, many of his people differ little in appearance from other Indians, except that they are decently clothed, and have a frank open way, and look you fair in the face; but some of his best might favourably compare with the people of an English village. This is especially the case with three or four of his eldest girls who are about to be married, who in their neat and plain English dresses are certainly attractive.

Dundas is going to do some baptizing and marrying. It is easier for Mr. Duncan to keep his young men straight than his young women, so he has not enough of the latter to meet the wants of his men, and he cannot approve of a Christian man marrying a heathen woman: this is but one of the many difficulties he has to contend with.

The result of Mr. Duncan's labours makes no very great show, at first; but when one compares his Indians with others it is difficult to realize that they are of the same race: the houses are of small logs, with strong uprights, and roofs of broad sheets of bark; inside, they are clean and orderly: some have stoves, in others a bed of gravel has been made in the middle of the floor, on which are the blazing logs, while a broad chimney made of bark comes down to the beams and conducts the smoke through the roof.

Nearly all the Indians use commonly such phrases as "Good morning, Sir", "Good night, Sir", "thank you, Sir", &c, and many understand what is said in English. In their worship, they use the Lord's prayer in our tongue, and several English texts: they sing nicely both in their own language and in ours, and in the latter their pronunciation is astonishingly correct; they even sing catches and rounds: I heard them sing, "see our oars with feathered spray", and a blind man might well have thought he was hearing a well trained English village school.

Mr. Duncan sends the children away with their parents on all their hunting and fishing excursions, in conformity with their usual custom: thus, although they lose some of their school time, they do not become effeminate, nor lose their expertness. Those who remain behind cultivate the gardens: the soil is particularly good, and although this is a wet place the rain soaks quickly through the earth. The harvest of potatoes this year has been very bountiful, more so than could have been expected, and other vegetables seem to thrive equally well.

October 31. This morning we returned from Fort Simpson, whither we went yesterday: the Fort is arranged on exactly the same plan as Fort Rupert, except that it is smaller, and has not such a good garden:[1] there are more Indians, and they show fewer signs of contact with civilization: the navigation is very dangerous to one unacquainted with the neighbourhood, all the rocks being of stone in strata set on its edge.

I do not know whether the above will give you any idea of what ugly looking rocks there are.

The deer here are exceedingly plentiful, cheap, and fat: venison is three halfpence a pound, and no English park could produce tenderer or fatter meat. Mr. Duncan has a tame young mountain sheep running about with his goats: it is a great curiosity with long hairy wool, large limbs, short body and neck, and bright wild stubborn eye: I am sorry to say that yesterday an Indian boy mischeivously threw a pair of shears at it: they accidentally struck him with the points foremost and entered his back: his hindquarters are paralysed, and it is doubtful whether he will live: he is not quite despaired of as he eats a little.

November 2. 1863. Yesterday, several of Mr. Duncan's Indians were baptized: on Saturday a number of names, of which I contributed not a few, were written down, and a selection from them fitted on to the Indians: I select a few with there [*sic*] Indian names, in order that you may form your own opinion as to whether they have benefitted by the change: they receive surnames as well as Christian names because many of their Chimseian names have heathenish or ludicrous meanings. Stohamloosl, Frederic Calvert. Wahanloosk, George Hills. Looahnahts, Frederic Verney. Pellahquahamnay, Edmund Verney. Thrahket, Adam Dundas. Pike, Robert Dundas. Maush, John Delaney. Comkaqwun, Richard Moody.[2]

November 7. Since writing the above some infant baptisms have taken place: Frederic and Lucy Calvert had their daughter baptized Lucy: Frederic Verney's wife, I regret to say, is not yet a Christian, and is therefore only known by the name of "Teaks": they have two sons called Edmund and Frederic.

Yesterday morning we left Metlakatlah: there the snow was not more than half way down the mountains; to-day we are steaming down Grenville Canal, and the snow is down to the water's edge. Mr. Duncan thinks that the climate of Fort Simpson and its neighbourhood is peculiarly mild in winter: I do not exactly see how it is to be accounted for, but he attributes it in some way to a return current of the N.E. trade wind: that part of the coast is more open to the ocean than further South where Queen Charlotte's Islands intervene.

I intended to have left Metlakatlah on the 5th and was called very early with a view to having the steam got up: I went on deck, and found that it was a lovely calm morning; the sun had not yet risen, and the stars shone brilliantly through the frosty air, but when I looked at my barometers, I found they had fallen considerably: I therefore delayed giving orders about the steam, and went to bed again: bye and bye I went on deck, at about seven: it was a beautiful morning, and the sun was shining warmly, but the barometer was lower than ever: we had a mild delicious day, the sun shining brightly while far off to the S.E. dense black clouds hung about the mountains, and the barometer remained very low: towards evening the glass began to rise, and as it continued rising all night, we started early the next morning, and then we steamed south about thirty miles into the tail end of that strong wind which the barometer had been indicating. Today is mild and calm, the barometer still rising.

I shot on our last day at Metlakatlah. I went away with Dundas in my canoe, with two of my men to paddle me: we came to the mouth of a long creek, fed by two streams at its head; Dundas took one side, and I took the other: presently I saw some stock ducks, about half a dozen, swimming about at the far end: I called gently to Dundas to be cautious: he did not hear me, but the ducks did, and rose, flying towards him: then they caught sight of him and swerved to my side of the creek: he fired both barrels and missed; I fired with an Eley's cartridge,[3] and brought down a drake: I think it was one of the most beautiful birds I ever saw: green, purple, and gold shot head; blue and white wings, dark green back and tail, bright red legs and feet: I have preserved the wings for those two ladies who asked me to bring them some feathers from these parts. Dundas gave me great credit for bringing down the drake, as it was rather a long shot: pray tell Uncle Frederic when you see him, that he may know that I improve in my shooting.

November 10. We left Metlakatlah on Friday last, and on the following day we met a Metlakatlah canoe, who informed us that liquor selling to Indians was going on at Kitamat; thither we proceeded, and anchored last night about twelve miles therefrom: soon after midnight, I despatched Mr. Marshall, the gunner, with an armed boat's crew, to the Indian village: when he arrived, he sent some men to the back of the house where the white man lived and some to the front, and knocked at the door; when it was opened, he entered, and while he was fumbling for a light, some whiskey was thrown out window, almost in the faces of our men at the back: at daylight we steamed up in the Grappler, and took on board the liquor seller, Frank by name, who is on board now:[4] I doubt whether we shall be able to get sufficient witnesses to convict him after all, as the Indians like whiskey and are unwilling to betray those who sell it to them. We have shocking bad weather, wind, rain, and Scotch mist continually, which interferes materially with the pleasure of our cruize.

November 15. 1863. This evening we have arrived at Carter's Bay, the first anchorage North of Milbank Sound; the barometer is rising now, after being for some days lower than I have seen it since I left England. I hope it augurs a fine day for crossing the Sound tomorrow.

It is an inestimable advantage to us to have Dundas on board for this cruize: he has this evening given us a capital sermon on James' quotation from the Psalms about keeping the tongue from evil, and the lips that they speak no guile:[5] the men were very attentive, and I am sure that I drank in every word of it.

This weather is very bad, and prevents our seeing the fine mountains we pass: the very heavy rains have however filled all the streams, and the most beautiful cascades abound: now that we are at anchor, and it is nearly calm, the sounds of waterfalls round us quite fills the air.

November 18. On the morning of the 16th we left Carters Bay, and arrived at Millbank early in the afternoon: there we made another fruitless effort to regain our lost anchor, and in the evening steamed down towards the anchorage at Bella Bella: this is where the H.B.Co. Fort McLaughlin used to be, but which now no longer exists:[6] the whole of the chart around Millbank Sound is peculiarly incorrect: at about 4.30. while steaming between two islands, the ship struck on a rock, about three feet below water: the engines were immediately reversed, and a bower anchor was laid out astern, but the tide was falling, and it was found impossible to move her: as the tide fell, her bow and starboard side forward were up high and dry on the rock, while her stern was in deep water: by degrees her stern sunk lower and lower until the water came in on to the deck through the stern hawseholes; then it crept slowly forward, half an inch at a time, until it reached the skylights over the gunner's and engineer's berths: the tops of the skylights were put on, and caulked down with tallow and spunyarn: then, the bilge water all ran aft, and the ship began to leak slightly in two or three places, owing to the unequal strain brought on her: by keeping the pumps going however, we kept this water under: then the water on the upper deck crept forward past the mizen mast to the companion hatch: fortunately I had on board a quantity of yellow cypress plank which is a beautiful soft fine-grained tough wood, not found in the South of Vancouver Island: I had it for using about the ship, and I am going to send a log home: we unshipped the after hatch, covered it with tarpaulin and battened it down with the yellow cypress plank: presently the water crept still further forward, covered the companion hatch, and flowing in over the taffrail, and through the port gangway washed the foot of the skylight over my cabin: at this time the main pump became partially choked, we pumped with the fire-engine, and prepared to bale with buckets: now the ship began rapidly to heel to port: I went to the port gangway and found the water fast rising to the gunwale; then with a violent heave and wrench she fell off the rock into the deeper water on her port side: I sprang on to the gunwale, holding on to the main rigging while the water swept along the deck, reaching up to my middle where I was: then she righted, the water flowed away leaving her nearly upright on a lower ledge of rock: soon after twelve she floated, and steam was raised.

But all this time the wind had been rising, and coming down in heavy squalls from the S.E:, the ship lying with her head about South, so even after she floated, it was with some little difficulty we succeeded in getting her clear of the rocks. Then we stood out into the main channel where we remained under weigh all night, with a fresh S.E. gale, with heavy squalls of rain and hail: in the morning we got an Indian who shewed us the proper channel into the anchorage whence I now write.

So you see our trip has not been without adventure, and considerable risk: had the ship not fallen off when she did the water might have advanced to the engineroom hatches, when the pumps could not have been worked to keep her free, and the hatches battened down would probably have leaked much: or had she remained on the rock where she first struck, I doubt whether she would have floated off until spring tides, and a gale of wind might have bumped her to pieces before then. It was mainly owing, under God's Providence, to the cheerfulness and alacrity of the officers and men that the ship was saved from becoming water-logged. I am afraid that her bottom will be found much damaged, and that it will take some time to repair her.

I do not enter into any details of the precautions taken to keep the ship from running on a rock, because no one would be inclined to exonerate me on account of what might be said by a shoregoing man, and him necessarily so partial as my own father: but I like *you* to know that I have never ceased to remember Sir Michael Seymour's advice to me, when he wished me good bye in the House of Commons:[7] it was to be cautious as a young man, but as rash as I please when I am an old one. It is for my professional superiors to judge how far I may be to blame for those two accidents, but I think I may fairly expect not to be censured for either: at least *you* will be glad to know that such is my honest private opinion.

This evening the ship has been beached, and we find the damage to be not so serious as had been expected: the starboard bilge-piece is just started, and part of the stem and false keel knocked away.

November 21. 1863. Fort Rupert. Yesterday morning we picked up the anchor we laid out when we struck on the rock, and steamed to Safety Cove, whence we started again this morning, arriving here at about half-past six in the evening.

The weather is now very calm and fine, a remarkable contrast to what we have had heretofore, and the barometer is higher than I have ever before seen it since I have been out here: as it is now full moon we have been able to do some of our running, the last two days, after dark.

December 2. 1863. We left Nanaimo for Victoria, this morning, and have anchored for the night at a place called Otter Bay: we hope to reach Victoria tomorrow.

At Nanaimo, we found the "Cameleon", and a few letters, but I suspect that the principal part of the mail is at Victoria waiting for us. I have one letter from you, dated September 12. I have been much grieved to hear of the death of dear Sir Henry Hope: he was the last friend I saw in England, and of course I thought then that I might never see him again.[8]

On arriving at Nanaimo, I found a new gunner, Mr. Russell, waiting to relieve my old gunner, Mr. Marshall, superseded at his own request: Mr. Marshall is a most valuable officer, and I shall feel his loss very much: he has been my right hand, and has known how to conduct the discipline of the ship with forbearance and moderation: I can not expect that Mr. Russell will be quite his equal, but I think he desires to do his best.[9] This change of gunners will be some sort of a little trial to every one on board, until things shake into their places again. I do not yet know how or when Mr. Marshall will go home, but I am sure that you will not mind shewing a little kindness, if you have the opportunity, to one to whom I am in many ways much indebted.

And I find they have made Captain Richards Hydrographer: I thought that perhaps Captain Spratt would have got it: I dare say Captain Richards would forward any letters or small parcels to me, but he will never be such a good friend as Admiral Washington: he is a great loss to the profession, and his place will not be easily filled.[10]

I do not yet know what will be done with the "Grappler." When the Cameleon returns to Esquimalt in about a week's time, a survey will be held on our bottom, and then we shall know more about it: I apprehend that our repairs will take about a month, when they are once taken in hand, so we shall not have much cruizing at present. I look forward with great pleasure to a return to civilized life, and to reading up a great batch of letters: besides this, I have no small anxiety to know whether I shall find any young rabbits, or whether the pigeons have been laying, and whether the ducks and chickens are all serene.

December 3. Victoria. We anchored here this afternoon, having left Nanaimo at noon yesterday: we went first into Esquimalt where I was sorry to learn that the bad weather had caused some little mortality among the farm yard: only four ducks are left, so from henceforth I shall abandon the proverb of a wet day being "fine weather for young ducks": but the chickens and turkeys have thriven wonderfully: one rabbit has departed this life, regretted by all who knew her, and I have further to mourn the loss of two infant pigeons deceased, under circumstances of a very distressing nature: they were devoured by rats: the parents, however are making preparations to replace them with all convenient speed.

Mr. and Mrs. Palmer did not spend their honeymoon at the Bower, because they thought it too small: I was rather disappointed at this, as I had taken some trouble in preparing it for them, but after all, of course I only wanted them to do what they liked best.

Claydon's son seems to be a very ungainly puppy; name, Nero: although his mother is white, he is a *coloured* dog: you will understand that this is a delicate way of hinting that he is black. During my absence, the Bower has been much improved: a ditch has been dug round two sides of the garden, which has already had the effect of making it much dryer, but it is hardly deep enough: some small yew and juniper trees have been planted, which will be a great improvement if they live: a fire has been lighted frequently in the new chimnies, and this has kept everything very dry and in good order.

I find here letters from you up to the end of August: probably tomorrow's steamer will bring more letters. You appear to have enjoyed your visit to Mr. Cumming Bruce very much: I wish I could have been with you, but I desire no lengthened residence in England until I have served for two or three years as Commander, to entitle me to post-captain's rank: I should not mind serving as lieutenant for an extra year, if I might obtain a command as soon as I am promoted to be a commander.

It is an inexpressible relief to me to be again anchored in Victoria: for the last two months I have felt a great, although doubtless a wholesome, strain on my mind: the continual bad weather has made it a very anxious time, and and [*sic*] I have no one to share my anxieties or responsibilities: I really think that another week would have made me quite ill: those to whom I have spoken on the subject assure me that I need fear no censure whatever for having twice been on shore: I must say that this is also my own conviction, but I shall be glad when I hear what the Admiral says about it: when all one's reports have to be in writing, it is not quite such plain sailing as it would be if the admiral were here: whatever he may say, I know *that you* will value my assurance that I did my best.

December 4. No news of the mail yet. I went out riding with His Excellency Sir James this afternoon, and gave him many details of my northward cruize: he was in good humour, good spirits, and good health.[11] I hear that he intends going to England when he is relieved: if he does, I make no doubt that you will know him: I dined with him this evening, so lost the day as regards other business. By the next steamer I intend to despatch two envelopes addressed to you: this letter will be enclosed in an envelope sent by Wells Fargo's express, because you will be anxious to hear news of my return: the other envelope is a yellow one, and will be sent the usual way: it will contain letters to be forwarded to other people: I shall be curious to know how much sooner this letter arrives than the other.

December 5. 1863. I have been much grieved to read in a paper of October 10. the death of Caroline Hanbury; it is mentioned in no home letters: what a terrible blow it must be to Robert, to be left with all those motherless bairns; if you have the opportunity, pray assure him of my affectionate sympathy: Aunt Abel must feel it deeply, and all my cousins:[12] it makes one ask oneself the solemn question, who shall be the next? if I am summoned, shall I be found ready? it is strange and mysterious to think of Car, Sir Henry Hope, and Mrs. Pinfold, enjoying with other loved ones, a holy fellowship above of which we can have no conception: Car was fond of me, and I loved her much: I wonder that you do not mention her loss in any letters, but I think I have missed some of your letters lately. I suppose that the mail steamer is sure to arrive tomorrow.

December 8. 1863. The mail arrived this morning, four days late, having been in some little danger, I believe, in a gale of wind outside. Your letter of October 6 has arrived, viâ New York, marked "insufficiently stamped", and then the mark erased with a pen.

The particulars of Car's death are very interesting: my roving life has prevented me from forming many intimacies, but there are tried friends to whom I look for advice when I come on shore, and whom I ask to help me in getting into wholesome society, and who are good enough to pardon any gaucheries that are the result of living afloat: of these staunch friends, Car was quite the first: when I was in London four years ago, she took me up; she put up with my shortcomings which grated on her refinement, and was a true friend: I looked forward trustingly to a renewal of that countenance at some future day, and if I could so love and value her, who knew her comparatively so little, I can form some estimate of the wide gap she has left in her immediate circle, a gap never to be filled even by time. For poor dear Robert I feel deeply: it must be difficult for him to realize that his loss is her gain, but that I am sure he will one day rejoice in, as we can now, I trust, speak of and feel dear Mamma's happiness.

Your affectionate Son,
Edmund Hope Verney

The Small Bower. Esquimalt. V.I.
December 10. 1863.

My dear Father,

Having yesterday despatched a letter to you from the "Grappler" I am not sorry to date this one from my own fireside: I am in a state of great bliss at the rest and quiet of this snug retreat: just before I left, I built a double chimney, and now in my bed-room and sitting-room are two blazing wood fires, which promise to keep the house quite warm enough during the winter. Of course I am not quite settled down yet, but in a few days I hope to be in a condition to ink paper freely.

December 12. Your letters of September 29. and October 14. did not reach me until I had despatched my letters by last mail. I learn that dear Emily is to winter at Torquay: how delighted she must be, dear child, as she will be so near you: I hope there will be some really nice people at Torquay this winter. From this place I have no news to send you: the admirable allegorical picture in Punch representing Britannia preparing for storms from all quarters truly represents the flying rumours we hear; alas! the Grappler is not a very splendid command, in case of war, nor is she on a station which is likely to occupy much public attention.[1]

We expect the Tribune in January: in a day or two, the Cameleon will probably return from Nanaimo, when a survey will be held on our bottom, and it will be decided what repairs are necessary.

December 18. The thirteenth was our first really wintry day, with frost and snow: since then it has been freezing and thawing, snowing and raining, until the country is in a state easier to conceive than to describe; when the rain commenced the snow was eighteen inches deep; it is raining to-day, and most of the snow is melted, but there are still some great heaps of it left, and the rain and melting snow are running in rivers in every direction.

Since I last wrote, I have been laid up with a severe cold, but am now much better: I shall keep quiet however until the end of the week, so as to try and get quite rid of it before I fall into my usual groove again. You know how dull one feels with a cold, and how disinclined for letter-writing, even to those one loves best.

December 20. The mail steamer arrived yesterday, and sailed again this morning: owing to a mistake my letters were not sent: she brought no English mail, only a few American letters, and I have heard no news of importance.

My Christmas dinner is to be at the McKenzies as it was last year: I hope you will have a happy family circle at Claydon, and write word to me about it; you will not have forgotten to bring "Brandy" in, when you drink George's health, although I fear that George's affection for poor Brandy will have cooled very much by this time. I have a nice letter from him.

December 23. It is quite disgraceful to see what a short letter I am going to send away by the mail that arrived this morning: my only excuse is that I have received no letters either by this steamer or the last, so that from letter to letter will have been a month. As the day after tomorrow is Christmas day, this letter must convey to you all, the compliments of the season, and hearty prayers for your happiness. A party of bachelors are coming here to celebrate Christmas eve tomorrow evening over a bowl of punch, to be followed, I suppose, by songs, and what is generally termed conviviality: I had a bowl of punch at my house-warming, the result of which was very satisfactory; that was in the summer.

Your affectionate Son,
Edmund Hope Verney

The Small Bower. Esquimalt. V.I.
Christmas Day. 1863.

My dear Father,

It is pleasant to think that they "miss me at home" and that somebody says "how sad to spend another Christmas without poor dear Edmund", and that a few weeks hence a letter will arrive from you, dated to-day, telling me what you are doing at this moment, 11.30. A.M. here, but about 7.45. P.M. with you, what toasts you honoured after dinner, who you[r] circle consisted of &c. Before my windows lies the "Grappler", the yard-arms and mast-heads adorned with bunches of evergreen, and a young fir-tree growing out of the funnel, while my porch and verandah are similarly decorated. I know that between each recurring Christmas we might more keep in mind the love of Our Heavenly Father which we this day celebrate. I rejoice greatly in having all your photographs, by which I bring you before me and think lovingly of you each on this day.

Dec. 26. This letter will be taken to England by Mr. Robert Burnaby: he is one of the principal merchants of Victoria, and greatly looked up to and respected: I have asked him to call upon you, because I can confidently recommend him to you as a man whose opinion is worth something: he is of the firm of Henderson and Burnaby, and a member of the House of Assembly: he is not such a young man as he looks, and if you are good enough to show him any little attention your kindness will not be misplaced: there are not many here of whom one can conscientiously and confidently speak as well: so many are either visionary or actuated by sordid motives in either praising up or depreciating these colonies, but I think Burnaby is sound and moderate.[1] I have been reading the Bishop's speech at Salisbury, and I really could not endorse all he says about B.C.: although of course he has been all over Cariboo, while I only went a few miles up the country, and must speak a good deal from hearsay.[2]

The serious winter has not yet commenced, although certain foreshadowings seem to indicate that it will be pretty severe.

Your affectionate Son,
Edmund Hope Verney

Burnaby takes home for me a little parcel addressed to you containing seeds for Mamma, and a marten skin for Aunt Fremantle.

E.H.V.

The Small Bower. Esquimalt. V.I.
December 28. 1863.

My dear Father,

In Royal Bay, just outside Esquimalt Harbour, lies the good ship "Rosedale" A.1. copper-bottomed, copper-fastened &c &c, Master, Philips: on board the said good ship is a log of yellow cypress wood, from Metlakatlah, addressed to you at the Claydon Station, Oxford and Bletchley Railway, freight and charges paid: the Rosedale will sail for Liverpool with the first fair wind. Now the last time I sent anything round the Horn, you asked after my financial condition, so to save myself a blowing up, I will say that during this year which is now so near its close, I have regularly drawn £20. per quarter less than my allowance: the past year having been remarkable for having four quarters, I am thus £80. to the good: In addition to this, the Admiralty, with their proverbial generous liberality, allow me £60. per annum, for keeping the Paymaster's accounts, the most complicated muddle ever invented, which have several times brought me to the verge of idiotcy: I have now been 18. months in the Grappler = £90., and my accounts are already passed up to the beginning of this year, and I hope soon to hear of their being passed up to May, so you see my finances are on the whole, flourishing, and will warrant my sending you a little stick.

Yellow cypress may be obtained at the north end of this island, but the finest grain is only to be procured further north: you will find it a soft wood, very easily worked or carved, of a bright yellow, with a fine close grain capable of receiving a high polish; it is also a tough wood: the Indians use it for making their paddles, and carved chests. If you wish to hear its praises sung, ask Captain Richards about it.[1]

I wish you would give up writing to me by Panama, and address your letters, "viâ New York and San Francisco" as there is now a daily mail between those places: even Admiralty letters are now sent that way: newspapers come by New York and Panama: the old route by St. Thomas' and Panama, has quite gone out of date, and is only used in writing to the Fleet, when it is uncertain on what part of the station the ship may be. I think that the Admiralty send a despatch bag now by New York and San Fran. You will probably be in town when you receive the letter, so perhaps you would not mind calling at Ridgway's and telling him to send my Army and Navy Gazettes, and Navy Lists, by New York and Panama, and to take care that they are sufficiently stamped.

My last letter to you dated Xmas day will probably reach you after this one, as a friend takes it home for me.

January 1. 1864. I feel as much bound to write a few words to you today as I do on Christmas day, to wish you a happy new year with every blessing: pray give my kind love and a happy new year to Mama.

January 3. The mail steamer, instead of being three or four days late, as usual, has arrived this afternoon, a day before she was due, therefore I close this letter to despatch it: I am happy to say that I am quite well; the weather is beautiful: a hard frost, a bright sun, a clear day, and no snow.

Tomorrow the Grappler will be beached that a survey may be held on her bottom.

Your affectionate Son,
Edmund Hope Verney

Dates of Army and Navy Gazettes, Nov. 7 and 14.

The Small Bower. Esquimalt. V.I.
January 10. 1864.

My dear Father,

My pigeon-house was yesterday plunged into the deepest grief by the untimely death of the two infant pigeons, which were frozen to death: this is the second pair of young ones that I have lost, and it is rather discouraging; their feathers were just beginning to grow.

The hard frost which has lasted for about ten days has this morning been succeeded by a dreary rain, and a considerable rise of the thermometer. I am reading with the greatest possible interest the report of your committee on Naval Promotion and Retirement: I wish you had sent me a copy: will you however be kind enough to put my name on a copy, in my room at home: when I command a larger ship some day, I should like to have it bound and in my library: I think it is calculated to do an immense deal of good, and ought to be extensively read throughout the profession: it is a great advantage for young officers to know the views held by their experienced seniors, and yet they are very difficult to get at: I cannot cross-question the Admiral when he condescends to ask me to dinner.

I am told that in the Gentleman's Magazine, somewhere about the year 1838, a Mr. G. Steinman Steinman wrote articles entitled, "Lives of eminent people in the time of Charles 2.nd", and that amongst others is an account of Sir Edmund Verney, did you ever hear of it?[1]

I believe that the picture of the lady who used to hang on the first floor of the old staircase, and whom we used to believe was Queen Elizabeth, has since turned out to be Mrs. Turner, so I send you a print of Mrs. Turner which I have picked up here, which I think will interest Mama. I also send you, from a daily paper, an account of the horrors of American steamboating, which tallies exactly with my experience.[2]

January 14. The Fraser river has been frozen up so that there has been but little communication with B.C., but the last few days have been so extremely mild that there is hardly any ice left now: the oaks and some of the bushes have begun to bud, and in one garden that I know of wall flowers have bloomed in the open air. I wrote to you a long time ago about a man of the name of Joseph Warner, a basket-maker in London: he has now arrived here in a large ship called the Napoleon III.[3]

My life is a very quiet one: the ship's bottom has been surveyed, and it has been decided that she must be hauled up on the ways to be repaired, but the senior officer here, Captain Hardinge, will not undertake the responsibility of such an expensive proceeding without the Admiral's sanction; the report of survey has not yet left this place, so I dare say we shall not hear from the Admiral for a couple of months, and then it will take at least a month to repair the ship, so I look forward to a quarter of a year's inactivity which, as you know, is very irksome to me. However, I find many objects of interest here and in Victoria, and must not grumble.

January 17. I send you a tracing of the chart of part of the coast of B.C., surveyed last summer by Captain Pender in the Beaver: Grappler Sound is up Wells' Pass; we anchored at the mouth of it on the fifth of October last.[4]

I saw the Governor yesterday: I told him that I thought I might reasonably expect to be promoted during the course of the year 1864: I told him that the first Lord's private-secretary had said, that a special recommendation from himself or the Admiral would materially aid my promotion: I said that during the time I had been out here I had wished not merely to do my bare duty, but had tried to forward the interests of the colony by such means as had been in my power, and that I had acquired a great regard for these colonies and should be sorry to leave: I said that if he thought I had acquired experience here which was valuable, and which my successor would take some time to acquire, it was just possible that the Admiralty would re-appoint me to the Grappler after promotion for a short time, at his request: he replied that he would take the first opportunity of forwarding my wishes. If my promotion were to arrive by the next mail, I should probably be placed on half-pay; I might study at the Naval College, but I should probably not get a ship until I had been a year or eighteen months a commander: this would be a sad pity, and it would be a great boon to be allowed to serve for a year or so as Commander in command of the Grappler: it would be a great favour, but the Admiralty might do it on the plea that the Governor recommended the importance of my services: you see, I am a magistrate for both colonies, and have some little experience of each, whereas my successor might be a style of man who cared very little for anything but the immediate duties of his profession. But on the other hand I should not like to be left for much more than a year in command of the Grappler, after promotion, because I should like to command some larger ship before being made a post-captain; so now I have done with the taboed subject: only when you go to the Duke of S. to thank him for my promotion, be it this year or the next, pitch into him very strong, to give me a ship at once.

Everything goes well with me, I am thankful to say. Mr. Marshall, my gunner was superseded, and left me about a month ago to go home round the Horn; I told him that I thought you would be glad to see him when he got home: he has been invaluable to me, and is far superior to the average of warrant officers: I do not know what I should have done without the aid of his advice and assistance in some of the critical circumstances in which we have been placed: his successor, Mr. Russell, promises well, but in a gunboat a warrant officer has duties and responsibilities for which he only becomes fitted by experience; in short he is first lieutenant. I shall be very glad if you see Mr. Marshall.

By the next steamer goes home Robert Burnaby Esqr, one of the principal merchants of Victoria: he bears a strong letter of recommendation and introduction from me to you.

Since I have been out here, I have from time to time sent you any quantity of seeds, but you have never told me whether you have been able to persuade any of them to grow: some time ago you went so far as to say that you would ask Black whether any had succeeded, but that is the last I have heard of it: every now and then your letters contain a paragraph to the effect that any seeds would be acceptable, and you throw it out as an entirely new suggestion that has just occurred to you, as if I had not already sent you about thirty or forty different kinds.[5]

January 18. 1864. The mail has this morning arrived, so Burnaby will be off to-day: she brings no letters at all, nor newspapers, nor, as far as I can hear, news of any kind.

Believe me,

Your affectionate Son,
Edmund Hope Verney

The Small Bower. Esquimalt. V.I.
January 23. 1864.

My dear Father,

The mail steamer that arrived on wednesday brought letters from you up to November 30., but Army and Navy Gazettes only to the 21st: I cannot think why I do not get as late newspapers as other people; the Cameleon has the Army and Navy Gazette up to the 28th.

I am delighted to hear you speak so favourably of Emily; she writes very cheerfully of herself: Lord Elgin's is certainly a severe loss which will be much felt I should think, quite a young man too I should say, comparatively: it is said here that Sir John Lawrence is to succeed him; you will, I suppose, be very glad if that is the case. It is also said that the Duke of Buckingham was offered the governorship of Jamaica, but declined to accept it unless the salary was raised: if this is true, I am surprised.[1]

I am afraid, from what I hear, that your beautiful horse "Moonlight" must be dead; I hope you will soon succeed in getting horses to suit you.

Tomorrow on Monday I go to San Juan in the Forward, with Lascelles and with Captain Hardinge: we shall probably be there for a couple of days, and I hope have some shooting, but the weather is very mild and wet, and the summer will be very acceptable when it comes: the weather is so mild that some of the bushes are already budding: the willows especially are covered with white buds. For the third time my pigeons are sitting, and I hope that this time I may succeed in safely rearing the young birds. Two of my autumn pullets are already laying eggs.

Your last letter enclosed to me one from Mrs. Hope Johnstone, in which she mentions having sent me her photograph, but the photograph did not come in your letter; pray tell me, Sir, what have you done with my photograph?[2]

January 27. If you or Emily are writing to Mrs. Price, pray tell her how delighted I was to read the names of her two daughters as having gained the first prizes for Bible Questions in the "Band of Hope Review."[3]

I suppose that you will be in town when this letter reaches you: if you have the opportunity, pray give the enclosed slip of paper to Lady Ducie: she will understand it.[4]

Of course, in a colony, one meets a great many people whom one cannot make out: there is here a Mr. Price, a man of about forty years of age, but looking younger: he is said to be a civil engineer, and to have been in the army, the navy, and the militia and to have a wife and children in England: he told me that he had been the Duke of Buckingham's fag at Eton, and that his father has some property at Westbury near Shalston, where he lives: can you tell me any thing about him? he is rather a spare, short, strong, wiry man: he says he knows you, knew me when I was "so high", and knows everybody else.[5]

February 4. The mail is now due and has probably only been delayed by the fogs which have prevailed today and yesterday. I know that my letters are stale and unprofitable, but I cannot invent news, and really nothing of any interest goes on here. The House of Assembly is discussing the salary for the new Governor, and it seems pretty clear that this colony cannot afford the luxury of a Governor all to itself: besides this I think there is a disposition to be mean and niggardly and to make the most of the colony's poverty as compared with the wealthier neighbour.

Gold is being discovered in several parts of this island, but not as yet to any very great extent: I believe that in two places it more than repays the labour of getting it out of the ground.

On Friday last, I went with the shareholders to visit the site of a proposed copper-mine on Lasqueti Island near Nanaimo: I have seen several places where it has been proposed to open mines, but I think none of them are likely to succeed at present: the shares are many of them held by mere speculators who are ready to sell out at the first rise in their value: where the current rate of interest on the best security is 1½ per cent per month, it is not worth any-one's while to invest largely in a mining company which will not pay anything for years: there are of course a few exceptions: it *is* worth the while of people in England to invest their capital in mines out here, as the current rate of interest in England is so much lower: I have no doubt that these two colonies are teeming with mineral wealth, but there is not capital here to work with. Burnaby is, I believe, going to form a company in England to work the Queen Charlotte Is. copper mines, and other companies for getting out minerals here are being formed at home, and I confidently predict that they will pay if the agents here are men of business, and upright, not such an easy thing to secure.[6]

Lascelles is going in very heavily for a new coal mine at Nanaimo, which will undoubtedly succeed if properly managed, and if sufficient capital is laid out; in short it will yield a fortune: but I have not confidence in the men at present associated with him in the speculation: an agent is going to England immediately to form the company & raise the capital.[7]

It is a great misfortune, that we have hitherto had no one out here whose opinion on the mineral wealth of the colonies commands sufficient respect: a man arrived some months ago, who was said to be great geologist; the newspapers gave him a flourish of trumpets, and great things were expected of him, but he is now known as a gambler and a drunkard; I may mention that we have grand arrivals from time to time; people come who are spoken of in the papers as "eminent naturalists", "well known geologists", "eminent or prominent citizens", "world-famed statesmen", "acquisitions to our shores" &c &c, but who slink away after a few months, leaving sometimes unpaid debts behind them: anything like a title, whether home or colonial is jumped at with avidity, and the bearer's personal appearance and manners are described with the minuteness one sees in the case of a celebrated bigamist or notorious swindler, ex. gra. Lord Milton or Hon. Malcolm Cameron.[8] Not one of the least benefits we should derive from a first-rate Governor would be that when an arrival is heralded with a grand flourish people would wait to see how the individual might be received by the Governor: I am afraid it is the case that the Governor and his family by no means give a tone to the society of the place and there is no one whose fiat is acknowledged as to where the great mysterious line shall be drawn.

A paragraph has gone the rounds of the English papers about the Princess of Wales reducing the crape on Her Majesty's bonnet; the story may not be true, but it is pretty and touching: I see that it has now found its way into the American papers: with slight variations I have read it in a San Francisco paper: the Queen is represented as having said "Lord! Alexandra, whatever have you been doing to my bonnet?"

You will be grieved to hear that the rats have for the third time destroyed my pigeon's progeny: two eggs have been broken and devoured; the most inviting of rat-traps, with a delicious banquet therein remains unheeded.

Feb. 5. 1864. Extraordinary to relate, the mail steamer has this day arrived, and brought me no letter; nor have I any newspaper. Adieu,

Your affectionate Son,
Edmund Hope Verney

The Small Bower. Esquimalt. V.I.
February 7. 1864.

My dear Father,

Yesterday morning the mail steamer departed: the principal news she brought was the birth of an heir to the Prince of Wales: we all wonder what he will be called; Duke of Dublin or Edinburgh I suppose. We also hear that Captain Kennedy is gazzetted governor, and that these Colonies will probably be more or less united: I begin to think that Union will be the wisest course, after all. Two Governors and two staffs of officials are an enormous expense, and if one can do the work would be an enormous waste of money.[1]

I was surprised to receive neither letter nor paper of any sort by last mail, but with the present bad arrangements for steamers, one should be surprised at nothing.

The weather here is extremely mild, too mild: many of the leaves of the more forward shrubs are already bursting forth, and some of the days lately have been very soft and balmy: this is not good, because a frost will do so much harm to the young leaves. A few day's sun would enable me to get my garden into some sort of order: the bower is in a very damp spot, surrounded by high trees, and does not quickly dry: as soon as it is practicable, I shall sow some grass seed, and endeavour to cultivate a lawn on some ground to the south of the house that has been prepared for that purpose: now the earth is to[o] wet to be touched with the rake or to be rolled.

Mr. McKenzie of Craig Flower has lent me a beautiful sturdy little pony: it is lent to me for an indefinite period: I have built some stables at the back of my house, of slab: slab is the exterior pieces of wood that are left after a tree has been sawn into planks: it is sold at the mills for a nominal price, as it is not worth the cost of carriage, and is used for firewood or for rough fencing: I had a raft of it made, and one of my boats towed it to my house; then a couple of my own men built the stables, and enclosed a small yard: I think that the knotted trunks of the slab make very handsome and picturesque stables, and inside they are, of course, as even as if they were built of plank: It is a great comfort to me to have a horse again, for I am sure that so much walking was injuring my knee, but I am afraid that I shall find keeping a horse quite as expensive a luxury as I did before.

This week I am going to prepare a box of curiosities to send home to you by the "Princess Royal": sending them away will rather denude my rooms, which are furnished and adorned with etceteras, so I must only hope soon to follow them.

February 9. We do not know what to think about the chances of peace or war: the latest papers speak of a general war in the spring as more than possible: I am afraid that in case of a European war, Vancouver Island will not be the best place for opportunities of professional distinction: perhaps that man deserves the greatest credit who humbly and steadily does his duty in an unheeded out-of-the-way part of the world, while others are rushing to excitement in pursuit of glory: assuredly the man who acts from a sense of duty must always stand higher than he who acts on impulse.[2]

If a European war were to break out, I should like to submit to the Admiralty my willingness to serve actively as junior lieutenant of a large ship, but at the same time my perfect readiness to remain here or to go any-where else where they might consider my services would be best bestowed: I hardly think that the system of volunteering for particular service is good in its results.

There is almost a crisis in Victoria at present: there actually seems to be no money in the place: everybody to whom even a small sum is owed clamours to be paid: a tradesman said to me yesterday when I went to pay a small bill; "I have large sums owing to me; I am deeply in debt, yet I have to go on buying goods on credit, and to go on giving credit to my customers: other people are doing it, and I must do the same or I shall be ruined." If there is a tolerably large immigration this spring, a few weeks will put everything to rights again.[3]

The value of land, the number of houses built, the amount of goods ordered from abroad are all regulated by the rate at which it is calculated that the colony *ought* to go ahead, and as long as there is a chance of its doing so people stick to their land, build new houses, and order in fresh goods: let that confidence be but shaken, and we shall have a grand crash: then would be the time to buy up land; for I have a perfect confidence in the ultimate prosperity of these colonies. If such a crash as I refer to were to come, I do not think it would last more than a week or two; capitalists from California would flock in, and buy up everything.

I have heard it said by intelligent men here, that it would well be worth the while of one of the great English banks to send out a partner and establish a bank here: there are in Victoria two chartered banks, but they hardly take the place of an English banker: it seems to me that if 3½ per cent can be got in England on the best security, and 18 per cent here on the best security, it would be worth while.

February 11. 1864. From sunrise to sunset yesterday, not a cloud was to be seen, and the air was warm and mild like summer: at night a slight frost, and this morning promises to be just such another day: few climates in this latitude can show such glorious days in February: trees and shrubs are already budding.

I have had lent to me the August number of a magazine called "Christian Work", published by Strahan and Co, 32. Ludgate Hill; it contains three most interesting articles; the first, "Impressions of an eye-witness in the Waldensian valleys," another, "The Army Chaplains, by an Army Chaplain"; the third is in the form of a long advertisement, which I was particularly requested to read, "Address to Christians throughout the World, by the Clergy of the Confederate States of America":[4] Now all three are well worth reading, but the one on Army Chaplains is the one that I think you would be sorry not to have read: I do not believe that it at all over-rates the zeal and efficiency of the Army Chaplains, but it does make one yearn to have something done for our poor sailors besides boxing them up in iron chests.

A chaplain of the name of Johnson has been appointed to the "Leopard":[5] his appointment is significantly remarked in the Colonial papers: he was here in the Topaze, a year or two or three ago, and was allowed to leave her quietly to avoid a courtmartial for drunkeness: yet he is again sent afloat, rather to the amazement of good folk here, who know all about him: I can speak quite impartially, because I never saw him, but heard of him from people on shore here and from the officers of the Topaze, long ago: perhaps the most melancholy part of the affair is that his re-appointment is not viewed by the navy here with indignation and disgust, but rather as a matter of course: indeed, I heard him spoken of as a "lucky fellow": this is a thing that a naval chaplain-general would prevent: the Article I have referred to points out the various ways in which the spiritual wants of the soldier are met: all these means are now I believe in operation in the navy, but to a very, very small extent: I fear, alas! that Naval Chaplains do not obtain that high estimation that in virtue of their holy office they ought.

The senior officer, Captain Hardinge, hesitates to incur the expense of repairing the "Grappler", until he has the authorization of the Admiral, which has not yet arrived: after we once begin, it will take a month or two to put us to rights, so in the meantime there lies the "Grappler" before my windows, a good 'un to look at, but a rum 'un to go. You know how extremely irksome to me is inactivity, and I do much regret that I see no prospect of its speed[y] termination.

Valentine's Day. 1864. The mail steamer arrived this morning, bringing me your letter of October 29, which must have been delayed on the road: my newspapers are only up to December 12. while other people have them upwards of a week later. Captain Hardinge, of the Cameleon, and our senior officer, is promoted: it used to be one of my dreams that perhaps I might obtain my promotion at the same time as him, and get appointed to the Cameleon, but I have well-nigh given up thinking of the future now: indeed it would be foolish to do so, when I have so much to be thankful for in the present: there are also several promotions of lieutenants and Commanders, although I have not yet seen the list.

I am very glad you have had Captain Kennedy staying at Claydon, but you do not tell me very much about him, or when we may expect him here: I like more than I can tell you, Aunt Helen's last present to me, "The Graver Thoughts of a Country Parson".[6] I am very glad that all accounts agree that you and Mamma are both well: Sir Henry Bruce's death is reported; he was a good man, and a gallant fellow.[7] Adieu,

Your affectionate Son,
Edmund Hope Verney

The Small Bower. Esquimalt. V.I.
February 15. 1864.

My dear Father,

You will remember a certain confidential memorandum sent by me to Admiral Washington, a week or ten days after my arrival in this colony, nearly two years ago; he wrote to me on the receipt of it to the effect that he would not fail to let it be known whence he had derived the information it contained; he is now alas! gone, and there have been since then two private secretaries to the First Lord; do you think it would be worth while to ask Captain Hall whether he ever heard of it, and to try and get a favourable mention of it noted in that book of the services of officers which is kept in the Duke's private office? I remember that I built many hopes on it at the time, but it seems long, long ago.[1]

We hear that Captain Kennedy left England on the 17th of last month, so we may expect him here in the early part of next month: you do not say what you are doing with our bishop, or how soon he is coming out again.

I always direct my letters to Claydon, although I suppose you to be in London at present and I have no doubt that you give orders to have them speedily forwarded: I enclose a note for Miss Hardinge, whose address Emily is sure to know.

February 18. Yesterday was the anniversary of my entering the Navy: yesterday I had been thirteen years at sea.

Yesterday evening my engineer-in-charge attempted to drown himself by jumping overboard when delirious: Mr. Russell, the gunner jumped after him, and with some difficulty succeeded in saving him: to my very great astonishment, the doctor declares that he is delirious from the effects of drink: since I have commanded the "Grappler", I have never known him even excited from the use of liquors: he has been in the ship nearly five years now, and I can understand that the monotony of being in such a small ship with only one, or, at the most, two messmates, and especially the weariness of these long winter evenings, the ship lying idle and unemployed, have injured his health, and that he has taken opium and spirits to induce sleep and while a-way the time. He has to-day gone to hospital, and I suppose he will not come back to us, as such a step would be safe for neither himself nor for us: if the doctor declares that he is suffering only from delirium tremens, I fear that he will have to be tried by a court-martial: he has always been a most zealous and efficient officer.[2]

February 19. The Cameleon returned from Nanaimo this afternoon: the mail is due tomorrow or Sunday, and will probably bring Captain Jones, Captain Hardinge's successor:[3] in the meantime all things glide along very evenly here, and considering their long spell of inactivity here, my men behave very fairly, and give not much trouble. Leaves are beginning to appear in a hesitating and doubtful sort of way, and the arch of honeysuckle over my front gate is putting forth vigorous shoots. The stream of adventurers to the mines has already made a start for Cariboo, and it seems as if this year was to be quite as forward a one as any former year: one of the signs of the march of civilization is that a woman who keeps a stationery shop in Victoria is going to establish a lending library on Williams' Creek: another, is the formation of the Antler Creek Bed Rock Flume Company (limited.) which I think may be considered a great stride in advance.

February 21. Today is as wet as a day can be: the mail arrived this morning bringing neither letters nor news, not having corresponded with the steamer at Panama. Hence I have no news to send you except that I am well and that one of my ducks had her left foot bitten by a rat three or four evenings ago: all my pullets have commenced laying and are going on as well as can be expected.

And so, with love to all, believe me,

Your affectionate Son,
Edmund Hope Verney

The Small Bower. Esquimalt. V.I.
March 1. 1864.

My dear Father,

Perhaps the two subjects at present uppermost in the colonial mind, are the banquet to be given to Sir James Douglas, and the reception to be given to Captain Kennedy: the banquet to Sir James is to take place on the tenth, and is a matter of comparatively plain sailing, but the arrangments connected with the reception of Captain Kennedy are a fruitful source of discussion and jealousy:[1] to a bystander like myself, the jealousies are unintelligible; it has been arranged that His Excellency is to go round to Victoria in the "Grappler," and the Committee of Managment orders that only the Colonial Secretary and Naval Officers shall accompany him in the gunboat: I am an inactive member of the General Committee of Managment, and I signified my cordial approval of an order which would relieve me of the embarassment of being pestered with applications for a passage round, but on the other hand I said that of course, as captain of my own ship, I reserved my right to invite any private friends of my own that I chose: this made some of the Committee furious, and they have threatened to change the programme, and convey H.E. to Victoria by land: I have not the slightest intention of inviting any-one at present, but I can imagine that circumstances might arise that would make me regret having pledged myself to invite no one: but there is terrible jealousy on the subject.

There is also a difficulty about the coloured people: the only volunteer rifle-corps in existence here is a corps consisting of coloured people, and I am sorry to say that the Committee of Managment have so worded their programme as to exclude them from the procession: I hope, however, that by a little wholesome agitation on their part they will obtain some recognition on the part of the people: strongly though I feel on behalf of the coloured population, it would not become me to appear as their champion on this occasion: I have been surprised and disappointed at the narrow-mindedness that has lately showed itself in connexion with the change of Governors, and the absurd jealousies between people who, one would have supposed, had nothing to be jealous of.[2]

March 4. Be it remembered that the first wild-flower, a little forget-me-not, appeared on the twenty-sixth of last month. I enclose to you the speech of Mr. McClure, the Vancouver Island delegate: the printed one is what he intended to say, and the written one is my short-hand report of what he did say: of course I know I am not very expert with my shorthand, but still the latter is the nearer the truth; the speech was very badly delivered to an audience containing scarcely one respectable person; it was received in silence, and the whole thing was about as dull as it well could be[.][3]

March 6. The mail steamer is due to-day, and a mail-day always unsettles us: the steamer comes and goes so quickly that one likes to be on the spot to answer any important letters by the return boat, and it is very unfortunate when she comes in on a Sunday as is too often the case; this is a sad mammon-worshipping place: many young men connected with the merchants offices &c were deprived of their half holiday yesterday, and will have to work for some hours at their desks to-day, Sunday, because the steamer is due to-day. This is an evil which I dare say the Governor will be able to check if he gives his attention to it. It is difficult for you to realize the desecration of the sabbath that is brought about in a thousand different ways by the arrival and departure of the mail steamer on a Sunday: the authorities can refuse to grant a clearance and so delay the departure until Monday but I am afraid they cannot prevent her from arriving on any day she pleases.

The increasing length of the days, and the approach of spring gladden my heart, and it is a relief to think that the long dreary winter evenings are concluded. No answer having as yet arrived from the Admiral, the repairs to the ship's bottom have not yet been taken in hand: after they are commenced, they will take at least a month to complete, and all this time I am enduring that state which is to me the most wearisome, the state of idleness and inactivity.

Is my name near the top of the list of candidates for the Traveller's Club? if not, how soon may I expect my name will come on? For several letters past, you have not mentioned how Miss Nightingale is; pray tell me. Our verse to-day, March 7., is Mark 6.31.

Believe me, Your affectionate Son,

Edmund Hope Verney[4]

The Small Bower. Esquimalt. V.I.
March 26. 1864.

My dear Father,

The Mail Steamer, by which the Governor arrived, departed this morning, taking away Captain Hardinge, late of the Cameleon. I mentioned in my letter to Aunt Fremantle my astonishment at Mrs. Kennedy's salutation that she was sorry I was going away, because I was promoted: we have now newspapers up to the thirtieth of January, which contain no mention of it, but it is a mystery to me what could have induced any one at San Francisco to say such a thing: I did not believe it at first, so it was no disappointment to me.

The Governor and his family have made decidedly a very favourable impression; he speaks well, and to the point, and one or two of his remarks were very much to the point; for instance "it is often better to be decidedly wrong than undecidedly right", and "I have more disposition to serve you than to govern you", and again "the surest passport to my regard will be to have served faithfully my predecessor": in short, I think he'll do.

You may suppose that I shall watch his reign with close attention, as perhaps I never have had the opportunity for a more valuable lesson. If I send you a copy of the newspaper, pray remark the delicate distinction between the conduct of Captain Jones and myself; he *escorted* Mrs. Kennedy, while I *gracefully assisted* Miss Kennedy.[1]

Many thanks for a United Service Magazine which arrived, probably from you: it contains an article on Lighthouses which is to me particularly interesting. Sometime ago you mentioned having sent me several numbers of that magazine, but they have never come to hand. What would you wish me to do about the "Isaiahs"? I have given away some copies, to let the book be known, but only one has been sold: the fact is that no one thinks of buying religious books here.

March 28. I have read a letter in the Army and Navy Gazette of the 2nd of January with great interest; as the subject is "Naval Chaplains", and the signature is W.R.F. I have no doubt that it emanates from my uncle; of course I agree with its sentiments, and deeply regret that the agitation on the subject which has been going on for the last two or three years has been productive of so little result. I cannot help thinking that that wonderful engine, the House of Commons, might produce the required result by bringing a little pressure to bear on their Lordships. The appointment of an efficient Naval Chaplain-General would give a spurt to all Chaplains that would send a thrill right through the service, and be sensibly felt by even the crew of a little gunboat in the uttermost parts of the earth. An efficient man, in the first instance would establish such a routine that a less efficient man hereafter would still be of great use.[2]

March 31. The mail steamer has this morning arrived, bringing English news to the second of last month viâ St. Thomas', and probably later news by New York. All the news you send me of Emily and others are most gratifying. I am sorry to say that the report of my being promoted got into the local papers, so I have to endure congratulations on the happy event.

I am sorry that Hankin has left the Service: he has arrived to-day: I always strongly disapproved of it when he spoke to me on the subject, and had hoped that his better sense would have guided him when he returned to England: however, we shall see how he prospers.[3]

I am happy to be able to add that I am very well, but no orders to repair the "Grappler" have yet arrived from the Admiral, and I shall be glad when that little matter is settled. Captain Kennedy shews me the greatest kindness: his troubles are about to begin, probably this afternoon and I shall watch his conduct with the greatest possible interest. His response, yesterday, to an address from the coloured volunteers, in which he expressed true British sentiments, will probably call forth a few strong letters in tomorrow's papers.[4]

It is remarkable how thoroughly he has made himself master of people and events here from information obtained before his arrival, and yet he receives all courteously, and makes no parade of being quite au fait, and behind the scenes.

Believe me, Your affectionate Son,

Edmund Hope Verney

Will you kindly telegraph to me, when I am promoted? If you write that you will, it will be a relief to me to know that.

Private

The Small Bower. Esquimalt. V.I.
March 26. 1864.

My dear Father,

Captain Kennedy seems disposed to be very kind to me: when I offered to-day to be of any use in my power if there was any-thing he might not like to ask any one else to do, he replied that when the time came he would ask me things he would not ask anyone else: I think I know what he meant.

I deeply value your affection for me which prompted you to send me such kind presents by the Governor: the knife is quite a chef-d'oeuvre, (if that is the way to spell it,) and the little lamp is a marvel of ingenuity; the books are very nice, and good books are dear here; the chocolate reminds me of many similar presents in bygone years, but the most charming of all is to see and converse with those who have so lately seen and conversed with you. When I left England you said something, which little speech has hung sadly and heavily on my heart ever since; when you gave me your skates you said "I shall never skate again"; it was with great delight and indeed relief that my letters told me of your skating last winter.

I agree with you that the daughters will make capital *Colonial* wives, and the mother seems to be really a good soul.[1] The Governor says there seems to be a strong feeling of nationality in California.

I rather hesitate to give Ommaney carte blanche to pay all bills, but according to your wish I enclose a note for him, which please read.

I get on capitally with Captain Jones, the senior officer, whom I like much; I think he is a really good man. I shall from time to time write you word about Captain K, and as you know him, you will be the more interested to know how he succeeds: I can imagine that there are people here to whom he will give great offence, and that the government will not at first be a bed of roses, but the two colonies being entirely distinct will simplify matters very much for him. I am afraid lest his two attractive daughters should gather a silly crowd about them, but I dare say that they and their mamma will be too wise to allow it; the whole family seem to stand in awe of their "Governor".

Your affectionate Son,
Edmund Hope Verney

I think Captain Kennedy might be a little more charitable to Sir James Douglas' shortcomings.

List of articles sent to England in the H.B.Co. Ship "Princess Royal." March. 1864.[1]

---

1. 1. Bale, containing a dozen birch-bark mats of Indian manufacture, from Metlahkatlah.
2. 1. Bundle of sticks.
3. 1. Chest, consisting of a large carved Indian chest, cased in fir plank, and containing,

1. Large carved Indian head-dress, with birds and beak complete.
1. Birch-bark basket, containing carved spoons, ad lib.
1. Indian drum.
4. Bird's wings.
1. Facetious devil on a pivot.
1. Mask of sea-monster, with plenty of jaw.
1. Hairy human mask.
1. Demon and child.
2. Hairy little devils.
1. Supercilious coxcomb.
1. Inquisitive bird with painful tail.
2. Small astonished head-dresses with mother-of-pearl eyes.
3. Ivory soul-catchers.
1. Carved slate bowl.
1. Ancient stone bowl.
1. Stone hammer.
2. Stone adzes
1. Elk-skin.
1. Indian bag, containing three carved wooden bowls.
1. Round basket, containing,
    1. Pipe of carved slate.
    2 Pairs of mocassins.
    3. Wooden combs.
    1. Lip-piece.
    1. Skin-bag, from Sitka.
    2. Mountain-Goats' horns.
1. Globular basket, containing,
    1. Model of an Indian chest, containing,
        1. Small basket, containing,
            1. Ivory charm.
        1. Ivory charm.
    1. Head-dress of bear's claws.
    1. Chief's funny-bone.
    1. Carved wooden pipe.
    1. Mysterious squeaker.
1. Small bird, with disproportioned beak and fish.
1. Fish-spear-head.
1. Carved and painted bowl.
1. Carved bowl, containing two fish-hooks.
2. Sets of gambling tools.
2. Medicine-man's rattles.
2. Deer's horns.
1. Large carved ladle.
1. Large and one small too-too.
5. Small common rattles.
1. Carved chiefs-rattle.
1. Fish, for head-dress.
1. Pair of leggings, with fringe of sea-parrots' beaks.

The case containing these articles should be opened carefully, so as not to injure the inner box: this inner box, as well as several of the carved bowls of quadrangular form, will be found to have sides made from one plank, bent round and joined at one angle only.

The contents of this box, when added to what was sent home in the Princess Royal last year, and when are added a few articles I have by me at present, will probably form one of the best collections of the curiosities of this country that has ever been sent to England; and as these things are becoming more rare every day, and more highly prized by their possessors, it is not probable that so good a collection can ever be formed again, except at great expense.

Edmund Hope Verney

The Small Bower. Esquimalt. V.I.
April 6. 1864.

My dear Father

Although the world revolves pretty much as usual to-day, I like to write to you on my birthday, and to remember that there are one or two people in existence who will specially think of me: to-day finds me six-and-twenty, and still a lieutenant; I used to expect to be a commander at four and twenty, but I dare say I should have made a very bad one. A banquet is to be given to Sir James Douglas on Friday, and I am going to New Westminster to attend it.

I enclose newspaper paragraphs for your amusement: the story about Earnest Walker is quite true; he is a University man, and one for whom I have some regard, although he makes a cut at me at the end of his story: we were fellow passengers from England.[1]

April 10. On Friday I attended the banquet given to Sir James Douglas at New Westminster: although much less pretentious than the Victoria banquet, it was more decorous, and creditable. Of course, there was not a single good speech, but then neither was there the gross violation of good taste that there was here. We sat down to table, about one hundred, including almost every respectable man in the colony: care was taken that those who were known to be rampantly hostile to the Governor should not obtain tickets.

Captain Kennedy continues to win golden opinions here; the action of the House of Assembly in refusing to provide him with a house, to allow him a private Secretary, or to pay the travelling expenses of his Secretary, does not, I think meet with the approbation of the people: the resolutions, which were not even couched in courteous language, were carried by the casting vote of the Speaker; he is a son in law of Sir James Douglas, and his speech on the occasion was gross, treasonable, and insolent: an indignation meeting on the subject, to condemn the course pursued by the Assembly, is to be held tomorrow evening.[2]

A great deal is being said here on the subject of non-sectarian education; I can hardly reconcile to myself that education should be afforded, and the bible forbidden, but in a colony where there is no state church it is a very difficult matter; were I at home I could form an opinion on the subject from books, or from conversation with intelligent men, but here are so few books, and fewer intelligent men. I think the Governor's view is to reduce the religion in the daily schools assisted by Government to a minimum, but to afford Government aid to Sunday Schools of all denominations. Unfortunately the adjective "non-sectarian" is sometimes practically interpreted "atheistic".

April 14. Yesterday afternoon the "Tribune" arrived under sail in Royal Bay, and was towed in to the anchorage by the "Forward". The mail steamer, which was not expected until Saturday, arrived last night, so I must prepare to close my letter: our summer appears to have begun now: to-day is the third really fine warm day, and everything in the vegetable line is springing forward. Nicol, the chaplain of the "Tribune", was in the Emerald; he is staying with me to-day at the Bower. His officers speak very highly of Guilford; they call him "a gem of a skipper", and indeed he seems so: he rarely uses the steam, but knocks his ship about everywhere under sail; he has certainly got a most delightful command: he is only about five years older than me, and five years senior to me in the Service; I am afraid I cannot expect such a fine command when I am a young captain; if ever indeed I am to be one at all.[3]

11. P.M. I have only time to glance over my letters; one from the Secretary puts my mind more at ease with regard to our misfortunes on our Northern cruize; home letters are very satisfactory.

Your affectionate Son,
Edmund Hope Verney

The Small Bower. Esquimalt. V.I.
April 16. 1864.

My dear Father,

We had a mail two days ago, and another having arrived to-day finds me quite unprepared with any letter to send to you, while the accumulated heap of unanswered letters is awful to contemplate: your latest date is February 29, very late news, while I have seen the "Times" of March 2.

The "Grappler" is at present beached for Lord Gilford to see what damage she has sustained, and I am in hopes that he will undertake the responsibility of having her repaired at once: we have now been idle for upwards of four months.

April 17. The mail steamer goes out this morning, and I feel ashamed that I have no long letter ready to send you. There is, I think, at present but one opinion of Captain Kennedy, namely that he is the right man in the right place, and that his administration will be of great benefit to the colony: he is a wonderfully clear-headed man, and has already acquired very great influence: the policy hitherto has been to avoid unpleasant subjects, to keep them quiet or to shuffle out of them; Captain Kennedy professes to be anxious to clear up everything, and to make public his opinions on every vexed question: I have no doubt that before very long he will be able to have everything his own way: his previous experience gives him great weight as hitherto there has been no one here to say what is usual in other colonies. The blue-book containing Mr. Langford's letters, &c is very interesting; I wonder you did not send it to me.[1]

Many thanks for the Claydon Almanac, with the Lighthouse engraving; it is peculiarly appropriate to my duties. Thank-you also for uncle's sermons, and the view from the rectory terrace, which arrived by governor Seymour: he is still in Victoria, but will go to New Westminster on Tuesday: he has been waiting for some arches &c to be completed. Our summer has at last fairly set in, so far at least that I think we have done with the bad winter weather.[2]

The last accounts of Emily are not so good as they might have been, and I shall be anxious to hear further of her.

Your affectionate Son,
Edmund Hope Verney

The Small Bower. Esquimalt. V.I.
April 17. 1864.

My dear Father,

Another letter shall be laid on the stocks at once, in order that the next mail shall not find me unprepared: I read in the latest papers of officers being promoted, of commands being given away, and of the prospect of a European war, and all make me feel my chances of advancement getting smaller and smaller, as the fresh pages of the book of history are written, and the remembrance of the Indian campaign becomes fainter and fainter: if we are involved in European war, I beg you, in my name, to ask the Admiralty to appoint me to some ship on active service, as I should be miserable out here.

The "Grappler" will be paid off in June: if the Admiralty pass me over, and do not promote me then, it will be a great slight; I know privately that they have written out to the Admiral to make arrangements for paying the gunboats off.

April 19. Having just got up, I look in vain for the Cameleon this morning; she sailed for the coast of Mexico at daylight. I think that her Commander, Theodore Morton Jones, is one of the nicest fellows I ever met in the Navy: we have been a good deal together since he came, and I shall miss him very much: the frequent change of senior officers is a great bore although indeed it is in some cases a relief.

April 21. Yesterday I rode out to Gold Stream with the Governor and thirteen others to see the quartz mining which has been lately begun there:[1] the most distant claim is about thirteen miles from Victoria on the road to Cowichan and Nanaimo; I had never been so far along that road before, and was much delighted with the beautiful views we opened out from time to time: the day was very fine, so the nearer hills of the Island and the more distant mountains of the Olympian Range were equally clear, and an occasional glimpse of the water in the Straits of Fuca made it a scene of great beauty: most of the trees and bushes are in leaf, while the least advanced are budding; a few days hence the under-wood will be so thick that some of the best points of view will be blocked up: the last two miles of road are but trail, while the nearer portion is passable for a light wagon.

From what we could gather it appeared that the Gold Stream would be a good quartz mining district, and lucrative when proper machinery shall have been erected: the gold in the quartz is generally invisible to the naked eye, only to be detected by its weight, or by amalgamating with quicksilver after the quartz has been crushed. The gold Stream itself is not dry during summer and promises to furnish the motive power for machinery, without which the diggings will never pay. After we had inspected the principal works, we sat down to a luncheon that had been prepared, and edified each other by making speeches, proposing toasts &c.

The Governor is desirous of encouraging exploring parties through the island, and has promised that from the Crown Lands Revenue two dollars shall be forthcoming for every one subscribed by the Public with this object: I have no doubt that an exploring party will be equipped and sent out in a very short time.[2] There appear to be some very hard-headed and intelligent men who have interests in the mines at Gold Stream, and I expect that they will make it pay.

April 23. I have been talking to one or two of my naval friends on the subject of promotion: now I want you to be so good as to ask for it definitely on the occasion of the Grappler being paid off, which will probably be in June: if you write me word that it is refused I shall apply for it by a memorial through the Admiral on the station, but I am told that it will be better to withold the memorial until I am sure I am not to be promoted without it: I need not go over the old ground of the services &- on which I base my claims for promotion: it is a fact that I have served in the ship, the Shannon, where every other officer senior or junior to me has made at least one rapid stride in the profession, while even if I am promoted immediately I shall have derived less benefit from Indian service than any other officer: I do indeed feel very strongly on the subject now, and will represent my own case if you can do nothing more for me, but I am advised that it would be better if I could get promotion without that. Gilford tells me that he got his last step by memorializing.

April 27. The mail steamer has arrived, bringing no English letters. I get on capitally with Gilford: if you have any midshipman friend, and you would like to see him made a sailor of, get him appointed to the Tribune; I do not believe that her superior as a man-of-war is afloat, and I know not where to look for her equal.

Your affectionate Son,
Edmund Hope Verney

The Small Bower. Esquimalt. V.I.
May 2. 1864.

My dear Father,

I enclose a letter to Captain Hall, which I leave entirely in your hands: burn it if you like: put it in an envelope as it is and send it to him, if you think that better: or please see him and deliver it to him if that seems best to you.

Sir James Douglas will return to England in a week or ten days, after an absence of fifty years: he will be accompanied by Mr. Young, the Colonial Secretary, accompanied by his wife and family: I hardly think he will remain long in England, as he will find himself such a stranger, and so utterly lost in the crowd: pray let me know if you see him. Let me thank you again for what you have so kindly done for me in the matter of the United Service Institution: it has caused me great pleasure; I have just received the official intimation of it.

Will you be so kind as to have my name put down for the "Public School Club": I may perhaps never join it, but I am anxious to belong to some Club when I come home, and I think you could get me proposed and seconded without much trouble.

I have to-day had a grand luncheon party, the Governor and his family, the McKenzies, and officers of the "Tribune": we had a charming day, bright sunshine and fresh breeze: after luncheon we went for a ramble in the woods, came back for a cup of tea, and separated: nobody was stiff with any-one else, which was a good thing, and the Governor had a long yarn with Mr. McKenzie, which was also a great point gained. Then I went for a short ride with the Governor and shewed him some of the country which he had not before visited: he has a great deal of very difficult work before him, and I hope he will do it well: I think that from what has been seen of him much is expected of him: he goes down well with people.

May 4. I am conscious of my shortcomings in the way of letter-writing: the steamer is expected tomorrow, and I have no respectable letter ready to send away: the details of my life would be uninteresting to you who know none of the people. I have had great misfortunes with my turkeys: nine young ones died a few days after they were born: I have now a hen sitting on turkey's eggs, and hope to be more successful next time: I have also failed hitherto in rearing my young pigeons: I think it has been owing to my having three gentlemen and one lady: so two gentlemen have been incarcerated.

I bought two goslings, a week old, and the rapidity with which they have grown is something quite remarkable: the quantity they eat is amazing: when they are tired of walking about and eating they lie down and eat all the grass within reach: they are very tame, never having known a mothers care, and walk into the kitchen and allow one to stroke them.

I have sixteen thriving young ducks, and two hens sitting on duck's eggs: one of them had a goose's egg, but the gosling unfortunately expired in its efforts to break open its shell: it was discovered with its beak sticking out. I have also a grouse egg being hatched: if a young grouse comes out, I shall cut off the outer bone of the wing at once; the wound will heal immediately but the bird will never be able to fly well.

Then my garden and early vegetables are coming forward very well, but I find that the weeds grow terribly fast. In about a week I intend to go and live on board the Grappler for a short time, to see that she is in good order: things have been allowed to work rather loosely during the winter, because it was no use contending against the ceaseless rain and cold; but now the summer has begun, we have painted the ship, and I wish her to be in first rate order by the time the Admiral arrives in the middle of this month. The trees are just fledged, and the country is looking about its best; the wild-flowers are abundant.

May 5. The mail steamer has arrived this morning, bringing, I fear, no English letters. Two of my men deserted last night, taking with them the ship's dingy: I dare say we shall not again see either men or boat: both the men were of indifferent character, but one was my cook, and consequently rather an important part of my establishment.

The more I see of Gilford, the more I admire him: the Tribune is certainly in first rate order, and he deserves infinite credit for having made her such a contrast to most ships of the present day: she reminds me of the good old days when I first entered the service, when every man and every officer had to do his duty, before pepper and mustard were served out.

Your affectionate Son,
Edmund Hope Verney

P.S. Rejoice with me: the man who deserted is not my cook, but another man of the same name.

E.H.V.

The Small Bower. Esquimalt. V.I.
May 6. 1864.

My dear Father,

The mail steamer that arrived and sailed again yesterday brought no news of any importance, and but very few letters: the comfort when one steamer brings no mail is that the next is sure to bring one, and possibly two. Tomorrow the "Grappler" will be ready for sea, and I am going to live on board for a few days, and take the ship out for a cruize, to expend our quarter's ammunition at a target, exercise under sail &c[.] Last night, Walker of Bella Coula left me: he is quite a different man now, and rapidly regaining his strength; but it will probably be a year before he can be pronounced cured: you will remember the newspaper account of his sufferings which I sent you.

May 7. Yesterday there was a meeting of the exploration Committee, of which I am a member: the Governor has said that for every dollar subscribed by the public for furthering the exploration of Vancouver Island, he will on behalf of the Government, put down two: in consequence of this offer, a public meeting was called, and the Vancouver Island Exploration Committee was appointed. A public meeting is to be held on Tuesday, to draw forth the opinions of practical men as to how exploration may be most efficiently and economically conducted: I expect that the meeting will be one of great interest: the idea at present is to send out two small parties at once, and later in the summer to despatch a larger party to those parts of the Island which the smaller parties may recommend should be more carefully explored: what is most wanted to be known about is agricultural land in the first instance, and coal and minerals subsequently: it certainly is remarkable how little is known of the Island at present, beyond the coast lines of the hydrographical survey.

May 9. On Saturday a lady gave a picnic at a place called Sangster's plains, a spot that may be reached by a long ride from Victoria, or by a comparatively short pull in a boat outside the harbour:[1] I was invited, and pulled out in my gig, and the gig's crew came up to see the fun: when amusement was at its height, a groom who had come out with one of the waggons, and was an old friend of mine called me aside and told me that he had heard my boat's crew making arrangments to desert and pull across to the American shore: I ran down to the boat and found them there, having provided wine and meat to take with them, so I got into the boat and we pulled on board. I am now trying to get the evidence of another man who overheard them talking, as I want to make quite sure of the fact before I punish them:

I mention this that you may see what disappointments one is subject to out here: of course, even the best men try to desert when they know that they can quadruple their wages by going in a merchant ship; but it is heart-breaking work to see those whom one has tried to make comfortable and to bring into a fair state of discipline trying to desert, and shewing that they are not to be trusted: about a week ago, two of my men took the dingy in the night and deserted to the American side; one of them was a young fellow of whom I had a very good opinion, but the other was a blackguard.

May 11. On Monday we went outside the harbour to fire at a target, and anchored for the night at a place called Parry Bay: early the next morning an Indian came alongside and pointed out to us two figures wrapped up in blankets in a canoe a little way off, paddled by two Indians, which figures he said were men-of-war's men: I sent out a boat and was very much delighted when she brought back two marines belonging to the "Tribune" who had been trying to desert: then we weighed with a glorious S.W.ly breeze, and cruized in the Straits under sail all day, exercising: I have not enjoyed myself as much for a long time as I did yesterday: the ship sailed far better than I had expected, and the breeze was glorious: in the afternoon we sailed into Esquimalt, and moored in our usual berth, not having had the fires lighted all day: I handed the two deserters over to the viscount's tender mercies.

May 14. The mail steamer that arrived this morning brought me no letters: this is the second mail by which I have not heard from you: the only news of importance that we have is that Admiral Denman is appointed to this station, and that he has selected Captain Christian for his flag captain.[2]

The Indians inland from Bute Inlet have massacred a party of fourteen men, and Gilford has this afternoon gone to New Westminster in the Forward to consult with Governor Seymour as to what is best to be done.[3]

Your affectionate Son,
Edmund Hope Verney

The Small Bower. Esquimalt. V.I.
May 20. 1864.

My dear Father,

As a mail steamer is now due, I must not allow myself to be surprised without even a letter begun, although, as usual, it is not easy to find much sensible matter to say.

A Russian corvette arrived here a day or two ago, bearing the flag of Admiral Popoff, who was here in another ship a year and a half ago:[1] he is a young man of about 42, who has got on rapidly on account of his services in Sebastopol: he called on me on board the "Grappler" this morning, and went round the ship; then he came down into my cabin, and looked at my nautical instruments &c: he particularly admired the small artificial horizon which was Uncle Fremantle's present to me when I left England: he also was much interested in seeing the pocket sextant that Miss Nightingale gave me, and enquired much about her: he was quite indignant when I shewed it to him, and asked him if he knew the name; he said that of course every-body had heard of Florence Nightingale at Scutari. The Admiral appeared to be an active and intelligent man, and pleasant to talk to, but I believe he is not popular in his own service; he is celebrated for giving good dinners, and has by this means won the hearts of the good people of San Francisco. He gives a grand dinner tonight, to which I am invited: he has on board a Prince with his wife and family who is going to Sitka as Governor, Prince Maksutoff: Governor Kennedy is invited with his family, so I suppose we shall be a large party.[2]

His ship, the Bogatyz, is a large corvette with a few very heavy guns: I think that large corvettes, with a few heavy guns, are a class of ship more highly thought of by other nations than by England: we rather stick to line-of-battle-ships and frigates, which have this advantage, that when ships are engaging yard-arm to yard-arm the guns on the battery deck can be fought without their crews being exposed to the fire of riflemen aloft: the same thing would hold good in engaging shore batteries at close ranges or if under a heavy fire of shell.

Admiral Kingcome may now be daily expected: he said he would arrive here at the middle or end of May. I am glad to hear that Admiral

Denman is appointed: I have no doubt that you will see him before he leaves England.

May 21. The mail steamer arrived this morning, bringing only a letter from Aunt Abel, dated March 31.: I have not yet heard of any news. Our dinner last night went off very satisfactorily, with but little stiffness of formality: the Princess Matsukoff had no pretension to classical beauty, but she was very attractive and "spirituelle": she is only 18, so is a great acquisition to the officers: there was a want of finish in the way the dinner was put on the table, but the food itself was admirable: it appeared as if the cook sent up whatever dish happened to be ready: there were no vegetables at all, and ices were followed by roast veal: we had each seven wine glasses, and seven different kinds of wine, pronounced to be marvellously good: after dinner we adjourned to the wardroom where was a piano, and we had music and singing. When the Governor's party went away the ships hull and spars were illuminated with blue-lights.

All the Russian officers spoke French, and most of them German and English: they seemed to be well educated and gentlemanlike, and would probably compare favourably with the naval officers of other nations: there was a courtliness about their manners which was decidedly French, without however that very finnikin air one sometimes sees.

The Admiral evidently takes great pride and interest in his profession: he shewed us some very valuable charts and sketches of Sebastopol executed during the seige, and shewing how intimately the Russians were acquainted with the positions of our approaches: he probably sails for Sitka tomorrow.

Now, adieu my dear Father: I am turning my attention more particularly this year to the raising of ducks, of which I hope to get about fifty: at present I have only twenty-eight, but I have four hens sitting on duck's eggs, and the ducks are still laying: Claydon has five lovely little puppies, all doing well.

My garden is very small, but it is neat, free from weeds, and in good order, and will supply me with what little I want during the summer.

Your affectionate Son,
Edmund Hope Verney

The Small Bower. Esquimalt. V.I.
May 25. 1864.

My dear Father,

The Admiral arrived yesterday in the "Sutlej": he is much disappointed at being superseded, but more especially at not being allowed to bring his flag at the fore to England: I must say that I am very sorry that honour has not been conceded to the gallant old fellow: such an old veteran is entitled to the sympathy of every-one, and that small thing would have brought much pride and pleasure to the honest old Admiral's heart. He has done his best conscientiously and feels he is not appreciated, a very bitter feeling for a man at his time of life.

I sincerely trust that the "Grappler" will now be taken in hand and repaired: the Ral talks of heaving her down, but there can be no doubt that the cheapest and most expeditious plan would be to let the whole thing out by contract, and have her hauled up on the slip at Victoria.

I have a good deal of work in hand just now, besides the "Grappler": I am a member of the "Exploration Committee", and Chairman of the sub-committee appointed to draw up regulations for and to conclude arrangements with the Exploring party: we hope to be able to get them all under weigh by the first of June: the conduct of the party is entrusted to a certain Dr. Brown, sent out by a Scotch botanical Society to collect seeds.[1]

June 4. I have just returned from a week's visit to Cowichan which I enjoyed exceedingly, visiting among my friends the settlers, who were most hospitable, and welcomed me very pleasantly. The mail arrived this morning bringing your letters of March 15. and 28. I am very glad you have met so many people from these parts, as you will have learnt so much about these Colonies: You ask what the Admiral has said about our going on shore: he has actually said not one word about it; he has not asked one question as to how it occurred: the fact is that I suspect he knows he ought not to have sent us north at that time of the year, and that he desires to do nothing that may draw the attention of the Admiralty to our serious damages:[2] I do not even know when he intends repairing us: I know he thinks of leaving it to Admiral Denman: I am becoming very heartily tired of the "Grappler"; she is very defective: she steams badly: her bottom is all knocked about, and we are so shorthanded that it is one incessant drive to keep the ship in even tolerable order, and it is really impossible to forget all about promotion: orders have arrived by this mail to pay the gunboats off, and I think they can hardly refuse me my promotion now.

I am very sorry to hear both from you and from Emily of her fever, which must be very trying to her, and cause you much anxiety: I trust that the worst of it is now over, and that the change of air may do her permanent good: I am not sure that a six month's cruize round the West Indies, or in some very distant place with her eldest brother would not do her a world of good.

With regard to what you say about Professor Jowett, I quite agree with you, and rather like to dwell on the simplest side of religion:[3] by all means let each one who has the ability study what may be called the scientific side, but let each pin his hopes of salvation to its simplicity: when the autumn comes on I will get you some more pine seeds, especially some yew seeds which a botanist has told me would be valuable in England.

Pray tell me about Aunt Dunsany: a letter a few months ago said that she was failing fast, but since then I have heard no more.[4] Your long letter has done me a great deal of good: a father's letters are, I suppose, always the most welcome to a son.

Acland of the Sutlej has been with me on my Cowichan cruize and I think enjoyed it thoroughly: he is a good youngster, better perhaps than most boys, but I tell him that he does not come up to what an Acland ought to be: I have recommended him to change his name, as he would make a very creditable Jones.[5]

I look forward to great trouble with the "Grappler": I see breakers ahead: paying her off will involve an immense amount of labour, of red tape, and winding up elaborate accounts: then there will be unpleasant work in getting a new ship's company, certainly not composed of the best men in the fleet, and breaking them in, with the expectation of being promoted shortly: however, I must not anticipate too much; sufficient unto the day is the evil thereof, and the green peas in my garden will be ripe next week.

Adieu, my dear Father; with love to Mama, believe me,

Your affectionate Son,
Edmund Hope Verney

H.M.S. Grappler. Cowichan. V.I.
June 8. 1864.

My dear Father,

The "Grappler" anchored here last night, having brought up the exploring party who are to commence by ascending the Cowichan river: they hoped to have started last night but the weather was very wet, and as it is raining hard to-day they are still on board: the barometer has now begun to rise so we shall probably have the fine weather again tomorrow: this rain which is so unpleasant to us is a great boon to the whole country: the summer began very early this year, the land was quite dried up and there was every prospect of an unproductive season: now however, I think it promises to be one of the best seasons we have had here.

I have a visitor staying with me, a Mr. Howell, whose father is superintendant of contracts I think in the War Office: he is a very nice fellow and a pleasant companion: his sister Mrs. Cruickshanks who lives in Victoria is also a very nice person: a man of the name of Bottomley, and a midshipman of the name of Donner from the Sutlej are also with me, and we hope to have two or three days cruize tomorrow if it clears up to shoot and fish among the mountains:[1] I had that same pleasure here last week, and enjoyed it much, only am not able to do as much as I could wish for fear of being laid up with my game knee. It is always a great pleasure to me to visit the Cowichan settlers, most of whom are my personal friends and always give me the warmest welcome. It is not generally known in Victoria what a thriving settlement this is, or how much is doing here, but I hope that shortly the Governor will visit Cowichan, and then people will take more interest in its welfare.

The Chronometer watch you gave me before I left England has been again cleaned and repaired to give it another chance; I will let you know if it goes any better: every watchmaker who looks at it says it is a beautiful watch and ought to keep most accurate time, but it has now cost me a third of its original cost in repairs, cleanings, &c.

June 14. I have a sad catastrophe to relate to you: I returned on Sunday evening after an absence of six days at Cowichan, and found that the marine left in charge of the Bower had deserted; wine, cider, ale, clothing &c are missing so that I am altogether a loser to the amount of £35. He has stolen that watch chain made of coins which I had collected at great trouble and expense. I am much vexed about the whole affair for many reasons: in the first place there are not many people who can afford to lose £35.: then I am vexed to have lost such a good, steady, industrious servant; and then I am vexed at the ingratitude of a man for whom I had done a great deal: I had lately doubled his wages at his own request: since he came to live on shore he had learnt both to read and to write, and of a Sunday evening lately we had been reading together a very nicely bound pilgrim's progress which I had given him, and which he has taken with him.[2] He bore a very high character, and I had great confidence in him: I am not surprised that he deserted, because I am not surprised at any one deserting from the low pay of the Navy when they can get at least four times as much on shore here, but I am surprised that he should have robbed me: he should at least have taken every care that I should not suffer from his desertion. Henry was aware that the man had been unsteady and keeping bad company for the last two or three months, but he did not caution me, but contented himself with threatening the man with being reported: I must own that I am also disappointed with Henry, but he seems sorry for it.

June 16. The mail arrived and departed yesterday, when this letter, by an oversight, was not sent.

Today the Russian corvette Bogatyz sails with Admiral Popoff & Mr. Fournhelm the ex-governor of Sitka, and wife & family: I had a good deal of talk with Mme. Fournhelm who begged to be most kindly remembered to Miss V.Z. Mme. F. is a very nice person, and speaks English perfectly, having lived for a long time in Devonshire: I told her that Emily & Miss V.Z. were living at Torquay, and she congratulated them on being in such a charming spot: she is now looking forward to the pleasure of returning to Europe after an absence of nearly six years, which I am afraid she has felt to be rather a banishment.[3]

June 22. I returned yesterday from Nanaimo whither I went to seize five Hydah Chiefs whose people were suspected of having shot some cows in the neighbourhood of Victoria.[4] Nanaimo is a place that is rapidly springing into importance: a month or two ago it was declared a port of entry, and since then it has already made a start: the Vancouver Coal Company are working the mines on a large and increasing scale: they have a railroad and a locomotive engine, and the value of land is rapidly increasing.

If any bishops or Governors are coming out here, or any one by whom you could send a parcel, will you be so good as to send me one dozen "Emerald polka-mazurka" and one dozen "Shannon's Brigade in India": the latter must be ordered on my account from Saunders and Otley, the former are either in London or at Claydon.[5]

The mail has arrived this afternoon, bringing two letters from you: one is dated April 15; the other is marked "viâ New York" and dated April 30: you say you are writing by New York as an experiment, and that you wish me to let you know the result: you see that New York brings letters upwards of a fortnight sooner in this instance: Mr. Ridgway has sent me my newspapers much more regularly lately, but even he does not send them by New York: my Army and Navy Gazette is dated April 23^{d}.

You hint that it might be advisable to come home a Lieutenant if there is no prospect of my coming home a Commander in a few months: I am afraid that it would be wrong to leave the "Grappler" until I am promoted, and it must not be thought of, even if it should keep me out here a year or two longer. The "Grappler" is ordered to be paid off on the 18th of next month, and possibly the Admiralty may take that opportunity of promoting me: when the "Grappler" has been paid off, I shall write an official letter to the Admiral asking him to move the L.C.A. to grant me my promotion: if he backs it strongly it may be successful: I suppose that this ministry can hardly last many months longer: if not perhaps the Duke might promote me just before going out, so "nil desperandum".

Please tell that bad girl Mary Ann Tyler that she has not written to her brother for nine months: she does not know how much absent brothers prize their sisters' letters, and I do. A Gunboat will probably have to take the Governor round the settlements shortly, and I hope that I may have this duty to perform: it would be very interesting to point out to him various objects of interest and to bring under his notice deserving settlers. An officer receiving a Governor on board is paid £3. a day for the first week, a guinea a day afterwards, and a guinea a day for each of his suite: a little help of this sort would be very opportune after my recent losses.

Pray give my love to Mama; I will answer her jolly long letter by next mail,

Your affectionate Son,
Edmund Hope Verney

H.M.S. Grappler. Fraser River. B.C.
June 27. 1864.

My dear Father,

Your letter of April 30. referring to some unwise letter of mine to Commodore Spencer, has puzzled me much: I always keep copies of letters of any importance, and I send you copies of the only two letters that I can find that are at all likely to be the one referred to, but in neither can I see a word to offend the most sensitive post-captain; show them to any of your naval friends, and ask whether they contain anything unbecoming or unusual for a young officer to write to his superior.[1] Captain Spencer may say what he likes, but he always behaved very badly to me from the first, allowing himself to be ruled and governed by others who were unworthy of his confidence, and who bore me animosity for reasons not worth entering into in a letter. Captain

Spencer's behavior to me on more than one occasion was quite contrary to the customary courtesy of the profession: since he and Captain Richards left the station, I have always got on capitally with the senior officer, whether Captain or admiral.

Your affectionate Son,
Edmund Hope Verney

(Copy) H.M.S. Grappler. Cowichan. V.I.
May 10. 1862 [*sic*].

Dear Commodore Spencer,

Tomorrow morning I intend to leave for New Westminster according to the orders I received from Captain Pike: if the tide flows tomorrow afternoon, as I expect, we ought to reach New Westminster in the evening. I will write from New Westminster as soon as the work there is completed.

I have taken advantage of my stay here to visit the interior part of this settlement, further from the coast than I have been before: it has been very gratifying to see the abundance of rich open prarie, the progress that the several farms have made, and the general contentment of the settlers. The only cause of complaint, and it appears to be a just one, is that the Governor has not yet paid the Indians for the land according to his promise; when they are hindered by the farmers from cutting down trees, or establishing themselves on new potatoe patches they plead the non-fulfilment of the Governor's promise, and an affair of this nature might at any time lead to a serious disturbance.

There are no complaints of the behaviour of any Indians belonging to tribes of the Cowichan valley, but a party of travelling Indians, generally from the north, have on more than one occasion been saucy to isolated settlers, and created a little alarm.

This afternoon we hear a rumour from the natives that there has been trouble at Comax, and that three settlers houses have been burnt; Indian rumours have generally some foundation, I think.

I am, dear Commodore Spencer,

Yours faithfully,
(Sd.) Edmund Hope Verney

[Copy] H.M.S. Grappler. New Westminster. B.C.
May 13. 1863.

Dear Commodore Spencer,

At Sunrise this morning we took on board the harbour-master, and proceeded to the mouth of the river to paint and re-adjust the buoys. There was some little delay on two occasions owing to the midship boiler giving way, but each time a wooden plug was inserted in the leaking tube, and the steam ready again under the half hour. The work was completed, and we returned to New Westminster this afternoon.

I intend to start for Nanaimo tomorrow morning, and to take in as much coal as convenient in the afternoon. On Friday I hope to go to the Comax settlement where there will probably be some cases of smuggling and liquor selling to Indians to be dealt with. I shall probably leave Port Augusta early on monday morning for Nanaimo, calling at Nanoose Harbour on the way, and fill up with coal. I hope thence to return to Victoria calling first at Saltspring Island. Tuesday will probably be occupied in coaling, so we might anchor at Saltspring Island on wednesday evening in Ganges Harbour. On thursday I shall proceed to Cowichan, and remain there one or two days before returning to Esquimalt.

I have entered into these details that you may have no difficulty in sending me orders at any time, and I shall adhere to the above arrangment as far as practicable.

I hope that the letter I sent to you from Cowichan arrived safely on Monday evening or tuesday morning.

I am &c

(Sd.) E.H.V.

H.M.S. Grappler. Victoria. V.I.
July 1. 1864.

My dear Father

Tomorrow we start for the Bentinck Arm to take dispatches to the Admiral: for the last week we have been engaged in unsuccessful attempts to get the Tribune afloat: she grounded on the sand-heads while trying to get out of the Fraser river about a fortnight ago: the Forward and Grappler were hastily sent for to lend their aid, and for nearly a week we did our best to help her off night after night: but at length the repeated strain upon our boilers caused them to give out, and important dispatches for the Admiral arriving from the Colonial-Secretary of British Columbia, we were ordered to repair our boilers here, and then proceed with all despatch to Bentinck Arm.[1]

I have been very glad to have a little work to do lately: our bottom has not yet been repaired, and if it is done at all, I do not think it will be during Admiral Kingcome's reign: in the mean time the ship is kept running about as usual, and certainly she *looks* all right, as all her damage is below water: as it was during November last that we got on shore, I think the action of the water on the unprotected wood must be doing a great deal of mischief, and certainly rotting the caulking, so do not be surprised if you hear that a good gale of wind has shaken her bottom out; however, there is not much probability of bad weather at this time of year.

The paying off of the gunboats will probably be postponed until August, as there is so much doing at present, which just increases the possibility of my being promoted before the crews are changed.

The newspapers and radicals of this colony, under the semblance of the deepest commiseration, crow over what they delight to call "the

Wreck of the Tribune": now, say they, must there be for ever an end of all pretence on the part of New Westminster and the Fraser River to vie with Victoria and Esquimalt, day after day does the paper ring some new change on this fruitful theme: the efforts to get the Tribune off have failed hitherto because the fates have appeared always adverse: she is now lightened of her guns, shot, ammunition, salt meat, and spare screw, and has her topmasts struck: she floats, or nearly floats every twenty-four hours, and every twenty-four hours she is moved a cable's length or more in the direction of the deep channel, but on two occasions a northerly gale has sprung up, and in a few minutes blown her back a distance that it had taken days to traverse: on other occasions the wind has not sprung up until the tide had fallen and allowed her to ground again, when of course it could do no harm. While on the one hand I am sorry to have to leave Gilford in his trouble, on the other I am glad to have done with such heavy night work that was most harrassing to both officers and men: I think a few days more will see the "Tribune" fairly afloat again, and it will then be seen whether her damage is bad or not: there is no doubt that she has been severely strained, and probably she will go down to San Francisco to be docked, but there are people here who ought to know something about it, and who declare that she is "hogged", and will never again be seaworthy. As may be supposed, poor Gilford is terribly vexed although he fights manfully against his vexation.[2]

No blame can attach to him for the ship having got on shore, I should think; there is certainly no credit due to the pilot who had charge of her when she grounded, or to the Harbour Master of New Westminster for the state of his buoys: it may also be asked what were the circumstances that rendered it necessary to send a ship drawing so much water up the Fraser at all, when gunboats or merchant steamers might have been procured.

I hardly know whether in your stirring European times you will care to hear of Colonial politics: there can be no doubt that Governor Seymour has become deeply imbued with the British Columbian feeling, and is a warm partizan of his own Colony: I hardly like to say that he has adopted the extreme British Columbian views of jealousy of V.I., but he has certainly gone in more heavily for B.C. than I should have expected: he is now at Bella Coula, and intends travelling through to Cariboo thence.

The House of Assembly here are making greater donkeys of themselves than ever; the best men will not stand for the House of Assembly: I think on the whole that I am now, after two years observation, prepared with an opinion which is this – The Colony of Vancouver Island should have its constitution taken from it, and it should be annexed to British Columbia; the United Colonies should then be governed by the same laws, by one Governor and a legislative Council like the Council of B.C. at present.

I think that on the whole Governor Kennedy is popular, but people do not yet understand him: of the two Governors he impresses me as being the best able to govern, but until he is provided with a suitable Government House, and treated with more courtesy by the House of Assembly he will not be understood: he has a heavy task to perform, and I conclude that all sensible men must agree that he is setting to work the right way about it.

Adieu, my dear Father; with love to Mama and all at home, believe me,

Your affectionate Son,
Edmund Hope Verney

H.M.S. Grappler. Bella. Coula. B.C.
July 8. 1864.

My dear Father,

We arrived here on wednesday, bringing despatches to the Admiral from the Colonial Secretary of B.C.: communications are received from Governor Seymour every four or five days, by the latest of which we hear that he has joined a party of volunteers from Alexandria: tomorrow or the next day we hope to hear that they are after the Indians.

On Sunday the Admiral starts for Esquimalt, leaving me here to communicate with the Governor, and possibly I may be here two, three, four, or five weeks: this letter will go down by the Sutlej, so if you do not hear of me shortly you will know that I am stowed away in this crack in British Columbia.

By the last mail orders arrived that Lascelles and I are to be reappointed to the Forward and Grappler, to complete our service of three years in the gunboats from the dates of our appointments: Lascelles' time will be up in November, mine in February: the orders do not state what is to happen to us at the expiration of that time, whether we are to be promoted, or merely superseded; of course if it merely means superseded I should like to be re-appointed and to remain here until I am promoted however long that may be: nevertheless I think they ought to promote me now on the ship's paying off: the "Grappler" is to be paid off as soon as we return to Esquimalt.

Will you be so good as to forward the accompanying letter: I only brought out enough clothes to last me for a year or eighteen months, and now I have not got a garment fit to be seen: in short I may say that I am a mere mass of rags, destitute of even the common necessaries of life: you will feel for me when I tell you that the very eau-de-cologne I brought out is all gone.

Adieu, my dear Father: with love to Mamma, believe me,

Your affectionate Son,
Edmund Hope Verney

July 9. The Sutlej sails for Esquimalt this evening, leaving me here to keep up communications with Governor Seymour: I may be here for perhaps three or four weeks, but not longer, because I have not provisions to last out: what I shall do with myself all the time, I am not prepared to say: a man named Howell, is with me, and we shall try what can be done with guns and fishing rods: such however is the ignorance in which the living creatures of these parts are steeped, that the most alluring flies that can be manufactured in London have no charms for them and their grovelling tastes are far more in favour of a piece of salmon roe, or some nasty entrails.

The Sutlej will lend us eleven marines, so we shall not be so short-handed as usual, and shall be able to get the ship very clean and to have plenty of drill: as soon as we return to Esquimalt, we shall be paid off and recommissioned: only one or two of the present crew will remain for the next commission, so I shall lose my most trusted men: altogether it is rather too bad leaving me to commence the new commission: if the L.C.A. mean to promote me at the end of my three years, they might just as well have given me the additional six months, and my promotion now.

We have been surprised to hear nothing of Admiral Denman; it is said that he has been travelling on the continent, and that as his address was not known the news of his appointment took a long time to reach him: if he brings Mrs. Denman out with him, they will be a great addition to Colonial Society.

Yesterday a prisoner was brought in, who had ventured down among the white men and the faithful Indians as a spy: he was recognized at once, pinioned, and brought down on board the Sutlej. I have been much interested in observing the salmon fishing; at this season of the year they come in from the sea and force their way up the rivers to deposit their spawn, and show a wonderful determination in darting up rapids: across the Bella Coula river a dam has been built of logs, boughs, trunks of trees &c, in which three or four clear places have been left: the water on the upper side of the dam is perhaps three or four feet higher than on the other, and finds its way between the logs or over them more or less along its whole length: but where the gaps have been left it rushes through with great speed, and it is for these gaps that the salmon make: these gaps are filled by a large rectangular wicker work basket or trough about six feet by twelve made with very large meshes only just close enough to keep the fish from escaping, so as to offer as little resistance to the water as possible: the lower side of this basket is not a right angle, but inclines inwards at an angle of about 45°; neither is it so high as the other three sides, which are perhaps five or six feet: the water rushes down through this basket, submerging the inclined side: the salmon springs up the little waterfall, over the inclined side, and into the basket: hence it could easily leap back again if it knew its danger, but its instinct teaches it only to ascend the stream, so it swims to the upper end of the basket and there pokes about seeking for egress: in the meantime it touches as it swims about three strings attached to the bottom of the basket and held at the other end by a boy who is on the look-out; he feels the contact, and at once the basket is raised out of the water, and the fish taken from it.

In this way the natives catch in one basket from a dozen to a dozen and a half salmon in an hour, often getting two at one haul: they are at once handed over to the women who clean them, cut them open and spread-eagle them on sticks, and dry them in the smoke of their fires: after this process they will keep for a long time, and if cooked after our fashion make a dish by no means to be despised.

It was one of these Bella Coula Indians that shot Ernest Walker last year, so although they are at present friendly to us, and likely to continue so, there must be among them many treacherous and bad individuals.

Their language is said to be the most harsh and guttural of those spoken by coast tribes, and the people the most barbarous and depraved, so we cannot plume ourselves on our allies: the inland tribes are very angry with them for the countenance they are shewing us, and the help they afford us in packing our provisions, and sey [*sic*] that as soon as this affair is settled they will exterminate every Bella Coula Indian.

E.H.V.

H.M.S. Grappler. Bella-Coula. B.C.
July 13. 1864

My dear Father,

With the prospect of being left here for two or three weeks to keep up communication with Governor Seymour and his corps of volunteers, I shall have plenty of time on my hands and intend to get up long arrears of correspondence: it is also a good opportunity for me to clean and paint ship and do many little things that cannot be done when the ship is continually under weigh.

A man of the name of Howell is with me on a visit: his father is superintendant of contracts in the war office, and his sister is married to a Mr. Cruickshank a broker in Victoria: he has been for some years in China and Japan, where his health gave way, and is a most agreable companion: I have also messing with me an assistant-surgeon named Atkinson, lent to the Grappler for the occasion; so we form a cosy little party.[1]

There is certainly not much to be done in the north Bentinck Arm: as yet we have discovered neither shooting nor fishing: there are one or two walks along trails involving an occasional stripping to the waist to ford streams, but they are for the most [*sic*] along trails through thick damp bush. There are picturesque waterfalls coming down through narrow gorges among the rocks overgrown on either side by scraggy pine trees and thick underbush with occasional open spaces of thick soft damp moss: and in some parts the streams fall brawling over fallen logs, which may be used as a bridge by the sure-footed but are mightly slimy. Then there are mountains which may be climbed, but the views from them are only of further hills and snow-capped mountains piled up one above another, in some places bare and precipitous in others covered only with the endless pine.

Perhaps our pleasantest pastime is picking berries: each takes a small pan and after first filling his stomach proceeds to fill his pan with some description of berry: these are brought on board and made into puddings or jams, thus affording delectable employment during the day, and agreable repast in the evening. No deer are to be bought from the natives, but plenty of salmon, some weighing seven or eight pounds.

Randal Plunkett writes to me to cut him a "bit of a thwig", a "shillelah": will you be kind enough to pick out one of the sticks I have sent home, if they have ever arrived, and send it to him with my love.

August 5. Today a vessel is to leave Esquimalt to come here to re-leave us; she will probably take four or five days to come up, and will bring letters, news papers, provisions, scandal, and other necessaries dear to the heart of one who has been quite out of the world for six weeks. Our time has passed merrily enough, between shooting, fishing, and picking berries: the shooting has been almost nil, and until the last week or ten days the fishing has been but a name.

Two or three days ago I caught a 10. lbs. salmon, and landed him quite exhausted after nearly half an hours work. I have a very good salmon-rod and line which I bought for a mere song a few weeks ago: it was made by a game-keeper in Wales, and given as a great treasure to a man who came out here, and was glad to sell it when he ran short of money: when I bought it I had no idea what a good one it was: just now there is very good fishing, both salmon and trout: the salmon come up the streams to spawn, and the trout follow the salmon to devour their spawn when they can get it: in fishing for trout we bait with salmon roe, and as we are rather short of provisions, a dish of trout for breakfast is a great treat: the salmon will rarely take bait at this time of year: we troll a spinning spoon bait across narrow places in the streams, or through the deep pools in the eddies, and in most cases hook the fish foul by the tail, the fin, the gills, or even in the back: a fish thus hooked has far more power than a fish hooked in the mouth, and this kind of fishing requires stronger tackle, and great care. Twice have I lost hooks and line: yesterday, I played a large fish for nearly half an hour, when he broke away from me, but luckily I saved my hooks.

The Admiral lent me ten marines before he left; so this long spell here has been a fine chance for getting the ship put to rights, and making all sorts of sailors dandifications, a list of which would, I fear, be thrown away upon a landsman: I spent one week on shore, and had my cabin painted throughout.

August 17. Still at Bella Coula. Why no vessel has arrived to relieve us, I cannot divine: either no vessel left Esquimalt on the fifth, or the vessel that left has got on shore or come to grief in some way: we have provisions to last about a week longer, and then we shall have to go down whether we are relieved or not. We are enjoying delicious weather, days of sunshine and nights of cloudless stars: I should be in no hurry to be relieved if the Captain's table was a little better supplied, but, poor fellow, he is running very short of provisions, and his steward cannot get much for him: he has my warm sympathy. I am effecting wonders in the "Grappler", left here with plenty of men, plenty of time, and fine weather: sailmakers, coopers, carpenters, and blacksmiths hard at work: we are unfortunately out of paint, so the painting has to stand over. On the second of July we left Victoria, so we have about six weeks mails due to us.

August 22. 1864. At length the "Forward" has arrived to relieve us, bringing a few letters, yours of May 1. – June 1. What you say about my appointment to the Royal Yacht disturbs me somewhat, and would disturb me more, did I think there was the least chance of my receiving the appointment: on the whole, I do not think I am likely to be selected: Leiningen will doubtless have some voice in the matter, and he knows that I am not cut out for a courtier.[2]

But besides that, there are other considerations; my promotion would be definitely postponed for two years: then I should be promoted one year after Scott who was in the Emerald with me, and is upwards of a year my junior: it would not be pleasant to have a man promoted over my head out of the same ship. Furthermore the intensely idle life of the Yacht and the "swelldom" it carries with it would probably be very bad for me, and very distasteful to me: I have always said that *this* is the best lieutenant's appointment in the service, and I do not make an exception even in favour of the Yacht: to a man who has once tasted the sweets of command, even junior lieutenant of the Yacht would be most galling: then in case of war, I should of course deeply regret being in the Yacht.

Here I am, not seeing as active service as I could wish, not being employed as continually as I could wish, but still doing something and learning something, and as far as my wishes are concerned, here I would remain until I am promoted, even for two or three years more. I love my profession far more than I have ever done before, and am well aware that I have many years carelessness to make up for, so I do not want to be shunted up through the Yacht. A lieutenant of the Yacht leads an idle life, and learns for two years nothing of a profession which it takes a life-time to acquire.

But, now on the other hand, it would be ungracious to refuse or rather decline what the Duke of Somerset terms "an honour": if the Duke feels that I cannot expect to be promoted for two years or more, he probably believes that he is doing me a great favour in submitting my name to the Queen: doubtless you, and those whom you have consulted are better judges of what is right than I can be: I can only say that as far as I know I would sooner serve two years more in the "Grappler" for my promotion than two years in the Yacht: I had rather serve as first lieutenant of the "Tribune" for two years than go to the Yacht: but as some conclusion must be arrived at, I arrive at this, that as the Duke's offer appears to have been made, as was my appointment to the "Grappler", *unsolicited*, it is my *duty* to accept it, and to trust that Providence will wisely order the issue.

And now that I have dismissed the matter in the above wise and oracular manner, it is to be remarked that this letter can probably not arrive until *after* the important question is decided: you say that the

Queen makes her choice in September: we shall start the day after tomorrow, the 24th, and my letter can not leave Esquimalt until September, but I am glad to think that if I am selected you will be proud and pleased, and if I am not your disappointment will be relieved by knowing how slight a boon it would have been to me. No one could appreciate more highly than I do the honour that *has* been conferred on me by the Duke's selection of my name for submission to the Queen; *that* honour would not be increased by its being further selected by the Queen, whose selection could be guided by no higher authority than that of the Duke: but I would rather show my appreciation of that honour by any active service than by service in the Yacht.

If I am not selected for the Yacht, and if in February next at the expiration of my three years I am not promoted, I only beg to be re-appointed to the "Grappler".

August 23. Your accounts of Emily are not, on the whole, very satisfactory: I trust that you and she may be guided as to what is right for the coming winter: I believe in Jamaica, and a visit to Mrs. Price. From what the Bishop of Columbia has written to these Colonies, I am sure that he has not met with the support he expected in England: there is plenty for him to do out here, and the sooner he returns the better. The Forward has brought us the news of the extraordinary discoveries of gold at Sooke, near Victoria: this will be a grand thing for the Colony: the discovery was made by the Exploring party sent out by the Exploration Committee.[3]

Thank you much for the hints you give me about the undesirability of frequenting the Government House too much: indeed I never thought of it in that light, and I see how right you are. I hear that Mr. Cary the Attorney-General is bankrupt, and will have to leave the colony.[4]

I am indeed sorry to hear of Aunt Dunsany's death, although I had expected it for a long time, in consequence of what you had written me word:[5] do you remember that a short time before I left England I gave her, by your advice, Mamma's white cornelian seal with "Eliza" on it? if I might have it again it would have a double value to me. While I congratulate Miss V.Z. on the brilliant appointment offered to her, I deeply feel how Emily will be distressed to lose her: where you will find any one to fill her place, I know not: our darling E. does not take readily to strangers.

May I ask you to be so good as to answer the letter from Mr. Coleman & Co. in such manner as you may be advised is best: I should think the book had better be transferred to Mr. Adams on the same terms as it was held by Saunders & Otley.[6] I shall also be much obliged if you will ask Ommaney to pay up my subscription to the Bucks Infirmary. And now I have answered all the points of your letters, so far: when a heavy batch of letters arrives, and especially if one has a black seal, I do feel grateful when I can read them over, and gather mainly pleasure from their contents.

August 29. 1864. We arrived at Nanaimo yesterday, and start for Bute Inlet tomorrow morning: I shall leave my letters here to be sent down to

Victoria by the first opportunity. I am very glad to have an opportunity of seeing Bute Inlet, the scenery of which I am told is very fine.

Your affectionate Son,
Edmund Hope Verney

Low Camp. Bute Inlet. B.C.
September 1. 1864.

My dear Father,[1]

We reached Bute Inlet in the "Grappler" yesterday afternoon, where we found the Sutlej's launch. The Sub-Lieutenant in charge of her had gone up the country with 23 men to a place called Harper's Ferry, about 30 miles up the Homathco River, to prevent the Chillicoaten Indians from coming here to fish.[2] I am now on my way to join him with 10 of my men. It is 2 days' march and we started this morning; and I now write from the ½ way House. It is about 8 P.M. and pitch dark. 3 or 4 camp fires are burning and I am lying under a rude shelter made of cedar bark, with a fire burning before the opening. The flickering fires fitfully light up the tall stems of the surrounding trees, principally cedar and spruce pine, among which the bayonet of the sentry gleams from time to time. Within 20 yards runs the muddy Homathco River whose waters of melted snow are bitterly cold. Several of my men have sore feet from the day's march. I have with great success prescribed sitting for 20 minutes with the feet in the running snow water, then allowing them to dry and rubbing them with dry soap. That was our cure in India.

We have with us a pack train of 5 or 6 mules and 2 packers who are bringing up our provisions, blankets, etc. We shall probably remain at the ferry for a week or 10 days. I have written to the Admiral to tell him what I have done, and I have no doubt that a party will be sent to relieve us. It is very important that the Indians should not be allowed to fish: I think there is nothing so likely to subdue them as the prospect of starvation in the winter. 8 of the murderers are said to be already given up, and I hope the others will be very shortly. The country here is wild and rugged in the extreme – more so than any parts of B.C. that I have yet seen. The hills are as usual of either granite or trap, and their sides are often perfectly smooth as if they had been polished down. Most of the forest that we have travelled through today has been comparatively free from underwood, the tall trees standing handsomely in low brush and weeds. Some of the rivers were very rapid and shewed that when swollen they must be very broad and swift. All were bridged except one that we had to ford.

September 3. At about ½ past 1 yesterday we reached the ferry, many of the men being very footsore. We employed the afternoon in endeavouring to launch the Scow, the big flat bottomed boat used for the ferry. All the ferries in this country are on the same principle. A stout hawser crosses the stream, having a large block on it, to which the scow is attached by ropes; by these last she is brought at an angle to the stream which carries her across, the large block running along the hawser. Our efforts to launch the scow were stopped by darkness coming on. This morning they were renewed, when suddenly, without any warning, she started out into the middle of the stream. 7 men were in her and either did not understand the management of the ropes or lost their presence of mind, for they veered too much off one rope so as to bring all the strain on the other. Both ropes broke, and away she went down the stream. I was in bed when Talbot, Sub-Lieutenant of the Sutlej, came and told me about it.[3]

Fortunately, the men made no attempt to leave the scow, so of course they were all right as she must bring up sooner or later and then they had only to get out and walk back. A couple of hours later one of the party returned, as pale as a sheet, the very picture of terror. He said that the scow struck against a rock, when he and another jumped out. He managed to land, and was so frightened that he hardly looked round, but ran back as fast as he could. He believed that the man who jumped with him had missed his footing, as he saw him struggling in the water. The other men were safe in the scow. Some hours afterwards five men appeared on the opposite bank of the river. The scow had drifted into shallow water, where they had all got out and walked up through the brush. Of the man who jumped first and missed his footing they had seen nothing, and I fear there is every reason to believe that he was drowned. A man went off after him on a pony this morning and has not yet returned, and 12 men are going to look for him tomorrow morning. While we expected to have got the scow afloat yesterday, either Talbot or myself were constantly in her. But this morning she went so unexpectedly that they had no one to look to for orders. Had either of us been in the boat, I believe that the ropes would not have been broken, or if they had that we could have kept the men quietly in the boat until it was safe to get out. But they seem to have had a panic and quite to have lost their presence of mind at seeing the boat dart down the river at headlong speed. It was enough to frighten them, although in point of fact there was little or no danger. The scow now lies perfectly safe on the sand nearly 10 miles down the river.

The man who was lost, named Nichless, was a great favourite in the camp. He belonged to the Sutlej, and was very steady, quiet and hard working.[4] An event like this cuts us all up when we are such a small party, and especially do I feel it, as the commanding officer by whose orders he was working. But the duty on which he was employed was a necessary one, and if we of the navy lose our lives in the execution of our duty, we can wish for no more honourable way of ending our days, even though that duty may be ordinary and common place. This has been a wet day and uncomfortable in every way, but we have established communication across the ferry by sending men across, slung on ropes, under the big block.

Your affectionate son,
E.H.V.

H.M.S. Grappler. Homathco River. B.C.
September 8. 1864.

My dear Father,

I forward a shorthand letter to you, written during my short expedition up the river: here is a continuation of it in longhand.

September 4. This afternoon I crossed the ferry with six men, and proceeded about four miles up the trail: after marching about one mile, we found the bushes stripped of their berries, shewing that the Indians had been there lately, but had not dared to venture nearer the ferry. The trail did not improve as we went further, but became hilly and rocky. A party went out from the camp this morning to see if they could find any traces of Joseph Nichless, but they came back in the afternoon, having found none.

September 5. At daylight this morning a party of eighteen men commenced crossing the Ferry; it took upwards of two hours for the whole party to cross, one man going over along the rope at a time: when we were all across, we detached advanced and rear guards, and marched up the trail: we ascended a high mountain, and descended it on the other side to the level of the river, where we came to "The Murderers' Camp". here were clothes scattered about, and the scene brought back to ones mind the dreadful accounts of the murder that appeared in the papers.[1] We went on to the end of the trail as far as it is yet finished, a distance from the Ferry of about twelve miles: here all the workmen's tools were lying about just as they had been left the night before the murder: the drill sticking in the rock, the hammer lying by it, and the fuze ready to ignite the powder: everything was there to complete the work that man could bring, only the human life was wanting.

I left the party at the end of the trail to return tomorrow, while with an escort of two men I returned to the camp at the Ferry, making a day's walk of five and twenty miles over very rough country, not a bad day's work for a poor cripple.

September 6. This morning at daylight I started from the ferry with an escort of two men and a baggage pony, and reached the "Grappler" before dark; thirty miles, not a bad walk for a cripple, after yesterday's exploit. However, I was pretty well done up, and my knee would not have held out for a third day.

September 8. Brings me back to the point whence this letter started. Last night arrived the "Beaver" with *no end* of letters[,] newspapers &c: not hurriedly may they be answered, but bye and bye I shall sit down before them like Lord Raglan before Sebastopol and overcome them in detail.[2]

Also arrived orders from Admiral Denman to return with the Sutlej's launch to Esquimalt, which orders however I shall not carry out until the return of the messenger sent with despatches to the Admiral on the first instant, informing him of our having advanced to the Ferry.

September 9. Now I pull out all your letters to look over and to answer them. Yours of May 11. tells me that it was at your solicitation that the Duke of Somerset submits my name to the Queen for the Yacht: however

I suppose it is all settled by this time and that her selection has been made: you say it is sure promotion at the end of a year: alas! no; two years. I have not seen Admiral Denman yet, but expect to return to Esquimalt in a week or ten days. I am sure it is very good of you to take so much trouble about the Yacht for me, and I am afraid you must be sadly bothered at getting no answer from me either by letter or telegraph, but you see I did not receive your letters in time for either. You will have by this time received my letter from Bentinck Arm telling you not to expect to hear from me for a few weeks.

Very many thanks for the copy of your letter about the Schleswig-Holstein war; I will read it with care.[3] Many thanks also for the book on the "Queen's English": I suppose that is the language spoken in the Yacht, with which it is necessary that every one of her officers should be in some degree acquainted: I think that book must have been sent to me by Mamma; she loves to put me to utter confusion with an Armstrong shell of that kind. I am much obliged for all you write about memorializing: I am by no means sure that it would be a wise thing: yet Gilford did it, and it got him his captain's step.

What bad news from New Zealand: poor Hay I see died of his wounds: he was midshipman and Naval Cadet in the "Havannah"; midshipman and mate in the "Britannia"; lieutenant and Commander in the "Shannon": I wonder whether you remember him at all.[4]

I am very grateful for your kind reception of Mr. Marshall: you do not say much about him, but I hope you were pleased with him: I owe him much for his zeal, good conduct, and assistance on board the "Grappler", more probably than he is aware of: when I first took command of the ship I wanted the help of such a man; now I have an inferior man, but I am able to stand alone: I hope he will go to Claydon.[5]

Your latest date is June 30. I wonder what Captain Hall will have said to my letter: probably some common-place official answer: I feel very strongly that I ought to be promoted *now*, not go to the Yacht for two years: I am afraid my letters do not make it clear enough, but what will they do with me if I am not appointed to the Yacht: I have grown quite a captain, and should be very very sorry to go to a large ship again. It is said that a larger class of gunboat is to be sent out here: I should like to command one of them: my experience of the very intricate pilotage of these waters would qualify me in some degree for such a command. I do not know whether these new ships are to be lieutenants or commanders commands. The Governor offered to make me President of the Pilot Board the other day, but there were a great many reasons why I thought it better to decline, so I am only a member and the Surveyor General is Chairman.

I see that a very interesting naval history has been published by a Mr. Younge: if I am not coming home immediately will you be good enough to forward to Mr. Ridgway the enclosed note ordering it?[6]

September 19. 1864. This morning we joined the "Sutlej" at Port Moody, and for the first time I have met the Commander in Chief:

nothing could be kinder than were he and Mrs. Denman: rather to my disappointment I am ordered to convey Mr. Duncan and Dr. Walker to Metlakatlah immediately: we shall start in four or five days when our boilers shall have been repaired: I do not like going up north at this time of year in those unsurveyed waters: I anticipate bad weather, and a repitition of this time last year: however, now I know the Channels, it will be easier work as far as the navigation is concerned.[7]

Yours of July 15. arrived to day: you ask about who have been promoted over my head; very few, thanks to my having lost no time as a midshipman, perhaps six or eight, but not more; they have been generally flag-lieutenants: I have passed over the heads of several cotemporaries, who have lost time by their own misconduct or neglect: but this is just what I complain of: my name stands on the Navy List with those of my cotemporaries; few have passed *me*, and I have only passed those who have lost time: *every* other officer of the "Shannon" gained some great advancment in his profession, while the Navy List shows that I gained none; while flag lieutenants are being promoted over my head; and, for instance, Lord Charles Scott who was a young midshipman in the "Pearl" in India, will be promoted out of the Yacht this time next year over my head: he has already gained upon me one year, because he was made lieutenant at once, without being a mate, for his services in the "Pearl". But I am weary of the subject, and I have no doubt many officers in the service have worse grievances than mine, with perhaps wives and families depending on them: only let me fight it out bravely out here till I am promoted: they may call me a lieutenant if they like, but let me remain Captain of the "Grappler:" everybody in the two Colonies knows Captain Verney.

I am very glad to hear you were pleased with Mr. Marshall; I should have been sorry if you had written coolly about him, very sorry. Charming notes from Emily and Mamma: from the former's letter I learn for the first time of the safe arrival in England of the large carvings I sent ever so long ago: do please put them up as gate-posts, or do something with them: give them to a museum if they are of no use to decorate dear Claydon.

If you do not hear from me for three or four weeks you will know that I have gone to Metlakatlah: you may be sure that I intend to come back as quickly as possible. Henry is pretty well, but he wants a deal of "rosining up." You will be amused to hear that Dr. Walker is, of all people in Victoria, my most particular aversion: it will do me a power of good, will it not, to have to live with him for some weeks cooped up in this little cabin.[8]

September 23. This afternoon we went for Nanaimo to coal and go on to Metlakahthla: Mr. Duncan and Dr. Walker are on board. We are going up on account of resistance offered by the crew of a small trading craft, the "Random", to Mr. Duncan's native constables, whereby one of them was killed: we take the doctor up to attend on the wounded men, and if we hear of the "Random" being in the neighbourhood we shall try to seize her, and to bring her down. Although I am not an advocate for Indian constables being slaughtered, I am not by any means clear that it is a wise thing to send Indian constables to apprehend white men: I am not sure that there are many white men who require apprehension who would accept it at the hands of an Indian, especially as that class of men is generally American, and holds coloured men in the most utter contempt.

September 24. 1864. I think we shall be ready to start for the North tomorrow: it is impossible to say how we shall get on, but if there is any Indian summer we ought to have returned by the end of October or beginning of November: I shall make all possible speed.

Thus then I say farewell for the present: if we have fine weather and get through our work quickly it will be a pleasant cruize.

Your affectionate Son,
Edmund Hope Verney

H.M.S. Grappler. Nass River. B.C.
Observatory Inlet. October 6. 1864.

My dear Father,

I wrote to you last from Nanaimo, where we took on board sixty tons of coal, and yesterday week started for Metlakatlah: we arrived at that place on Tuesday, having had strong southerly gales all the way: there we landed Dr. Walker and came on yesterday to Fort Simpson, leaving again this morning for Nass River: we tried to get up the river this afternoon but the water was very shallow, and there was some little sea, so I thought it hardly prudent to persevere: if it is fine tomorrow I shall make another attempt: we want to get up the river to call upon the Nass Indians, and to see the Rev. Mr. Doolen, the missionary:[1] Mr. Duncan is on board with me, and if we cannot get the ship up the river we shall probably go up by boat.

Dr. Walker is attending to the sick at Metlakatlah, who are all three going on well. I enclose you two letters written to Mr. Duncan by an Indian girl while he was at Victoria: they are very touching and shew the intense love his people bear him.[2]

October 9. The weather did not admit of our ascending the Nass River, so we returned to Metlakatlah the day before yesterday: repairs to the boilers will keep us here until wednesday.

There is no doubt that this is a wet place, and yet milder in winter than any neighbouring spot: at Nass, for instance, about sixty miles hence, the snow in winter is six or eight feet deep, and the cold is so severe that the Indians hardly leave their houses: the Hudson's Bay Company had a fort there which was abandoned chiefly on account of the cold and bad weather:[3] I think that the climate of Metlakatlah must be influenced by some warm current coming round the north end of Queen Charlotte's Islands: last spring the mail steamers from San Francisco to Victoria encountered severe gales of wind, and were compelled to throw overboard their deck cargoes, consisting partly of boxes of apples: these apples were picked up by the Indians in large quantities on the shores of Dundas Island, about twenty miles from this: a cask of butter was also found floating about, and, I regret to add, was appropriated by Mr. Duncan without any payment of customs dues, or study of the laws of flotsam and jetsam.

There is a good deal of improvement here since my visit last year: a substantial mission house has been built in front of the church, in the English style, which will when completed inside, be a fit place for a clergyman and his family: indeed I think the mission has reached that stage when a married clergyman with a family is more wanted than a single man.

Perhaps Mr. Duncan's management of the young women is one of the most wonderful and most successful of his works, and at the same time not the best appreciated by the public: to take into his own house, and to entertain at his own table young women at the most critical ages, is a task that few young men would care to undertake: and yet I will venture to say that few ladies would have turned out such good specimens of virtuous, modest, and attractive young women as he has been able to give in marriage to his Indian young men: two that I have seen are really charming, their bright black eyes beaming with pure affection: Mr. Duncan must be a remarkable man that for years he has had young women living alone with him in his house, and no white man or Indian has dared to breathe a taint on his name: the Indian mothers know that there is no place in this world where their daughters are so safe as in Mr. Duncan's house, and that he will see that in due time they are provided with the best husbands: he generally has five or six girls living with him, who love him devotedly as their father: Mr. Cunningham, the missionary under Mr. Duncan, has just married one of these girls.[4]

I am buying one or two curiosities, but very few: I sent you a really good collection at the beginning of this year, and there is no object in getting more of the same: I shall however get a dozen or so of mats, which I think you will always be glad to have.

October 14. Yesterday morning we left Metlakatlah, with a high and rising barometer, and are already a hundred miles on our way to Victoria: to get calms and a high barometer at this time of year is indeed fortunate, and if this weather lasts for two or three days, I hope to be by that time in surveyed waters again. Every mile that we get further south, we are so much nearer to milder climate, civilization, and the Small Bower: we cannot however go at full speed as we must economize coal.[5]

The Small Bower. Esquimalt. V.I.
October 27. 1864.

My dear Father,

I returned from Metlakatlah this day week, but cannot say that I am yet in my right mind: for the first two or three days I was quite overwhelmed with business; the Grappler to be paid off, the Lighthouse accounts five months in arrears, and the affairs of the Exploration Commitee to be wound up; gradually I am sifting things, and putting them into some sort of order preparatory to commencing work in earnest.

My pile of unanswered letters is appalling, but of course yours of July 31. and August 15. and 31. have the first claim.

I am now finding out how important it is that an officer should be intimately acquainted with all the details of his profession: I am seriously thinking of giving up everything else, and studying nothing that is not professional, and especially being up in all petty details: I ought to have been a first lieutenant.

My re-appointment to the Grappler has arrived, with an intimation that my three years will have expired on the 25th of February next: if I am then ordered home and not promoted, I think I ought to go as first-lieutenant in some ship.

Pray take care of Mary Ann Tyler, for my sake; you know she is my protegè [*sic*]: Henry tells me that she has left Claydon: why did she leave? can she not be brought back? I am sure she is loyal and true, and ought not easily to be allowed to slip through our fingers.[1]

The Admiral and Mrs. Denman are very kind to me; I hope to know more of him: but they leave for the South in two or three weeks. The Bishop is very much needed here, he is laying up sorrow for himself by staying away so long; I am sure he will be grieved and shocked when he returns, and I think he will say he ought to have returned sooner.

The two Colonies ought to be united immediately: I have not time now to enter into the matter, but I see the blackest squalls to windward: union will be forced by the very serious difficulties that will arise, unless it comes before: the jealousy and hostility at present existing will appear to you incredible when I have time to write to you about it: you will think there must be something in the Colonial air conducive to insanity: if the Colonies are united, there can be no doubt which Governor will be retained. What I have gathered induces me to hope that there is an idea of speedy union at the Colonial Office: I have no doubt that Governor Seymour will oppose it.

I rejoice to hear of the safe arrival of my curios: pray *use* them. I do not the least expect to be appointed to the Yacht. I have a few more curios to send some day, but I have another packet of seeds for you: a botanist assures me that they are well worth sending home, so do not despise these because the others turned out worthless. Have the seeds of the Wellingtonea Gigantea thriven?

Your remarks about the loss of my chain of gold coins amuse me: be it known that I have not worn it half a dozen times since I left England; indeed I do not remember ever to have worn it. I did not give it to Emily for a bandeaux for her hair, because I always intended it for my wife whom I intend to love better than Emily, if possible; so you see the loss is hers, poor creature; and you should keep your sympathy for her some day, instead of laughing at me.

Then for the last few years you have insisted that I am personally vain: now you know I will not admit that at any price: I may be culpably vain about myself in some ways, but I maintain that a man cannot consider himself good-looking and a bewitching creature generally, without at least being aware of the fact. Now I am certainly not conscious of entertaining these sentiments of self-admiration: on the other hand, I am not prepared to say that I consider myself an ungainly and repulsive object, because in truth I have not considered the matter either way: I will however make a note of it, as a subject for future reflection, when I can get a plate glass mirror to reflect straight, and when I have time to reflect.

What you say about my letters to Captain Spencer relieves me much: I am glad I sent you copies of them, and that you see they contained nothing very outrageous.

At Metlakatlah Mr. Duncan gave me a goat, and I bought from an Indian, a tame wild goose: on our passage down these made great friends: the goose would fly furiously at the goat, and make believe to peck its eyes out, when Nanny would butt the goose over, by way of annihilating it; but they never hurt each other: why two such dissimilar creatures should strike up a friendship, I know not; – unless indeed it might be because they both begin with G.

I wrote word to you that my friend Howell stayed with me on board the "Grappler" for about three months: I shall write to him and ask him to call on you: I think I may venture to say that you will like him: we became very intimate: we scarcely agreed on any point, and in many ways he did me a great deal of good: he is full of charity towards all men & I am not. He left for England by the steamer before last, but intends to dawdle home.

The "Grappler" will go on the slip in a week or so: at present we are clearing everything out of her, to lighten her as much as possible: I do not expect that she will be ready for sea much before 1865. We are to pay off on the last day of this month.

Oct. 31. 1864. This day is the last of this Commission: the ship is to be paid off today:[2] one great weight has been removed from my mind by the fact that the ship's steward, the man who keeps the accounts, has volunteered for twelve months of the next commission: he has been a bad character, and on one occasion that you will perhaps remember, played me false, and nearly got me into very serious trouble: since then I have learnt how to keep a continual check on his work, and the result has been that his good qualities have become invaluable to me, and I have found the means of checking him from going far wrong: nevertheless he has always made himself out a martyr and me a tyrant until last saturday when he found he was really going to England, and I was trying to get another ship's steward: then he came to me with tears in his eyes, acknowledged that he had always been justly punished, and volunteered to remain in the ship as long as I did. I must confess that I was much pleased; not merely pleased to retain such an able secretary, but pleased that he acknowledged his fault: for when a man of even the worst character persists in declaring he has been unjustly punished, it bothers me awfully.

We had an earthquake on Saturday: not a very severe shock, hardly as bad as the one at Lisbon, but still enough to make a man sneeze: some of the brick and plaster houses in town were a good deal shaken: I was shaving at the time, and very glad to rush out in to the middle of my grass plot, whence in the still early morning I heard it grumbling and rolling away past Esquimalt to the southward: no harm was done to the bower.

November 2. The Admiralty having notified to me on my re-appointment that my term of service, three years, will have expired in February next, I have no doubt that I shall then be either promoted or superseded: Lascelles' three years will expire this month, and we shall see what they do with him: After having thought about it, I think there is no doubt that I have been out here long enough; but if in February I am still left in the "Grappler", and neither promoted nor superseded, I am by no means sure that it will be wise to apply to come home: I think it would be better to leave myself entirely in the hands of their Lordships: perhaps they will leave me a few months longer and then promote me: if they *order* me home they must pay my passage, and then I can ask for promotion or another good appointment with a better face than if I had come home at my own request.

November 5. Of the New Zealand promotions, Hotham is to be promoted as soon as he has served his two years as lieutenant: this is of course a very extraordinary favour for war services, but this is the category in which I always hoped my services would come: but it is useless writing about it, as I know you have done all you can: If I am not promoted in February next, when my three years will have expired, I assure you, my dear Father, I shall have been very badly treated, but of course I must just serve on and on until I am promoted: if they order me home without promotion, in February, I shall apply for the coast of Africa, and they shall see I am in earnest.

Swann, who is promoted for N.Z. was two months junior to me as lieutenant, and senior to me as a midshipman in the "Arethusa": he is a man of no interest.[3]

Nov. 7. The Secretary asked me a day or two ago whether I should be willing to accept the appointment of flag-lieutenant, in case Sir. L. Loraine should get a death-vacancy: I declined.[4] He did not say that he was authorized to ask me. I do not know how much longer their Lordships intend to keep me a lieutenant, but as I have gone on for so long I wish the rest of it to be in the regular course of service: this sentence is hardly grammatical but you will understand what I mean.

The mail due yesterday has not arrived yet: it is just possible that she may bring news of this year's appointments to the Yacht.

Governor Seymour gives a grand ball tomorrow, in honour of the Prince of Wales' birthday: I am going over to New Westminster on that account, for I belong as much to one colony as to the other. As I sleep this evening on board the steamer that runs to New Westminster, I close this letter now, before the arrival of the mail.

Your affectionate Son,
Edmund Hope Verney

Nov. 7. 1864.

The Small Bower. Esquimalt. V.I.
November 13. 1864.

My dear Father,

A mail steamer is expected today or tomorrow, and that I may not be quite unprepared for her arrival, I start a letter now.

The "Grappler" went round to Victoria the day before yesterday; this afternoon she will be beached that the bottom may be examined, and a contract made for the repairs: tomorrow she will be hauled up altogether out of the water. I hear that Charteris is promoted out of the yacht.[1] Will you be so good as to forward the two enclosed scraps to Uncle Frederic. The last mail brought me no letters from any one: I suppose that no news must be always taken to be good news.

November 17. The mail steamer that arrived to-day is the second that has brought me no letter from you: she brought me however one from Mr. Marshall: I am very glad to find that my recommendation of him has been of some use to him: I was very much afraid that my rank being so low my recommendation would have been thought nothing of.

The "Grappler" is now half way up the slip at Victoria: tomorrow a survey is to be held on her: the Admiral has some idea of recommending the Admiralty to sell her, as it will cost a great deal to repair her out here: when he receives the report of the surveying officers tomorrow he will decide this: if he does desire to sell her, it would take at least three months for permission to arrive from England, during which time I should be idler than ever: if he repairs her it will take about six weeks or two months to do that, so in any case I am likely to be pretty quiet at Victoria or at the Bower, for some weeks to come. I hope to get a week or two's leave and run away somewhere, perhaps to see the mills at Alberni.[2]

Nothing could be kinder or more really friendly than the conduct of the Admiral and Mrs. Denman to me: it is delightful to meet such people out here.

Your affectionate Son,
Edmund Hope Verney

The Small Bower. Esquimalt. V.I.
November 22. 1864.

My dear Father,

The mail steamer has arrived this evening, a day before she was expected, and as I have something rather important to tell you, I shall send this letter by New York.

The fact to be told is that the Admiral is writing home by this mail to recommend that the "Grappler" be sold, as, owing to the high price of labour out here, it would cost two thousand pounds to repair her. What the Admiralty will do with me I know not, but to every father who has a son in the Navy I would say, if your son performs a gallant act, go the Admiralty and ask for his promotion: if the Yellow Fever attacks your son's ship, go the Admiralty and ask for his promotion; if your son's ship is ordered to be paid off, or ordered not to be paid off, or ordered to be sold, or to be broken up, in short in every circumstance of life, wherever you can find a peg to hang it on, go to the Admiralty and point out that in this remarkable and very exceptional case, they cannot, of course, refuse to promote your son.

The Admiralty's answer as to what is to be done with the "Grappler" cannot arrive here before the end of February or the beginning of March, before which time my three years in the "Grappler" will have expired, therefore if they wish to promote me here is now such a chance as they may not soon get again, and I advise them to seize it. You may say that this is my advice.

I have not been able to find out exactly what the Admiral has said in his despatch, but the Secretary told me that so far from attributing any blame to me for the damage that the vessel has received he had said rather the reverse, and he does not think that the Admiralty will even order any enquiry to be held about it.

And now, my dear Father, we must look the matter fairly in the face, and see what is to be done if I am not promoted: in the first place there can be no manner of doubt that I must go on serving: I must not come and spend some months with you on shore: I must try to get another independent command at once, as, after the "Grappler" I should much prefer being my own captain. A subordinate position fits a man for command, but a command hardly fits him to fill again a subordinate position.

Your letter of September 16. from Kingston arrived this evening: Emily seems to have been charmed with the place. The end of your letter had been torn off: I wonder what it was about: it must have been delightfully interesting, I am sure.

You will pity me, laid up for at least three months of idleness, and then I know not what. Henry was trimming off a walking-stick a few days ago, with the blades open at both ends of his knife: as might have been expected, he has cut his hand severely, but it is going on well, and will be all right in a week or two, the doctor says.

Your affectionate Son,
Edmund Hope Verney

The Small Bower. Esquimalt. V.I.
November 29. 1864.

My dear Father,

On Saturday the Grappler was hauled off the slip at Victoria, and on Sunday morning we steamed round to Esquimalt where the little craft will lay until the pleasure of the L.C.A. be known: then I presume she will be paid off again and sold, and her Commander will be ordered to – – ? We shall only have six or eight hands on board, and only perhaps run to San Juan or to the Lighthouse, so my office will be nearly a sinecure.

A few days ago, I attended a meeting held in Victoria for the purpose of establishing a mechanic's Institute: it was attended chiefly by working men, and after several preliminary resolutions had been passed a committee of management was elected, each name being voted for by a show of hands: I was very much pleased indeed to be elected on this Committee; a working sawyer proposed my name, and I was elected by working men: I had the greatest number of votes with the exception of, I think, three people whose names were carried by acclamation: I have often been on Committees of one sort or another before, but my name has probably been put down by some friend or with some definite object which has never given me half so much pleasure as I experienced on this occasion.[1]

In september last, I seized on suspicion of smuggling a schooner with eighty gallons of whiskey on board: I sent her to New Westminster where she was let go by the custom-house officer, and I am now threatened with an action for damages for her detention: I have written to Governor Seymour to ask that the Government of British Columbia, on whose behalf I was acting, may defend me: but a law-suit is a great nuisance any way.[2]

Will you be so good as to send to me some copies of my polka-mazurka, and of the "Shannon's Brigade in India": I much want to give them away to friends out here. All the copies of the music that are left are either at Claydon or in South Street: the books must be obtained in my name from the publishers. I want to give a copy to the mechanics' Institute library, when it is formed, and there is also a mechanics' Institute at Nanaimo to which I should like to give a copy.

December 2. The Sutlej's departure for the South is now postponed until after the arrival of the next mail; which will probably be on Tuesday next: I do not think that Mrs. Denman at all likes the idea of rough weather or is in any hurry to leave so snug an anchorage as Esquimalt.

We have had no snow yet nor as much rain as is usual, and I think we shall shortly have hard frosts and fine weather: keeping wind and frost out of the Bower is an admirable exercise for my ingenuity: it might be got over by papering the house inside, but that would be a great expense, so I get the old charts from the ships, and nail them up with little tacks, so they are at once useful and ornamental: one side of my bedroom shows a number of charts so cut and fitted to each other as to represent the Pacific Ocean, the keyhole of the door being a few miles south of the Friendly Islands; my skates and fishing tackle hang on Kamschatka, while the evening dress I wore last night still shelters South California.

December 5. The mail steamer is now due, and I believe that the Admiral will sail in the Sutlej the day after she arrives: the winter has so far treated us very kindly, advancing but slowly and treating us to here and there a warm sunny day, while the roads are not yet at their worst, and the ditch round my house is still dry. I have a very kind letter from Governor Seymour, who says he will at once see what can be done for me about that affair of the schooner Nonpareil.

I venture to suggest to you to send a present of books to our Mechanics' Institute: I am a member of the Library Committee, and we will undertake to pay the freight: the Admiralty will send free of charge a box to the care of the Consul at Panama, who will send it up by a man-of-war: I ask you this because I think you may have some duplicate copies of books at Claydon, which you would not mind giving, or on the other hand if you have no books to give, of course the Victoria Mechanics' Institute can have no sort of claim on you.[3]

December 7. This day the mail is expected, and as soon as she comes, the Admiral will sail. He and Mrs. Denman have certainly been particularly kind to me. A certain Dr. Ash is going home, and I have asked him to call on you: I think you will find him a shrewd sensible man, able to give you valuable and reliable information about the Colony: he goes home to attend to the sale of some spars and lumber, three or four shiploads of which he has sent round the Horn.[4]

December 8. 1864. The mail steamer is late this time, but she will probably be in to-day: The master of the "Tribune", Bond, is going home by her; he is a fine fellow;[5] how I wish I was going; I do feel a little homesick sometimes, because I fancy I am worthy of something a little better than a gunboat, and I want a more active life: however, I suppose that patience will bring it all in good time.

Yesterday I discovered that the remarkable friendliness Admiral Denman has exhibited towards me is in a great measure due to Lord Dunsany:[6] I do not write to him, but I dare say you will see him some day, and you may tell him that his kind word spoken in my behalf has made many things smooth, and given me many a pleasant hour: in a few hours, the Admiral will be sailing South, and very possibly I shall have gone before he returns in the spring, but I cannot fail to remember that he is [*sic*] more than once quite gone out of his way to be civil to me.

This morning the first snow appears, having fallen during the night: for the last two or three days it has been freezing hard, and I had hoped we should have had some ice without snow. My little house is not easily kept warm now: although I can keep the thermometer up to 60, the cold air pours in at all the cracks and ensures a free supply of oxygen.

The orders for the disposal of the Grappler will probably arrive here in March, so I may really hope to be home in the summer: I have not yet heard when George is likely to come home: it would be very jolly if we could all be at home again together, but if it is not to be, let us at any rate so pass through our probation here that we shall *all* be united in our permanent home: I find it difficult to think that I shall ever like Heaven more than Claydon, and this just shows how determinedly men set their hearts on things below, because of course I know better. What a crafty dawg I am! I have found out what the Admiral wrote home about me, although, of course, what he writes in his despatches is supposed to be a secret: he said he did not think that I was to blame for the ship having got on shore, as it was in unsurveyed waters, and that he considered me a diligent and meritorious officer: with all my craftiness, I cannot be quite sure that those were his words, but it was very like that at any rate; that ought to do me some good with the L.C.A.

December 9. 1864. The mail did arrive this morning, at last, bringing me among other good things a glorious long letter from Mama, and a box of clothes from Stone. Likewise also your letter of October 2. I hope Mr. Marshall will now be promoted, and appointed to some good ship. I am anxious to hear the result of Fred's examination: George's promotion was capital news, so now I hope all your sons will make a move up.

I am delighted to hear how well your volunteers' dinner went off: I wish I could have been with you: when you have us all at home again, you must give another. I was charmed to get my box of clothes so soon from Stone: I wrote for them from Bentinck Arm exactly this day five months, and they left England on the 17th of October: they have just arrived in time, as I have really "nothing to wear".

Your affectionate Son,
Edmund Hope Verney

Private.

The Small Bower. Esquimalt. V.I.
December 7. 1864.

My dear Father,

I write you a few private words about the Admiral and Mrs. Denman. I had an idea that the Admiral was one of the leading men of the profession: well, he is not: he does not go in for it heart and soul; he hates business: he is absurdly grave about trifles, and treats lightly important matters. He is a man who requires to be managed, but it requires a great deal of tact to manage him: he is sometimes unreasonable in his likes and dislikes which are rather strong. Mrs. Denman is a great deal too profuse in her endearments, the result of which is that the Commander in Chief is very generally referred to as "Dear Josey", except when he is spoken of as "Josey Dear".

As regards the management of the Fleet I do not think that he will be very successful: he starts with the idea that he is going to do every-thing himself, attend to matters of detail, be very energetic, painstaking, and laborious: but after an hour or two's work he will throw aside all his papers, and go on shore for a drive: his poor secretary, who has never been one before, nor ever even been in a secretary's office, complains bitterly that the Admiral will never write drafts of his letters, but only alters all the secretary's drafts, and that he can seldom get him to attend to business; this would not be so bad if the Admiral would form a more just estimate of himself: he brought with him a man who had never been a secretary before, because he intended to work hard himself as Uncle Hope does; but seeing how little work he does, he ought to have brought a first-rate secretary. Mrs. Denman's presence on board is voted an intolerable nuisance by the officers, and doubtless the men too, although personally she is very much liked: she has more than once interrupted me when I have had business with the Admiral, and sent everything clean out of his head.[1]

However, he is a gentleman, and that covers a multitude of sins: he suffers from diabetes, which must be a sad trial to him and to her too: nothing could exceed the kindness I have received from both of them, and I am very grateful to them for it, and to you and Mama who have doubtless had a hand in it.

Your affectionate Son,
Edmund Hope Verney

I have found out a secret that perhaps you knew before: Admiral Denman is the author of that celebrated pamphlet "Admiralty Administration its faults and defaults."[2]

The Small Bower. Esquimalt. V.I.
December 11. 1864.

My dear Father,

Yesterday morning the "Sutlej" sailed for the South, and I lost good friends in Admiral and Mrs. Denman; nevertheless I was not sorry to see the flagship's stern as she steamed out of the harbour, for after she has been here for six months we get tired of her; there is always more formality and etiquette in the presence of the flagship, and after one has got everything one wants it is rather wearisome to have to dance attendance on the Admiral every morning. I dare say when the spring comes, I shall be glad enough to see the Sutlej's smoke coming round the Race Rocks, if I am still here.

Poor old Bridgman, the bishop's butler, is seriously ill: I believe I may say he has had no sleep for a fortnight: directly he begins to doze off, he chokes himself, and starts up nearly suffocated: I do not know exactly what is the matter with him, but those are the symptoms, and the doctors look very grave about him.

How much the Bishop is wanted here, you cannot conceive: perhaps if I were in a better position to judge, I should think differently, but at present I doubt whether the good he is doing in England can outweigh the evil of his absence. We hear that the diocese is to be divided, and that there is to be a bishop of New Westminster, but I should have thought that one bishop was enough.[1]

It is an Englishman's privilege to grumble: I want to grumble, so I take for my text the following extract from the letter of Mr. Stone, the tailor at Portsmouth: "According to your request I informed Sir Harry that I was about to send to you, and in reply he stated that he had nothing to enclose:" what! Papa got *nothing* to enclose to his big boy? not even a bunch of dried leaves from Claydon? not even a wee pot of home-made jam or butter? not even an old file of the county papers with the account of the volunteer's dinner [in] it? not a new pamphlet or a half-finished sketch out of Mama's portfolio? he should have seen his boy's face when he threw out the pretty new uniforms one after the other; and found *nothing* else in the box: he did not want a bag full of silver and gold, but he *was* so silly and childish as to want some little token although he is nearly twenty-seven, and certainly ought to have been more matter-of-fact.

December 14. 10.30. A.M. I have just watched the Charybdis steam out of the harbour, taking with her to England some eight or ten of the Grappler's best men: I think it is time for me to go now: these men who are gone are all the best men, and nearly all petty officers, the men who for the last two and a half years have been my best friends, my advisers in doubt or difficulty, men whom I have grown very much attached to: I wonder whether they are as sorry to leave me as I am to lose them. It is a fine thing for a Captain to bring his ship into Spithead after a three years commission, to pay her off with credit, and to bid farewell to his ship's company on his quarter-deck, but it is a melancholy thing to lose them here and there, half a dozen at a time, and to be himself left behind to plod on as before, to make new sympathies, and to work on again. I look forward to the possibility and even to the probability of meeting the Charybdis on her arrival in England, and seeing my gallant fellows again before they are dispersed. If I am not at home, and you are in the neighbourhood of the Charybdis on her arrival, I am sure you would be pleased with my men.

In the charge of Glasson, the chaplain, I have sent you a bale containing Indian mats, &c, and also a pair of elk-horns: they are addressed to South Street: Captain Turnour, who is well-known as a most popular fellow, has put the horns in his cabin for me, so that they will not be knocked about.[2]

December 15. In the Army and Navy Gazette of the 23^{d} of October, I saw that the Hon. Albert Denison has been appointed to the Yacht, this year:[3] it did not even relieve me from any uncertainty to see it, for to tell you the truth I had ceased to feel any anxiety on the subject, and had almost forgotten it. I hope it will not have been an anxiety and disappointment to you. By this mail I shall send you another packet of seeds: I send them just as I received them: I do not even open the packet, but I forward them just as they arrived at my office: they have been given to me by Dr. Brown, or rather Mr. Brown M.B., who commanded the exploring party during the summer, and is a professed botanist: now please tell Mama that if these seeds do not turn out to be really very valuable, I shall have done all I can, and I shall send no more: so, there!

December 17. 1864. Did you ever receive a log of wood, of yellow cypress, that I sent home to you in some sailing ship that left here a year or a year and a half ago? I sent nothing else at that time, there was just the one log of wood. Yesterday afternoon the Mechanics' Institute was opened, and I must say, although I am a party concerned, that I think all the arrangements for the comfort of the members are admirable: there are two large rooms, with wash room &c adjoining: one room is a reading room, with desks and newspapers; the other, rather smaller, is a library, with bookshelves and periodicals; in the latter neither smoking nor talking is allowed.[4]

December 21. The mail steamer has arrived this morning, so I must prepare my instalment of letters to travel that road that I wish I were about to travel myself, and which I now look forward to travelling before very long. Indeed, I shall be glad to visit Mr. Edwin Saunders at 13A.[5]

Only one letter, and that an official one, has come by the mail, so for the present Adieu: the direct steamer will probably be here the day after tomorrow, with news well into the beginning of November.

With love to Mama, believe me,

Your affectionate Son,
Edmund Hope Verney

The Small Bower. Esquimalt. V.I.
December 23. 1864.

My dear Father,

The mail steamer arrived to-day, and I send you a few lines because I know you like to hear something by every mail, but as I wrote to you by the mail three days ago, I have not much to relate.

The only event of any real importance that has taken place in the interim is that "Catherine", the goat Mr. Duncan gave me at Metlakatlah, presented me yesterday with twins; her Ladyship is going on as well as can be expected.

Your letters of October 14. and 24. have arrived, and newspapers to November 6: letters viâ Southampton are always a week or two behind New York, and now-a-days everything comes by New York except the heavy official mails. I can quite understand why you have not gone to Malta with Emily: I can think of many reasons why you would think it more right to deny yourself this pleasure. Nobody tells me definitely that Fred did not succeed in his Baliol examination, but sundry allusions to "poor Freddy" lead me to divine the cause of his poverty. Well! I too will sympathise with the boy, and say "poor Freddy" for I would sooner face an enemy's frigate any day than a board of examiners.

I am glad that you have seen the Bishop again, and liked him; it is not only in England that comments are made on the absenteeism of colonial Bishops: one of the papers here had a pretty strong leading article on the subject a day or two ago. A letter for Mr. Despard Pemberton came in one of the envelopes to-day, but I know not whose, and no one alludes in any way thereto: I shall forward it to him: it looks like Aunt Helen's handwriting. How I wish I was with you at Claydon to fill a little of the gap caused by Emily's absence: please God, we shall make a happy family party in the summer. I quite agree with you that if it seems to be my duty to come home in February or March, there is every reason why I should not seek to remain out, but it will be a bitter pill to come home still a lieutenant: here it does not matter so much, as I am practically a captain.

I will tell you a good friend I have at the Admiralty, whom I think you do not know; Mr. James G. Noel, one of the clerks: he was Admiral

Pelham's Secretary, and I should be very glad to hear that you have seen him on one of your visits to the Admiralty, after you have seen "the man at the foot of the stairs": I am sure he would do anything he could for me, or tell you if there is anything further we can do: I have a very friendly letter from him by this mail.

Pray tell Emily, when you write to her that I have received her long long letter, and that of course it will take some little time to write a long long answer: you see a long short-hand letter is really a formidable thing. Christmass is drawing very near indeed, and I know our thoughts will be with each other on that day: George in India, Emily at Malta, Edmund in V.I.: could a family be more scattered? However there are four of us together, where they will be no more scattered: may the others be united with them one day.

Your affectionate Son,
Edmund Hope Verney

The Small Bower. Esquimalt. V.I.
December 25. 1864.

I believe it is usual, my dear Father, always to write a few lines to you on Xmas day when I am absent, but surely I did not last Xmas expect to have now written from this house: however, I wish you a merry Xmas and a happy new year, and I trust that your Christmas day to-day has been one of peace and pleasure: with me it is 7. P.M. so now with you it is about 3. A.M., and you are all snoring in your beds, and trying to sleep off the effects of your heavy indigestible Christmas dinners.

I have been dining soberly at Craig Flower, as usual, but tomorrow we are to keep high holiday: a holiday is proclaimed in town, the shops are to be shut, and the public offices are to be closed, and tomorrow I go to Craig Flower again, for Christmas fare, charades &c: I dare say you and Freddy, and Uncle & Aunt Fremantle, and Uncle Frederic have dined together, and, thought lovingly of the absent ones.

January 1. 1865. A happy new year to you. A few nights ago a man tried to rob my hen-roost: Henry heard him first, jumped out of bed and gave chase, but the scoundrel escaped over the fence.

I have received a hint that if money is forthcoming I can get my chain back again, the chain of small gold coins that I lost when the marine deserted in the summer: I have communicated with the police, but do not know whether I shall be able to get it or not.

Did you ever get an answer from Uncle Hope to your proposition that I should pay him a visit on my way home?[1] If you hear that the "Grappler" is to be sold, and that I am coming home, please continue to write to me for some time, as I shall have to remain for a few weeks to square off the accounts &c, and the family news I gather from American newspapers is not explicit. Will you be so good as to send the enclosed note to Captain Hardinge: I do not know his address, but Noel, or some one at the Admiralty will know where to find him.

January 8. The mail steamer, not yet arrived, was expected both yesterday and the day before: by this mail you will receive another packet of seeds, with specimens of foliage attached: so now if none of my Vancouver Island seeds suc-*seed*, it will not be my fault: I have done all I can.

We had some sharp frost a fortnight ago, but now the weather is as mild as spring: I assure you that the day before yesterday was absolutely a hot day: not a cloud was to be seen and people in winter garments were complaining of the heat: the ground now is thoroughly soaked, and when once that has taken place, it takes weeks to dry it again, and a few fine days make little or no difference in the state of the roads; so far, this has been a remarkably fine winter. Tomorrow if the weather is fine, I am going to take the Governor for a day's cruize off the south coast of the island.

January 10. 1865. Just as we were starting yesterday for our pleasant little cruize, expecting to have the Governor and a little party of friends on board, and having provided luncheon &c, the engineer forgot to open the discharge valve, and blew the top of the condenser off: fortunately no one was hurt; but the repair of this will lay the ship up again for some time longer.

The mail steamer came in yesterday at dusk, bringing your letter of November 16.: although sent through the Admiralty, it came viâ New York: if the Admiralty would always send your letters viâ N.Y. what a good thing it would be. One of the disadvantages of being so far from home is the vagueness of news: no one has yet told me that Fred was plucked in his examination for Balliol, but I know it certainly now, from putting together all the allusions to him, and now something in Mama's letter intimates that the Bishop is going to be married; but she does not distinctly say *our* bishop, nor does she say whom he is going to marry: she says "we are rejoicing greatly over the Bishop's marriage", and there it ends.[2]

I am grieved to hear from Aunt Fremantle of poor Mrs. Price's death: I suppose that the disposal of Lady Dunsany's was a great boon to the Prices, and must have been a relief to our dear friend.[3] I am going to New Westminster in a day or two to spend a few days with Governor Seymour, so if I miss a mail, you will understand the reason. I shall be very glad to come home, I assure you: I do not think it would be mentally healthful for me to stay out here longer.

Your affectionate Son,
Edmund Hope Verney

Government House. B.C.
January 13. 1865.

My dear Father,

I arrived here from V.I. yesterday, with Pender of the "Beaver". We remain here until wednesday: when we reached New Westminster, the Governor came down for us and our baggage in the little steamer "Leviathan", an extraordinary little screw boat that he has as his yacht.

And now I am in for a week's thorough change, which I expect will do me all the good in the world.

There is certainly a marvellous difference between the climates of Victoria and New Westminster: at Victoria we had wonderful spring-like weather, with the thermometer standing at 58° in the shade, on the south side of the house; here it is very cold, with a good deal of snow on the ground: at the bower I have been sitting reading in the verandah, here I am cowering over the fire.

The B.C. Legislative Council has just opened, and yesterday the Governor made his speech, a remarkably good one in my humble opinion: he promises to do a great deal for the Colony, to draw direct trade, instead of its all passing through Victoria: a good road that is being made from the West End of N.W.ter to the entrance of Burrard Inlet will encourage ocean-going ships to come there, and certain alterations are to be made in the Tariff with the same object:[1] it is impossible to do anything for the benefit of B.C. without appearing desirous of damaging V.I. for the simple reason that all B.C. trade has hitherto been through V.I., and every act done by the B.C. Government for the benefit of that colony only fosters bitterness with V.I., and increases the difficulties of future union. The movement on the East side of the Rocky Mountains in favour of federal Union, and recent events in Australia, ought surely to show both the Imperial Government and the local Governments the advantages and indeed ultimate necessity of union, and the heart-burnings and troubles that are being laid up for the colonists by its delay. But there are none so blind as those that wo'nt hear.[2]

January 16. On Saturday, the Governor took us up the river in the Leviathan to Langley, where we saw the old fort and buildings of the Hudson's Bay Company.[3]

January 22. 1865. What a bad correspondent I am; I am sure it is time for me to come home and be licked into shape again. I came back from New Westminster on Thursday: my visit was just one week's waste of time; breakfast at 10. A.M.: cocktails before dinner, and mulled port at two in the morning: if I had stayed there another week I think I should have started a short black pipe. But nevertheless I saw a good deal, and learnt a good deal. The Bishop's marriage has taken most people by surprise, but every-one says and agrees that he ought to have a wife. Have you heard of his proposed division of the diocese? it gives unmixed dissatisfaction, both in B.C. and in V.I.: even his own clergy cannot defend it, and I think his proposal has been a very serious false step: he ought to have known the strong feelings and jealousies between the two colonies, and that the only possible division of the diocese must be conterminous with the colonies themselves: this is one of the evils of his long absence: no man here in his right senses would have dreamt of such a division of the diocese as the Bishop has proposed, and for my part, I cannot understand his doing what he has: it has caused quite an outcry.[4]

Governor Seymour is doing a great deal for British Columbia, and is very popular: Governor Kennedy and his House of Assembly do not pull together; how their difference will end, I hardly know, but I am inclined to think it will result in total Union of Vancouver Island with British Columbia, the best thing that can happen: there is a strong party here in favour of abolishing the free port which has always been the chief obstacle to Union.

So far, Governor Seymour's government appears to have been the most successful, but then he has had much the easiest part to play, and we must remember that Governor Kennedy's game is not yet played out: a few months must give him either a victory or a defeat, and I think it will be the former.

Jan. 24. 10.30 P.M. I have just returned home from delivering at the Mechanics' Institute, my lecture "Ocean's Signposts": it was well received.[5] I hear the gun of the mail-steamer, so close my letter, and probably tomorrow morning it will be bounding homewards to you, where the writer would fain follow it.

Your affectionate Son,
Edmund Hope Verney

The Small Bower. Esquimalt. V.I.
January 28. 1865.

My dear Father,

Governor Kennedy was very much pleased with your letter to him: he shewed it to me, and, I am sure, thought a great deal of it. You will probably have heard that a wonderful change has come over the feelings of people here, that they are willing to surrender their cherished free port, and that yesterday the House of Assembly voted by a majority of one third of the House in favour of unconditional Union with British Columbia.[1] Not but what this move has been, and is still being, strongly opposed by the Wharf Street merchants of Victoria, those to whom the ships that arrive here are consigned; in their Chamber of Commerce they have by a majority of twenty to one passed resolutions strongly in favour of retaining the free port, and they have petitioned the House of Assembly on the subject, but it has been of no avail; the general feeling in favour of Union and a tariff has been too strong, and the Chamber of Commerce is believed to be actuated by selfish and not patriotic motives; it is said that the abolition of the free port will severely test the stability of more than one of the leading Wharf Street mercantile houses.

There is no doubt that there has been a great deal of over-trading, a great deal of over-speculation, and of trading on borrowed capital: the abolition of the free port will bring things to a crisis at once, although in any case I believe it would have been inevitable sooner or later, and will, I trust, bring about a more healthy tone in trade.

The estimates are now passing through the House of Assembly, and the members are shewing a more conciliatory spirit towards the Governor than they have yet done. My estimates, the Lighthouse Estimates, are nearly the last.

After two weeks of summer in the middle of winter came a severe frost, making as good and smooth ice, as the most ardent skater could desire; this was succeeded, the night before last, by a heavy fall of eight inches of snow; yesterday I hired a sleigh, and for the first time in my life, went out sleighing. This snow has been converted into slosh, by to-day's ceaseless rain, and this evening as I look out of my Western window, I see the brilliant orange clouds melting away, and the clear blue sky shining and giving promise of a lovely day tomorrow: the barometer, though low, is steadily rising, so I have faith in my prediction. There lies the "Tribune", ready for sea, to sail either tonight or tomorrow morning, and then we shall be left with Captain Jones for our senior officer.

I hope that you always glance over any open letters I send to be forwarded, as you may perhaps pick up various items of news this way.

February 5. I feel my time in this Colony growing very short now: I suppose that the orders to sell the "Grappler" will arrive here towards the end of this month or the beginning of next. We are having a wonderfully fine winter, the finest I have seen, and weather makes all the difference to one in any lonely little shanty. It is very pleasant to have Captain Jones here, he is such a charming fellow: he is good enough to come and see me pretty often, and we walk together some-times, and go out peacocking in Victoria.

The House of Assembly has this year reduced my salary by £50., but it has not cut down anything else in the Lighthouse Estimates, I am happy to say: one item I had introduced for the first time, £30. a year for a library: I have already a Lighthouse Library of nearly 300 volumes, which I collected from my friends, and now although £30. will not go far out here, it will enable us to take in some periodicals, and get some of our most worn books bound: I applied for money for this object last year, but the late Governor would not approve it.

By the way, did you ever hear that the chief difference between a young maid and an old one is that one is careless and happy, while the other is hairless, and cappy?

February 6. I was beginning to write short-hand in a fit of absence of mind. On getting up this morning, I see the mail steamer alongside the wharf, so she must have come in during the night. I had no letters by the last mail, so I hope to get some to-day, but of all the uncertain things of this world there is nothing beats the Vancouver mails. If this glorious weather continues tomorrow, I am going to take the Governor out to the Lighthouse on the Race Rocks.

9. A.M. Your letters of November 30. and December 15. arrived just now; also a long letter from Browne, the late Secretary. After Admiral Kingcome had left, I wrote a very short official letter to him just asking plainly that if he was satisfied with my services while under his command, he would move their Lordships to grant me my promotion on the ship being paid off: I gather from Browne's letter that he did so, with very favourable remarks: well! every little helps.

I trust that the choice of Christchurch for Freddy may prove to have been the right one: I was under the impression that Christchurch was likely to give a man expensive tastes and habits. I fully expect to be ordered home in a few weeks, but I dare say I shall not leave here for *at least* a month after the orders arrive. You see, *two* mails from you have reached me today; a man has gone to the post-office and not yet returned; if you have written by New York, he will bring me yet a third mail: your letters generally come in the Admiralty despatch bag, but New York letters always come through the post-office.

If I am promoted this spring, I shall not be surprised: I quite expect it; but I really believe that it will be no disappointment to me if I am not.

10. A.M. The letters have arrived from the post-office, bringing me the Army and Navy Gazette of December 10., and two letters from British Columbia. Now, adieu: I am just going on board to despatch my official correspondence for this mail, and then I am going to town to work in my office; although they have cut down my salary £50.

With much love to Mamma and Fred, and hoping you are quite well as this leaves me at present, believe me, Your affectionate Son,

Edmund Hope Verney

February 6. 1865.

The Small Bower. Esquimalt. V.I.
February 8. 1865.

My dear Father,

Yesterday we went to the Race Rocks Lighthouse in the "Grappler", taking the Governor, Miss Kennedy, and two or three gentlemen: I dare say this may prove the last cruize of the "Grappler", if she is to be sold immediately, and I am happy to say that she did well, and we had as glorious a day as you can imagine: the water was as smooth as a lake, and the beautiful mountains with their snow-covered tops were as distinct as I have ever seen them.

There is an artist here, a Mr. Coleman, whom I have known for the last two years: some years ago he published a book of tinted lithographs of views of Mont Blanc, which he has three times ascended: I wish you would ask to see it some day in London, as I think you would be pleased with it: it is called "Scenes from the Snow-fields" by E.J. Coleman, published by Longman & Co: poor Mr. Coleman, having never been brought up to hard work, is really in some distress here, and has rather poor health, but I like him, and believe him to be a thoroughly honest fellow.[1]

February 13. I am glad to hear that Lady Gwendolen Herbert is better: is it thought that she will ever be really well and strong again?

(February 18.) Yesterday completed my 14th year in Her Majesty's Service, and found me still wearing a lieutenant's uniform: perhaps I may have the same story to tell this time next year.

An election, which has just taken place to determine the question of unconditional Union with British Columbia, has resulted in the return of the two candidates favourable thereto, although one of the other candidates was a very superior and well educated man.[2] I must own that it is my conviction that a few months hence will see Vancouver Island annexed to British Columbia, and deprived of its representative Government; and a capital thing that will be: we colonists are too young for representative Institutions, and we abuse instead of using them.

This is Saturday, and it is stated that the mail steamer left Portland on Monday: in this case she should have been here on Wednesday, and fears are entertained that she may have come to grief during the past stormy weak [*sic*]: the American mail-steamers in the Pacific are proverbially unsafe, and generally overcrowded. The severity of the winter has now passed away; the days are sensibly lengthening out, and the mid-day sun has some power, and in a very few days we shall probably see the beginning of our glorious season of wild flowers.

Parson Dundas is coming down to stay with me on Monday, as he is now houseless: Archdeacon Gilson moves into St. John's Rectory, and Dundas will go home soon after the Bishop's arrival: he received from his Sunday-school teachers and children a farewell address, and a small presentation of plate: I think I told you some time ago that the Petty Officers of the "Grappler" gave Dundas a bible, "unbeknownst" to me; that is always a good and safe present for a parson, in case he has not got one.[3]

February 19. My eyes are constantly wandering to the harbour's mouth, but no mail appears as yet: I hope there has been no calamity. Captain Jones has lent me Captain Gronow's book, which I think is very jolly to read: his anecdotes bring one back to such an interesting time: he must be a very queer old fellow: I should like to see him: I dare say he knew Sir Harry Calvert, although I see no mention made of him:[4] I have sent to Mr. Duncan some of your remarks on Metlakatlah, as you suggested.

February 19. This afternoon the mail steamer has arrived, not bringing any particular news however. I do not expect to hear the Grappler's fate before the first or second mail in March, but to-day Admiralty letters have arrived dated December 30.

Governor Seymour has asked me to pay him another visit at New Westminster: the Kennedys are going, and the Council is going to give a ball, and there is to be a grand battue shooting: I think I shall very likely go.

Good bye, my dear Father, with much love to Mamma, believe me,

Your affectionate Son,
Edmund Hope Verney

The Small Bower. Esquimalt. V.I.
February 22. 1865.

My dear Father,

This evening the mail steamer has arrived, and the only news I have yet seen is not altogether favourable to me: I see in the Navy List for this year that Lascelles has been superseded from the "Forward", but has not been promoted: Fox of the "Sutlej" is, I see, appointed to command the "Forward": this augurs badly for me, for how can I expect my promotion, if they do not promote Lascelles who is nearly two years my senior?[1]

No letters have come from you this time: in future, four steamers a month will leave San Francisco, but two will stop short at Portland, and two only will come on to Victoria: the object of this is to force through Portland and U.S. Territory the traffic to the newly discovered mines at Kootenay:[2] the next mail is the one by which I hope to hear the fate of the "Grappler", and by which the Bishop ought to arrive, but she will probably not be here for nearly a month.

Will you kindly forward the enclosed letter to Browne, with one of the photographs of the Small Bower: the destination of each photograph is marked on its back, and I think you will be glad to receive yours.[3]

You may notice the elk horns over the porch, and the deer's horns on each post of the verandah; also my coxswain, Russell, standing before the fowl-house: the window under the verandah is my bed-room window; the glass door under the verandah opens from my sitting room, of whose window you have an oblique view: my dining room is entered from the porch, or from the kitchen behind: I hope you will be able to understand my arrangements, with the assistance of the plan: when I came to the house, it consisted of merely the dining and sitting-rooms: the "Grappler's" men built the rest, including porch, verandah, chimney &c: so whereas it did front west, it now fronts south.

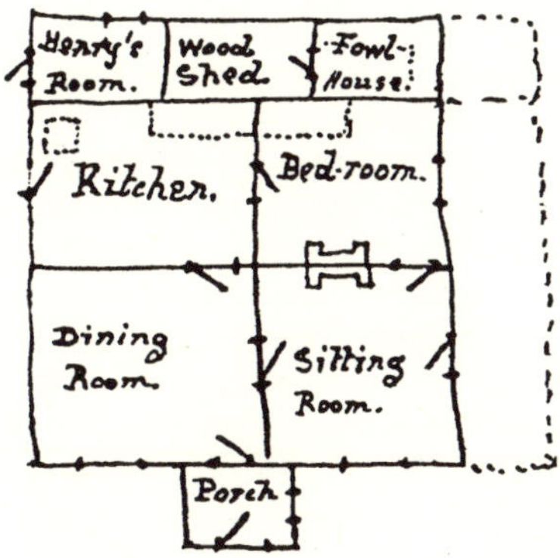

Your affectionate Son,
Edmund Hope Verney

Private

Government House. New Westminster. B.C.
February 26. 1865.

My dear Father,

Yesterday evening I came over here with Governor Kennedy and his family in the colonial tug, the Sir James Douglas. The reason of our invasion of this Colony is a round of gaities & dissipations, centering round a ball to be given by the Legislative council on Tuesday.

It is very interesting to converse with the Governors of the rival Colonies, and to hear the same question discussed from different points of view, and I think that at length I begin to see a way by which Union could be effected to the satisfaction of both Colonies. British Columbians in general, and the people of New Westminster in particular, object to Union on this reasonable ground, that they dread being brought under the dominion of some of the Victorian demagogues, who, in the Vancouver Island House of Assembly, have so troubled Governor Kennedy's course: there are also in British Columbia many, I am sorry to say, whose opposition to Union is based on purely selfish motives, one of the commonest of which is having town lots in, or suburban lots around, New Westminster, and I think there is no doubt that if Union is effected New Westminster will never grow to great importance, even if retained as the seat of Government. But there are in New Westminster, as in Victoria, characters equally capable of becoming a nuisance: a representative Government should be granted to a colony only when public opinion and public feeling will keep such noxious characters from becoming representative men: British Columbia is a crown colony, and the objectionable individuals have not therefore here had the opportunity of rising to the surface, although their existence is well known. Vancouver Island should never have had representative institutions granted it, and I believe that the commission of this great error lies at the door of Sir James Douglas:[1] now however, almost unsought for, certainly quite unexpectedly, the Vancouver Island House of Assembly surrender their constitution: unsolicited they come back to the Imperial Government and say that they will accept whatever arrangements may be made for them, unconditionally, so that they be united to British Columbia.

Now let the Imperial Government seize this opportunity: if they let it slip now they may never have such a chance again: let the laws and constitution of Vancouver Island be cancelled, with one clean sweep, and let it be simply annexed to British Columbia: I believe that this is now *the* thing to be done: I believe that so far from such a step being unpopular in Victoria, it would be received with gratitude by the thinking part of the community, and with but little surprise by any: let the seat of Government be for the present at New Westminster, with a Government House at Victoria for the Governor to make use of when he sees fit, but let him on no account ever be *compelled* to live there: let him nominate and have elected to his Legislative Council a few members, as he does in this Colony now, and it is my firm belief that with British Columbia and Vancouver Island as one Crown Colony, under a firm despotic Government in two or three years these bitter animosities will have ceased, and probably the country will be ready for representative Government. I think it is a matter of little importance which Governor is retained, although perhaps a man with a wife and family is generally a better father of a country: certainly, as far as leading society is concerned, Governor Kennedy and his family are the most desirable, but I am inclined to think that in his office, with his pen in his hand, Mr. Seymour is the cleverer of the two.

You may not agree with me: those whom you may meet may not be of my opinion; but I have a strong conviction that I am not far wrong, and that there are few people who are less prejudiced than myself, and who have had, at the same time, equal opportunities of forming an impartial opinion, on this question of Union. I do not think that either of the

Governors agree with my views, but I think both are agreed that it must ultimately end in Union.

March 8. I returned to the Bower on Friday last since when I have been laid up with a slight attack of fever and neuralgic toothache. While at New Westminster, I heard the question of Union very fully discussed: I understand, although of course this is private, that both the Governors are opposed to immediate Union, and that Mr. Kennedy is opposed to even ultimate Union. With regard to Mr. Seymour I firmly believe that he is opposed to Union solely from prejudice: he has been so good as to argue the subject with me most freely, and to allow me to speak to him about it quite without reserve, and his main argument is that B.C. has been unfairly used for so long that it is only fair now to give her a chance to show what she can do alone: I admit that she has been unfairly treated but I conceive that to be no argument against Union: it would be unfair to B.C. to delay the Union: towns would spring up and settlements would be formed on the strength of certain custom-houses, ports of entry, &c, which would be changed on the colonies being united, and this would be wrong: New Westminster itself will spring up to some little commercial importance if the colonies are kept separate, and then probably fall again when they are united: does not every argument of common sense and of reason tell against Mr. Seymour's proposition of keeping the colonies separate for a year or two and then uniting them? surely it requires no great knowledge of state-craft to see that if they are to be united it should be done at once: that they should never have been separated, and that it is absurd to say that the surest way to ultimate Union is to keep them separate two or three years longer: Mr. Seymour acknowledges that he is prejudiced, he acknowledges that he hates Victoria, and the Victorians, and I am convinced that he will some day see that his present view of affairs is wrong and distorted.

My conversations on politics with Mr. Kennedy consist in his laying down the law and my listening: there is no such thing as an argument with him on any subject; he effectually silences even if he does not convince: as a private individual, nothing can exceed his kindness to me, in *many many* ways, and I am much indebted to him, but as a statesman, I do not believe in him one bit: his enemies say that he is opposed to Union because he does not want to find himself without a government: a man with a family cannot afford that, and I believe he has little or no private means. Mr. Kennedy has certainly had a particularly difficult game to play, but then I do not think he has played it particularly well. Now Mr. Seymour has had a comparatively easy game to play, and he has played it remarkably well.

So now I have come to the conclusion that Vancouver Island should be annexed to British Columbia, and that the United Colonies should be governed by Mr. Seymour: I think he is a very clever man, and will be equal to the difficult points that will arise in such a case, and if he comes to England for a spare rib at the end of this year, as it is currently reported that he will, so much the better.[2]

A great deal depends, of course, on the personal character of Mr. Cardwell: if he is a man who shirks responsibility, he will of course shelter himself behind the united opinions of both Governors against immediate Union: but he may be a man who will see that such an opportunity as this may not occur again, and he may narrowly study the reasons which the Governors give for their decisions, and weigh both the given reasons and others that may suggest themselves, and in the latter case I can hardly think he would be adverse to Union.[3]

As much that I have written has been derived from private conversations, I am sure you will be very careful who sees this letter. The mail steamer bringing the Bishop will probably arrive tomorrow morning, and I trust I shall then hear the "Grappler's" fate[.]

March 10. 1865. The mail steamer arrived this morning, bringing the Bishop and his wife, and your letters of December 31., and January 13. and 16., but not the news of the "Grappler's" fate that I had expected: your letter would make me hopeful, but that I am determined not to hope and so not to be disappointed: you see they have superseded Lascelles, and not promoted him, so what chance have I who am nearly two years his junior.

You ask my opinions about the fray with the Indians in Clayoquot Sound, the picture of which appeared in the Illustrated London News: I am not qualified to give an opinion as I was away North at the time, and have heard very little about it, but all who understand these Indians agree that if treated properly by those who do understand them, it is seldom necessary to resort to violence.[4]

As I find this letter is already headed "private", I can reply quite freely to some of the remarks in your long letter of Jan. 13. I think I have an aptitude for official life, and I have thought that I might do well as a Secretary to some man in an official position: I understand a little about writing official letters, and the system on which those things are carried on: as Secretary to the Lighthouse Board here I have had a good deal to do, a good many official letters to write, and some £1500 a year to manage, and keep strict account of, and I flatter myself that my office is in every respect a model office, and I think, as I said before, that if the work is not too heavy and sedentary, I have some aptitude for office work: I think I could have made a pretty good Secretary to the Royal Commission on Lighthouses, for instance, but if what I say sounds very vain, pray forgive me: I am trying to convey an idea from my own mind to yours.

About marriage, I think I quite understand all you say, but I am for many reasons very anxious to get a wife: of course, she must be such a person as you describe, and I cannot expect that I shall find such a person at once, or that every one will be willing to have me; moreover, of course I must not marry until I am a commander, but being almost seven and twenty, I do not wish to put it off much longer: if I come home this spring and am not promoted, I must go afloat again at once, and serve until I am: it is my only chance. I think I can control my inclinations in marriage: I have never yet seen any one I really desired to marry, and I have always understood that it would hardly be right for me to marry a lady without at least as much fortune as my mother had.[5]

I am sure that the Bishop and Mrs. Hills are very grateful to you for sending them to Claydon: it was such a nice thing to do, and when I heard of it I was as glad as if any one had given me eight pence. It is a great blessing to be in a position to be able to do such a thing: they both speak most warmly of Mama's kindness to them, and I dare say they were not sorry to have her in the house. I hope you will not have sent my shorthand letter to Bishop Kip: I sent *you* a shorthand copy of my answer to his letter which I thought impertinent, and I wanted you to see how I had answered it: I thought Freddy would translate it for you. Bishop Kip does not know shorthand.

As you seem to have no doubt about it, I shall try to see Uncle Hope on my way home, but if I have the least cause to think he is not glad to see me, I shall take myself off again very quickly. He most certainly made an indefinite promise to ask for my promotion when he returned from China, and I think I remember his very words: now he says nothing of the kind took place: I do not so much mind his not having asked, or my not having been promoted, but what must he think of me? He must suppose I have a fertile brain to have invented such a thing; and he certainly said something to that effect. My route home will depend upon the orders I receive from the admiralty: if I am not promoted I shall perhaps be *ordered* home at the public expense, and perhaps appointed to some ship in England, in which case I should most likely have to go straight home.

Now I have answered all your letters by this mail, and I shall eagerly look forward to the next one to learn what is to become of me: all your letters speak confidently of my immediate return without giving any reason for expecting it: I think if you had heard anything definite you would probably have mentioned it. Tomorrow Dundas and I go to lunch with the Bishop, and I shall hear more about Claydon from Mrs. Hills; this morning we had not very long for conversation.

I shall think of you in your electioneering troubles, and if my good wishes can be of any use to you you shall have them, but pray remember, you *must not* be beaten at any price: it is worth a great deal more than £400 or £600 to you, even if you have to borrow the money: I wish I could authorize you to borrow it on the estate.[6]

With love to Mama, and *my* thanks for her kindness to the Bishop and his wife, believe me,

Your affectionate Son,
Edmund Hope Verney

The Small Bower. Esquimalt. V.I.
March 15. 1865.

My dear Father,[1]

I have to-day been writing to Admiral Kingcome, to thank him for his kind mention of me to the Admiralty: in addition to what you told me, I heard more about it from the Bishop. Our steamers are now reduced from three a month to two, and those two both touch at Portland on their way North, so we have no longer a direct steamer from San Francisco. The object of this, of course, is that the Rush to the Kootenie diggings this year may be viâ Portland and the American territory. Of course we are quite at the mercy of the Americans, as we have no English line of steamers. You will doubtless have heard how miserably uncomfortable the Bishop and Mrs. Hills were on board the American steamers.

Our next steamer will be due in about a week from now, when I ought to hear the "Grappler's" fate, if she hits it off with the Atlantic Steamers. Captain Jones has to-day gone out for a cruize in the Cameleon, and will be absent about a week, returning in time for the mail. Dundas, who is still staying with me, starts for England by the next steamer: he intends dawdling some time in California, so if my orders arrive in time, I hope to pick him up there. My route home must depend in a great measure upon the orders I receive: at any rate I hope to see New York on the way, and if practicable, the Salt Lake City: as I should travel with nothing but a pair of saddle-bags, one route would be as cheap as another, and I have not a farthing to spend in travelling royally. I hope you will be very kind to my friend Tom Howell, if he calls on you: his last letter to me was dated from Montreal, but I have no doubt he will return to England soon.

March 17. Mr. Kennedy being an Irish man, and this being St. Patricks Day, Emily's birthday, and the day on which I have twice left England in a ship called the "Shannon", there is an Irishman's ball in Victoria this evening; the day has been made much of; a St. Patrick's Society has been formed, and the orthodox amount of whiskey has been imbibed. I cannot make up my mind whether I ought to send the enclosed letter to Mr. Howell or not, so I leave it open for you to read, and for you to forward it or to burn it as you think expedient: I am so afraid lest Mr. Howell should consider it an impertinent intrusion. Mrs. Cruickshank has confided to me a great deal of her private affairs, a great deal more than is hinted at in my letter, but I fear that with even what I have said he may think I ought to have minded my own business: however, I am sure you will do what is right: if you burn the letter, it will make no difference, as no one will ever know that I wrote it.[2]

March 23. A letter from San Francisco states that we are to have only one steamer a month in future: this is a good thing as it will rouse the people here, and shew them that of course the Americans only seek their own interest, and that if we are to be well served we must subsidize a line of steamers.

March 24. Alas! Alas! the "Oregon" has arrived to-day bringing letters to January 28, but none for me: you can understand how eagerly I now look for letters: possibly I may gather something from the English newspapers when I see them tomorrow: I think I must have forgotten to beg for a speedy answer to my letters sent by the first mail in December.

We hear from the "Sutlej" at Valparaiso, where she arrived on the 25th of January after a rapid passage of 45. days: two men fell overboard off

Cape Flattery, but were picked up. Dundas goes by the steamer tomorrow morning: I too begin to have a yearning to be off, now that I know I *may* long for it: before, I knew I *must* not, and so I actually *did* not, but now I know I really am going soon, the yearning and longing for it are quite irrepressible at times: there is no harm in writing this now, as you will know that I am on my way home when you receive this: I shall not scruple to make use of the telegraph to let you know my whereabouts, and I am sorry you have never used it to me: it would be very jolly just now to know my fate. With love to Mamma and all your party,

Your affectionate Son,
Edmund Hope Verney

Private

The Small Bower. Esquimalt. V.I.
March 23. 1865.

My dear Father,

As time goes on, I become only more and more convinced of the one step that ought now to be taken with regard to these Colonies: there is in my mind no doubt that they ought to be at once united and placed under the Governor of British Columbia: Mr. Kennedy would make a good Governor, but there are many reasons why I should choose Mr. Seymour if the responsibility rested with me: it is my conviction, not hastily formed, that the people of this Colony are prepared for the step I have indicated, and that the House of Assembly is very generally felt to be only an obstruction: the united Colony should be under the form of Government of British Columbia; as far as I can understand the matter, I believe that the question of Union has by the last act of the House of Assembly been placed in the hands of the Secretary of State or of the House of Commons, and I am convinced that the Union in toto should be at once effected: I believe that strictly speaking the resolutions should have come from both Houses of the colonial Legislature: the Upper House has passed a neutral resolution, carried by the official majority against the recorded protest of the independent members of Council, and I *know* that this action of the official members was due to the pressure exerted by the Governor in his executive Council: the reasons he gave for opposing immediate Union were deemed so insufficient as to give rise to its being said that he dreads being again unemployed, with a family to provide for: I am afraid he is by no means popular, and I must confess that I am not able to understand his policy: he remains passive under his House of Assembly, appearing to desire [to] leave them to themselves, to get themselves into a worse and worse mess: I really think that they would be manageable under a firm rule: I begin to think that Mr. Kennedy is just the opposite of what he appears to be, that his character is the reverse of what he thinks it is, and of what his appearance and manner would indicate; yet withal he is as kind to me personally as ever.

Your affectionate Son,
Edmund Hope Verney

The Small Bower. Esquimalt. V.I.
March 26. 1865.

My dear Father,

Did I growl and grumble tremendously in the letter I sent off to you yesterday by Dundas? I know I intended to do so, because I thought I ought to have heard something from you about the fate of the "Grappler", and Mrs. Hills had letters dated the 28th of January: curiously enough I had positively no letters from England either private or official, and as the senior Officer received no despatch bag I think there must have been some mistake about the mails, as there so often is.

Dundas was a great loss: he had been staying with me upwards of a month, and I miss him much; he has been away from home for six years, so he is anxious to get back: many people, well known here, left by the same steamer; I think he said he had about twenty friends on board. I never saw a man so universally esteemed and regretted, and really his place will not be filled, as there is no one here who is at all the same stamp of man: there was one very nice little fellow called Knipe now gone home, and there is Sheepshanks, who is coming out again in June or July; but those are three men who are, as it were, in a class by themselves, and of a different stamp to the rest of the clergy.[1]

March 27. The spring may be said fairly to have set in now: everything is budding, and in sheltered places there are leaves quite out: the frogs are croaking vigorously, which is always a good sign, and I have seen one or two specimens of a small blue flower, like a forget-me-not: the young grass too has begun to shoot, and the milk is already richer: two or three leaves of the honeysuckle over my gate have begun to show, and the little rose-tree in my garden is covered with young spring shoots.

April 4. A steamer has arrived to-day from Olympia, bringing telegraphic news that the mail-steamer may be expected during the night, or tomorrow morning: I can hardly doubt that this steamer will bring me some orders about going home. On Sunday I found the first lillies, the first wild flowers of the year: I think that this year, the spring is nearly a month behind what it was last year; but it has at length taken the turn and the last few days have been quite fine.

April 5. 1865. Alas! still no orders about the "Grappler". I wonder you have not telegraphed to me: none of my letters are dated later than the end of January, while most people have letters to the end of February. Mrs. Kennedy has a letter which says "I see you have lost the gun-boats and that Captain Verney is coming home".

At the best, I see no prospect of getting away from here for six weeks, even if my orders come by the next mail.

With much love to all, and especially to our dear George,[2] believe me,

Your affectionate Son,
Edmund Hope Verney

Private

The Small Bower. Esquimalt. V.I.
March 26. 1865.

My dear Father,

While I eschew politics as much as possible here, and perhaps few people know that I take much interest in that subject, I have taken some pains to form an opinion on the subject of the Union of these Colonies: the more I learn about it, the more convinced I am that *the* thing to be done now is to unite them, as I have said in former letters. Last night I dined with Mr. Kennedy, and when he was conversing with the Bishop on this subject, I asked him when he thought Union ought to take place; he said, "the sooner the better; when two people are to be married it can't be done too soon". I was very much surprised to hear him express himself so decidedly and publickly when Mr. Seymour has told me privately that Mr. Kennedy is opposed to Union, and when I know that Mr. Kennedy maintained other views in his executive council, which is, as perhaps you are aware, a secret and not a public council; of whose proceedings I am not supposed to know anything: I think Mr. Kennedy rather expects Union, but perhaps it would not be politic for him to say what he thinks: the Colony is at present unquestionably not fit for representative government.

April 4. 1865. I could not now pick out in this Colony fifteen men who would make tolerably good M.P.s: that is to say fifteen men who are respectable, of good character, sufficiently well off to be somewhat independent, having an average amount of common sense, and able to spare the time from dollar-making; and of the best I could pick out, not more than one or two *would* serve in the Legislative Assembly; how absurd then to have a House of Assembly at all!

April 5. Your letter of January 30. arrived this morning. I sympathize with you deeply in your trouble about poor dear George, but now you have him at home, I trust it will all come right.

Your affectionate Son,
Edmund Hope Verney

Private.

The Small Bower. Esquimalt. V.I.
April 11. 1865.

My dear Father,

The mail steamer that arrived six days ago brought your letter of January 31. and tomorrow morning another steamer is expected: we are not often favoured with two steamers in seven days. I hardly expect that the steamers will bring any news about the "Grappler", as so short a time has elapsed since the last one, but there is always a chance.

I hear a little about Claydon from the episcopal bride: it appears that the inside of the house is perfect, but that the outside is not in keeping; but then the money spent on the inside is an expense which, once incurred, is complete, whereas if everything were made to correspond outside, it would involve a continual outlay in gardeners, park-keepers, and people of that sort.[1] Your expectation that I shall have left Vancouver Island before the arrival of your letter alarms me somewhat; I hope it does not mean that you are going to cease writing. You would doubtless easily learn from the Admiralty what orders have been sent to me, and you would arrange your correspondence accordingly: I never hope to hear of promotion by these steamers, because I think that you would send such good news as that by telegraph.

I shall anxiously expect news of George: it would be a great disappointment to me to hear of his going back to India without my seeing him, but I cannot help thinking that now he is at home his leave may stretch out to a year: it would be a sad pity to travel six thousand miles home, and to return without seeing all his friends, and reviving old associations.

The Bishop was very much pleased with his brown biscuits: they lasted him, or rather her, nearly all the way to Esquimalt, one of the first things the E.B. told me was what a comfort your biscuits had been to her, and how she could hardly have got along at all without them, the fare was at times so bad. I think he has made a wonderfully good choice in every way, and that she will be a wonderful acquisition to the Colony: of course at first married people are wont to be somewhat affectionate, but yet when all that wears off I think she will make him a happy man, and that it will be seen that he has drawn a prize in the lottery. Now, adieu until the arrival of the steamer tomorrow morning. I am *very* sorry to see by the papers that Uncle Frederic has withdrawn from Aylesbury, but it appears that he could not help it: I hope he may be successful in some other borough, where the electors are free and independent.

April 13. As I lay in bed this morning at six, there arrived to me my letters from the steamer which came in last night, or during the night: your latest date is February 16., but still no orders about the Grappler. How curious that you acknowledge the receipt of my letters to December 21. in which I tell you that winter is just setting [*sic*] , which acknowledgement I receive just as the winter is going away on the 13th of April: so one may fairly say that we have here a short four months' winter.

I have thought over, a good deal, what I have said in my letters to George: you see, on the one hand I know that they will not arrive until long after the event, whatever it may be, and so they will be out of date, and perhaps bore him dreadfully, but on the other hand, my heart is full of him, and of the deepest concern in his affairs, and if I only write to him in general terms he will not know how my heart yearns with affection towards him: now please tell him, that if he has not been pleased with my letters this was the dilemma I was in, and that I concluded on the whole to send them: but one thing is unalterable, whoever he may marry, and that is my love to him, and the sacred charge I undertook, and have so wickedly neglected, when on my mother's dying bed I told her she need not speak as I knew all she had to say: she would have told me to cultivate the affections of my brothers and sisters, and win their confidence, a duty I have hardly attempted to fulfil.

The little parting address to the Mechanics' Institute, which you recommend, is exactly what I had intended, and I shall prepare it whenever I see any prospect of leaving the Colony, of which I see none immediate at present: no orders have come by this mail and you do not mention that any have even been sent: I suppose some one at the Admiralty would tell you about it. Many thanks for the implied promise of a few books for the Mechanics' Institute: if they come out at all soon, I shall not have left the Colony.

I am very glad you have seen Dr. Ash, and I hope you liked him: I am a little amused at your advice about seeing everything worth seeing on my way home: you do not remember what a frightfully expensive thing travelling is on this coast: I have lived well up to my income out here, and you have, of course, heard what an expensive place this is: my position too has involved subscriptions to all kinds of things: the Admiralty owe me £180. which will not be paid until my store accounts are passed; and for that amount I shall have to overdraw on Ommaney: besides this I shall have to overdraw for my passage home, making a total of perhaps four or five hundred pounds, because it will be a great expense sending home Henry and my luggage: I only tell you this, because I wish to have no secrets from you, on these matters, but I ought to have no expenses at home after I come back; when my accounts are passed, the Admiralty will pay up £180, and I believe they will allow me ⅔ of my expense of coming home, so I shall clear it all off before long. I shall tell Ommaney that if he is alarmed at my over-drawing so much, he may tell you about it, but indeed I have always told him to keep nothing from you.

The long and short of it is that I ought to have saved money here, and could very easily have done it; but I began by thinking I should be here a very short time, so I went much into society, and lived well up to my income, determined to make the most of my time, and while I do honestly regret not having lived economically, I know I have had the full worth of the money. Please do not tell Mama anything about my affairs, or she will scarify me.

It is impossible to say what I may do when the time comes, but my present idea is to send Henry with my luggage viâ Panama and Southampton: to send one box of necessaries, coats & white shirts &c from Panama &c to await my arrival at New York: to travel with only a pair of saddle-bags, and always by land; from here by steamer to Olympia, and thence by land to San Francisco viâ Portland; then to Salt Lake City and New York: there to dress like a Christian again, dig out Uncle Hope, and so home. But my orders from the Admiralty, or some letter from you, or fifty other things may entirely change all this.

Now I must conclude my letter as the mail steamer sails at noon, and I am still as much in the dark as ever, as to when I may expect to get away: if the orders have been sent to the Admiral, he will not be here until the middle of next month, in which case I should not be home till the end of

August; but I have no doubt it will all be for the best. I am living very quietly now, and every day that I remain on full pay puts money into my pocket, so there is a bright side to every picture, you see. What I hear of Miss Hinde, by this mail, seems to show both her and George in a somewhat better light, but doubtless that, like other things, will be ordered for the best.[2]

Your affectionate Son,
Edmund Hope Verney

The Small Bower. Esquimalt. V.I.
April 14. 1865.

My dear Father,

Being Good Friday, Henry made me some hot cross buns for breakfast: I hope you were not neglected in that line this morning, and that your buns were as good as mine. I have been to town to Church, after which I lunched with the Bishop, and have now returned home to my solitary den.

At about the same time that Mr. Marshall left the "Grappler", Mr. Clarke, the Gunner of the "Forward", obtained his discharge from the service: he remained here for some time without employment, and at length got command of the "Sir James Douglas", the Government tug attached to the Dredger. I have been having some talk with him, and although his pay is £20. a month he assures me that he heartily wishes he were back in the Royal Navy: he will probably try to get reinstated, and I think he will succeed: he says that he is now convinced that there is no position in the world where a sailor is so well cared for as the Royal Navy, and that he would never have left it had he known as much as he knows now: I think that such testimony outweighs that of the many grumblers who are safe in the service and intend to stick there: still I cannot make out why there is so much difficulty in manning our ships in England.[1]

I think anxiously of your election: when I wrote to you from H.M.S. Shannon at the Cape of Good Hope, I gave you the M.P. on your letter, feeling sure that you would be successful, and I have still the same faith, and cannot believe that the Buckingham electors will be such gooses as to throw you over[.][2] The wild flowers are coming out: I have bouquets in each room, and yesterday two humming-birds were seen.

April 19. Yesterday morning we received the news of the death of Lincoln, which has created a great sensation here, as may be supposed: but when these events happen suddenly the feelings are not at once aroused, and I expect that today one will have a better idea of the effect it has on the Americans. The men of war in this harbour have their colours half-masts, and the U.S. flag at the main half-mast, and an "oration" is to be delivered in the theatre to-day by an American, on the subject. People seem to think that the murder of Lincoln will make little or no political difference, or that it will only make things harder for the South, but since the beginning of the civil war, prophets have been nonplussed.[3]

April 23. I am going to send you twelve copies of the Report of the Vancouver Island Exploration Committee. There is one thing in it I wish to explain: it was no doing of mine that my name stands first on the list of the Committee: I was not present at the meeting where that was settled, and did not know of it until I saw the List printed: I believe it was done because I was Chairman of the sub-committee.

I suggest to you to send copies as follows. To Captain Richards, the Hydrographer. Admiral Fitzroy. Admiral Kingcome, whose address used to be 16 Athenaeum St. Plymouth. The Geographical Society. Colonel Moody? Arthur Mills. Lord Lauderdale? The United Service Institution? Mr. James R. Greenway Brown R.N. Secretary to Admiral Frederick, at Cork. Arthur Kinnaird, for the Library of the British North American Association.[4]

April 28. A mail steamer is due either tonight or tomorrow morning, so I scratch a line to assure you of my well-being, so far. Yesterday I rode with Captain Jones and Doctor Farrelly of the Hospital to North Saanich and back, a distance altogether of upwards of forty miles, so today I feel somewhat tired and stiff.[5] The more I see of Captain Jones, the more I like him, and I esteem it a great privilege to have met such a man in my own profession; I am glad to think that Uncle Hope liked him. What a deal there is to learn in this world; I mean in every day occurrences, apart from the arts and sciences! What an awfully wise old cock Methuselum must have been! (Suttle yoak.)

I am reading "Goulburns thoughts on personal religion.": I suppose you must have seen it, but it strikes me as being one of the most remarkable books I have ever read: that man must have studied himself deeply, as well as well as [*sic*] other people: a book more to the point, I never read: I should think it must go straight home to nine people out of ten, and it seems to be a book exactly suited to the failings of this busy age.[6] How little time do even the best men give up to learning, compared to the time they spend in teaching: and where there is no self-culture, how can there be growth? Mr. Duncan told me how much he had lost by the ceaseless demands of his mission-work upon his time, leaving little or no time for reading: with how few of us are the devotions of the day, I mean the private devotions, the first care, to which laziness and all sorts of business and worldly duties must give way?

I am also reading with the deepest interest, Yonge's Naval History;[7] that is the one subject on which ignorance in a Naval Officer is inexcusable, and I am shocked to find how little I know about it: I am anxious to add "Nelson's Despatches" to my library when I come home: from the few extracts Mr. Yonge gives, I should think they were anything but formal. I have found that eating meat but once a day, and almost total abstinence from wine &c is a great help to overcome laziness, to which in my solitary life I have become prone: this is in the evening when the lamps are lighted, and the pine logs burn brightly: for the last eighteen months, I think, I have risen at six every morning. I wish I had a wife.

May 4. 1865. The mail steamer arrived to-day, bringing at length something definite in the shape of Admiral Grey's letter to you saying that he will send orders to the senior officer here to pay the "Grappler" off:[8] but here the matter ends, for I dined this evening with Captain Jones, and he has not received those orders: there has been some confusion among the mail-bags this time, so it is just possible that the letter containing these orders may turn up tomorrow, otherwise it will not arrive until the next steamer.

Well now! suppose the orders *do* turn up tomorrow, I should not be able to get away until the first mail in June: it will take nearly a month to square up everything and pay the ship off: then a speedy passage from this to England is six weeks: I dare say I should be nearly three months, at any rate two and a half, so at the quickest you must not expect to see me before the middle of August. I am afraid that you will cease writing to me long before I leave this.

And now, about my journey home. Salt Lake City is one third of the way from San Francisco to New York: my intention is to see all that is to be seen in the neighbourhood of San Francisco, and then to travel across the plains by Utah to St. Louis, and not to come by Panama at all. At New York I should find out where Uncle Hope is, and that would determine my movements thence.

Of course all this is going to cost a great deal of money, but I shall write to Ommaney to prepare him for being drawn largely on: if I borrow three or four hundred pounds, and invest it in travel, I think the dividend It will pay to my mind worth more than the interest I pay for it: the debt may be paid off some day, but the opportunity for storing the mind may not occur again. Of course I shall write to you constantly, and keep you informed of my movements, by letter or telegraph.

I look forward most joyfully to seeing you again, and I do hope George will still be with you: I long to see my dear brother again. This continued delay and uncertainty about my return is very bothering: since I have been in the Navy, good fortune has never come to me quickly: I have always expected it, or known of it indirectly, long beforehand: if I were to receive my promotion tomorrow morning, it would not be unexpected.

I do not hear that Uncle Frederic is going to stand for any place in Parliament. If you telegraph to me to hurry home, of course I shall do so.

Your affectionate Son,
Edmund Hope Verney

The Small Bower. Esquimalt. V.I.
May 7. 1865.

My dear Father,

Enclosed is a copy of a telegram which I shall send to New Westminster tomorrow: if you are clever enough to think of it you will see that an answering telegram to the care of the Consul at San Francisco would be sure to catch me, but probably if you do notice that, you will have nothing of importance to telegraph: however, I hope to find letters waiting at New York.

I hope to leave this by the first mail in June, so as to reach San Francisco about the 10th: then I may spend a week seeing the sights in that neighbourhood; I allow three weeks for crossing the plains viâ the Salt Lake City, so that would bring me to New York about the 10th of July: my movements then will depend upon what I hear from you, and where Uncle Hope is, but I might well expect to be at home early in August.

On Friday night the letter to the senior Officer referred to in Sir Frederick Grey's note, turned up at Lascelles' cottage, of all places in the world, so yesterday morning Captain Jones shewed it to me, and gave me the orders to pay off: so there lies the "Grappler" before my windows, with her long white paying-off pendant floating in the bright sunshine, a ship's length astern, emblem of the hope long deferred on which Naval Officers have to exist. I believe that Archdeacon Wright and his family will probably leave for England either by the last mail in this month or the first mail in next.[1] I hope it may have occurred to you to send me one or two letters of introduction to people at New York.

May 9. I begin to gather up my traps ready for my departure, and I fear it will be a bit of a wrench when the moment comes, and I have very little self-command at such moments, I always find. It is mournful to look at the flowers whose fruit I shall not see, and the faces that have beamed kindly on me for three years, now to be lost sight of, and alas! to think of opportunities neglected, of zeal grown cold, of pure and high thoughts and aspirations tarnished, to think of the good and happy time here I had pictured to myself, and the sad shortcomings and failings of the reality; ah well! it cannot be denied that that life in a colony has a tendency to drag one down, especially one living so much alone as I have; I am conscious of having fought against it, but I am also conscious of having given in: I trust never again to have to undergo such a test, and if I have not been very victorious, I have learnt much from failure.

May 12. Tomorrow we shall haul down the "Grappler's" pendant, and until I leave for England, I shall be borne on the books of the "Cameleon" or of the "Sutlej" if she arrives. Perhaps I may get away by the last mail in this month, after all, but I fear it will be too much hurry to attempt it, and it would be a pity to leave anything undone.

May 13. The "Grappler's" pendant was hauled down at sunset this evening: I saw it come down, and have it now safely in my possession: you shall see it when I come home; probably the only genuine bit of the old craft that you will ever see.[2] As the Flag-ship has not arrived yet, Sir Frederick Grey's orders to the senior officer here have expedited matters considerably.

May 15. The mail steamer came in this morning as it came in this day three years ago when I first arrived in the Colony. I was glad to get your letter of March 15, and so to find that you had not quite left off writing to me: there is nothing particular in your letter or in Mama's scrap at the end of it requiring to be answered. The "Sutlej" arrived on Sunday morning, and the Admiral told me he had had a long letter from you which he had answered as lengthily. I am very glad to receive the generally good accounts you send of all except poor Mama: I fear she has suffered a good deal during the winter. I have no doubt that I shall leave by the first mail in June, which will perhaps be the next steamer we shall have.

Your affectionate Son,
Edmund Hope Verney

Copy

From,
Lieutenant Verney. R.N.
Vancouver Island
To,
Sir Harry Verney Bart. M.P.
Claydon House.
Bucks.
England.

I start early in June. Address to the care of the Consul, New York.

May 6. 1865.

The Small Bower. Esquimalt. V.I.
May 21. 1865.

My dear Father,

It seems right that I should have some sort of a letter ready to send to you by every mail, even when I have not much to say: the next steamer will probably be here on wednesday or Thursday, and the following one is the one by which I hope to get away: archdeacon Wright goes by the first, with his wife and family: they are now all staying at the Bishop's: it has been very kind of him and Mrs. Hills to take them in, as it was really no joke, and has only been accomplished by dint of great compression.

It is a horrid bore, having to move: I had quite settled down for life, I find, although I was not aware of it, and now I am quite unhappy at parting with each chair and little &c: it will be a great relief when I find myself fairly on board the steamer. People are very kind, at saying good bye, and kind expressions crop up from unexpected quarters: some people on whom I have always looked coldly, and whom I have treated with studied reserve, quite melt one with the heartiness of their expressions: I have probably not more than another fortnight before me here, at the outside, so I must seize every opportunity of taking the pleasantest farewells, to leave behind me as few enemies as may be.

Tomorrow I am going to New Westminster for the Queen's birthday, to say good-bye to my friends there, and to see the grand gathering of Indians that is expected: it will be a fine sight.[1] The closing of the "Grappler's" accounts is going on but slowly, and may possibly detain me later than the first mail in June, but I feel pretty sure that I shall be able to get away then: there are two men hard at work. Pray tell our dear Emily that I do not write to her because I know she is at Claydon, and able to see my letters to you: I suppose too that we shall probably meet a week or two after you receive this: my first resting place in England will most likely be London, to do at once whatever has to be done at the Admiralty: I dare say I shall be able to get a room either at South Street or in St. James' Place: you ask me to telegraph as soon as I am in England, and I will do so.[2] I close this letter now in case I am not back from N.W. in time for the steamer.

Your affectionate Son,
Edmund Hope Verney

The Small Bower. Esquimalt. V.I.
June 3. 1865.

Dear Father,
I leave by the steamer this afternoon.

Edmund Hope Verney

Notes to Letters

The dates given at the head of these notes are those that appear at the opening of the letters, that is the earliest date in letters that have two or more dates.

May 15, 1862

1 Alfred H.P. Helby (d. 1902) commanded the *Grappler* from 1860 to 1862, when he was promoted from lieutenant to commander and returned to England. Lieut. Hon. Horace D. Lascelles (1835-69), a younger son of the third Earl of Harewood, commanded the second gunboat stationed at Esquimalt, HMS *Forward*. EHV mentions two other naval vessels in this letter: HMS *Charybdis*, a steam corvette commanded by Captain Hon. George Keane until 1863 and then by Captain Edward Turnour; and HMS *Hecate*, a paddle sloop engaged in coastal surveys under Captain George H. Richards.

2 The Cariboo gold rush, which began in 1860-61, reached its height during the spring and summer of 1862. For its impact on Victoria see G.P.V. and Helen Akrigg, *British Columbia Chronicle 1847-71* (Vancouver: Discovery Press, 1977), and Derek Pethick, *Victoria: The Fort* (Vancouver: Mitchell Press, 1968).

3 For George Hills (1816-1895), first Bishop of Columbia, see Jean Friesen in the *DCB*, and for his connection with the Verneys see the Introduction, 12-14, above. In his unpublished diary Bishop Hills records that EHV visited him on May 13: "I was pleased to find him well disposed & anxious to use his influence upon his fellow men to lead them to the service of God" (Archives of the Anglican Diocese of British Columbia, Vancouver School of Theology, BCARS microfilm, A796).

4 On EHV's views of the native Indians see the Introduction, above. Before leaving England he had read George Vancouver's *A Voyage of Discovery to the Pacific Ocean and Round the World*, with its engraved illustrations, and he appears later to have had a copy of the first edition (London 1798) with him in British Columbia: see his letters of August 11 1862 and October 14 1863. The smallpox epidemic which broke out in Victoria in March and raged during the spring and summer of 1862 was the worst catastrophe ever to afflict the native Indians of the west coast, reducing their numbers by more than half, according to common estimates. See Grant Keddie, "The Victoria Smallpox Crisis of 1862," *Discovery: Friends of the Royal British Columbia Museum Quarterly Review*, XXI.4 (Autumn 1993), 6-7.

5 For information about EHV's family, his relatives, and his personal servant, Henry Tyler, see the Introduction, 8-10, 19, 55n, above.

6 Kenneth McKenzie (1811-74) was bailiff of Craigflower Farm for the Puget Sound Agricultural Company, established by the Hudson's Bay Company; see W.R. Sampson in the *DCB*. Rev. Charles Thomas Woods (1825-95) was an Anglican clergyman in Esquimalt and at St. John's, Victoria, and headmaster of the Boys Collegiate School in Victoria, later archdeacon and rector in New Westminster.

May 25, 1862

1 EHV follows the common English practice during the period of terming conifers in general pines. What he means by "calcilaria" is debatable, since calceolaria is not found in the region.

2 A letter of Marie Hardinge (July 18 1862) at Claydon House indicates that she was a friend or companion especially of EHV's sister Emily.

3 James Douglas (1803-77) had been governor of Vancouver Island since 1851 and governor of the separate colony of British Columbia since 1858.

4 Arthur Mills (1816-98) was Conservative M.P. for Taunton (1857-65) and later for Exeter. A letter to him from EHV, August 30 1862, is in BCARS, Colonial Correspondence, F1214.

5 The episcopal residence, Bishop's Close, was like St. John's Church a prefabricated iron structure brought out from England.

6 Rear-Admiral Robert Fitzroy (1805-65), FRS, is best remembered for the important scientific surveys he conducted as captain of the *Beagle* in the 1820s and 1830s.

7 See EHV's later reference to the Davies family, keepers of the Race Rocks lighthouse, in his letter of October 15 1862.

8 As EHV's letters indicate, his second master, Sub-Lieutenant George Tomlin, soon transferred to another ship and was not replaced on the *Grappler*.

9 EHV alludes to Stephen Foster's well-known song, "Old Folks at Home".

June 1, 1862 (Private)

1 Rear-Admiral Lord Clarence Paget (1811-95), a son of the first Marquis of Anglesey, was First Secretary at the Admiralty in London.

2 According to the *Grappler* muster book (PRO, ADM 38 8204), John G. Marshall was born at Portsmouth and was twenty-five years old when he joined the ship in 1859. EHV's letters show the importance of this gunner's role as very able chief warrant officer on the *Grappler*.

3 John Washington (1800-63), who had actually been promoted from captain to rear-admiral in April 1862, was the Royal Navy's Hydrographer from 1855 to 1863. His letter of July 16 1862 thanking EHV for charts and descriptions and plans of forts at San Francisco is preserved at Claydon House.

June 1, 1862

1 John Stone was in business as "Naval Outfitter" at Portsea, Portsmouth. EHV's mother, Eliza, Lady Verney, was the author of *Practical Thoughts on the First Forty Chapters of the Book of the Prophet Isaiah*, published in London in 1858.

2 quiver full: Psalm 127.5.

3 Alan Herbert (1836-1907), M.D., a son of the third Earl of Carnarvon, practised medicine in Paris. Edmond de Grancey was a French naval officer who had become a friend of EHV during the Crimean War; he was killed in 1870 in the Franco-Prussian War.

4 William Lane Booker as British Consul had been helpful to EHV during his visit to San Francisco.

5 Davie: see the Introduction, 20, 55n, above.

6 Western is not further identified in the correspondence but John Norman sent EHV on Vancouver Island a strongly religious letter on June 12 1862.

7 our book: *The Shannon's Brigade in India.*

8 In his diary Bishop Hills records that St. Paul's Church in Nanaimo was opened on June 8, 1862, although the consecration was postponed because the title to the land had not been transferred.

JUNE 16, 1862

1 As a result of the dispute about possession of San Juan Island and the "Pig War" of 1859, Britain and the United States maintained garrisons at opposite ends of the island from 1860 until 1872 when San Juan was awarded to the United States.

2 For Tomlin see the Introduction, 20, above, and note to letter of May 25 1862. The commander-in-chief of the Pacific Station was Rear-Admiral Sir Thomas Maitland (1803-78), later eleventh Earl of Lauderdale.

3 Reports of Emigration and Immigration Commissioners were published annually as Sessional Papers of Parliament.

4 The *Army and Navy Gazette* was published weekly in London, on Saturdays as EHV indicates on July 17.

5 The *Colonist* reported on June 10 the arrival of the *Lady Young* from New Zealand with a cargo of miners, oranges, and coconuts. The Salmon River gold rush was in Washington Territory. The gold rush this spring and summer to British territory on the Stikine River was rapidly followed by disillusionment.

JUNE 27, 1862

1 Uncle Hammersley was presumably a great-uncle, as Sir Harry Verney's mother was a Hammersley.

JULY 2, 1862

1 William I. Kip (1811-93) was first bishop of the Protestant Episcopal Church in California; see the *DAB*. In 1860 with an introduction from Bishop Hills he had visited the Verneys in England, and EHV had recently visited him in San Francisco.

2 William A.G. Young (c. 1827-85), Colonial Secretary of British Columbia and Acting Colonial Secretary of Vancouver Island, was married to Douglas' niece, Cecilia Cowan Cameron. EHV makes some disparaging remarks about him but he had a distinguished career as a colonial administrator and was later knighted. See the *DCB*.

3 Colonel Richard C. Moody (1813-87) was in command of the detachment of Royal Engineers in British Columbia from 1858 to 1863. See the *DCB*.

4 The log of the *Grappler* records that the ship grazed on a rock near Laurel Point on May 16 (PRO, ADM 53 8157).

JULY 17, 1862

1 George Monckton-Arundell, sixth Viscount Galway (1805-76), an Irish peer who sat in the Commons, was no doubt familiar to Sir Harry Verney as the M.P. for East Retford. The steam frigate HMS *Bacchante* was Admiral Maitland's flagship.

2 Until 1864 the Royal Navy had ten grades of admiral, ranked by three squadron colours, red, white, and blue. See Michael Lewis, *The Navy in Transition 1814-64, A Social History* (London: Hodder & Stoughton, 1965), 126.

3 Admiral Sir James Hope, who was engaged in naval actions during the Taiping War in China, wrote EHV in a letter from Shanghai on May 2, 1862 that he had been wounded in the leg.

July 20, 1862

1 The mother of James Douglas' wife, Amelia Connolly (1812-90), was the daughter of a Cree chief. Other contemporary reports give a less prejudiced and more sympathetic view of Mrs. Douglas and her daughters. EHV is expressing a common opinion, however, in criticizing W.A.G. Young for holding too many official positions.

2 Dr. John Helmcken (1824-1920), Speaker of the Vancouver Island House of Assembly, was married to Cecilia Douglas (1834-65). He scarcely regarded himself as an infidel. His relations with Douglas were for a time strained not only because of political differences but because of a dispute about a land purchase Helmcken wanted to make. See his *Reminiscences*, 199.

3 Alice (1844-1913), who was actually the fourth daughter of the Douglases, eloped in August, 1861 with Charles Good (1832-1920), clerk to the Colonial Secretary of British Columbia, later Acting Colonial Secretary. The marriage ended in divorce in 1883.

4 Agnes (1841-1928), third daughter of the Douglases, married Arthur T. Bushby (1835-75), Registrar General for Deeds for British Columbia; see the *DCB*. The Attorney General was George H. Cary (1832-66); see the *DCB*.

5 David Cameron (1804-72), Chief Justice of the Supreme Court of Vancouver Island, was married to Douglas' sister, Cecilia Douglas Cowan; see the *DCB*.

August 3, 1862

1 HMS *Devastation*, a paddle sloop, had Commander John Pike as its captain.

2 Lambton L.L. Bevan is listed among the midshipmen in the muster book of HMS *Bacchante* in 1862 (PRO, ADM 38 5649).

3 On this speech and Verney's subsequent part in the founding of the Cowichan settlement, see the Introduction, 27, above.

August 7, 1862

1 In order to urge the establishment by the British government of a shipping line between Panama and Victoria, Sir Harry Verney in a speech in the House of Commons on June 13 (*Hansard's Parliamentary Debates*, 1862, col. 545) and in a letter in *The Times* on June 19 (p. 9) quoted EHV's letters from Acapulco on April 16 and San Francisco on April 27 regarding the dangerous and overcrowded conditions prevailing on American ships. He cited the letters as those of "a passenger" and "an officer," without explicitly identifying his son as the author.

2 On the origins of the Columbia Emigration Society of London, see Frank A. Peake, *The Anglican Church in British Columbia* (Vancouver: Mitchell Press, 1959), 39-40, and Jackie Lay, "To Columbia on the Tynemouth: The Emigration of Single Women and Girls in 1862," in *In her own Right: Selected Essays on Women's History in B.C.*, ed. Barbara Latham and Cathy Kess (Victoria: Camosun College, 1980), 19-41, and Joan Weir, *Catalysts and Watchdogs: B.C.'s Men of God: 1836-1871* (Victoria: Sono Nis, 1995), 66-76. On EHV's membership in the local committee see the Introduction, 28-29, above. Among his letters of July 1862 is EHV's

shorthand version of a passage in a letter from his father dated March 18 1862, in which Sir Harry Verney declared that the "Columbians" should send over gold to pay for the passages of emigrants sent out from England: emigration schemes he considered were to the advantage of "Columbia" rather than England, and the Columbians should pay the costs.

3 As a result of the situation EHV describes, members of St. John's Church in Victoria long held that their bells had been stolen by Holy Trinity Church in New Westminster. See Stuart Underhill, *The Iron Church* (Victoria: Braemar Books, 1984), 15.

4 Little seems to be known of Sarjeant the secretary, but Angela Burdett-Coutts was a generous benefactor of the scheme, as she had been of the Columbia Mission and bishopric, and additional funds were raised at a concert in London in July.

5 On the arrival of the "brideship" *Tynemouth*, see EHV's letter of September 20.

August 11, 1862

1 "Port Angelos" or "Angelo" is of course Port Angeles, Washington. Woodhall, Herts, was the country residence of EHV's aunt and late uncle, the Abel Smiths.

2 Rev. Alexander C. Garrett (1832-1924) arrived in 1860 as Anglican missionary to the Songhees in Victoria. He served in Esquimalt, and later in Nanaimo, and eventually became Bishop of Dallas, Texas.

August 16, 1862

1 Rev. Richard L. Lowe, after two years as an Anglican clergyman at Nanaimo, became the first incumbent of St. Stephen's, Saanich, in 1862 and served there and on Saltspring until his return to England in 1865. "Axener" is probably Christian Ochsner, a Victoria brewer, who according to the assessment rolls held land in Saanich in the early 1860s. Union Bay is now Patricia Bay.

2 As Verney indicates, the settlers going to Cowichan on HMS *Hecate* were accompanied by Governor Douglas, Attorney General Cary, and the Surveyor General, Joseph D. Pemberton.

3 The SS *Golden Gate* (not "Age") bound from San Francisco to Panama, with inadequate life boats and pumps that did not work, lost 170 passengers as a result of a fire at sea on July 27, 1862.

4 On Henry Tyler's sister, see the Introduction, 18, above.

5 Henry P. Wright (1816-92) was Archdeacon of Columbia, residing in New Westminster.

6 The *Memorial de Sainte Hélène* of Emanuel, Count de Las Casas was published in an English translation: *Journal of the Private Life and Conversations of the Emperor Napoleon at Saint Helena* (London: Henry Colburn, 1823).

7 Sir Arthur Helps published anonymously a series of three works with the title *Friends in Council*, dialogues on various social and intellectual subjects, the third and last in 1859. *The Recreations of a Country Parson*, also anonymous, was by Andrew K.H. Boyd, a moralistic work first published in 1859.

August 22, 1862

1 The panoramic photograph (actually a linked series) is preserved at Claydon House and reproduced in the present edition. I have not located any complete copy in British Columbia, but some separated parts are held by BCARS and the Victoria City Archives. Most of the features EHV describes such as the government buildings commonly known as the "Birdcages" are easily identified. He

gives information that helps date the photograph: it must have been taken prior to the loss of SS *Cariboo* by explosion near the entrance to Victoria Harbour on August 2, 1861, and presumably prior to December 1860, when palisades of Fort Victoria were pulled down (Pethick, *Victoria: The Fort*, 209).

August 30, 1862

1 Elliott is mentioned again on October 11 but (like Bell and Hastings, July 17 and September 22) he is not clearly identified.

2 Father Peter Rondeault (1827?-1900), an Oblate priest, arrived on Vancouver Island in 1858 and soon afterwards began to work as a missionary at Cowichan, where he remained for the rest of his life.

September 14, 1862

1 EHV's quotation is from the work by de Las Casas he mentions in his letter of August 20. Napoleon is represented in it as claiming to possess courage of "*the two o'clock in the morning kind*", that is "unprepared courage, that which is necessary on an unexpected occasion, and which, in spite of the most unforseen events, leaves full freedom of judgment and decision" (vol. I, pt. 2, p. 8, in the translation published by Colburn in 1823).

2 The Captain of the steam sloop HMS *Mutine* was Commander William Graham. Captain (later Vice-Admiral Sir) George H. Richards (1820-96), commander of the survey vessel HMS *Hecate*, charted much of the British Columbia coast and had a distinguished career as a hydrographer.

3 B. Woodd & Sons were wine merchants with premises at 34-35 New Bond Street, London.

4 For these various extra-naval activities, see the Introduction above.

September 20, 1862

1 With his letters about this date EHV enclosed eleven clippings from Victoria newspapers, including one from the *Colonist* on September 13 praising him for his assistance to the Cowichan settlers, two from the *Colonist* on September 19 about the arrival of the *Tynemouth*, one from the *Daily Evening Press* on September 22 in which the Immigration Committee was criticized for its lack of preparation to receive the immigrants, and letters from John Marshall, Gilbert Sproat, and Robert Burnaby in the *Press* and *Colonist* on September 23 refuting this criticism. On the newspaper discussion, the preparation of the Marine Barracks by the crew of the *Grappler*, and the entertainment of the immigrants aboard the ship, see the Introduction, 29, above.

2 In a clipping titled "The Regatta" from the *Press*, September 21, EHV underlined the names of the winning gigs from the *Grappler*: "Emerald" and "Ariel."

3 Rev. William Scott and his wife were placed in charge of the female immigrants on the *Tynemouth* by the Emigration Society in London, and after their arrival he delivered one of the addresses to them in Christ Church Cathedral mentioned in the next letter. The captain of the *Tynemouth* was Arthur Hellyer.

September 22, 1862

1 Victoria was incorporated as a city in August 1862, with Thomas Harris as the first mayor. There was no city hall, and the courtroom of the Police Barracks served as the council chamber. EHV enclosed clippings from the *Press*, September 16 and 17, about a ludicrous battle for the use of this room between magistrate A.F. Pemberton and the new mayor and council.

2 EHV enclosed a clipping from the *Colonist*, September 18, "Naval Magistrates," in which an anonymous letter writer criticizes him as a non-resident and naval officer for sitting as a magistrate in Victoria, but in which he is defended in an appended editorial comment.

OCTOBER 11, 1862

1 Mme. Goldschmidt was the married name of the famous singer, the "Swedish Nightingale," Jenny Lind (1820-87).

2 On the part played by EHV and the *Grappler* in the foundation of the Comox settlement, see the Introduction, 27-28, above. On October 25, 1862 the *Colonist* stated that the seamen of the *Grappler* expressed discontent that the colonial government had offered them no remuneration for additional work in the settlement expedition.

OCTOBER 13, 1862

1 This Everard must have been a son of Rev. Salisbury Everard, vicar of Swaffenham, Norfolk, whose wife, Charlotte Chester, was a niece of Henry Wilson, eleventh Baron Berners (1797-1871), and of his sister, Mrs. Abbot Upcher of Sheringham, Norfolk. See Sir Bernard Burke, *A Genealogical and Heraldic Dictionary of the Peerage and Baronetage of the British Empire* (London, 1866) under Berners, and Burke's *Landed Gentry* (London, 1868) under Everard and Upcher. The Salisbury Everards' eldest son was Louis (b. 1841). According to an advertisement in the *Colonist*, March 9, 1863, Louis Everard was for a time in the nursery business in Victoria.

2 Lord Walter Kerr (1839-1927), a son of the seventh Marquis of Lothian, served with EHV on HMS *Shannon* and in the naval brigade in the Indian Mutiny, and again as lieutenant on HMS *Emerald*, and went on to have a distinguished naval career; see the *DNB*. Several of his letters of the early 1860s to EHV are at Claydon House.

3 EHV's occasional replacement of "Tynemouth" with "Teignmouth" no doubt reflects the fact that he was more familiar with Devonshire than Tyneside.

OCTOBER 14, 1862

1 Fears about a possible naval threat to Vancouver Island from "monitors" at San Francisco were occasionally expressed by the Victoria newspapers. On his return journey to England on June 19, 1865 EHV sent Admiral Denman a report from San Francisco about the turret ship USS *Camanche*, stating that the vessel was really suitable only for smooth waters and harbour defence, and that it would be somewhat hazardous to navigate it to Esquimalt (PRO, ADM 1 5924).

2 EHV's list of improvements is quite up-to-date; for example, the new gas system was first turned on September 29.

OCTOBER 15, 1862

1 Rev. Robert J. Dundas (1832-1904), who became EHV's closest friend among the local Anglican clergy, served on Vancouver Island from 1859 to 1865. He was the first rector of St. John's in Victoria, and also took services in Esquimalt.

2 George Davies, assisted by his wife Rosina, was the first full-time lighthouse keeper on the west coast at Fisgard, 1860-61. His period at Race Rocks, 1861-66, culminated in tragedy after EHV's departure from the coast. See Donald Graham, *Keepers of the Light* (Madeira Park: Harbour, 1985), 12-22.

3 Malcolm Cameron (1808-76), a politician from Ontario, went on a mission to England in 1862-63 to present the grievances of mainland British Columbia and appeal for a more representative form of government, accompanied by Leonard McClure from Vancouver Island.

4 Gustav A.C. Bencke held the rank of assistant engineer on the *Grappler*, and rose on another vessel to chief engineer in 1878. Bishop Hills' diary records that he conducted some exploration of the Comox district on October 30, 1862. Major Charles Cumming Bruce (1790-1875), a Scottish M.P., was a friend of Sir Harry Verney. His son-in-law was James Bruce, eighth Earl of Elgin (1811-63).

5 HMS *Topaze*, commanded by Captain Hon. John W.S. Spencer, and HMS *Tribune*, commanded by Captain Lord Gilford, were both classified as steam sloops.

October 18, 1862

1 For a succinct account of the San Juan boundary dispute, see Akrigg, *British Columbia Chronicle 1847-1871*, 99-101. The marked chart which EHV enclosed with this letter is preserved at Claydon House, together with a manuscript copy of the Oregon Treaty of 1846. Like others on Vancouver Island, EHV believed that the Columbia River really should have been the international boundary.

November 1, 1862

1 This visit to the Comox settlement is recorded in some detail in Bishop Hills' diary. "Stewarts Island" is Stuart Island in the San Juan group then claimed by Britain but now American territory. Port Augusta is the old naval name for Comox Harbour.

2 A letter at Claydon House from Bishop Hills to Sir Harry Verney dated from the *Grappler* at Deep Bay on October 30 includes an account of the Comox visit and praise of EHV's dedication to the good of others and to God's work.

3 EHV expresses the view of the Yuclatas: Lekwiltok (Kwakiutls or Kwakwaka'wakw) from the Cape Mudge area, that was common at the time. See Gough, *Gunboat Frontier*, 132, and Robert Galois, *Kwakwaka'wakw Settlements, 1775-1920: A Geographical Analysis and Gazetteer* (Vancouver: University of British Columbia Press, 1994), 234-35.

4 Rev. John Booth Good (1833-1916) served in Nanaimo as Anglican missionary and later rector of St. Paul's between 1861 and 1866; he then went to Lytton but eventually returned to Nanaimo.

November 11, 1862

1 The occasion was the celebration the twenty-first birthday of the Prince of Wales, later King Edward VII.

2 Attorney General Cary was an unpopular figure. Showing increasing signs of mental instability, and charged with financial irregularities, he was eventually forced to resign in the summer of 1864.

November 1, 1862 (Private)

1 EHV's transcript of these religious meditations is preserved at Claydon House.

2 While the date at the head of this letter is November 1, the final paragraph refers to EHV's speech of November 10, and must have been added after that occasion.

3 Major-General Sir Henry Havelock (1795-1857) was the popular British hero of the Indian Mutiny campaigns, during which he succumbed to disease.

November 21, 1862

1 The clipping enclosed from the *British Columbian* of New Westminster has not been found.

2 The estate of the de Granceys was at Grancey-le-Chateau, 44 kilometers north of Dijon.

3 The reference is to Henrietta Herbert, Countess of Carnarvon, widow of the third earl, and two of her children, Alan Herbert (cf. June 1 1862, above), and Lady Gwendolen Herbert.

4 James Ridgeway was a bookseller at 169 Picadilly, London.

November 23, 1862

1 Cf. EHV's earlier references to Colonial Secretary W.A.G. Young, Chief Justice David Cameron, and Attorney General George Cary. Joseph Despard Pemberton (1821-93) was Hudson's Bay Company surveyor on Vancouver Island from 1851 to 1859 and colonial Surveyor General from 1859 to 1864; see Richard Mackie's article on him in the *DCB*. Alexander Watson (d. 1892) was Treasurer of Vancouver Island 1861-66. Edward G. Alston (1832-72) was appointed Registrar of Titles for Vancouver Island in 1861, and later served as Attorney General of British Columbia at the time of Confederation; see Dorothy Blakey Smith's article on him in the *DCB*.

November 29, 1862

1 The enclosed clippings with the letter redated December 4 are "Towing Out Vessels" from the *Colonist*, November 29, a letter signed M.W.K. defending EHV against criticism in the *Chronicle* for interfering with commerce by towing out a bark with the *Grappler*, and praising him for his assistance on other occasions to commercial vessels in trouble; and "Com. Verney" from the *Colonist*, December 3, defending EHV against the *Chronicle*'s criticism of his sitting as magistrate in Victoria. In a subsequent letter he enclosed "Still Harping on my Daughter," on the same theme, from the *Colonist*, December 6.

December 8, 1862

1 Isaiah: see June 1, above, and note. The other tracts are never identified.

2 *The Leisure Hour: A Family Journal of Instruction and Recreation* was published weekly in London; *The Sunday at Home: A Family Magazine for Sabbath Reading* was published monthly in London; *Good Words* edited by Norman Macleod was published monthly by Strahan in London and Edinburgh. All three journals were congenial to those with Evangelical religious views.

3 Octavius Ommanney was a Navy Agent at 14 Great George Street, London, and other members of his family had the same occupation.

4 Bishop Kip's son, whose name is not given, was secretary with the American legation in Japan. The clipping EHV encloses is the first of a series titled "Legation Life in Japan," published anonymously in the *San Francisco Bulletin*.

5 As EHV indicates, the Royal Navy at this time leased as a survey vessel the historic Hudson's Bay Company's *Beaver*, which arrived in 1836, the first steamship on the Pacific coast. See Derek Pethick, *S.S. Beaver: The Ship that Saved the West* (Vancouver, 1970), and James P. Delgado, *The Beaver: First Steamship on the West Coast* (Victoria, 1993). Daniel Pender (c. 1833-91) carried out important coastal surveys between 1863 and 1870, and was later promoted to captain. "Bonwich" is Charles Bonwick, whose name was placed on several coastal points as a result of his service on the *Beaver*; see John Walbran, *British Columbia*

Coast Names (Ottawa: Government Printer, 1909), 57-58. The *Grappler*'s remaining engineers were George Fitzgerald and Gustav Bencke; cf. October 20, above.

December 20, 1862

1 Confederate forces inflicted heavy losses on the Army of the Potomac at the Battle of Fredericksburg on the Rappahannock River on December 13. Later estimates put the Union losses at 1,284 killed and a total of 12,653 casualties.

December 24, 1862

1 Captain (later Vice-Admiral) Hon. John W.S. Spencer (1816-88), a younger son of Baron Churchill and grandson of the dukes of Marlborough and Grafton, had recently arrived in HMS *Topaze* to serve as senior officer at Esquimalt.

2 The scene of the Christmas festivities, the McKenzies' Craigflower farmhouse, is now a museum. EHV also received an invitation for Christmas dinner from the Cridges, and preserved Mary Cridge's note.

3 Edward Seymour, Duke of Somerset (1804-85), was First Lord of the Admiralty from 1859 to 1866.

4 George Price (1842-1926) was the son of friends of the Verneys, and connected with them through the family of Lord Dunsany. He was in fact promoted to lieutenant in the Navy in August 1862; he later became captain and served as M.P. for Devonport. See Michael Stenton and Stephen Lees, *Who's Who of British Members of Parliament* (Hassocks and Atlantic Highlands: Harvester/Humanities, 1978), II, 291.

5 For Rev. Charles T. Woods see May 15 above, and note. John Cross was the Verneys' tenant on a farm of the Claydon estate; he is probably mentioned here as a churchwarden. EHV's uncle, Rev. William Fremantle, was vicar of East Claydon, as well as rector of Middle Claydon.

6 EHV liked to receive the *Navy Lists* but he did not always peruse them with much care: Sackett Hope, who joined the Navy in 1814 and was promoted to captain in 1840, had become a rear-admiral in 1860. The earls of Hopetoun were heads of the Scottish family of Hope to which EHV's mother belonged.

January 6, 1863

1 The two gunboat commanders were very different in character. Lascelles was liked by many in Victoria because of his lack of moral pretensions. See Terry Reksten, *'More English than the English': A Very Social History of Victoria* (Victoria: Orca Books, 1986), 53-54. His racing exploits were frequently reported in the *Colonist*. When he forwarded the logbook of HMS *Forward* for 1860-61 to the Admiralty he inadvertently included between the leaves the card of a Victoria race meeting: the Beacon Hill Sweepstakes and Naval Stakes on October 3 and 4, 1861 (PRO, ADM 53 8026). The paymaster of HMS *Topaze* was Henry N. Scaife, and the captain of marines was James Shute.

2 The journal EHV mentions here, begun in July 1862 and continued until 1870, with numerous brief entries, is preserved at Claydon House. It is in shorthand, apart from proper names and dates.

3 On the arrival of the second "brideship" the *Robert Lowe* see the Introduction, 29, above. Rev. William S. Reece remained on Vancouver Island for ten years before returning to England. He became missionary clergyman at Cowichan, and in 1868 was made Archdeacon of Vancouver (i.e., Vancouver Island), where he caused controversy by his advocacy of High Anglican ritualism.

4 Abraham Lincoln issued the Emancipation Proclamation on January 1, 1863.

5 Under the heading "Bridal Feast" the *Colonist* on January 16 gave a more discreet account of the Poineer-Shaw wedding: "The company was very large and the entertainment of the most *recherche* description, and gave unqualified satisfaction." The ball in the evening is mentioned without the details EHV gives.
6 The *Report of the Commissioners Appointed to Inquire into the Condition and Management of Lights, Buoys, and Beacons*, a royal commission, was published as a Sessional Paper of Parliament in 1861.
7 These clippings from the *San Francisco Bulletin* are preserved with EHV's letters.
8 Dr. Peter Wallace was a surgeon attached to the naval hospital at Esquimalt.

January 26, 1863

1 Cotton workers in Lancashire suffered acute unemployment and impoverishment when the Civil War cut off supplies of American cotton. Subscription lists for their benefit in Victoria were frequently published in the *Colonist* in 1863.
2 Captain (later Admiral) Alfred P. Ryder now succeeded Captain John Moore in the key position of Private Secretary to the First Lord of the Admiralty. He had previously been in command of HMS *Hero*. He was the nephew of Dudley Ryder, first Earl of Harrowby, whose daughter Louise married Hon. George Fortescue of Bocconoc, Cornwall; they had four daughters as well as four sons.
3 The *Colonist*'s report of EHV's work to establish this school is cited in the Introduction, 31, above.
4 William Bridgeman served as Bishop Hills' butler, and his wife as housekeeper.
5 The chronometer of which the unreliability caused EHV perpetual concern was presumably supplied by M.F. Dent, "Watch, Clock, and Chronometer Maker to the Queen," 33-34 Cockspur Street, London, or E. Dent & Co., at 61 Strand, who also advertised nautical instruments.

February 5, 1863

1 Admiral Washington's letter allowing EHV expenses for the charts and useful information he gathered in San Francisco is dated December 16 1862. L.C.A.: Lord Commissioners of the Admiralty.

February 8, 1863

1 doubtful sex: probably a facetious misreading of Genesis 6.19 in the King James Version, on the creatures taken into the ark: "they shall be male and female."
2 Edward was probably one of the nine sons of Lieutenant-Colonel Henry Packe of Twyford Hall, Norfolk.
3 EHV plays here on the word "spiral" in allusion to the building of a new spire on the parish church of St. Michael, Steeple Claydon, a village of the Verney estate. Cf. his letter of December 21 1862; and see Nikolaus Pevsner, E. Williamson, and G. Brandwood, *The Buildings of England: Buckinghamshire* (London: Penguin, 1994), 643.
4 Sir James Paget, FRS, of Harewood Place, Hanover Square, London, was Surgeon Extraordinary to the Queen. James and Robert Ceely were surgeons in Aylesbury, Buckingham.
5 Sir Thomas Fremantle (1798-1890), later first Baron Cottesloe, was the brother of EHV's uncle, Rev. William Fremantle. He was chairman of the Customs Board, and had an estate at Swanbourne near Claydon. See the *DNB*.

FEBRUARY 20, 1863

1 The bill of lading signed by William Kingcome, master of the Hudson's Bay Company barque *Princess Royal*, on February 24, 1863 for Verney's shipment of "Two packages Indian Carvings/ One bundle Sticks/ One Case/ One pair of Deer horns – loose", freight charged £10, is preserved in the Hudson's Bay Company Archives, Provincial Archives of Manitoba (B 226/2/1, 292, 305-07). I am indebted to Dr. Richard Mackie for this reference. Cf. March 9 1863.

2 Dr. Charles Forbes was the surgeon of HMS *Topaze*.

3 Richard Carter appears in the *Navy Lists* at this date as a commander, serving under Captain Cumming on HMS *Emerald*.

4 The chief of the Songhees and his wife were commonly known in Victoria as King and Queen Freezy.

5 On the later fate of these artefacts, see the Introduction, 43, 58n above.

FEBRUARY 24, 1863

1 Hon. Anthony Evelyn Ashley (1836-1907), a younger son of the seventh Earl of Shaftesbury, served for a time as private secretary to Lord Palmerston.

2 The only extracts from California newspapers preserved with EHV's letters are Kip's articles on Japan that have already been noted.

MARCH 8, 1863

1 The insurrection against Russian rule in Poland broke out in January 1863 and continued for fifteen months before it was finally repressed.

2 William Schaw Lindsay was a leading British shipowner, and a Member of Parliament, in which he supported the Confederate cause.

3 The conclusion of this letter is missing.

MARCH 14, 1863

1 Dr. John Ash (1821-86) settled with his wife Dorothy in Victoria, where he practised medicine and became active in politics, holding cabinet positions in British Columbia after Confederation; see the *DCB*. EHV had served under Captain Arthur Cumming on HMS *Emerald*.

2 There are a number of portrait photographs of EHV both at Claydon House and BCARS. This one is no doubt BCARS 7434, probably by G.R. Fardon.

MARCH 30, 1863

1 William Duncan (1832-1918) arrived on the coast as a lay Anglican missionary of the Church Missionary Society in 1857. After several years at Fort Simpson he moved with his converts seventeen miles to the south in the spring of 1862 and founded the settlement at Metlakatla which became famous.

2 The marriage of the Prince of Wales to Princess Alexandra of Denmark took place on March 10.

3 Hon. Malcolm Cameron, who had gone to England to express the political grievances and desires of residents of mainland British Columbia, completed his mission and returned to Canada in February.

4 Admiral Sir James Hope, returning from China, was appointed later this year naval commander-in-chief for North America and the West Indies.

APRIL 8, 1863

1 Rev. C.T. Woods' note of April 6 enclosed with this letter congratulates EHV not only on his own and Mrs. Woods' behalf but on that of the McKenzie family and Mr. Watson (presumably Alexander).

2 The Registrar of the Supreme Court of Vancouver Island was Thomas Williams. The suspicion of a defalcation seems never to have been made public. On Chief Justice Cameron cf. July 20 and November 23 1862.

3 Captain Richard C. Mayne's *Four Years in British Columbia and Vancouver Island* was published by John Murray in London in 1862.

4 On April 4 two Americans, Bill Brady and John Henley, were attacked at Bedwell Harbour on Pender Island by Cowichan Indians. Brady was killed, and Henley was wounded but managed to escape to Victoria. On April 8 Frederick Marks and his daughter, Caroline Harvey, were killed on Mayne Island. At Governor Douglas' request on April 15 Lascelles went with HMS *Forward* to try to find and apprehend those responsible for the killings. For these and subsequent events in what became known as the Lemalchi affair, see Barry Gough, *Gunboat Frontier*, 139-47.

APRIL 20, 1863

1 Mary Jane Kinnaird (1816-88), the wife of EHV's relative, Arthur, later tenth Baron Kinnaird, was known for her interest in religious and educational works and support of "female emigration"; see the *DNB* entry for Arthur Kinnaird. The marriage of Jane Anne Saunders to Samuel Nesbitt took place on April 16. Nesbitt continued to prosper with a contract to supply the Navy with bread and biscuits, and built one of Victoria's grandest houses, Erin Hall, sometimes known facetiously as Cracker Castle. After his death in 1881 his wife successfully carried on the business. Jordayne Cave Browne Cave was, like Emily Berry, a passenger on the *Tynemouth* but did not marry her; in 1867 he married Charlotte Wright. After serving as a lay Anglican catechist at Nanaimo, Comox, and New Westminster, he was ordained as an Anglican priest in 1868 and served as a clergyman at Saanich before returning to England in 1870.

2 Commander Edward Hardinge (1830-94) was captain of the steam sloop HMS *Cameleon*.

3 hope deferred: Proverbs 13.12.

APRIL 26, 1863

1 Admiral Island is Saltspring. The attack by HMS *Forward* on the Lemalchi village on Kuper Island took place on April 15. See Gough, *Gunboat Frontier*, 141-42.

2 Edward Cridge (1817-1913) came to Victoria as Hudson's Bay Company chaplain in 1851, and subsequently became rector and dean at Christ Church. As the result of a dispute about ritual with Bishop Hills, in 1874 he led a famous secession from the Church of England in Victoria, and became bishop of the Reformed Episcopal Church.

3 Dr. Alexander Turnbull was assistant surgeon and Arthur K. Wilson acting lieutenant on HMS *Topaze*.

MAY 1, 1863

1 This naval mission was intended to give reassurance to the isolated settlers at Cowichan and Comox in the aftermath of the murders in the Gulf Islands.

2 The punitive destruction of the Lemalchi village followed Governor Douglas' instruction that while care should be taken of Indian lives Indian property might be attacked. See Gough, *Gunboat Frontier*, 141.

3 Reference is to the murder of Frederick Marks and his young married daughter – not wife, Caroline Harvey.

May 5, 1863

1 The surrendered men were wanted for the murder of Brady. Modeste Demers (1809-71), a native of Quebec, came as missionary priest to the Oregon territory in 1838, and was consecrated Roman Catholic Bishop of Vancouver Island in 1847. See Jean Usher in the *DCB*.

2 The Vancouver Island Superintendent of Police present here was Horace Smith. Mrs. Macnamara has not been definitely identified, but William McNamara served at this period as private secretary to Governor Douglas.

3 Bishop Hills went to England to raise money for his diocese, remaining there until March 1865.

4 Dr. John V. Seddall was staff assistant surgeon with the Royal Engineers in New Westminster.

5 Charles S. Nicol after a period on the mainland went to Nanaimo in 1860 as manager of the Hudson's Bay Company mines, and remained as manager after the mines were acquired by the Vancouver Coal Mining and Land Company from 1862 to 1869. An anonymous and undated children's book titled *The Prince and the Outlaw* is listed in *Fiction, Folklore, Fantasy and Poetry for Children* (New York: R.R. Bowker & Company, 1986), II, 2191.

6 EHV was evidently kept too busy in the search for the fugitives to attempt a full account of the complicated Lemalchi affair. The ship's log (ADM 53 8159) shows that the search took the *Grappler* to Kuper Island on May 20, to the Chemainus and Cowichan areas between May 21 and 23, and with the *Forward* to Montague Harbour on Galiano Island on May 24. The outcome was that some of the wanted men were never found; a number were taken, with the help of some groups of Indians, and put on trial in Victoria; and several were hanged. See Gough, *Gunboat Frontier*, 144-47.

May 29, 1863

1 On EHV's claims to promotion see the Introduction, 25-26, above: the senior mate (or sub-lieutenant) here is EHV himself. William C. Wilson, who had been a lieutenant when EHV served with him on HMS *Shannon*, was promoted to captain in March 1863.

2 James G. Noel was secretary of Rear-Admiral Hon. Frederick T. Pelham (1808-December 1861), a Lord Commissioner of the Admiralty, the younger brother of Sir Harry Verney's friend, the Earl of Chichester.

3 Captain James J. McCleverty was commander of HMS *Terrible*, under whom EHV served in the Mediterranean and Black seas. In *The Shannon's Brigade in India* EHV records his meetings with General Sir James Outram (1803-March 11, 1863), who led the British army that repressed the Indian Mutiny.

4 Sir Harry Verney was a member of the committee established by the House of Commons on February 24, 1863, which published its conclusions on July 24, 1863: *Report From the Select Committee on the Navy (Promotion and Retirement)*, a Sessional Paper. In this letter, as previously, the Duke of S. is the Duke of Somerset, First Lord of the Admiralty, and Lord Clarence is Lord Clarence Paget, Secretary of the Admiralty.

5 Reference is to Rev. Henry P. Wright, Archdeacon of Columbia, in New Westminster.
6 The biblical text is in shorthand.
7 Sarah, eldest daughter of Sir William Medlycott, Bt., of Ven House, Somerset, married on May 23, 1863 Captain Joshua Betty, R.A.
8 Rear-Admiral John Kingcome (d. 1871), who succeeded Sir Thomas Maitland as commander-in-chief of the Pacific Station, had entered the Navy in 1808, and served in the Napoleonic wars and on the Great Lakes in the War of 1812. His secretary was James R.G. Browne, and the captain of his flagship, HMS *Sutlej*, a steam sloop of 31 guns with a crew of over 500, was Captain Matthew Connolly.
9 Mrs. Pinfold: see the Introduction, 43, 58n and note, above.
10 pleasant places: Psalm 16.6.

June 21, 1863

1 The phrases EHV quotes do not occur in the collect he cites.
2 James Beeby was Accountant-General of the Navy, at Somerset House in London.
3 Admiral Maitland had recently succeeded to the earldom of Lauderdale.

June 29, 1863

1 The steward is listed in the *Grappler* muster book for the period as Christopher F. Haddy (PRO, ADM 38 8204).
2 Alexander D. Woodd is listed as a midshipman in the muster book of HMS *Sutlej* (PRO, ADM 38 7210). Basil T. Woodd (1815-95) of Conyngham Hall was Conservative M.P. for Knaresborough.
3 The Royal Naval Female School at Richmond, later at Isleworth, for the daughters of naval and marine officers, admitted those of limited means at low fees.

July 14, 1863

1 Except for the first and last paragraphs, the original of this letter is written in Gurney's shorthand, apart from dates, proper names, and a few other words. The text given here follows a transcript by Douglas Lister, in which a few slight errors in EHV's shorthand have been corrected and some additional paragraphing has been supplied.
2 Captain Robert Mann Parsons, in British Columbia with the Royal Engineers from 1858 to 1863, had been in charge of road building on parts of the route EHV was about to travel. On Archdeacon Henry P. Wright and Rev. W.S. Reece see the notes to the letters of August 16 1862 and January 6 1863. The Hudson's Bay Company's *Otter* arrived in 1853, the second steamship in coastal service after the *Beaver*. See Norman Hacking and W.K. Lamb, *The Princess Story, A Century and a Half of West Coast Shipping* (Vancouver: Mitchell Press, 1970), 47-51. For information about the *Governor Douglas* and other vessels mentioned in this letter, see Norman Hacking, "Steamboating on the Fraser in the 'Sixties," *British Columbia Historical Quarterly*, X (1946), 1-41.
3 On the inward part of his journey, EHV followed the Harrison-Lillooet Trail, made in 1858 by a volunteer crew of miners and later improved by the Royal Engineers, to by-pass the hazards of the Fraser Canyon by using a series of lakes linked by streams and portages; it became obsolete when the road through the Fraser Canyon was completed later in 1863. EHV's account of travel by this route may be compared with that of another traveller a year

earlier: "Harry Guillod's Journal of a Trip to Cariboo, 1862," ed. Dorothy Blakey Smith, *British Columbia Historical Quarterly*, XIX (1955), 187-232. See also Branwen C. Patenaude, *Trails to Gold* (Victoria: Horsdal & Schubart, 1995), which includes information about many of the roadhouses EHV mentions throughout his journey. Port Douglas, on Little Harrison Lake at the head of Harrison Lake, the settlement that served the trail, was considered as mile 0 in the naming of the roadhouses, as Lillooet was for the Cariboo Road. John Boles Gaggin (c. 1831-67) was magistrate there, and Rev. James Gammage served there as Anglican missionary and incumbent of St. Mark's Church, 1859-63.

4 A younger son of Simon, John Fraser became shareholder in a Cariboo mine and made many friends in Barkerville, but in May 1865 he succumbed to depression, as a result of financial reverses and disappointment in love, and apparently committed suicide. He is buried at Barkerville.

5 Seaton: properly spelled Seton. Rev. Robert Christopher Lundin Brown was Anglican missionary and incumbent of St. Mary's Church, Lillooet, 1860-65.

6 From Lillooet EHV followed the wagon road to Clinton, before returning via Ashcroft and Lytton to Yale. E.T. Dodge's correspondence with government officials in 1864-66 on the condition of the Harrison-Lillooet Trail is in BCARS, Colonial Correspondence, F477. Captain John Martley (c. 1828-96), a retired British army officer, founded the Grange Ranch at Pavilion.

7 la plate: written thus in longhand, presumably derived from *le prêtre*.

8 The Gold Escort established by Governor Douglas in 1861 to protect shipments of gold from the Cariboo was discontinued in 1862 but revived in 1863.

9 Scotty's roadhouse was kept by William Donaldson, an Orkney man. McLean's Hat Creek Post was founded by the Hudson's Bay Company trader, Donald McLean, whose sons later formed the notorious McLean gang. Clement Francis Cornwall (1836-1910), later lieutenant governor of British Columbia, with his brother Henry Pennant Cornwall acquired the property they named Ashcroft in 1862 and opened a roadhouse there in April 1863.

10 Henry Spencer Palmer (1838-93), later a major-general, served as lieutenant of the Royal Engineers between 1858 and 1863 in British Columbia, where he is best remembered for his survey of "Palmer's Trail" between Fort Alexandria and Bella Coola. Dr. Noble R. Oliver, a surgeon trained in the United States, practised medicine in New Westminster and the Cariboo and held an appointment with the Lands and Works Department. See *A Pioneer Gentlewoman in British Columbia: The Recollections of Susan Allison*, ed. Margaret Ormsby (Vancouver: University of British Columbia Press, 1991), 7, 92.

11 This may possibly have been John Wilson (1832-1904), later known as "the cattle king" when he became a large scale rancher in this area and supplier to coastal butchers. He was actually born in England but brought by his family to the United States at an early age. "Nincomin" is Nicomen.

12 Frank Laumeister made an unsuccessful attempt to introduce camels as pack animals on the Cariboo Road in the summer of 1862.

13 Henry Maynard Ball (1825-97) was magistrate at Lytton.

14 wailed: written thus in longhand, for "whaled."

15 Rev. Ebenezer Robson (1835-1911), a prominent Methodist clergyman, whose elder brother John later became premier of British Columbia, served at Nanaimo in 1860-63 and at Yale and the Cariboo in 1863-66.

16 Joseph W. Trutch (1826-1904), later knighted as lieutenant governor of British Columbia, was trained as an engineer and with his brother John held the contract for building the Alexandra suspension bridge which carried the

Cariboo Road across the Fraser near Spuzzum. Construction was completed in September 1863. See Robin Fisher's article on Joseph Trutch in the *DCB*.

17 Edward Howard Sanders (1832-1902) was magistrate at Yale. His wife Annie (1844-77) was the daughter of William, brother of Admiral Sir Fairfax Moresby (whose son John served as a naval officer on Vancouver Island in 1851-52 and later also became an admiral). Henry Reeve, a lay Anglican missionary, used his previous experience in China while working among Chinese miners in the Yale area.

18 On July 30 the *Colonist* reprinted the news which appeared in the *British Columbian* of New Westminster a day earlier: "The steamer Hope arrived from up-river yesterday, having on board the fag-end of the Escort, Lieut. Verny [*sic*], R.N., two camels and a number of return miners," together with treasure from the goldfields.

AUGUST 3, 1863

1 Like Bradshaw's series of railway maps and timetables, *Deitrischen and Hannay's Royal Almanack* (London, Edward Cleaver), published annually, was a well known work. It provided numerous listings of official persons, including British army and navy lists, as well as monthly calendars of astronomical and astrological information and a wide variety of other material. The title-page in 1863 gives the price as sixpence. The first two volumes of Alexander Kinglake's *The Invasion of the Crimea* were published in London and Edinburgh in 1863. The last sentence here is written in Gurney's shorthand, which Sir Harry Verney did not read; it is no doubt intended for EHV's sister Emily.

2 Benjamin Dyke Acland is listed as a midshipman in the muster books of HMS *Sutlej* (PRO, ADM 38 7210). Born in 1847, he was the son of Rev. Peter Leopold Dyke Acland, vicar of Broadclyst, Devonshire, and a grandson of Sir Thomas Dyke Acland, tenth baronet, M.P., the politically active head of a well known Devonshire family, who was a life-long friend of Sir Harry Verney. Sir Thomas' daughter Agnes was married to EHV's friend, Arthur Mills, See Burke's *Peerage and Baronetage* (1866), 11.

3 For the Parliamentary Committee on the Navy (Promotion and Retirement) and its *Report*, see May 29 1863 and note, above. In his evidence before the committee on May 12, 1863 Sir James Hope stated that on going to China he decided that he would bestow patronage "solely for the good of the public service," and that he therefore refrained from appointing as his flag lieutenant "my own nephew, who is now at Vancouver's Island in command of a gunboat, and who is a very good officer, and one in whose welfare I am naturally more personally interested than in that of any other" (*Report*, 112).

4 Like the *Army and Navy Gazette*, the *United Service Gazette* was published weekly in London, and it included listings of postings and promotions, as well as articles on subjects of military and naval interest, for example the current war in New Zealand. *The Weekly Dispatch*, also published in London, was probably EHV's main source for English news, such as parliamentary debates, which it reported quite fully, and his best source too for international news, supplemented by the more up-to-date Victoria and San Francisco newspapers.

5 Sir Eardley Culling Eardley (1805-May 21 1863), third baronet, had a family connection with EHV's Fremantle relatives, and in 1865 his daughter Frances married Robert Hanbury and became the stepmother of EHV's cousins.

6 EHV was right in predicting that Lord Walter Kerr "will get on." He became First Sea Lord in 1899 and Admiral of the Fleet in 1904. It is not clear why the name Seymour appears in the list of officers rapidly promoted, but Frederick A.

Maxse (1833-1900) set a record: lieutenant in 1852, promoted to commander as aide-de-camp to Lord Raglan in 1855, and to captain in 1857; he later became a rear-admiral. James E. Erskine, b. 1838, became sub-lieutenant in 1858, lieutenant in 1859 and commander in August 1862, and later a full admiral.

August 8, 1863

1 James Douglas had recorded his exploration of the Stikine area in June 1840 in his "Diary of a Trip to the Northwest Coast," April 22-October 2, 1840 (BCARS, A/B/40/D75). In March 1863 he was informed by the Colonial Secretary, the Duke of Newcastle, that he would be replaced as governor, and reports to this effect soon began appearing in Victoria papers, but he remained in office for another year. See Margaret Ormsby's article on Douglas in the *DCB*.

August 18, 1863

1 See *Hansard's Parliamentary Debates*, House of Lords, July 1, 1863, cols. 47-62. In this debate, which was on the British Columbia Boundaries Bill, the remarks of Richard Hely-Hutchinson, Earl of Donoughmore, and the Colonial Secretary, Henry Pelham Clinton, Duke of Newcastle, were just as misinformed as EHV alleges.

2 Rev. Constantine Pritchard of Teignmouth, described by Sir Harry Verney in a letter of January 27 1863 as "one of the most distinguished of Balliol scholars," was tutoring EHV's youngest brother, Frederick.

3 The family of the Webbs had many branches in the Claydon area, including a number of employees and tenants of the Verneys.

4 Hon. Randall Plunkett (1848-83) was the eldest son of the sixteenth Baron Dunsany; he suffered poor health and did not live long enough to succeed to the title

September 2, 1863

1 Thetis Island in Esquimalt Harbour later disappeared when the naval dry dock was constructed.

September 4, 1863

1 See *Hansard's Parliamentary Debates*, House of Commons, July 10, 1863, cols. 574-77. The Colonial Under-Secretary, Chichester Fortescue, defended Douglas and other Vancouver Island officials against criticism based on charges made earlier by Edward Langford and more recently by Leonard McClure. EHV had sent his father the clipping of a letter by McClure to John Copland printed in the *Colonist* on April 4, 1863, in which McClure boasted of having brought about Douglas' replacement as governor. Fortescue now stated it was true Douglas would be replaced but that he would retire with honour, having served a term much longer than normal.

2 Edward Langford (1809-95) came to Victoria in 1851 as bailiff of Colwood Farm for the Puget Sound Agricultural Company, a subsidiary of the Hudson's Bay Company, but he proved very extravagant, and his contract was terminated after five years. He became a bitter opponent of Douglas, returning to England in 1860. See the *DCB*. In response to demands in the Commons debate of July 10, 1863, *Correspondence Between Mr. Langford and the Colonial Department, Relative to Alleged Abuses in the Government of Vancouver's Island* was issued as a Sessional Paper on July 24.

3 Cf. EHV's earlier comments on the colonial officials, July 20 and November 23 1862. Those not previously mentioned are Benjamin W. Pearse (1832-1902), Pemberton's assistant and later successor as Surveyor General; Henry P. Crease (1823-1905), later knighted, Attorney General and later Justice of the Supreme Court of British Columbia; and Matthew Baillie Begbie (1819-94), later knighted, who became a famous figure as judge and later Chief Justice of British Columbia. All three are included in the *DCB*.

SEPTEMBER 12, 1863

1 For Lieutenant Henry Palmer see the notes to the letter of July 14 1863. On October 7, 1863 he married in New Westminster the daughter of Archdeacon H.P. Wright, Mary Jane, who was still alive to be interviewed by the *Colonist* on November 9, 1930.

2 On September 9 the *Colonist* reported that Admiral Kingcome would leave for a six months cruise in HMS *Sutlej*, and be temporarily replaced at Esquimalt by Captain Lord Gilford in HMS *Tribune*. According to the *Colonist* on September 21 when Commander Hardinge returned from his visit to the west coast in HMS *Cameleon* he reported that the Natives at Nootka Sound said a schooner whose loss he was investigating sank in a storm; they were "quiet and disposed to be very friendly."

3 Lieutenant Edward Stanley Adeane (1836-1902) of Babraham, Cambridge, was promoted to commander in September 1864 and later became a full admiral; some letters of his sister Jane are at Claydon House.

SEPTEMBER 17, 1863

1 Fort Rupert near Port Hardy on northern Vancouver Island was founded in 1849 by the Hudson's Bay Company in order to work the island's first coal mine, as well as to serve as a trading post. Later anthropologists found the Kwakiutl (Kwakwaka'wakw) Indians of this area much more interesting than EHV thought them to be.

2 Copies of EHV's official reports on this northern cruise are in BCARS, Colonial Correspondence, F108.5 and in the *Grappler* letterbook at Claydon House. An anonymous narrative of the voyage, presumably the work of EHV or Dundas, was published in the *Colonist* with the title "Return of the Grappler" on December 4, 1863, and an account by Dundas of the visit to Metlakatla was included in the *Fifth Annual Report of the Columbia Mission* (London 1864). Because of bad weather the cruise was not extended to the Queen Charlotte Islands.

OCTOBER 1, 1863

1 It seems to have been this meeting with the *Beaver* that prompted Pender to place many names connected with EHV on the charts of the areas he currently surveyed; see the Introduction, 10-12, above. Robert Cunningham (1837-1905), at this time in charge of the *Carolena*, came to the coast in 1862 as an assistant to Duncan in the mission at Metlakatla; he later became a prominent businessman, store and cannery owner, at Port Essington on the Skeena. In a letter of October 3 from "Newitty" (Nahwitti) he reported to Duncan the meeting with EHV: "Mr Verney was very kind to me & the Indians who are with me", and informed Duncan that Hewson had been lent as pilot to HMS *Grappler* (Duncan MSS, microfilm BCARS, ADD MS 2758).

2 Vancouver described the Burke Channel area of the central British Columbia coast he reached on August 14, 1792: "as desolate inhospitable a country as the most melancholy creature could be desirous of inhabiting," and commented:

"The common shellfish, such as muscles, clams and cockles ... that had been so highly essential to our health and maintenance in all our former excursions, were scarcely found, any where here, to exist." EHV's volume and page reference are accurate for the first edition of Vancouver's *Voyage of Discovery* (London 1798).

3 The arrival of the *Grappler* and visit of EHV and Rev. Robert Dundas to Metlakatla are recorded, although without much detail, in Duncan's journal for the period (microfilm BCARS, ADD MS 2758).

4 The Hudson's Bay Company's steamship *Labouchere* arrived in 1859 and made many trading voyages to the north coast. See Hacking and Lamb, *The Princess Story*, 56-60.

October 29, 1863

1 The Hudson's Bay Company Fort Simpson was founded in 1831 and moved to its current site in 1834.

2 The sources of most of the new names are obvious, including Bishop Hills, Colonel Moody, and EHV's uncle, Frederic Calvert. John Delaney was quartermaster of the *Grappler*, according to the muster books. Adam Dundas may have been related to Robert; a naval officer of the name, who had served in the Pacific on HMS *Modeste* in the 1840s, married one of the Hope family to which EHV was related. An unforeseen result of this renaming was that when dissension developed in the community after the move in 1887 to New Metlakatla, Alaska, some of the leaders of the opposition to Duncan bore the surnames Verney and Calvert.

3 Eley Brothers were well known English manufacturers of ammunition.

4 The arrested man was Frank Armstrong, an agent of Charles V. Baranovich, who was frequently in trouble for his involvement in the illicit liquor trade. On December 4 Baranovich's lawyer M.W.T. Drake wrote to Governor Douglas arguing that the arrest and subsequent fine were unjustified, and on December 30 EHV wrote Colonial Secretary Young to the contrary; see BCARS, Colonial Correspondence, F1214.

5 See Psalm 34.13 and James 3.6-8.

6 Fort McLoughlin near Bella Bella was founded in 1833 and abandoned in 1843. EHV's narrative of the grounding of the *Grappler* in his letter is more detailed than but consistent with the account in the ship's log (PRO, ADM 53 8159). The *Grappler* letterbook at Claydon House has a copy of EHV's official report on the incident to Commander Hardinge.

7 Vice-Admiral Sir Michael Seymour (1802-87) commanded the China station when EHV served there; he was M.P. for Devonport from 1859 to February 1863, when he resigned his seat to become naval commander-in-chief at Portsmouth. See the *DNB*.

8 Rear-Admiral Sir Henry Hope (b. 1787), a cousin of EHV's grandfather Sir George Hope, served as aide-de-camp to William IV and Queen Victoria.

9 The new gunner was John George Russell, whose seniority dated from December 1862.

10 Captain George Richards was appointed Hydrographer to the Royal Navy in succession to Admiral Washington in September 1863. Like Richards, Captain Thomas Spratt had conducted extensive naval surveys.

11 To mark his distinguished service and impending retirement Douglas was knighted, K.C.B., on August 14.

12 Caroline, eldest daughter of EHV's aunt and uncle, the Abel Smiths, died on October 4, 1863, leaving several young children. Her husband, Robert Hanbury, was Liberal M.P. for Middlesex, 1857-67.

December 10, 1863

1 The cartoon by Sir John Tenniel in *Punch,* October 17, 1863, p. 159, shows Britannia raising a storm signal, with clouds labelled Germany Denmark, Russia Poland, Prussia Austria, France Russia, and Mexico America.

Christmas Day, 1863

1 Robert Burnaby (1828-78) arrived on the coast from England in 1858, founded the Victoria firm of Henderson and Burnaby, commission merchants, engaged in other business enterprises, was active in civic affairs and served ably as a member of the House of Assembly of Vancouver Island for five years, and left his name at prominent places on the map of British Columbia. See the *DCB.*

2 Extracts from Bishop Hills' speeches in England about British Columbia were subsequently published in the *Fifth Annual Report of the Columbia Mission* (London 1864).

December 28, 1863

1 The false cypress commonly known as yellow cedar (*Chamaecyparis nootkatensis*) grows at sea level on the northern British Columbia coast but only at higher altitudes on the southern coast; planks of it had helped save the *Grappler* when on the rocks in Milbanke Sound in November. In a letter to EHV on February 16 1865 Sir Harry Verney eventually reported the arrival of the log in England.

January 10, 1864

1 G. Steinman Steinman's "Memoir of Sir Edmund Verney" was published in *The Gentleman's Magazine,* N.S., II, in July 1834. EHV sometimes laments his lack of historical knowledge, but it is surprising that he appears here to assign to the reign of Charles II his famous namesake, who was killed in 1642 defending the royal standard of Charles I. The monument to the standard bearer in the church of All Saints adjacent to Claydon House was undoubtedly familiar to him from his earliest years.

2 This clipping, titled "Passenger Ships Between New York and San Francisco," is from the Victoria *Evening Express,* December 29, 1863, reprinted from the New York *Herald.*

3 Joseph Warner: see October 15 1862, above.

4 This chart, preserved at Claydon House, shows the group of coastal names commemorating EHV and his family; see the Introduction, 10-12, above.

5 Robert Black is listed as the head gardener at Claydon House in the 1861 census.

January 23, 1864

1 James Bruce, Earl of Elgin (1811-63), former Governor General of Canada, died in office as Viceroy of India on November 20. He had been taken to Hong Kong and Calcutta on HMS *Shannon* when EHV served on that ship in 1857. On Lawrence, his successor, see the Introduction, 16, and note, above. Richard Grenville, Duke of Buckingham (1823-89), later became Colonial Secretary and Governor of Madras but not of Jamaica.

2 The Hope-Johnstones were among EHV's numerous relatives in the Scottish family of Hope to which his mother belonged. See Edward Walford, *The County Families of the United Kingdom* (London: Robert Hardwicke, 1865), 515.

3 Emily, Mrs. George Price of Worthy Park, Jamaica, a daughter of the fourteenth Baron Dunsany, had been a friend of EHV's mother; he mentions her son George on December 27 1862. *The Band of Hope Review*, N.S., III (April 1 1863), 111, lists her daughters Lolotte, aged fourteen, and Emily, aged sixteen, as prize winners.

4 Lady Ducie is either the wife of Henry Reynolds-Moreton, third Earl of Ducie, or the widow of Henry, second earl; several of the latter's sons were naval officers.

5 This Mr. Price is not further identified in the surviving correspondence.

6 See EHV's description of the gold diggings at Goldstream, April 21 1864. In the Queen Charlotte Islands Burnaby Island was named as a result of Robert Burnaby's involvement in copper mining there.

7 The Harewood mine, south of Nanaimo, named for Lascelles' family, the earls of Harewood, was never very successful, and Lascelles' investment proved unprofitable, in contrast to the rich reward gained by the naval officers who provided Robert Dunsmuir with his capital in 1871. On August 28, 1864 the *Grappler* took aboard some coal for trial from "The Harewood C.M. Comp.," in addition to its main supply from the Douglas Pit at Nanaimo, according to the ship's log (PRO, ADM 53 8160).

8 William Wentworth-Fitzwilliam, Viscount Milton (1839-77), reached Victoria in the autumn of 1863 at the end of the overland journey described by him and Dr. W.B. Cheadle in *The North-west Passage by Land* (London 1865).

February 7, 1864

1 Prince Albert Victor, who was given the title Duke of Clarence, was born on January 8, 1864; he died in 1892. On Governor (later Sir) Arthur E. Kennedy (1809-83), who had previously served as governor of Sierra Leone and Western Australia, see Robert Smith's article in the *DCB*.

2 The Schleswig-Holstein crisis, which culminated in Prussia's invasion of the duchies and seizure of them from Denmark in the spring of 1864, for a time seemed to threaten a wider European conflict.

3 On the economic crisis in Victoria upon the decline of the Cariboo gold rush see Reksten, *'More English than the English,'* 69-70.

4 In *Christian Work Throughout the World*, vol. I, no VI (August 1863), the titles of the first two (unsigned) articles are as EHV gives them; the third article is "The Churches in the Confederacy. By the Rev. Dr. Hoge of Richmond," written to defend Southern views.

5 Edward M. Johnstone appears in the *Navy Lists* as chaplain on HMS *Leopard*.

6 *The Graver Thoughts of a Country Parson* (London: Alexander Strahan, 1863), an anonymously published popular religious work, was by Andrew Boyd, whose *Recreations of a Country Parson* EHV had read in August 1862.

7 Admiral Sir Henry Bruce (1792-1863), who died on December 23, had entered the Navy in 1803 and served as a midshipman at the Battle of Trafalgar. Best remembered for his capture of Lagos in 1851 and suppression of the slave trade in west Africa, he commanded the Pacific Station 1855-57. See the obituary in *The Gentleman's Magazine*, N.S. XVI (February 1864), 249-50.

February 15, 1864

1 Cf. EHV's earlier references to this memorandum, June 1 and 27 1862. Captain Robert Hall had succeeded Captain Ryder as Private Secretary to the First Lord of the Admiralty.

2 The engineer was George Fitzgerald. His attempted suicide is the subject of an official letter on March 14 by EHV, copied into the *Grappler* letterbook at Claydon House. The records show that Fitzgerald recovered sufficiently to return to duty on the *Grappler*, and eventually became a chief engineer.

3 Commander (later Vice-Admiral) Theodore Morton Jones (1828-95), arriving now to take up his new command, had been appointed on December 14 as Commander (now Captain) Edward Hardinge's successor as captain of HMS *Cameleon* and senior officer at Esquimalt.

March 1, 1864

1 On EHV's involvement in these arrangements, see the Introduction, 36, above.

2 The exclusion from the welcoming procession of the Victoria Pioneer Rifle Corps, often known as the African Rifles, occasioned a long and heated correspondence in the *Colonist*. Letter writers generally declared that the discrimination was un-British and prompted by American residents in Victoria, but some suggested that this was not the whole picture.

3 EHV's longhand transcript of McClure's speech is preserved with this letter. In most respects his version is consistent with the long and detailed version published in the *Colonist* on March 3, 1864 with the heading "Meeting in the Theatre." According to both versions, McClure and Cameron were courteously received by the Colonial Secretary, the Duke of Newcastle, when they made their criticism of abuses in recent years in the governments of Vancouver Island and British Columbia, but they felt some disappointment when the duke expressed reservations about granting responsible government to colonies with such small populations, and they regretted the subsequent lack of progress in Parliament. EHV's version, however, has blunter criticism than the *Colonist*'s about discrepancies between views the duke expressed in conversation and in later speeches in the House of Lords, and it contains much fiercer criticism of the Colonial Under-Secretary, Chichester Fortescue. According to EHV, McClure declared:

> Through the agency of Mr. Pemberton, there had been a misunderstanding between Mr. Fortescue and myself; he made many rash and insulting insinuations against me in the House: I met him in the lobby of the House; he was personally unknown to me, because I had never been able to see him at the Colonial Office as he was away in the country enjoying the sweets of connubial felicity with his newly-married wife, instead of attending to his work.

After McClure had met Fortescue and pointed out his errors to him, according to this account, the under-secretary "did not make his retraction in the House of Commons as he ought to have done" but McClure then wrote to the leading journals, which caused M.P.'s to take up his subject, with the result: "when I saw Mr. Fortescue wince under the remarks of members of the House, I really felt pity for that unfortunate individual."

4 At least one letter appears to be missing here, which presumably included an account of the banquet for Sir James Douglas in Victoria on March 10, and the first account of the arrival of Governor Kennedy on March 25, unless the gap is explained by the letter to Aunt Fremantle EHV mentions on March 26.

March 26, 1864

1 EHV enclosed a clipping from the *Colonist* of March 26, "Arrival of Governor Kennedy," describing the manner in which the new governor was brought

around from Esquimalt in HMS *Grappler* on the previous day. EHV and Pender are described as "gracefully assisting" the governor's two daughters in landing. With a subsequent letter EHV enclosed "Chinese Address to the Governor" from the *Colonist* of April 5.

2 EHV's periodical reference on March 26 may be an error, as no article on lighthouses had recently appeared in either *Colburn's United Service Magazine* or the *United Service Gazette*. W.R.F.'s "Naval Chaplains," in the *Army and Navy Gazette* on January 2 as EHV states, is an appeal for the appointment of a naval chaplain-general.

3 Philip J. Hankin (b. 1836) arrived on Vancouver Island in 1857 with HMS *Plumper*, and later served there as a lieutenant in HMS *Hecate*. He resigned in England from the navy in January 1864 and returned to Vancouver Island. He served as Superintendent of Police under Kennedy, and later became Colonial Secretary of British Columbia. See Walbran, *British Columbia Coast Names*, 225-26.

4 On March 31 the *Colonist* reported that Governor Kennedy had assured the members of the Pioneer Rifle Corps of his opposition to colour discrimination, and advised them that with patience they would in time overcome the prejudice.

March 26, 1864 (Private)

1 The elder of the two Kennedy daughters, Elizabeth, in 1867 married Lord Gilford, and became Countess of Clanwilliam when her husband inherited the earldom. The younger daughter, Georgiana, did not marry.

List of articles sent to England

1 This list of artefacts here placed at the end of the March letters may have been attached to a letter, now missing, earlier this month.

April 6, 1864

1 The clipping from the *Colonist* of April 5, titled "Thrilling Narrative," gives the story by Ernest Walker, a settler on Bentinck Arm, of an attack the previous December by Indians on him and a companion while the two were engaged in a hunting expedition, in which the companion was killed and Walker wounded. He was subsequently rescued by Indians from Bella Bella. The account concludes: "Mr. Walker gives it as his conviction that had the gunboat Grappler taken the Indians who committed previous murders, on the occasion of the visit of the gunboat to that locality, this unfortunate affair would never have happened." On November 20, 1863 the *Colonist* had published a report from Bentinck Arm maintaining that the *Grappler* on its northern voyage should have taken strong action against Indians there alleged to have committed murders; the *Colonist* repeated this assertion on June 1, 1864.

2 In his speech on April 7 Helmcken hinted at the possibility of Vancouver Island joining the United States if the British Government did not meet the expenses of the governor. EHV's outrage was widely shared, as the account of the Victoria "Monster Meeting" in the *Colonist* on April 12 shows. Helmcken denied that he was ever an annexationist.

3 The chaplain of HMS *Tribune* was Rev. Frederick W. Nikoll. The commander of the ship was Richard J. Meade, Captain Viscount Gilford (or Gillford), later Earl of Clanwilliam (1832-1907), who eventually became Admiral of the Fleet. Lord Charles Beresford, who served as a midshipman on the *Tribune* a year or

two later, describes Gilford as one of the finest seamen and his ship as one of the sharpest in the service, and comments on his love of going under sail. See *Memoirs of Lord Charles Beresford* (London: Methuen, 1914), 61.

April 16, 1864

1 For this blue book see September 4 1863 and note, above.

2 On Frederick Seymour (1820-69), the new governor of mainland British Columbia, see Margaret Ormsby's article in the *DCB*. No copy of the Claydon Almanack mentioned here has come to light. Rev. William R. Fremantle's numerous published sermons are listed in the *British Library Catalogue*.

April 17, 1864

1 The discovery of gold at Goldstream in October 1863 caused a minor gold rush.

2 On the Vancouver Island Exploration Expedition, see the Introduction, 29-30, above.

May 6, 1864

1 Sangster's Plains was at Esquimalt Lagoon.

2 Admiral Kingcome's successor in command of the Pacific Station was Rear-Admiral Hon. Joseph Denman (1810-74), second son of Lord Chief Justice Baron Denman. He made his reputation in suppression of the slave trade in west Africa 1840-41, and had recently been in command of the royal yacht *Victoria and Albert*. He did not in fact appoint Christian; the captain of his flagship, HMS *Sutlej*, remained Captain Trevenen P. Coode, who had already succeeded Matthew Connolly under Kingcome.

3 News reached Victoria on May 11 of the "Bute Inlet Massacre," in which on April 30 fourteen men working on a road projected by Alfred Waddington from the inlet to the Cariboo gold fields were killed by Chilcotin Indians, the beginning of what became known as the "Chilcotin War."

May 20, 1864

1 Admiral Ivan Popov was commander of the Russian fleet in the Pacific.

2 Prince Dimitrii Maksutov took office at Sitka this month as last chief administrator of the Russian American Company, in effect Russian governor of Alaska, 1864-67.

May 25, 1864

1 On Robert Brown (1842-95) see John Hayman's introduction to his edition, *Robert Brown*; as EHV notes on December 17, he was actually M.B., not M.D.

2 After examination of the *Grappler*'s damage Admiral Kingcome had finally reported on March 7, 1864 to the Secretary of the Admiralty that during its cruise on the northern coast "the 'Grappler' grounded twice, and sustained some damage to her Port bilge, and Main and False keels, but she does not make any water. I have ordered the defects to be undertaken at once, and hope the Gunboat will soon be again ready for sea and efficient" (PRO, ADM 1 5878, f. 230). He did not suggest any fault on EHV's part, and evidently did not see any need to hold a formal enquiry such as was subsequently held following the much publicized grounding of HMS *Tribune* at the mouth of the Fraser River.

3 Benjamin Jowett (1817-93), Regius Professor of Greek at Oxford, was one of the authors of *Essays and Reviews* (1860), which caused great controversy by

its critical examination of aspects of the Bible and Christian doctrine. He was later Master of Balliol, and a frequent visitor to Florence Nightingale at Claydon House.

4 On Lady Dunsany see below, August 23 and note.

5 Cf. the earlier reference to Benjamin Acland, August 3 1863. EHV may have in mind the West Country saying that the human species consists of men, women, and Aclands. The most distinguished member of the family, Dr. (later Sir) Henry W. Acland, Regius Professor of Medicine at Oxford, was a friend of Sir Harry Verney and sometimes served the family as a doctor.

June 8, 1864

1 Thomas Howell, whose son was also named Thomas, appears in the *Army Lists* as Director of Contracts. On the Cruickshanks see below, March 17 1865 and note. Bottomley remains unidentified (although a lieutenant of Marines of that name served on HMS *Bacchante*). C.S. Donner is listed as a midshipman in muster books of HMS *Sutlej*.

2 John Bunyan's *The Pilgrim's Progress* (1678) remained a popular devotional work during the Victorian period.

3 Ivan Furuhelm (as the name should be) was Maksutov's predecessor as chief administrator of the Russian American Company, 1859-64. Miss V.Z., who seems to have been a companion of Emily Verney, is unidentified.

4 A group of Haidas camped on the Songhees Reserve was suspected of shooting and wounding two cows belonging to the Anglican missionary there, Rev. A.C. Garrett. The *Grappler*, sent with a police sergeant in pursuit of the chiefs, apprehended them at Nanaimo and brought them back to Victoria. Four of them subsequently got away to the north again without waiting for the investigation to be concluded. See the *Colonist*, June 18, 20, 22, 24, 25, July 1.

5 The "Emerald polka-mazurka" was presumably composed by EHV himself for the band of HMS *Emerald*, but I have not seen any copy.

June 27, 1864

1 The copies of the two official letters which follow are given just as they were sent to Sir Harry Verney, but the first should no doubt be dated 1863, like the second, rather than 1862.

July 1, 1864

1 On June 18 HMS *Sutlej* had brought to Bella Coola Governor Seymour with a volunteer military force, which was to proceed eastward while another force moved westward from Fort Alexandria, in the attempt to apprehend those responsible for the "Bute Inlet Massacre" and other recent killings in the Chilcotin.

2 On the grounding of HMS *Tribune*, see for example the *Colonist*, June 24, titled "Naval Disaster," June 27 and July 1.

July 13, 1864

1 The assistant surgeon was Thomas Atkinson from HMS *Sutlej*.

2 Sir Harry Verney had discussed with the First Lord of the Admiralty, the Duke of Somerset, the possibility of EHV's being appointed to the royal yacht. Prince Ernest of Leiningen (1830-1904), whose father was a half-brother of Queen Victoria, was captain of the yacht *Victoria and Albert*; he had been EHV's shipmate on HMS *Britannia* during the Crimean War. Lord Charles

Scott (1839-1911), mentioned in the next paragraph, a son of the Duke of Buccleuch, was serving as lieutenant on the royal yacht.

3 The discovery of gold on the Leech River near Sooke by the Vancouver Island Exploration Expedition resulted in a rush and much temporary excitement followed by widespread disappointment.

4 Cary's financial difficulties forced him to sell his dwelling, Cary Castle, which Governor Kennedy acquired as his official residence. He left the colony in September 1865 and died insane in England the following July.

5 Eliza, widow of the fourteenth Baron Dunsany, died on April 30, 1864. She was EHV's great-aunt, a sister of Georgiana, wife of Admiral Sir George Hope.

6 EHV probably refers here to arrangements with publishers for the disposal of unsold copies of *The Shannon's Brigade in India*; only one edition was published.

September 1, 1864

1 The original of this letter is in Gurney's shorthand, with the exception of dates, proper names, and a few other words. The text given here follows a transcript made by Douglas Lister. An earlier transcript preserved with the original at Claydon House was presumably made by a member of the Verney family at the time the letter was received but it has some minor errors and omissions.

2 Governor Kennedy wrote to Sir Harry Verney on September 6 explaining that the *Grappler*, currently out of postal range, was at Bute Inlet blockading the fishing of the Chilcotin Indians.

3 The sub-lieutenant was Charles W. Talbot.

4 According to the muster book of HMS *Sutlej* (PRO, ADM 38 9128), Joseph Nickless, A.B., had joined the Navy for ten years in 1856; he is marked "first class for conduct" and "excellent." A copy of EHV's report of September 6 on the drowning is in BCARS, Colonial Correspondence, F1223.

September 8, 1864

1 EHV describes the scene of the "Bute Inlet Massacre" of April 30.

2 Fitzroy Somerset, Baron Raglan (1788-1855), was commander of the British Army in the Crimea.

3 Sir Harry Verney, who had visited Schleswig-Holstein to study farming methods, published *Denmark and the Duchies. A Letter to One of his Constituents* (London: William Ridgeway, 1864), in which he showed himself more sympathetic to German opinion than to the Danish claims to the duchies, and he expressed similar views in Commons debates in the early months of 1864. Within a year he reversed his position and became highly critical of the aggression of Prussia under Bismarck; see *Hansard's Parliamentary Debates*, April 7, 1865, cols. 926-29.

4 Commander Edward Hay of HMS *Harrier* died of wounds on April 30 received in an attack on a Maori stronghold in the Waikato War.

5 Sir Harry Verney's assurance about Marshall's favourable reception at Claydon House in his letter of November 30 is quoted in the Introduction, 17, above.

6 For Yonge's *History of the British Navy*, see April 28 1865 and note below.

7 As EHV goes on to indicate, he was sent on this mission in response to William Duncan's request after one of his Indian constables had been killed and others wounded by the crew of the trading schooner *Random*. Dr. David Walker

accompanied him to minister to the wounded constables. Copies of EHV's official reports on this northern cruise are in BCARS, Colonial Correspondence, F1214, which also contains Walker's reports on his medical work at Metlakatla, and F1223, and in the *Grappler* letterbook at Claydon House. William Duncan in his diary gives an account of the voyage, writing for example on October 1: "Commander Verney is very kind to me"; and he provides a detailed record of EHV's visit to Metlakatla: see the Introduction, 40, above.

8 David Walker (1837-1917), a native of Belfast, trained in medicine in Dublin, was best known for his participation in an Arctic expedition in 1859 seeking to learn the fate of Sir John Franklin. EHV's "aversion" is never explained.

October 6, 1864

1 Robert Doolan was Anglican missionary on the Nass, 1864-67.

2 These letters are no longer to be found.

3 The Hudson's Bay Company Fort Simpson was at first on the Nass, between 1831 and 1834.

4 According to Duncan's diary, Cunningham announced to him and Verney when they landed at Metlakatla on October 4 his marriage to Elizabeth Ryan. Sir Harry Verney commented in a letter to EHV on December 16 1864 that he feared this marriage was contrary to Duncan's purpose, which was the betterment of the Indians rather than the provision of wives for missionaries, but he hoped it would have the result of attracting the Indians to "intimacy with our own people."

5 The end of this letter is missing. According to the ship's log (PRO, ADM 53 8160), the *Grappler* grounded in the Salmon River, Johnstone Strait, on October 17, but reached Nanaimo on October 19 and Esquimalt on October 21.

October 27, 1864

1 For the explanation about Mary Ann Tyler see the Introduction, 18, above.

2 The *Grappler* was immediately recommissioned but as EHV laments the end of the current commission meant the loss of his most experienced men and much financial accounting and other paper work.

3 John W. Hotham was promoted to commander on July 1 and John T. Swann was likewise promoted on July 14, 1864.

4 Sir Lambton Loraine, Bart., was flag lieutenant on HMS *Sutlej.*

November 13, 1864

1 Hon. Frederick Charteris, who had been serving as a lieutenant on the royal yacht *Victoria and Albert*, was promoted to commander on August 31, 1864.

2 EHV's friend Gilbert M. Sproat had been one of the founders of the mill at Alberni in 1860; but this excursion evidently did not take place.

November 29, 1864

1 On EHV and the Mechanics Institute, see the Introduction, 30, above.

2 Letters relating to the litigation following EHV's seizing of the schooner *Nonpariel* are in BCARS, Colonial Correspondence, F1214; F333.15 is a letter of December 16 from Colonial Secretary Birch of British Columbia to the Attorney General giving EHV Governor Seymour's support.

3 Sir Harry Verney's letters show that he decided to delay his response to the request for books until EHV could make the selections himself on his return to England.

4 On Dr. Ash see March 14 1863 and note, above.
5 Henry Bond was master of HMS *Tribune*.
6 Edward Plunkett, sixteenth Baron Dunsany (1808-89), was a rear-admiral.

December 7, 1864

1 The admiral's wife, Grace, daughter of Jesse W. Russell of Staffordshire and Northamptonshire, appears in at least one memorable photograph on the deck of HMS *Sutlej*, surrounded by the ship's officers. His secretary was William E.L. Veale.
2 The anonymously published *Admiralty Administration: Its Faults and Defaults* (London: Longman, Green, Longman, and Roberts, 1861) warns of the rapid increase in French sea power under Napoleon III, and makes sweeping criticisms of current British naval administration, including the rapid turnover in first lords and the lack of system in manning ships.

December 11, 1864

1 On the plan to divide the diocese, see January 22 1865 and note, below.
2 Rev. Henry Glasson was chaplain and Captain Edward Turnour captain of HMS *Charybdis*.
3 Lieutenant Hon. Albert Denison was a son of the first Baron Londesborough.
4 EHV describes the first location of the Mechanics Institute on Langley Street.
5 Edwin Saunders of 13A George Street, Hanover Square, is listed in London directories of the period as surgeon dentist.

December 25, 1864

1 Sir James Hope, who was promoted from rear-admiral to vice-admiral in September 1864, was now based in Halifax as commander of the North American and West Indian station.
2 At the beginning of January 1865, Bishop Hills married Maria, daughter of Vice-Admiral Sir Richard King; the honeymoon was spent at Claydon House.
3 Mrs. George Price was a daughter of the late Lady Dunsany. See January 27 and August 23 1864 above.

January 13, 1865

1 Governor Seymour's speech at the opening of the Legislative Council is given fully and highly praised in the *British Columbian* of New Westminster on January 14. The Royal Engineers had already made a trail to Burrard Inlet in 1859.
2 While the Charlottetown and Quebec conferences of September and October 1864 led to Canadian confederation in 1867, the corresponding movement in Australia actually made much less progress during this period, and federation there was not achieved until 1901.
3 Old Fort Langley was founded in 1827; New Fort Langley was the site of the proclamation of the colony of British Columbia on November 19, 1858.
4 Governor Seymour's liking for cocktails was to prove fatal; he died as a result of alcoholism in June 1869. One of Bishop Hills' proposals was to make Vancouver Island and the coast of British Columbia into one diocese, and the interior of British Columbia into a second; but the diocese remained undivided until 1879 when it was split into three. See Frank Peake, *The Anglican Church in British Columbia*, 51-53.
5 On this lecture see the Introduction, 30, above.

JANUARY 28, 1865

1 On January 27 the Vancouver Island House of Assembly passed a resolution in favour of union with British Columbia.

FEBRUARY 8, 1865

1 On Edmund Coleman (1823?-92) see John Hayman, "Where Flowers Forever Bloom, A Victorian Artist at the Edge of the Pacific," *The Beaver*, LXVI.2 (April-May 1986), 27-35. Coleman's *Scenes from the Snow-Fields: Being Illustrations of the Upper Ice-World of Mont Blanc* was published in London by Longman, Brown, Green, Longmans and Roberts in 1859.

2 In the election for the House of Assembly in Victoria on February 13 Amor De Cosmos and Leonard McClure, who favoured union, defeated G.M. Sproat and C.B. Young, who opposed it.

3 Rev. Samuel Gilson, Archdeacon of Vancouver, 1864-66, succeeded Dundas as rector of St. John's in Victoria. Dundas preached his farewell sermon on March 19, and left for England a few days later.

4 Rees Howell Gronow published *Reminiscences of Captain Gronow* in London in 1861 and further volumes of his memoirs followed in 1863, 1865 and 1866. The first volume dealt with the period of the Napoleonic wars and Regency.

FEBRUARY 22, 1865

1 Lascelles' successor as commander of HMS *Forward* was Lieutenant Henry Fox. EHV found Lascelles staying in the same hotel as himself in San Francisco on June 23, suffering from a painful eye affliction, which obliged him to remain in a darkened room. He returned to England by an easier route than EHV, and resigned from the Navy before returning to Vancouver Island, where he died in 1869.

2 On the Kootenay gold discovery and the supply route through American territory, see Akrigg, *British Columbia Chronicle 1847-71*, 311-13.

3 A copy of this photograph is reproduced in the present edition from an album at Claydon House.

FEBRUARY 26, 1865

1 In introducing a representative element in the government of Vancouver Island in 1856, a House of Assembly with elected members, Douglas had in fact followed the instructions of the Colonial Office.

2 In England on January 27, 1866 Governor Seymour married Florence Maria Stapleton.

3 Edward Cardwell, later Viscount Cardwell (1813-86), was Colonial Secretary 1864-68.

4 After the captain and the two crew members of the trading sloop *Kingfisher* were killed and the vessel plundered and burned, Admiral Denman mounted a controversial attack on the Ahousats at Clayoquot Sound between October 2 and 12, 1864, in which at least fifteen Indians were killed and several villages destroyed. See Gough, *Gunboat Frontier*, 114-22. The report in the *Illustrated London News*, XLV (December 31 1864), 664, was titled "Conflict with the Indians of Vancouver Island," and was accompanied by two engravings, the larger of which was titled "The Boats of H.M.S. Sutlej and Devastation attacking an Indian Village in Clayoquot Sound, Vancouver Island."

5 On January 13 1865 Sir Harry Verney wrote to EHV that the latter would be "seriously embarrassed" if he married a woman who had less than his

mother's fortune. Sir Harry illustrated this point by stating that he was having to go in debt to meet election expenses of at least £500 or £600, and that if he was not M.P. he would be made sheriff, which would cost him about £400.

6 Sir Harry Verney's letters show that he anticipated the calling of the general election of the summer of 1865 well in advance of the dissolution of Parliament on July 6.

March 15, 1865

1 Pasted at the head of this letter is a photograph in the *carte de visite* format which EHV has labelled "A Chief of the Eucletaw Tribe. V.I." The photographer can be identified from the backdrop as George Robertson, Victoria Theatre Photographic Gallery (information from David Mattison, BCARS).

2 The problems of George Cruickshank, the son-in-law of Thomas Howell of the War Office and brother-in-law of EHV's friend Tom Howell (June 8 1864), were subsequently given a great deal of publicity in Victoria newspapers. Active in politics and civic affairs, and in business as a broker, Cruickshank had previously been an accountant with the Bank of British Columbia in June 1863 when five thousand dollars was stolen. In the early months of 1865 his mind became unbalanced; he confessed to the theft and was arrested on May 11; but he was acquitted in a trial by jury in July on the ground that he was insane and that his confession was not credible. He never recovered his mental health and died two and a half years later in Scotland. See the *Colonist*, May 12 and 13, July 21 and 22, 1865, and February 11, 1868.

March 26, 1865

1 Rev. Christopher Knipe (1834-96), in British Columbia from 1860 to 1865, served as Anglican missionary in the Cariboo gold fields and at Alberni. Rev. John Sheepshanks (1834-1912) served as Anglican clergyman in New Westminster and elsewhere in British Columbia between 1859 and 1867; he later became Bishop of Norwich. See D. Wallace Duthie, ed., *A Bishop in the Rough* (London 1909).

2 EHV's younger brother George had arrived home on leave from the army in India. He wished to marry a young woman he had met in India but was opposed by his father and stepmother, partly on grounds of youth and inadequate income. Two of his letters on this subject to EHV on Vancouver Island are preserved. The Verney family correspondence on this reads very much like a novel by Anthony Trollope.

April 11, 1865

1 The unfavourable comment on the "outside" at Claydon House by Mrs. Hills, the episcopal bride (referred to as E.B. in the fourth paragraph), prompted one of Parthenope Verney's most indignant letters to EHV *en route* to England on July 14. She declared that Mrs. Hills should have realized that ground near the house was unfinished because of construction of a terrace and road alterations which could not be completed during the winter.

2 Eventually George overcame the family opposition and married Miss Hinde, the daughter of Colonel (later General) John Hinde.

April 14, 1865

1 The Vancouver Island government steamship *Sir James Douglas* was launched in Victoria on January 7, 1865 (cf. February 26 above). It provided communica-

tion and transport to coastal settlements and performed many other important functions for over twenty-five years. Its first captain, William R. Clarke (1834-94) did not return to the Navy but later became harbour master at Victoria. See E.W. Wright, ed., *Lewis and Dryden's Marine History of the Pacific Northwest* (Seattle: Superior Publishing, 1967; first published 1895), 139.

2 EHV learned from the newspapers that his father had been re- elected when he reached Chicago in his overland journey on August 12.

3 The report of Lincoln's assassination on April 14 reached Victoria quickly by way of Seattle which already had a telegraph line, and was among the first news to reach New Westminster when the telegraph was completed to that place on April 20; cf. EHV's use of the new telegraph on May 7.

4 Robert Brown's report, *Vancouver Island. Exploration*, was published in Victoria by authority of the government by Harries and Company in 1864. The names of most of the recipients EHV proposes for his copies occur in earlier letters. Rear-Admiral Charles Frederick was one of the Lord Commissioners of the Admiralty. For Arthur Kinnaird, later tenth Baron Kinnaird (1814-87), see the *DNB*. In an annotation pencilled at the end of the letter, Sir Harry Verney added to the list the Travellers Club and Colonial Secretary Cardwell. Admiral Kingcome's letter of thanks to Sir Harry Verney, dated from Weymouth on July 6, expressed the hope "your excellent son" may be rewarded "with the promotion he highly deserves."

5 James Farrely, an assistant surgeon on HMS *Sutlej*, was assigned to the naval hospital at Esquimalt.

6 Edward M. Goulburn's *Thoughts on Personal Religion, Being a Treatise on the Christian Life in its Two Chief Elements, Devotion and Practice* (London: Rivington) was published in 1862; the author was a prebendary of St. Paul's.

7 Charles D. Yonge's *The History of the British Navy from the Earliest Period to the Present Time* (London: Richard Bentley) was published in two volumes in 1863.

8 Vice-Admiral Hon. Sir Frederick Grey was a Lord Commissioner of the Admiralty. His letter to which EHV refers, dated February 28, is among Sir Harry Verney's papers.

May 7, 1865

1 Archdeacon H.P. Wright returned with his family to England in May 1865, but came back and served as Archdeacon of Vancouver Island from 1877 to 1880.

2 The last entry in the log of HMS *Grappler*, made on May 13 at 7.24 p.m., reads: "Ship placed out of Commission/ Hauled down Pendant" (PRO, ADM 53 8385). The vessel was then put on the sale list at Esquimalt, and replaced later in the year by the larger and faster gunboat, HMS *Sparrowhawk*. After its sale and conversion in 1868 the *Grappler* was used in the commercial coastal trade until its destruction by fire with heavy loss of life in Seymour Narrows in 1883.

May 21, 1865

1 A photograph at Claydon House taken by Charles Gentile on May 24 which shows EHV with Governor Seymour, the British Columbia Colonial Secretary, Arthur Birch, Commander T. Morton Jones, Daniel Pender, and a group of Indian chiefs is reproduced in the present edition.

2 While 32 South Street was Sir Harry Verney's London house, 9 St. James Place was the lodging of EHV's uncle, Frederic Calvert. According to a letter of September 10 he wrote after landing at Liverpool, EHV eventually decided to spend just one night in London, at Fenton's Hotel, and after calling at the Admiralty on September 11, to go on to Claydon House the same afternoon.

Index

Aboriginal or First Nations subjects are listed, in accordance with the terminology of Verney's period, under the heading "Indians, Native." Ships are indexed by name under the heading "Ships." Indexing of notes is selective.

THE PIONEERS OF BRITISH COLUMBIA

The Reminiscences of Doctor John Sebastian Helmcken
edited by Dorothy Blakey Smith

A Pioneer Gentlewoman in British Columbia: The Recollections of Susan Allison
edited by Margaret A. Ormsby

God's Galloping Girl: The Peace River Diaries of Monica Storrs, 1929-1931
edited by W.L. Morton

Overland from Canada to British Columbia
edited by Joanne Leduc

Letters from Windermere, 1912-1914
edited by R. Cole Harris and Elizabeth Phillips

The Journals of George M. Dawson: British Columbia, 1875-1878
edited by Douglas Cole and Bradley Lockner

They Call Me Father: Memoirs of Father Nicolas Coccola
edited by Margaret Whitehead

Robert Brown and the Vancouver Island Exploring Expedition
edited by John Hayman

Alex Lord's British Columbia: Recollections of a Rural School Inspector, 1915-36
edited by John Calam

To the Charlottes: George Dawson's 1878 Survey of the Queen Charlotte Islands
edited by Douglas Cole and Bradley Lockner

Vancouver Island Letters of Edmund Hope Verney, 1862-65
edited by Allan Pritchard